AMERICA AND IRELAND,
1776–1976

AMERICA AND IRELAND, 1776-1976

The American Identity
and the
Irish Connection

THE PROCEEDINGS OF THE UNITED STATES
BICENTENNIAL CONFERENCE OF
CUMANN MERRIMAN, ENNIS, AUGUST 1976

CON HOWARD, EXECUTIVE EDITOR
EDITED BY
DAVID NOEL DOYLE AND
OWEN DUDLEY EDWARDS

GP

GREENWOOD PRESS
WESTPORT, CONNECTICUT • LONDON, ENGLAND

Grateful acknowledgment is made to the following:

"The Fall of Rome" reprinted with permission of
Random House, Inc., from *W.H. Auden:
Collected Poems*, edited by Edward Mendelson.
Copyright 1976.

Lines from "Spenser's Ireland" reprinted with
permission of Macmillan Publishing Co., Inc., and
Faber and Faber, Limited, from *Collected Poems*
by Marianne Moore. Copyright 1941 by Marianne
Moore, renewed 1969 by Marianne Moore.

Library of Congress Cataloging in Publication Data

Main entry under title:

America and Ireland, 1776-1976.

    Includes bibliographical references and index.
    1. United States—Relations (general) with
Ireland—Congresses. 2. Ireland—Relations
(general) with the United States—Congresses.
3. Irish Americans—Congresses. I. Doyle,
David Noel. II. Edwards, Owen Dudley.
III. Cumann Merriman.
E183.8.I6A47   301.29'73'0415   79-7066
ISBN 0-313-21119-1 lib. bdg.

Library of Congress Catalog Card Number: 79-7066
ISBN: 0-313-21119-1

First published in 1980

Greenwood Press
A division of Congressional Information Service, Inc.
88 Post Road West, Westport, Connecticut 06880

Printed in the United States of America

10 9 8 7 6 5 4 3 2

CONTENTS

FOREWORD
MICHAEL O'KENNEDY

This volume is an important contribution to Irish-American studies. The essays that it contains from so many distinguished scholars, Irish and American, and Ambassador Shannon's perceptive introduction open to us the great diversity of the Irish experience in the United States and convey some sense of the magnitude of the contribution which Irishmen and Irish Americans have given in every field of endeavor in their adopted home.

At a time when opportunities were denied to them at home, America provided a road to material progress to millions of Irishmen and women. There they could develop as far as their abilities would take them. At the same time their achievements in their new home provided a source of inspiration to those who stayed behind, clear proof of what they themselves could achieve in freedom.

Although Irish emigration to the United States has all but ceased, the ties forged in the past two centuries remain as firm as ever. The Irish-American consciousness is strong. Publications such as the present one will enable them to take stock of their achievement.

The United States of America is one of the great nations in history. It has contributed enormously to the material and intellectual development of the modern world. It has done so by absorbing within its frontiers the energies and skills of people from many countries. We are proud that our fellow countrymen have contributed to the building of America. We are happy that our kinsmen there have not forgotten their identity or their origins. These facts augur well for the further development of the deep and abiding friendship that unites our two nations.

I am happy to pay tribute to the organizers of the Merriman School, which gave birth to this volume.

MICHAEL O'KENNEDY
Minister for Foreign Affairs of Ireland, 1977–79
currently Minister for Finance

EDITORIAL NOTE

Since it was envisaged that this work be a substantive guide to the field of Irish/American connections, Dr. Doyle has provided bibliographical notes to all contributions bearing directly upon such relationships, and footnoted the final editorial survey, which is an overview of recent publications. In the interests of uniformity the editors have embodied the remaining documentation provided by contributors in these bibliographies. Those papers which were reflective rather than historical were left without references, as their authors intended. Finally, the editors left all contributions substantially unaltered as a necessary record of the conference proceedings, and do not necessarily concur with all the views expressed in them. They especially wish to thank James Sabin of Greenwood Press for hs exemplary patience; Mrs. Pat Foley for her equally good-natured typing and retyping; the librarians of University College, Dublin, Edinburgh University, Columbia University, and the National Library of Ireland for bibliographic assistance; the officers of Cumann Merriman for encouragement and support; Con Howard and Professor Denis Donoghue for acting as advisers and diplomats extraordinary to this project: without their aid it would have ground to a standstill on several occasions; and above all the scholars whose participation made the original occasion so rewarding, and gives this work what variety and distinction it enjoys. All of us found encouragement in Ambassador William Shannon's and Foreign Minister Michael O'Kennedy's interest and participation in the work. Our deepest thanks are due to Bonnie Dudley Edwards for masterly editorial work on some of this volume and to Dr. Patrick Henchy without whose aid it could not have appeared.

D. N. D.
O. D. E.

INTRODUCTION

WILLIAM V. SHANNON

Ireland, a small nation on the western rim of Europe, and the United States, a vast continent-wide nation in North America, have had a disproportionately significant and intimate association. This volume of essays by more than a score of distinguished historians and critics from both sides of the Atlantic examines that association from several different perspectives. The bicentenary of American independence provided the occasion for this collaborative effort. In 1976, the Merriman Summer School—taking its name from the brilliant eighteenth-century Irish poet Brian Merriman, and held annually in County Clare, Ireland—devoted itself to the theme "Ireland and America, 1776–1976." The outcome is this intellectually exciting book, one sure to inform and challenge anyone interested in the history of the two countries.

Wisely, the aim of neither the organizers of the conference nor the editors of this volume has been unanimity or consensus. Rather, they have sought fresh thinking, new insights, the vitality of vigorous controversy. In this, they have succeeded. As with any good critical examination of the issues and state of knowledge in a given field, one concludes the reading of this book stimulated by the richness and complexity of what is known about the past and at the same time eager to learn the results of ongoing and future research.

The interplay between Ireland and the United States derives much of its character and color from the relationship of each of them to a third nation—England. The thirteen states that formed the American nation were all English-speaking communities created by an outburst of English colonizing energy in the century and a quarter between the founding of Virginia in 1607 and Georgia in 1732. English naval and military successes ensured that despite earlier Spanish settlements in Florida and the Southwest, the new American nation would be English in its language and in many of its legal and political institutions.

The same thrusting English impulse for dominion and colonization that produced the American settlements in those centuries was also felt in Ireland and with far less happy results. The Irish, unlike the American Indians, could not be exterminated or driven westward. They were too numerous, too concentrated, too resilient. But having suffered periodic military defeats, the Irish were deprived of legal title to their best lands, which were then "planted" with English and Scottish settlers much as if Ireland were, indeed, a virgin territory. Death or exile was the fate of many thousands of native Irish in the seventeenth century, while most of those who survived sank into abject poverty and servitude.

This catastrophe produced a sense of broken nationhood from which the Irish people still suffer. Beginning in the late nineteenth century and continuing into the present, Irish people have tried to reach across the chasm of those centuries of defeat and occupation and link up once again with an Irish language almost eradicated and a rich Irish culture that flourished in the early medieval period. The Ardagh Chalice, the Tara Brooch, and other Irish art treasures exhibited in the United States in 1977–79 are examples of that culture. Irish monks had conserved Greek and Latin learning and were instrumental in keeping it alive in the darkened Europe of the ninth and tenth centuries. One scholar has written: "Whoever on the continent in the days of Charles the Bald (in the ninth century) knew Greek was an Irishman, or at least his knowledge was transmitted to him through an Irishman, or the report which endows him with this glory is false."

English conquest, effectively consolidated in the Elizabethan and Cromwellian periods, meant not only the loss of lands, political independence, and cultural heritage but also introduced deep religious divisions that still wound the national consciousness. The cause of the Protestant Reformation became identified with the political fact of English rule. This made it impossible for the native Catholic Irish to intermarry with and gradually absorb the English settlers as they had earlier absorbed Scandinavian and Norman invaders. The plantation of thousands of Presbyterian Scots in Ulster introduced yet a third religious influence. In America, the concept of a neutral secular state eventually took hold and religious tolerance became a national tradition. In Ireland, tolerance was as urgently needed, but instead politics and religion became intertwined to the detriment of both.

Meanwhile, English economic imperialism toward Irish textile manufacturers served to alienate both the Protestant and Catholic communities. Since Belfast was particularly hard-hit, the result was heavy emigration from Ulster to the American colonies. These were descendants of the people imported into Ulster by King James I to help ensure Ireland's loyalty. On their transplantation to America, they became the most resourceful and implacable enemies of the Crown. These recently emigrated Protestant Irish were in the forefront of the political struggles leading up to the American Revolution and in the subsequent fighting.

"The American War was lost by Irish emigrants," Lord Mountjoy observed with some exaggeration. "These emigrants are fresh in the recollection of every gentleman in this House; and when the unhappy differences took place, I am assured, from the best authority, the major part of the American army was composed of Irish; and that the Irish language was as commonly spoken in the American ranks as English."

Americans, aided by their enormous distance from England, achieved relatively easily the national independence of which Irishmen dreamed and were to go on dreaming for another 150 years. For Americans, French naval intervention—invariably tardy or insufficient in Irish struggles—was timely and decisive. From the very beginning of its nationhood, therefore, America beckoned to Irishmen as a gleaming symbol of success and power, contrasting so starkly with the reality of their own gray political frustration and black defeat.

These Protestant Irish were to play a major role in the political and cultural life of the American nation. Nine of the signers of the Declaration of Independence were of Irish ancestry, including four who were born in Ireland: Charles Thomson, secretary to Congress, born in Derry, James Smith, a Dubliner, George Taylor, from Ulster, and Matthew Thornton, from Limerick.

Fourteen American presidents from John Adams to Jimmy Carter have traced all or part of their lineage to Protestant Irish forebears. Three of them were sons of Irish emigrants. Andrew Jackson's parents were born in County Antrim; James Buchanan's father was born in Donegal, and Chester Arthur's father in Antrim. When President Jackson visited Boston in 1833, he was greeted by the Charitable Irish Society there. He said on that occasion,

I feel grateful, sir, at the testimony of respect shown me by the Charitable Irish Society of this city. It is with great pleasure that I see so many of the countrymen of my father assembled on this occasion. I have always been proud of my ancestry and of being descended from that noble race.

Place names in America such as Belfast, Maine, and Londonderry, New Hampshire, also testify to this Ulster influence. By 1730, Pennsylvania had townships named Derry, Donegal, Tyrone, Coleraine, and Fermanagh. Similar names are scattered throughout the American South.

The Irish people have always had a keen interest in education, and Irish Presbyterians have been particularly zealous. Of the 207 permanent colleges established in the United States before the Civil War, 49 were founded by Presbyterians.

Originally, Catholic and Protestant immigrants from Ireland made little or no distinction among themselves along religious lines. Thus when the Friendly Sons of St. Patrick, a fraternal group, was organized in Philadelphia in 1771, the first president was Stephen Moylan, whose brother was a Catholic bishop, and the second president was John M. Nesbitt, an Ulster Presbyterian. In the late nineteenth century, however, perhaps to distinguish themselves from the much larger numbers of Catholic Irish immigrants of the Famine generation, some Protestant Irish began to denominate themselves as Scots-Irish. This is a term of dubious accuracy that obscures as much as it clarifies. As Peter B. Sheridan of the Library of Congress's Research Service noted in his monograph, *The Protestant Irish Heritage in America* (July 1977), "not all Irish Protestants were of Scottish origin and they did not all come from Northern Ireland." President Arthur's father, for example, came from County Antrim, but he was an Episcopalian, not a Presbyterian, and his forebears originated in England.

To measure quantitatively the presence of the Protestant Irish in American life today is virtually impossible. A minority of them survives in discernible communities in the mountainous areas of North Carolina, Virginia, West Virginia, and Kentucky. They are the direct descendants of the pioneers of the Revolutionary War period. But the greater number of the Protestant Irish have over the generations intermarried with other Americans of English, Scottish, German, or other lineages and have disappeared as a distinct ethnic group. It would be erroneous therefore to equate all the descendants of the Protestant Irish immigrants with impoverished mountaineers. Although two Irish Protestant empire builders—Andrew Mellon and Henry Ford— were exceptional figures, many others have been highly successful if less conspicuous.

When the American Revolution broke out, the Irish response was—as Professor John A. Murphy makes clear—decidedly ambiguous. The most eloquent and incisive arguments made in Britain on behalf of the Americans were voiced by the greatest Irishman of the age, Edmund Burke. Irish Protestants were generally sympathetic toward the American cause, for they saw the American cause as their own writ large. The British government made concessions in 1782 to "Grattan's Parliament" in order to stave off Irish unrest. Irish Catholics may have been equally sympathetic, but many of them saw a short-run advantage for Ireland —and Catholic emancipation— by overtly professing their loyalty to the British Crown.

The next phase of Irish-American relations began in 1845 with the onset of the Great Famine and the sudden, wholesale emigration of Irish people to Canada and the United States. In his essay, Cormac O'Grada clarifies the many difficult issues concerning the origins and nature of that great emigration.

In the first U.S. census in 1790, analysis suggests that of the 3,172,444 white persons (ignoring the black slaves for this purpose), between 10 percent and 20 percent were of Irish origin, from both Northern and Southern Ireland. The predominantly Protestant immigration had virtually ceased by the early nineteenth century. Between 1820 and 1930—when immigration to the United States dwindled sharply because of the Great Depression—5.5 million Irish people emigrated to the United States. This group was predominantly Catholic. Several of the essays evaluate the consequences for American society of this second wave of Irish immigrants in diverse fields such as politics, military affairs, literature, labor unionism, business, and religion.

Much of the behavior of the American Irish is comprehensible only in terms of a reaction against the social and economic circumstances prevailing in Ireland and against British political dominion in "the old country." The Irish, having been overwhelmingly a rural people at home, became overwhelmingly an urban people in the United States. It was as if they felt that because the land had rejected them in Ireland in the terrible famines, they would now reject the land. The aggressiveness, high spirits, and self-confidence that had found so few constructive outlets in Ireland—where political and economic power were monopolies of the Anglo-Irish ascendancy—burst forth in the United States. Professor James Walsh's chapter on the Irish in California is particularly interesting for the vivid picture it affords of individual Irishmen making the leap in one generation from depressed peasants to spectacularly successful mining millionaire or crusading U.S. senator. In the United States, the immigrants were able to transform the meaning of the term "the fighting Irish" from one of opprobrium to one of self-esteem. They altered their image from the feckless, inconsequent, defeated Paddies of *Punch* cartoons and English satire to a tough, successful, warily respected people.

Having spent themselves in so many lost nationalist causes in their native land, the Irish in America pursued political success and power with ruthlessness and avidity. As Professor Thomas Brown observes, the Irish did not invent the urban political machine; it existed before their arrival, and it evolved in some cities such as Cincinnati, Ohio, where they were never dominant. But in those cities where Irish were numerous—Boston, New York, Jersey City, Chicago, San Francisco—they displayed remarkable skills in organizing the urban poor and deploying their strength. Their political organizations were usually "more effective, more functional, more successful" than rival machines. They made "Tammany" a byword for this kind of political craft in the seventy years between the end of the Civil War and the onset of the New Deal. They organized people "not on the basis of their conscience but on the basis of their interests." For that reason, their political machines were regarded by other Americans as subversive of the democratic political process and legal procedures and the term "an Irish politician" became one of disdain. But, if viewed pragmatically, these Irish politician" machines were essentially conservative institutions that succeeded in stabilizing the great American metropolises and made possible the orderly expansion of public services and the urban economy.

The Irish in their transatlantic journey did not lose their capacity to laugh at themselves or to see the deeper tragic implications of the human predicament. Professor Charles Fanning in his entertaining and perceptive chapter on Finley Peter Dunne's "Mr. Dooley" illuminates a neglected aspect of the work of that great satirist. The dramatist Eugene O'Neill, the

novelists James T. Farrell and F. Scott Fitzgerald, and the short-story writer
Flannery O'Connor are four American writers whose work derives in
different ways from their Irish heritage and who have tried to come to grips
with the universal elements in human experience by lavishing detailed attention on specific people, places, and communities. Like other great writers
from Turgenev to Jane Austen, they found the world in a parish, whether
that parish be a tormented corner of New London, Connecticut, or the
South Side of Chicago or the French Riviera or rural Georgia. These American writers shared with their Irish counterparts the "difficult but stimulating
problem of inheriting a tongue without a tradition." Irish writers had almost lost contact with the rich tradition of Gaelic, which declined during
the oppression of the seventeenth and eighteenth centuries and almost
disappeared during the nineteenth with the introduction of the national
schools where English was compulsory and Gaelic ignored. They thus
entered upon the use of the English language without a natural tradition of
their own. Similarly, American writers inherited English but had to evolve
metaphors and rhetoric to fit a unique society in a vast, raw, new continent
quite different from Shakespeare's "sceptered isle."

Unwittingly, Irish Catholic immigrants introduced into American life an
international dimension that is only now being seen in its true significance.
Because of their religious and political differences with England, the Irish
looked to the mainland of Europe—to Rome for religious guidance and
inspiration and to France and Spain for political succor. Although the
prevailing ethos of American life was English and Protestant and increasingly
secular, the American Catholic Irish through their churches and schools
kept alive a viable if minority tradition that was European and Catholic and
religious. Now that the United States is a global power and Ireland is an
active member of the European Community and the United Nations, this
minority tradition has gained fresh relevance. Ireland, which in the medieval
era was "a land of saints and scholars," a conservator of the ancient learning
of Greece and Rome, has become in the twentieth century a source of
religious missionaries for Nigeria, Peru, and India. It has become, too, an
active agent in mankind's search for a just world order. As President John F.
Kennedy said in his address to the Irish Parliament in June 1963: "From
Cork to the Congo, from Galway to the Gaza Strip, from this legislative
assembly to the United Nations, Ireland is sending its most talented men to
do the world's most important work—the work of peace."

In a sense, this export of talent is in keeping with an historic Irish role. But you
no longer go as exiles and emigrants, but for the service of your country and, indeed,
of all men. Like the Irish missionaries of medieval days, like the wild geese after
the Battle of the Boyne, you are not content to sit by your fireside while others are in
need of your help. Nor are you content with the recollections of the past when you
face the responsibilities of the present.

This Irish commitment to internationalism makes the United States and Ireland amicable comrades in the search for world order. In reaching out for a larger role in Europe, Ireland is not turning its back on the United States. On the contrary, European union and strength have long been cherished goals of American foreign policy.

Because of the traditionally close relationship between Ireland and the United States, it was logical for another American president—Jimmy Carter— to express his "deep personal concern" about the sectarian violence wracking Northern Ireland and to pledge in August 1977 that if the two communities there—with the help of the British and Irish governments—could reach a political settlement, the United States stood ready to offer economic assistance in the form of job-creating investment. The Carter statement was the natural gesture of one who sees a friendly neighbor beset by trouble. Since Ireland had exported so much of its wealth—the brains, energies, and talents of millions of its sons and daughters—to the United States, President Carter's offer was in the nature of a modest recompense. In the fraternal spirit in which it was offered, the Carter initiative was welcomed by the overwhelming majority of people in both Protestant and Catholic communities, North and South. Out of old intimacy had come new hope. From succeeding pages of this book, readers can better understand how this close, complex, and enduring relationship took form and has developed for more than three centuries.

PART ONE
THE
AMERICAN
IDENTITY

EDMUND BURKE AND THE AMERICAN REVOLUTION

CONOR CRUISE O'BRIEN

Let us begin by considering two-well known lines from W. B. Yeats's poem "The Seven Sages."

> American colonies, Ireland, France and India
> Harried, and Burke's great melody against it.

What was *it*? I shall come back to that question. For the moment let us note the implied acknowledgment of Burke's consistency; a just acknowledgment of something that has been unjustly impugned. In other ways, I think Yeats's lines somewhat misleading. The key words "harried" and "melody" suggest a Burke concerned to stir emotions by his eloquence on behalf of the persecuted. Burke could do that: he did it for the victims of the Irish Penal Laws, for the Begums of Oudh and, most famously, for Marie Antoinette of France. He knew well how to play on the emotions, but on the whole he used this skill sparingly. The great bulk of his writings and speeches consists of reasoned arguments. And nowhere is this more evident than in his speeches aimed at averting the conflict in America.

In all his great campaigns there was, as Yeats discerned, one constant target. That target—Yeats's "it"—was the misuse of power. But the forms of the misuse of power differed in the different cases mentioned, and Burke's manner of approaching the different cases differs also. In his impeachment of Warren Hastings he used rhetorical devices to excess: In his last writings on the French Revolution—the *Letters on a Regicide Peace*— there is a reckless abandonment to crusading fury. Emotions perhaps equally powerful, or even more so, working generally under greater restraints; the Burkian veils are often present in his writings on Ireland. But in none of the great themes that he treated is he more consistently rational and free from pathos than in his speeches and writings on America in the period before the outbreak of war.

The sufferings of the colonists are not his theme, nor does he dwell on the brutalities of the agents of George III. In the most striking of the rare cases (before the war, that is) in which he backs his case by an appeal to an emotion on behalf of the Americans, the emotion he appeals to is not pity. It is admiration. It is also by implication, fear. "Timidity, with regard to the well-being of our country," he had written, "is heroic virtue." The passage I refer to is the famous one about the whalers in *On Conciliation with America*. It will be familiar to many of you: I quote a part:

No sea but what is vexed by their fisheries. No climate that is not witness to their toils. Neither the perseverance of Holland, nor the activity of France, nor the dexterous and firm sagacity of English enterprise, ever carried the most perilous mode of hard industry to the extent to which it has been pushed by this recent people; a people who are still, as it were, but in the gristle, and not yet hardened into the bone of manhood.

Burke's concern, in relation to America, was not primarily with the Americans, though it was also with them. It was primarily with the interests of Great Britain (including Ireland). His objection to the policies of Grenville, or North, or George III himself, in relation to America was not that these policies were oppressive or unconstitutional, but that they were dangerously foolish. The particular form of misuse of power with which he was concerned in this case was misuse through folly, ignorance, and complacency, rather than through greed or cruelty. Basically, he thought that, if military conflict could not be averted, Britain would be the loser—not necessarily on the field of battle but in relation to its long-term interests. "Victory" as he wrote during the war, "would only vary the mode of our ruin." In reaching this conclusion he had taken into account not merely the resources of the colonies, and the energies of the colonists, but also the *feelings* of the colonists. He does not share those feelings, but he has taken the measure of their force. Thus he has this to say, on the tea tax: "No man ever doubted that the commodity of tea could bear an imposition of three-pence. But no commodity will bear three-pence, or will bear a penny, when the general feelings of men are irritated, and two millions of people are resolved not to pay." (I may add in parenthesis that this passage is much more characteristic of Burke's usual manner than the "melody" of that too-famous flourish about the queen of France; or even than the whaling passage, one of the purplest patches in his American writings.)

This commonsense, down-to-earth Burke, concerned with practical interests and assessment of forces, may perhaps seem and indeed be, a less noble figure than the lamenting harpist of "The Seven Sages." Yet if one has come to distrust the plangent strain in politics, one turns with relief from that distorted Yeatsian Burke—recognizable though some of the features are—

to the real Burke of the American Revolutionary period. I have spoken of his common sense, but this is not quite the right word. It comes out as common sense, especially as we read it in retrospect, because the plain and robust style in which it is often (though not always) expressed can make his propositions appear to be obvious. But they were not obvious at the time to most people, and it took a quite uncommon energy of mind to lay hold of those propositions, and to state them so that they now seem obvious. It also took uncommon largeness of mind in the contemplation of the great scale of the interests involved, uncommon industry in the mastery of detail, and uncommon deftness in the passage from great to small.

Considering all these qualities, and considering also the lucidity and generosity of mind—even in the weighing of interests—which shine out from, for example, the speech *On American Taxation* (1774) and *On Conciliation with America* (1775), I for one do not wonder at the admiration which so many nineteenth-century thinkers had for Burke's political wisdom. Other views have to be taken into consideration, however. In general, in relation to Burke, Sir Lewis Namier's frequent disparagements *en passant*— rather like those of T. S. Eliot on Milton—have exerted a certain influence. People like to quote biting remarks made by one eminent person about another. What interests us here specifically however is Burke's view of America, and that has been forcefully criticized by modern writers, including Burke's American biographer, Carl B. Cone.

As is well known, Burke's party, the Rockingham Whigs, when in office in 1766, had accompanied their concession to American feeling—the repeal of the Stamp Act—by a Declaratory Act asserting the supremacy of Parliament, and its right to tax. This combination is believed to have been Burke's idea, and he defended it for years afterward, notably in his great speech *On American Taxation* of 19 April 1774. In *Burke and the Nature of Politics: The Age of the American Revolution*, Dr. Cone finds that this speech has been praised extravagantly. He thinks its "gorgeous rhetoric" and "wonderful imagery" have combined with other factors, such as its "apparent reasonableness and magnanimity" to persuade men that Burke's recommendations offered a solution to the American colonies. Dr Cone considers this judgment "open to question." He notes that Burke offered, at this time, only one specific proposal: the removal of the tax on tea. He wonders how long Americans would have remained satisfied with that concession, and also "how far men in control of a government should withdraw from a position they believe is constitutionally sound." He thinks that Burke's "gliding over the matter" ignored "the basic problem." "Either the colonies were subordinate in all cases whatsoever, or they were not. Burke tried to have it both ways." Dr. Cone concludes: "The imperial constitution needed amending by granting to the colonial assemblies not merely the privilege, but indeed the right to tax. Even the Rockingham party, under whose guidance Burke thought the quarrel could be ended, was not prepared to grant this."

I think this line of argument worth considering, both directly on its merits and for two other reasons. The first is that it is characteristic of a certain current of twentieth-century academic depreciation of what nineteenth-century Englishmen thought of as Burke's wisdom. And the second is that this depreciation, both in the degree that it is justifiable, and in the degree to which it is excessive, encourages us to think again about the nature of Burke's political thought and action, the question of his *wisdom*.

The language of Burke's biographer about Burke's language reveals a distance between the biographer and his subject. "Gorgeous rhetoric" would apply well enough to some of the anti-Jacobin writings of Burke's old age. It fits only isolated passages in his writings and speeches on America. Nor is the reasonableness of *On American Taxation* only "apparent "; it is incontrovertibly there, and reasoned argument and the fire of conviction, not gorgeous trappings, make the force of the speech. Judgments about magnanimity have to be more subjective, but I do not know where anyone who would deny real magnanimity to Burke's American utterances would look for examples of that quality in political history.

It is true of course that there is something sophistical, and even slightly ludicrous, in the combination of an insistence on the right to tax, with an equal insistence on the inexpediency of exercising that right. It reminds one a little of the Catholic theologian who reconciled the strict eschatology of his church with his personal humane feelings by managing to believe in "an eternal Hell eternally empty." As compared with Burke's balancing act, Chatham's rejection of the right to tax Americans at all seems more consistent —just as the same Chatham was more consistent during the war itself when he continued to refuse to contemplate independence for America, long after Burke and his friends had dropped the right to tax, and resigned themselves to the inevitability of independence. But Burke was not trying to win competitions in intellectual consistency; he was trying, in the first place, to avert a war, and then, when that failed, he was trying to shorten one. The propositions that were needed to shorten the war were not the same as those which, if adopted, might have averted it. The price of the Sibylline books was subject to inflation.

As I have indicated, I think Burke's nineteenth-century admirers were right in speaking of his wisdom. Where they were wrong—and most un-Burkian—was in tending to minimize the importance of the contexts in which that wisdom had to express itself. We may properly say that Burke was a *wise* politician, but we have also to redistribute the emphasis and say that he was a wise *politician*. The noun also qualifies the adjective. Burke worked in a particular political context, with particular political friends and enemies, for particular political objectives. His words should be judged by political standards and not just by academic ones. If a student "glides over" something in an exam paper, his examiners will rightly conclude that this is because the student does not know the answer. But a politician may well "glide over" a particular question because he *does* know the answer. Politicians talking among themselves like to use the word "political" as a term of praise, and I have observed that they are especially apt to use this term about statements which successfully glide over those themes over which the speaker wishes to glide. We have Burke's own word for it that he thought such glidings permissible. "Falsehood and delusion are allowed in no case whatsoever," he wrote in the first of the *Letters on a Regicide Peace*, "but as in the exercise of all the virtues there is an economy of truth. It is a sort of temperance by which a man speaks truth with measure that he may tell it the longer." I might add that if a politician claims to be more truthful than that, it may safely be inferred that he is in fact showing himself to be less truthful.

In emphasizing the need for the repeal of the tea tax, Burke was concentrating on a step which he thought within the bounds of political possibility in Britain, and among things politically possible in Britain, the most likely, to abate the fever in America. On the question of rights, he "economized"; the Rockingham Whigs who had carried the Declaratory Act as an adjunct deemed necessary to a conciliatory measure, were not well placed on him by party. "Party divisions," he had written in 1769, "whether end of conciliation. Burke believed in party, and he accepted the limitations placed on him by party. "Party division," he had written in 1768, "whether on the whole operating for good or evil, are an inseparable part of free government." The assertion of the *right* to tax in the Declaratory Act is un-Burkian *if taken by itself*. The repeal of the Stamp Act, on the other hand, was the most important achievement of Burke's policy of practical conciliation. I believe it is legitimate to infer that a number of Burke's associates in the Rockingham party would not have gone along with the repeal of the Stamp Act if it were not combined with the declaration. And Burke had to defend the policy, and the record, of his party—a policy and record which he had strongly influenced, but had not been alone in influencing. Wisdom informs his speeches, but the practical restraints of political action, and the very nature of the objective which both wisdom and practicality dictated, filtered the expression of that wisdom. Burke had to take acount of the views and the prejudices both of those whom he was trying to persuade, and of those with whom he acted. Dr. Cone, very oddly, rebukes him simultaneously *both* for not going the whole way with the colonists—by advocating the repudiation of the right to tax, in 1774—*and also* for failing to convince the majority of the House of Commons. But if he had gone the whole way with the colonists, he would have failed to convince his own friends, let alone a majority in the House of Commons. The idea that any opposition speech could have convinced such a majority at that time is a strange one, and Burke certainly entertained no such notion. He showed clearly, near the beginning of his speech, that he knew how the vote would go, when, having appealed to "experience" he added "and would to God there was no other arbiter to decide on the vote with which the house is to conclude this day." By the "other arbiter" he meant, of course, the influence of George III and his ministers over the parliamentary majority.

On that April day, Burke did not hope to sway the majority in the House of Commons. He did believe that, as time revealed the folly of North's course, and thereby also the wisdom of the conciliatory policy of the Rockinghams, Rockingham would come back to power. That did happen, but only after the total defeat of Britain in the war, and when it happened Lord Rockingham promptly died. In the meantime Burke had lost his own seat at Bristol, as an indirect consequence of the war he had sought to avert. In his political life Edmund Burke had much wisdom, but little luck.

In an essay on Burke's writings on the French Revolution, I have stressed the relevance of Burke's Irish origins. I believe these origins are also relevant to his writings and speeches on the American Revolution, but relevant in a different way. In the case of the French Revolution, what was mainly relevant were Burke's Catholic associations and sympathies: the Catholicism of his mother and her Nagle relatives, of his wife's father, and possibly the abjured Catholicism of his own father. (One of Burke's American editors, Elliott Barkan, defines his religious background in rather quaint language. Burke he says "was reared in his father's religion, Anglicanism, but his mother, a Roman Catholic, nevertheless managed to instill in him a deep belief in the existence of God"). With these connections—and the word "connection" is a key word with him—he was incensed by the triumphant anti-Catholicism of the initial British welcome for the news of the French Revolution. A sermon by Dr. Price in that vein provided the detonator for the great explosion of Burke's *Reflections on the Revolution in France.*

In the case of the American Revolution it is Burke's general Irishness, not specifically his Irish Catholic connections, which is relevant. There was no Irish Catholic welcome for the American Revolution, corresponding to the English Protestant welcome for the French one. In Ireland, it was Protestants, not Catholics, who welcomed the agitation which preceded the American Revolution. I confess that if I were addressing an Irish-American audience in this bicentennial year, that is one topic on which I might well practice an economy of truth, that my address might last the longer. Irish Protestants tended to favor the American cause, in that period, both on Whig principles and as favorable to the winning of concessions from England—the process that led to the relative autonomy of Grattan's Parliament, which was of course an exclusively Protestant body. The Irish Catholic leaders, on the other hand, saw in the proceedings which led to the Revolution the possibility of winning concessions for themselves, as against the Protestant

Ascendancy, by the directly opposite course: that of demonstrating their loyalty to the Crown. The whole justification of the Penal Laws and the Protestant Ascendancy had been the presumption that Irish Catholics were disloyal, because of their Jacobite past. The proceedings in America, and the response of many Irish Protestants to those proceedings, seemed to the Catholic leaders a golden opportunity of demonstrating that the boot was on the other foot: that it was *Catholics* who were loyal and *Protestants* disloyal. This was the response of Catholic leaders; it need not of course be assumed that the mass of Catholics were praying for victory for George III. We do not know what the mass of Catholics felt about the matter, but given the state of relations between Catholics and Protestants in Ireland at the time, it may, I think, safely be assumed that a course which aroused demonstrative enthusiasm among Protestants would *ipso facto* receive at best a tepid reception among Catholics. These were the conditions that permitted the Catholic leaders safely to display so much loyalty at this period to the British Crown in its dealings with the American rebels.

Burke was a moderate Whig, with strong Irish Catholic connections and affections. This involved tensions, since Whiggery generally was anti-Catholic, and Irish Whiggery vehemently and vindictively so. One might say loosely, but I think meaningfully, that in the case of the French Revolution the Irish Catholic side of Burke won, whereas in the case of the American Revolution the Whig won. It is instructive to compare the use of the word "Protestant" in the two relevant periods of Burke's life. In the context of the period preceding the American Revolution it is a term of praise: the virtues and achievements of the settlers are linked to their Protestantism. But by the time of the French Revolution, Burke is using the term in hostile and derisive ways: not of course hostile to the Church of England, but hostile to those who emphasize the divisions between the church and Rome.

There were, of course, differences in his personal situation. At the time of his major speeches aimed at averting the American Revolution, Burke is in his mid-forties, ambitions and hopeful of the return of the Rockinghams to power. He was mindful of Whig orthodoxy, and knew that his own was suspect because of his Catholic origins. By the time he came to write the *Reflections*, the need for such economies was no longer so pressing. Burke was over sixty, Rockinghan was dead, Pitt was minister, Fox leader of Burke's party, Burke himself derided in the House of Commons. He had lost his seat at Bristol in 1780 for reasons connected with both Ireland and Catholicism, and in attempting to defend himself in these sensitive areas had revealed his real opinions much more openly than he had thought prudent— or than actually *was* prudent—in the period before the American war. By 1790 the pressures of party ties and of ambition, and indeed of hope, were relaxed. He could express much more of his personal feelings, even those connected with his Irish Catholic origins, covered in the mid-seventies with that "politic well wrought veil" of whose propriety he spoke in another context.

This is not, however, to say that, if he had felt free to express such feelings on the eve of the American Revolution, his response to the American events would have been different in substance. In comparing his responses to the two revolutions, the differences in his personal situation have to be noted. But there is also a difference in the nature of the challenges. The character of the French Revolution itself, and of British responses to it, involved attacks on Catholicism. No such direct challenge was involved in the process leading to the American revolution although such a challenge did emerge during the American war and partly in consequence of it. As between George III and the colonists—two contending sets of Protestants—the Irish Catholic leaders took the line which they thought most advantageous to themselves and their people, which was the line of loyalty. Burke might well have approved, for people in their position, a tactic so obviously dictated by prudence, "the god of this lower world." But his own position was different. He was a member of the British Parliament and of the established church. He might, and indeed did, share many of the feelings of the Irish Catholics— of the class from which they drew their leadership—but he did not have to be swayed by their tactics. As far as Ireland was concerned, what he hoped to see, as appeared a little later, was a kind of double enfranchisement: Ireland itself on an equal footing with England, and Irish Catholics on an equal footing with Protestants, distinctions being based on social class and property, not on religion. As far as he was concerned, the cause of conciliation with America was fully consonant with the first of these objectives—which indeed in *On Conciliation* he misleadingly presented as if already attained— and not inconsistent with the second.

The discriminatory laws against Irish trade were analogous to the laws to which the colonists objected, and were applied by the metropolis with uniform indifference to the feelings of the dependencies. Irish resentment against the discriminatory laws was not affected by religion. Catholics of the class to which Burke's Nagle relatives belonged hated these laws quite as much as Protestants did. Burke's Irishness—however guarded its expression at the time of his writings of the mid-seventies—gave him a firsthand understanding of how people in dependencies can feel about such laws, and about the indifference which such laws at best reflect. His American writings are reasonable but they emphasize the importance of feelings, whereas his adversaries, and some of his friends, emphasize intellectual concepts: duties, rights.

Burke was conscious that the state of feelings would be decisive in the circumstances. Both as agent for New York (1770–75) and as a conscientious legislator, he had studied America enough to know that it could not be governed against its will. He knew that if American feelings continued to be ignored and trampled on, the result would be a disaster for Britain. No one knew better than he the importance of feelings in political affairs. And he had to share some of the feelings of Americans. In his American writings of before the war, these feelings are masked where he refers to Ireland. At one point he goes beyond "economy of truth" and seems to fall into that "falsehood and delusion" which he thought "permitted in no case whatever," and which indeed he very rarely falls into. The passage I refer to is that idyllic picture of Anglo-Irish constitutional relations which he draws in *On Conciliation:*

Ireland has ever had from the beginning a separate, but not an independent, legislature; which, far from distracting, promoted the union of the whole. Everything was sweetly and harmoniously disposed through both islands for the conservation of English dominion, and the communication of English liberties.

Nobody knew better than Burke—as his later writings reveal and indeed very much later— how far the sweet harmony described was from the reality. But that that reality was present to Burke's mind, in the American context, is evident from, among other passages, the following generalization in the *Letter to the Sheriffs of Bristol* (1777): "When any community is subordinately connected with another, the great danger of the connection is the extreme pride and self-complacency of the superior, which in all matters of controversy will probably decide in its own favour."

The American Revolution, in its inception, had not touched the nerve of the Catholic question. But the reverberations of the American war did so. Ironically that war both stimulated policies toward Ireland which Burke favored, and also severely damaged Burke's career. Keeping Ireland quiet for the duration became an important part of British policy.

Ireland at the beginning of the war was more than quiet: it was helpful. Not only did Catholics enlist but—more surprisingly—the Protestant Parliament, to Burke's indignation, voted supplies for the war in America although these were opposed by the Patriot party, whose influence later grew. Burke who had hoped to see Ireland become, by mediation, "the balance of the Empire" was disappointed and embittered by that vote. Yet a war of which he disapproved, and Irish reaction to it of which he also disapproved, produced consequences which he could not help supporting although as a result of skillful or fortunate combinations of displays of loyalty and implied threats in Ireland, it became expedient to allow concessions—some of them proposed by Burke's friends—to both Irelands: some economic and later constitutional concessions, beneficial in practice mainly to Protestants, and some relaxations of the anti-Catholic penal code.

The combined concessions, both sets of which Burke was known to favor, were unpopular in his Bristol constituency, as in other parts of Britain. Anti-

Irish and anti-Catholic feelings became inflamed. The Gordon riots in the summer of 1780 put Burke's life in danger. The linked questions of Burke's Irishness and of his (suspect) attitude to Catholicism now became painfully relevant. When he had been elected for Bristol in 1774, his attitude toward America had been popular in a city whose trade with the colonies was important. But already by 1778 and even more by 1780, he was in trouble because of the Irish consequences, which he favored, of the war he had sought to avert. His previous "gliding over" of the Irish reality, and his own relations to it, will no longer serve. He stops gliding and defends himself manfully, from 1778 to 1780. In defending his votes to his constituents, in 1778 he both departs from his earlier idyllic picture of Ireland—he now refers to "the vicious system of its internal policy"—and reveals the real, though partly subterranean, continuity of his thinking on Ireland and America:

I oppose the American measures upon the very same principle on which I support those that relate to Ireland. God forbid that our conduct should demonstrate to the world that Great Britain can in no instance whatever be brought to a sense of rational and equitable policy, but by coercion and force of arms.

By 1780 he was speaking even more plainly. "To read what was approaching in Ireland in the black and bloody characters of the American War, was a painful but a necessary part of my public duty" (speech at Bristol prior to the election).

The prevailing tone of the England of George III in relation to America had to remind such an Irishman as Burke of that England's tone toward Ireland also, and indeed his Bristol constituents reminded him of it—a tone which boded no good for any of the countries concerned.

Burke's counsels in relation to America went altogether unheeded after 1766, and came to be honored only in retrospect. The policies he favored for Ireland were partially implemented, but as near panic measures under the pressures of the American war, and Burke was damaged by the backlash against those measures. More than a decade later, under the pressures of the war with France, similar but greater concessions to Ireland were followed by a recoil, the dismissal of the reforming Lord Fitzwilliam in 1795. Burke, who had foreseen the disaster in America, in the closing years of his life foresaw disaster in Ireland. That disaster came in the year after his death, 1798. In that sense, Yeats was right.

Because of America and of Ireland, Burke lost his seat at Bristol, and with it much of the weight he had acquired in the practical politics of Great Britain. During the remainder of his political life, as a member for a pocket borough, he never recovered the standing and contemporary influence which he enjoyed from 1774 to 1780, as the representative of a great trading city.

It was a heavy loss to him: But he knew also that he had won something.

I shall conclude by quoting possibly the most moving words that Burke ever spoke. Those in which he acknowledged his probable impending defeat, on the eve of the election of 9 September 1780, must move us still:

And now, Gentlemen, on this serious day, when I come, as it were, to make up my account with you, let me take to myself some degree of honest pride on the nature of the charges that are against me. I do not here stand before you accused of venality, or of neglect of duty. It is not said, that, in the long period of my service, I have, in a single instance, sacrificed the slightest of your interests to my ambition, or to my fortune. It is not alleged, that to gratify any anger, or revenge of my own, or of my party, I have had a share in wronging or oppressing any description of men, or any man in any description. No! the charges against me, are all of one kind, that I have pushed the principles of general justice and benevolence too far; further than a cautious policy would warrant; and further than the opinions of many would go along with me. In every accident which may happen through life, in pain, in sorrow, in depression and distress—I will call to mind this accusation; and be comforted.

FOR FURTHER READING

The principal source is the edition of Burke's letters, still appearing: Thomas W. Copeland, ed., and associates, *The Correspondence of Edmund Burke*, 10 vols. to date (Cambridge and Chicago, 1958–77). The collected works have been variously reprinted, but not in a modern edition: *The Writings and Speeches of Edmund Burke*, 12 vols.(Boston, 1901). Convenient editions on select topics include Matthew Arnold, ed., Edmund Burke, *Letters, Speeches and Tracts on Irish Affairs* (London, 1881; New York, 1976); Brian W. Hill, ed., Edmund Burke, *On Government, Politics and Society* (London, 1975); L. I. Bredvold and R. G. Ross, eds., *The Philosophy of Edmund Burke* (Ann Arbor, Mich., 1960), together with the Dent/Dutton Everyman editions, *Speeches and Letters on American Affairs* and *Reflections on the Revolution in France*. Among commentaries more germane to the present treatment are the following: Carl B. Cone, *Burke and the Nature of Politics*, 2 vols. (Lexington, Ky., 1957, 1964); Ross T. S. Hoffman, *Edmund Burke: New York Agent* (Philadelphia, 1956), and his "Burke as a Practical Politician," in Peter H. Stanlis, ed., *The Relevance of Burke* (New York, 1964); T. H. D. Mahoney, *Edmund Burke and Ireland* (Oxford, 1960); Bertram Newman, *Edmund Burke* (London, 1927); and Burleigh Taylor Wilkins, *The Problem of Burke's Political Philosophy* (Oxford, 1967). M. R. O'Connell, *Irish Politics and Social Conflict in the Age of the American Revolution* (Philadelphia, 1965), provides the Irish background, and there are good studies of the English ideological background to Burke's reactions: Colin C. Bonwick, *English Radicals and the American Revolution* (Chapel Hill, N.C., 1977); John Brewer, *Party Ideology and Popular Politics* (Cambridge, 1976); George Guttridge, *English Whiggism and the American Revolution* (Berkeley, Calif., 1942). On the English political background, Bernard Donoghue, *British Politics and the American Revolution* (London, 1964), betters the work of the same title by C. R. Ritcheson (Norman, Okla., 1954); Piers Mackesy, *The War for America, 1775–1783* (London, 1964), provides the best account of the decision making against which Burke reacted.

THE WRITERS OF THE AMERICAN REVOLUTION– VARIATIONS ON A THEME BY AUDEN

OWEN DUDLEY EDWARDS

The piers are pummelled by the waves;
In a lonely field the rain
Lashes an abandoned train;
Outlaws fill the mountain caves.

There is nothing very odd about the alienation of intellectuals: it is their natural condition in society. What was odd about the intellectuals during the American Revolution was that so many of them found it as the answer to their alienation. Fulfillment of that kind is unusual. We expect diverse responses from intellectuals. The very term suggests independence of mind. Hence a mass, almost lemming-like, movement toward a popular front in the 1790s or the 1930s may arouse our suspicions. The life of the mind is not to be confused with Radical *chic.* It is reasonable to see Lenin, Trotsky, Mao, and Ho Chi Minh as intellectuals; but we would not allow the term to their unthinking followers. The Irish intellectuals responded to the insurrection of 1916 and the movement that followed it in various ways, but despite the vigor, extent, and diversity of the Irish Renaissance the fraction who really supported it and were fulfilled by it is very small. The most outstanding figures—Yeats, Shaw, O'Casey, AE, Joyce, George Moore, Lady Gregory, Douglas Hyde, James Stephens—opposed the Easter Rising and its sequel or else offered ambiguities in comment of truly Empsonian complexity. The only really remarkable intellectual of maturity who supported it was Connolly, and the only remarkable intellectual in the making to participate was MacDonagh. The term cannot be applied to other votaries unless it is cheapened.

Sir Lewis Namier called 1848 the revolution of the intellectuals: English was not his first language, and here it betrayed him. On his definition of it, 1848 was an *intellectual revolution*, a revolution concerned with textbook constitutional questions, a revolution dictated by scraps of paper, and theoretical considerations, but not a revolution driven by great minds.

Great minds may have played minor roles, and other great minds may have made approving noises, especially when it was safely over. But it was not a revolution of the intellectuals.

But the American Revolution was. Professor Bernard Bailyn, Dr. Gordon Wood, and their fellows have shown us how dominated by political ideology the whole event was. It had other causes, but it does acquire a particular interest when we acknowledge that some of the foremost minds of their own or any other time found their greatest fruition in it, and these men were not its camp followers, but its leaders. John Adams would speak, many years later, of the Revolution being in the hearts and minds of the people: well, it was in his heart, and those of Jefferson, Paine, Franklin, Hamilton, and other great writers, and because they were great writers, it quickly entered other hearts and minds.

Professor Henry Steele Commager has recently spelled out the identity of the American Enlightenment and the American Revolution. Obviously, not every Enlightener maintained himself at all times in the vanguard of the Revolutionary movement. Franklin trimmed on occasion. John Dickinson was forward in the late 1760s but not in the mid-1770s. And the defenders of Loyalism had some men of very remarkable intellect among them—Boucher, Seabury, Jonathan Sewall, Daniel Leonard. Indeed the high intellectual quality of the pamphlet war preceding the outbreak of hostilities obtained its stature because such giants entered the battlefield on the Loyalist side.

The question which sometimes stumps the fairly cool student, especially the cool English student—why did they revolt?—gets new meaning here. The colonial revolt was in part bred by hysteria, misunderstanding, malice, bigotry, and disappointment at frustration of expectations. But the intellectuals' position is in some ways that of minds too big and free ranging to accept the position of subordination to which their colonial status assigned them.

It was one of the misfortunes of London rule that the metropolis never learned, then or later, to accustom itself to decisive, if transient, loss of intellectual supremacy before challenges from its provinces. Contemporary with the American revolt another enlightenment, the Scottish, was as vigorously asserting its intellectual superiority to London, and London was taking it less kindly than she took American pretensions. But geographical proximity enabled the Scots to succeed in their attempt to dominate the English mind; the Americans were neither numerous enough nor near enough to do so. Yet the life of the mind in America was as honored as it was in Scotland and more formally than in England. Massachusetts Bay distinguished itself as the first society in the history of the world to found its own institution of higher education, Harvard, within six years of its own birth. That tradition tells us a great deal, and advises us that if ever the intellectuals decided to revolt, something would be heard of the matter.

The very largeness of their own backcountry appealed to the grandeur of mind they saw within themselves. In that sense the Quebec Act was an intolerable threat to intellectual *lebensraum*. If they were being reduced to an intellectual nursery, their initial response was childish and bad tempered, with all the bogeys of French rule and Popish establishments they conjured up. And there was certainly much old anti-Catholic feeling to be stirred up. Yet while John Adams, Jefferson, and Hamilton could express bitter anti-Catholic sentiments, especially when opening up a propaganda salvo and before moving from the emotional to the intellectual content of their arguments, they had no difficulties in finding themselves alongside the Catholic Carrolls of Carrollton, clerical or lay, in the cause of the Revolution. The Continental Congress of 1774 produced propaganda so anti-Catholic as to win vociferous Irish Protestant support; but it was not hypocrisy, on the deepest level, which eroded that sentiment. The Revolution took its votaries farther, save for those whom it threw aside in a recoil. If the intellectuals were obsessed by Rome, it was in the last analysis less from fears of papal Rome than from dreams of republican Rome. Classical analogies were gratifying to dignity, nor did they restrict geographical horizons.

> Fantastic grow the evening gowns;
> Agents of the Fisc pursue
> Absconding tax-defaulters through
> The sewers of provincial towns.

To argue an eighteenth-century budding of a Whitmanesque propheticism of American largeness is not to question the greed of the whole business. The American Revolution was sordid enough in much of its motivation, whether on the part of those who wanted a freer hand over their black slaves, or those who wanted to shake off London's restraining hand hindering rough-and-ready colonial solutions to the Indian problem, or those who squandered their inheritances at London gaming tables in doubly doomed attempts to outbid London in sophistication and East India in cutting a dash, or those whose intellect was largely nourished on diets of political paranoia no longer very salable at home but still possessing some durability in the remoter regions. And although our intellectuals had little to do with these matters, they found a judicious silence sometimes profitable. We would hardly term Sam Adams an intellectual; but the real intellectuals, such as John Adams, knew that Sam Adams had his uses and that a Revolutionary Providence—as opposed to the old Massachusetts Providence from whom John Adams had moved so far—had its purposes in making Sam Adams. Sam Adams's methods were not those a fastidious intellectual might wish to copy or even observe; but at a time of crisis one did not pedantically pick him up on every peccadillo. Paine had a decent record on slavery before he threw himself into pamphlet warfare against British rule;

but he tended to lose sight of it, especially since it was clear that the Revolution would not end slavery. Its long shadows might. Jefferson's long career is a record of fascinating ambiguities on both slavery and the Indians; suffice it to say that his name could be taken by slaveholder and abolitionist, by missionary and apostle of genocide. What he could not be called from the grave to support was racial equality. John Adams was far less ambiguous on race than Jefferson, and both blacks and Indians found his son their great champion; but neither Adams had much enthusiasm for Jefferson's democratic theorizing, in the context of whites or anyone else.

The American Revolution and its intellectuals, then, were a revolution and intellectuals whose consciences were not as good as they might have been. In the cases of the intellectuals, this tended to increase the force of their writing. They had to ascend high ground; they needed to conceal the fact that, as they stood, their feet were muddy and their shoes not very protective against damp. Thus the desirable returns from smuggling had to become a theory of maritime empire, economic independence, capitalist enterprise, and the freedom of mankind. Loyalist critics were quick to nail the eloquence of the defense to the muddy origins from which it sought to escape; the intellectuals of Revolution had to choose more mountainous terrain than ever, whence either to inflate their lungs with unknown ozone of liberty, or to discharge their finer and more destructive shots against their vociferous opponents. It might be that the intellectual himself had his own past record to escape: Franklin's political skeletons included much more than his Loyalist son; if John Adams was high-minded, he knew that any defense of a cause led by his cousin Sam involved a vast area requiring deep fortifications; and so on. Rhetoric became self-sustaining, and self-advancing. Its momentum shifted from a defense of certain economic pleas in the 1760s to an activity independent of any narrow economic benefits in the 1770s. Neither the Economic Man nor the Reasonable Man, those two great hideous exemplars of self-interest, could be expected to support the cause of American independence in 1776. If the stakes were still in some respects economic, they were now so much from the economics of dream as to keep the matter in the intellectuals' hands.

So far we have been talking about intellectuals; but the form of their intellect was literary. The eighteenth century was a great age of rhetoric, but whatever claims may be uttered for the colonial assemblies as bodies reaching under their own momentum a condition of quasi independence, he would be a brave man who would argue—from the material evidence we have—that the oratory of the legislative chambers of colonial America outstripped that of Burke in Westminster or Grattan in College Green. Indeed the orators of the American Revolution are generally argued as having been superficial and rather frothy figures. Had the colonists ever got representation at Westminster, at least to the extent of declaiming before the House of Commons, their speakers would hardly have put up a strong show against the home team. The British and Irish advocates of conciliation did their work on a level the colonial orators could not have equaled. Even on frothy eloquence Patrick Henry could hardly compete with the Irish Parliament, and as to depth of thought in oratory the Americans possessed no one remotely comparable to Burke. Their best speeches were essays read in public. It was the war of the pen against the tongue.

They were writers, then, the greatest of them, and they deserve some analysis as writers. But if together they achieve an awe-inspiring unity of teamwork and purpose, taken individually the symbolism which confronts the reader of their publications is very varied. Their ambition to express and win acceptance of their intellectual prowess is a vital common factor, and tells us much of the nature of their alienation. But that alienation needs to be looked at in its origins and character in individual cases. For they were extraordinarily different people. In communications, in climate, in socio-economic background, the American colonies were sundered and hence so were their intellectuals; most of these writers had certain common bases of belief, certain common ideological yardsticks, certain common political superstitions, certain common attitudes to history, to their heritage, and to their own place in English-speaking culture. Even there, differences can be discerned. And if we go below that, the differences become immense. If we examine the most obvious five among our intellectuals—John Adams, Paine, Franklin, Hamilton, Jefferson—they differ in age, length of residence, experience of England, previous political activity, religion, economic and social background. Jefferson has been termed an aristocrat without too much straining of the term; Adam's father was a respectable small-town worthy; Franklin was self-made, if well-to-do, by the time of the Declaration; Paine was a refugee from ill-starred excise work and corset making; Hamilton was neither English nor American nor legitimate nor, perhaps, even totally white.

What confronts us from their most important revolutionary writings? I want to play with one word in each case, and explore them for the rest of this essay. The words are "love," "science," "hate," "gain," and "magic."

> Private rites of magic send
> The temple prostitutes to sleep
> All the literati keep
> An imaginary friend.

Amid the enormous mass of pamphleteering on the American Revolution the *Novanglus* papers of John Adams hold a special place. They lack the brilliance of Paine's *Common Sense*, the succinctness of Jefferson's *Summary View*, the economic shrewdness of Hamilton's *Farmer Refuted*, the pioneer originality of James Otis's work, the legal profundity of James Wilson's writings, the breadth of resource of Franklin's scattered screeds, the exact appropriateness to a specific development of John Dickinson's *Letters of a Pennsylvania Farmer*. They are not even complete: the last papers of the series were lost in the confusion in the printers after fighting broke out on Lexington Green, and the conclusion—if they were the conclusion—has never been seen since then. They commence superficially, and their early pages have some flavor of local party vendetta and parochial bigotry. Yet as a totality they bring together more that is great than their fellows. If Adams is eclipsed by others at individual points, his entire work reaches the heights in area after area. Wilson could argue the legal aspects more cogently and originally, but Adams's use of the law and constitution of England brought a richness and life to his argument which the other lacks. It is ironic, although not unnatural, that the Scotsman used his British sources with the dry perfection of a scholar, whereas the New Englander conveyed his derivation from a whole history of the evolution of liberty with all the love, identification, and sureness of touch that any British reader could demand. Whatever the weakness of his hold on the British and Irish present, he could capture their past with a professionalism extraordinary in one who had never left America.

It contains much else. There is invective of a high order, personal and political; there is a masterly theory of the constitutional relationship of Parliament to colonies which anticipated the idea of the British Commonwealth, and which retained enough life to inspire a clash of giants in the field of political science—Charles Howard McIlwain and Robert Livingston Schuyler—a century and a half later; there is an eloquent defense of the Continental Congress of 1774 and an implied presaging of the much more positive accomplishments of its successor in 1775, Adams being a delegate of major import in both; there is an initial preoccupation with Massachusetts which ultimately elevates both quarrel and locality to great human questions; above all, there is life.

Adams, aged thirty-nine, returned from that Congress of 1774 in November. Delighted with the support from the other delegates for beleaguered Massachusetts, while conscious of the restraint which distinguished many of them from its emissaries, his euphoria suffered a shock of discovery that the Loyalist writers were no more ready to let Congress win by default than were the Loyalist leaders. "I found the *Massachusetts Gazette* teeming with political speculation," he wrote in 1819, "and Massachusettensis shining like the moon among the lesser stars." Indeed, the *Massachusettensis* letters have won many plaudits from their own time to ours as one of the most effective Loyalist tracts of the entire controversy. The author followed Swift's prescription: he used the point of his pen, not the feather. "I saw the small seed of sedition, when it was implanted: it was as a grain of mustard. I have watched the plant until it has become a great tree; the vilest reptiles that crawl upon the earth, are concealed at the root. . . ."

"I instantly knew the writer to be my friend Sewall," recalled Adams, "and was told his work excited great exultation among the tories and many gloomy apprehensions among the whigs." Well it might. "A smuggler and a whig," remarked the Loyalist in his fourth letter, dated 2 January 1775,

are cousin-germans, the offspring of two sisters, avarice and ambition. They had been playing into each others hands a long time. The smuggler received protection from the whig; and he, in turn, received support from the smuggler. The illicit trader now demanded protection from his kinsman, and it would have been unnatural in him to have refused it; and beside, an opportunity presented of strengthening his own interest. The consignees were connected with the tories, and that was a further stimulus. . . .

Thus *Massachusettensis* on the origins of the Boston Tea Party.

Of Sewall, the octogenarian Adams tells us that his father "was unfortunate; died young, leaving his son destitute; but as the child had discovered a pregnant genius, he was educated by the charitable contributions of his friends." Jonathan Sewall was twenty-nine when the two men met; Adams was twenty-two.

In 1757 and 1758 he attended the supreme court in Worcester, and spent his evenings with me. . . . Here commenced between Mr. Sewall and me a personal friendship, which continued, with none but political interruptions, till his death. . . . We attended the courts in Boston, Cambridge, Charlestown and Concord; lived together, frequently slept in the same chambers, and not seldom in the same bed.

Very few of their letters have survived: It may be that most were destroyed when the Revolution made them enemies. One of Sewall's which remains was written on 13 February 1760:

Cicero's name has been handed down through many ages with admiration and applause. So may yours . . . if, in the estimation of the world, a man's worth riseth in proportion to the greatness of his country, who knows but in future ages, when New England shall have risen to its intended grandeur, it shall be as carefully recorded among the registers of the *literati*, that Adams flourished in the second century after the *exode* of its first settlers from Great Britain, as it is now that Cicero was born in the six hundred and forty-seventh year after the building of Rome?

The older man, charming, urbane, quick-witted, was clearly attracted and amused by the eagerness of Adams, and knew that the gruff, shy Adams hero-worshiped him. One feels he suspected, without being too resentful of it, that Adams was brighter than he was, which Adams probably did not suspect. A touch of cynicism led Sewall to know himself to be ambitious, yet to believe Adams to be more so. Yet that letter seems to enjoy the temptation of his young admirer toward ambition. It is hard to imagine Sewall not also enjoying Adams's answer:

I expect to be totally forgotten within seventy years from the present hour, unless the insertion of my name in the college catalogue should luckily preserve it longer. Yet, though I have very few hopes, I am not ashamed to own that a prospect of an immortality in the memories of all the worthy, to the end of time, would be a high gratification to my wishes.

As Adams remembered it, Sewall was the one who first took alarm from the proceedings of the British government, and that as early as 1759, with the rumor "that the English would now new-model the Colonies, demolish the charters, and reduce all to royal governments." His version of that conversation with Sewall began with the latter's urgent "John," and he interrupted himself to add, "He always called me John, and I him Jonathan; and I often said to him, I wish my name were David."

America must resist the English, and by force, Adams recalled Sewall telling him. They argued as to which of them should write in the newspapers advising militia training; Adams, according to himself, felt Sewall was the man, but Sewall, he said, feared offending influential patrons. The panic died down, and in 1762 Sewall became engaged to Esther Quincy, with Adams very nearly following suit immediately by proposing to her first cousin in the heat of the moment. He pulled back in time, and married Esther's more distant relative Abigail Smith several years later. The Quincy engagement had to be a long one for Sewall, and Adams saw him almost every weekend as a result. "During all these years, there was a constant correspondence between us, and he concealed nothing from me, so that I knew him by his style whenever he appeared in print."

Sewall was slowly drawn into the Loyalist camp. By 1767 he was indeed writing publicly, if pseudonymously, about Boston fears of governmental repression, but as an object of ridicule, not as a basis for concern. Adams replied, also under a pseudonym: "though a few individuals may perceive the approaches of arbitrary power, and may truly publish their perceptions to the people, yet it is well-known, the people are not persuaded without the utmost difficulty to attend to facts and evidence."

If Sewall was becoming elitist, Adams's position was hardly that of a democrat. Their old friendship was not weakened by the controversy, nor were Sewall's new friendships. Adams in 1819 recalled his friend's being commissioned in 1768 by Governor Francis Bernard, the recent target of the younger man's invective, to offer him the post of advocate-general in the admiralty court, "which I decidedly and peremptorily, though respectfully, refused." Nevertheless, "we continued our friendship and confidential intercourse, though professedly in boxes of politics as opposite as east and west, until the year 1774. I had then been chosen a delegate to Congress." Sewall, he remembered, vigorously warned him against going. Now political debate had gone far beyond elegant fencing as a precursor to job offers. It meant an inevitable breach. Adams's recollection of his own parting words was:

"I see we must part, and with a bleeding heart I say, I fear forever; but you may depend upon it, this adieu is the sharpest thorn on which I ever set my foot."

Congress followed, and then the return, and the *Massachusettensis* letters. Sewall's embrace of Loyalism, its obviously likely consequence in an ultimate severance, and that event when it happened, added a bitterness to John Adams's hatred of the Loyalist clique whom he believed to have ensnared his friend—a hatred which went far beyond the political norm for so honest a man. Professor Bailyn, at the close of his essay on Paine cited later, speaks of Adams's "intense hatred of the Hutchinson-Oliver establishment in Boston, a hatred that any reader of Adams' diary can follow in innumerable blistering pages of that wonderful book, and that led to some of the main triggering events of the Revolution." But although he finds a "sense" of this hatred in common with that of Paine, its origin was not, and its object far more limited.

One can see in Adams's grief a sense of tragic fitness that the leading literary adversary of his Congress should be his lost friend. And his wife, Abigail, gave him no chance to spare the fallen idol. On 25 January 1775 she wrote to Mercy Otis Warren: "Every act of cunning and chicanery is made use of by the execrable Massachuttensis 'to make the worse appear the better reasoning. . . .'" She at least had found an analogy for him: true to her Puritan heritage, she was quoting—almost accurately—from the second book of *Paradise Lost*, the original subject of the words being one of Satan's lesser counselors, the fiend Belial,

I do not think it unlikely that he receives a share of the money we are told was sent as a bribe for the Leaders of the people. "Sly, undermining Tool" representing the Whigs as men of desperate fortunes, as tho' Truth could not be told only by men of fortunes and pensioners. When is it ever told by them? Are not pensions and places productive of a most narrow sordid and mercenary Spirit, and are we not told that they are granted more for Ministerial than publick Services?—Help me to a Name befitting the character of this Miscreant!

Was this the product only of revolutionary ardor, and of wifely resentment against the traducer of her husband and his congressional colleagues? Or was there also a vestige of old resentment against her husband's Jonathan, senior to her by sixteen years and hitherto unassailable? At all events, whether under her duress, or with a determination to work out to its most bitter end the blasting of his friendship, John Adams began the *Novanglus* papers:

Massachusettensis, whose pen can wheedle with the tongue of King Richard III, in his first paper, threatens you with the vengeance of Great Britain, and assures you, that if she had no authority over you, yet she would support her claims by her fleets and armies, Canadians and Indians. In his next, he alters his tone, and soothes you with the generosity, justice and humanity of the nation. I shall leave him to show how a nation can claim an authority which they have not by right, and support it by fire and sword, and yet be generous and right.

In his fourth letter Massachusettensis had written:

Had a Cromwell, whom some amongst us deify and imitate, in all his imitable perfections, had the guidance of the national ire; unless compensation had been made to the sufferers immediately upon its being demanded, your proud capital had been levelled with the dust; not content with that, rivers of blood would have been shed to make atonement for the injured honour of the nation.

Novanglus could hardly have whipped himself into greater rage than shows in his reply:

Is it any breach of charity to suppose that such an event as this would have been a gratification to this writer? Can we otherwise account for his indulging himself in a thought so diabolical? Will he set up Cromwell as a model for his deified lords, Bute, Mansfield and North? To what strains of malevolence, to what flights of diabolical fury, is not tory rage capable of transporting men?

Massachusettensis sardonically recognized his adversary:

He slides into a most virulent attack upon particular persons, by names, with such incomparable ease, that shows him to be a great proficient in the modern art of detraction and calumny.

Even the old compliments on Adams's learning now seemed destined to be replayed with cruel irony:

Novanglus strives to hide the inconsistencies of his hypothesis, under a huge pile of learning. Surely he is not to learn, that arguments drawn from obsolete maxims, raked out of the ruins of the feudal system, or from principles of absolute monarchy, will not conclude to the present constitution of government. . . .

But Adams could still recall a little of the old laughter:

I am no more of a lawyer than Massachusettensis, but have taken his advice, and conversed with many lawyers upon our subject, some honest, some dishonest, some living, some dead, and am willing to lay before you what I had learned from them.

The violence which John Adams had to do to himself in making war against his own friend, and in choosing so dramatically between his Jonathan and his America, is what lifts the *Novanglus* papers so high. Seldom has so much learning been joined to so much passion. And it was the personal sacrifice he made rather than the abstract sense of patriotism which gave them that radical fury normally found in shallower minds of the era, such as Sam Adams or Patrick Henry, or, at a far greater extreme, Tom Paine. *Novanglus* is a work of genius, and like so many works of genius, it is the greater because it was born of personal grief.

Massachusettensis laid down his pen on 3 April. Lexington, and the loss of the last work of Novanglus, followed. Thence Adams returned to Philadelphia for the second Congress, and then for the third with its Declaration of Independence, and after that he was bound for European diplomacy in the cause of the embattled infant country. Sewall went into exile. Peace had been signed for five years when they met again. Adams was now the first United States minister to the Court of St. James. Sewall in 1788 came to London en route for Halifax, Nova Scotia. Adams in 1819 was clearly as moved by what followed as he had been at the time.

I inquired for his lodgings, and instantly drove to them, laying aside all etiquette to make him a visit. I ordered my servant to announce John Adams, was instantly admitted, and both of us, forgetting that we had ever been enemies, embraced each other as cordially as ever.

Sewall, writing to a friend shortly after that meeting, was more sardonic, and more bitter. His road, after all, had proved the harder. But the colder spirit was once more kindled by the warmer one:

Adams has a heart formed for friendship, and susceptible of its finest feelings; he is humane, generous and open—warm in his friendly attachments tho' perhaps rather implacable to those whom he thinks his enemies . . . if he could but play backgammon, I declare I would chuse him, in preference to all the Men in the world, for my *fidus Achates* in my projected Asylum: and I believe he would soon find it the happiest state. . . .

The faithful Achates, dearest companion of Aeneas in his search for a new fatherland. But Adams had the presidency before him; Sewall only Nova Scotia, and death. Whatever they did talk about at that reconciliation, it was not the famous controversy. Because, if they had, Adams would have discovered that Sewall was not Massachusettensis. Yet the younger man persisted in the belief that he was for another thirty years, and duly put Sewall's name beside his own on the title page when he republished the two works in 1819. Had Adams known in 1775 what he never learned until 1821, that his opponent was the arrogant, opulent Daniel Leonard, a mere acquaintance whom he grew to value less with each new experience of his company, we might very well still have had the *Novanglus* papers. But would they have had such profundity in their ardor, such striving for excellence to impress a venerated adversary, such savage indignation, ennobling fury, immortal fire? Leonard could never have meant to him what Sewall did, as an enemy any more than as a friend. But Sewall he mourned to the last as "evidently broken down by his anxieties, and probably dying of a broken heart."

"Jonathan, thou wast slain in thine high places. I am distressed for thee, my brother Jonathan; very pleasant has thou been unto me; thy love to me was wonderful, passing the love of women . . ." (2 Samuel I. 26).

> Cerebrotonic Cato may
> Extol the Ancient Disciplines,
> But the muscle-bound Marines
> Mutiny for food and pay.

A division between father and son over the American Revolution might seem more likely to produce works of genius, born in pain, than a war against a friend, imaginary or otherwise, but the evidence will hardly sustain such a thesis in Benjamin Franklin's case. His relations with his natural son, Governor William Franklin of New Jersey, were agreeable, affectionate and businesslike; he regretted their division. But love, as opposed to warm affection, or sexual enthusiasm, was never Franklin's master. There is symbolic justice in D. H. Lawrence's having written the most profound attack on him yet made, however unjust Lawrence himself may have been in specifics.

When Conan Doyle was still trying to present Sherlock Holmes as the man of science alone (he humanized him from *The Sign of Four* onward), he had Stamford remark:

Holmes is a little too scientific for my tastes—it approaches to cold-bloodedness. I could imagine his giving a friend a little pinch of the latest vegetable alkaloid, not out of malevolence, you understand, but simply out of a spirit of inquiry in order to have an accurate idea of the effects. To do him justice, I think that he would take it himself with the same readiness. He appears to have a passion for definite and exact knowledge.

Franklin, like Holmes, was not only a scientist in the modern sense of the term: he was also a social scientist, using the same cold-bloodedness in the same way. The twentieth-century divorce of the two callings blinds us to the extent that, in his outlook, they were the same thing. The famous "Poor Richard" postulates have excited admiration and condemnation on the plane of morality. They have, in fact, nothing to do with morality, save where morality can be seen as an ingredient in a scientific formula.

Franklin has been called a friend to England, and to its enlargement, the first British Empire. Can we imagine our Philadelphian Holmes experimenting on that friend? If we view the somewhat inconsistent pattern of Franklin's writings and actions respecting the mother country, the Empire, and the North American colonies as a series of scientific experiments, it certainly accounts for many things. Various explanations have been suggested— a desire for popularity, self-interest with special reference to land speculation— but the *form* of his writing militates in favor of the scientific explanation. The Stamp Act impresses him as an experiment; it is tested; it proves strongly negative in result; he proceeds to argue its converse. In politics, this is inconsistency; in science, it is sense. His contemporary polemicists in action against the British government devote their deepest reflection to the English ideological roots of their self-justifications: Franklin finds an analogy between British policy in America and a possible policy for Frederick the Great toward Britain, and argues his case so well that it briefly imposes on British readers. In other American hands such an analogy might do as hyperbole, but in Franklin's the satire is so measured as to be plausible. English he may have felt, but it was not a feeling compounded of saturation in tradition, or of a sense of himself working out the logic of English constitutional history, as was true of John Adams, nor was his break a conscious self-rupture from that history, as was that of Tom Paine. On the most positive level, his schemes of pan-colonial union are coldly experimental. The very fact that his road to revolution was pursued in London for the ten years before Lexington increased the tendency. He was physically far removed from the confusing distractions of field research, and even at the outset could not hope to speak with authority on American popular sentiment, as the Stamp Act crisis proved. His experiments had all the dangers, and all the comfort, of paper work. He was primarily an armchair theorist, or at least a blackboard one. He could get results quickly, as he did on the Stamp Act, but most of the time he had to reconcile himself to garbled reports of results, or none.

It was this which enabled him to grapple with theoretical extremes, where the American polemicists, in most instances, made such heavy weather of their ideological progress toward rebellion. In almost all instances American propagandists could not bring themselves actually to deny any authority to Parliament over the colonies until the 1770s: the step, however convenient to their ambitions, involved a flirtation with royal prerogatives which, as good children of the Glorious Revolution, they naturally contemplated with inward trepidation. It was all very well to say that such reservation of royal authority was purely nominal; it still might seem to go against the spirit of Locke and the Williamite settlement. Franklin, wiping the failure of the Stamp Act experiment from his fingers, at once began to consider the denial of parliamentary authority. He also—virtually simultaneously—found it possible to cooperate in the fight to repeal the Stamp Act with its proviso of parliamentary rights of taxation. Different experiments might proceed concurrently: indeed, it was advantageous that they should. It saved time, and doubled the likelihood of results.

It is this cold-blooded experimentalism which accounts for Franklin's proving such an able propagandist, and a shrewd diplomat, during his French mission throughout the formal war for independence.

Accordingly, Franklin's place in the propaganda war before the Revolution was an odd one. He was always much more concerned with trying the effects of a theory, an argument, an analogy, an intrigue, than in sweeping under the momentum of conviction to ideological proclamation, as John Adams, Tom Paine, and even Alexander Hamilton did. He fed arguments, documents, experiences, theories into the hands of his correspondents rather than giving himself the indulgence of devising elaborate creeds.

Inevitably, it left out of account how far his experiments were appropriate for his human subjects (apart from any quick reactions he might obtain from a vociferous minority). The scientist can hardly abandon his researches on such a plea as that. In any case, "Poor Richard" had prescribed an entire secular code whose experimental character its author made very clear by the speed with which he broke it when it suited him. He would certainly never have wished to know one-hundredth of the contemporaries that work would influence—after all, he wanted a good circulation for it —much less judge its effects on them.

His scientific enthusiam had nothing to do with personal austerity. He wanted position, money to maintain it, and associates to enhance it. That position was necessary to enable his experiments to take place. Ideally, he would have influenced London, Dublin, Edinburgh, Boston, and Philadelphia politics and society. It was annoying when his field of operations in London began to be circumscribed by what must have seemed arbitrary and unscientific turns of political fortune. His close friend Shelburne could not maintain office; his favor in the eyes of Chatham proved only a wink from a falling star; his fellow agent Edmund Burke left office with the Rockinghams, not to return for fifteen years; his respectful reception from the Commons gave way to his vilification in the finest invective at the disposal of Sir Alexander Wedderburn. Moreover, as hostility to America increased, Franklin himself became more disgusted at the provincialism of the metropolis. He was a great scientist; London seemed increasingly ready to regard him as a dishonest hayseed.

Ultimately, for him, American independence meant recognition of American science, in his own person. France honored him, above all as a *savant*. The severance of the link with London disposed of the perpetual problem of having to prove his provincial status no bar to intellectual eminence. The glory was agreeable, but it was his knowledge he wanted honored, not himself, difficult though it often was even for a scientist to distinguish between these entities.

The Godwin family were much aware of the American conflict, and if little Mary was not born until after Franklin's death, she would have known of him as the most famous scientist of his century, above all in the field of electricity and its uses. And when she chose to immortalize a scientist in her famous novel, the first syllable of his name was the first of Franklin's, the second closely akin to Franklin's second. The positive accomplishments of the Baron Frankenstein were considerable, however much the human factor negated the full revelation of his triumph. Franklin had reason to worry about the human factor too. After the United States Constitutional Convention in Philadelphia he answered a question from a man in the street as to the nature of the being which had been brought to birth: "a republic." But with the prudence born of eighty-odd years' experience of human effects on scientific experiment, he added: "if you can keep it."

> Caesar's double-bed is warm
> As an unimportant clerk
> Writes I DO NOT LIKE MY WORK
> On a pink official form.

"The bearer, Mr. Thomas Paine, is very well recommended to me, as an ingenious, worthy young man," wrote Franklin to his son-in-law Richard Bache on 30 September 1774. "He goes to Pennsylvania with a view of settling there. I request you to give him your best advice and countenance. . . ." It is one of Franklin's experiments whose results are open to our scrutiny, and once set in motion by him it acquired its own momentum. This was accomplished when the scientist had himself returned, and set Paine to work on a history of the Anglo-American quarrel. Paine transformed the brief into one for a philippic demanding American independence, and on 10 January 1776 *Common Sense* was published.

Elsewhere in these sketches my interpretation has been largely my own, but on *Common Sense* Professor Bernard Bailyn has said what has to be said, in his Library of Congress lecture of 1973 (published in the Library's *Fundamental Testaments of the American Revolution*). His work is a masterpiece. He points out that

on the major questions Paine performed a task more basic than arguing points in favor of independence (though he did that too); he shifted the premises of the questions and forced thoughtful readers to come at them from different angles of vision and hence to open for scrutiny what had previously been considered to be the firm premises of the controversy.

Franklin, by now quite ready to contemplate independence, was self-congratulatory: the effect of the pamphlet was "prodigious" in colonies hitherto unready for the final step. Professor Bailyn is cautious on this; events between January and July 1776 had their own effects independently of Paine's highly popular work. But he points to its special character "something bizarre, outsized, unique . . . which sets it off from the rest of the pamphlet literature of the Revolution" and "helps us understand .   .   . something essential in the Revolution as a whole"—and beyond the questioning of common premises, and the extraordinarily "emotional intensity and lyric appeal" of certain passages, he diagnoses a larger quality:

> The dominant tone of *Common Sense* is that of rage. It was written by an enraged man—not someone who had reasoned doubts about the English constitution and the related establishment in America, but someone who hated them both. . . . The verbal surface of the pamphlet is heated, and it burned into the consciousness of contemporaries, because below it was the flaming conviction . . . that the whole of organized society and government was stupid and cruel and that it survived only because the atrocities it systematically imposed on humanity had been papered over with a veneer of mythology and superstition that numbed the mind and kept people from rising against the evils that oppressed them.

Professor Bailyn finds Swift, rather than any of Paine's American fellow pamphleteers, the comparable case. "For Swift too had been a verbal killer. . . . " But he contrasts the Swiftian irony, the rapier-like subtlety, with Paine's language—"violent, slashing, angry, indignant."

It is a most useful comparison; the depth of feeling, the appeal to fundamental human responses, the savage indignation, are shared. But the contrast is instructive too. Macaulay in his essay on the War of the Succession in Spain summed up Swift as "the apostate politician, the ribald priest, the perjured lover, a heart burning with hatred against the whole human race, a mind richly stored with images from the dunghill and the lazar-house" (he was more sympathetic and more perceptive in his treatment of Swift in later essays, and in the *History*). The last two terms concern us.

Urination, defecation, flatulence all preoccupy Swift in much of his writing. In one way this is realism; Swift sees to it that Gulliver performs his normal bodily functions with a regularity lacking among the heroes of most fictions from his day to ours. Nevertheless Swift is obsessive about it. *Common Sense* shows a comparable obsession, but a different one:

> as a man who is attached to a *prostitute* is unfitted to choose or judge a wife, so any prepossession in favour of a *rotten* constitution of government will *disable* us from discerning a good one [italics mine].

And again:

> Ye that tell us of harmony and reconciliation, can ye restore to us the time that is past? Can ye give to prostitution its former innocence? Neither can ye reconcile Britain and America.

And a moment later:

> As well can the lover forgive the ravisher of his mistress, as the [North American] continent forgive the murders of Britain.

Paine was seeking to convert an audience, by emotion rather than by logic, but still to convert. His pamphlet may have been intended to shock, but he also went to great lengths to win possible common ground by an almost fundamentalist use of the Bible in support of his case. Paine was religious, and was sufficiently preoccupied by religion to a degree that his obsessiveness on that matter cost him the friendship of the cautious Jefferson during that statesman's presidency. Professor R. R. Palmer in the second volume of his great *Age of the Democratic Revolution* remarks of *The Rights of Man*: "There are more Biblical echoes in Thomas Paine than in Edmund Burke, appeals to Genesis and St. Paul to argue for human equality and the unity of mankind." But in *Common Sense* Paine allowed his audience to assume a commitment to Scripture he was far from holding; perhaps a bad conscience on this, and even on use of Scripture in *The Rights of Man*, helps account for his desperate anxiety to publicize his real beliefs toward the end of his life. In any event he made vast concessions in *Common Sense* to attitudes of his putative audience which he did not share. One must therefore assume that sexual imagery which could not but repel was forced from him, not by contrivance, but by conviction. He had to speak those words.

The imagery suggests a very different universal outlook to that of Swift. If anything, the persistence of Swift's stress on Man's disencumbering himself of urine, wind, and excrement symbolizes an insistence that the baser wastes must be purged from human nature. Paine's imagery is not that of purge, although he is calling for political severance: it is rather that of irreversible sexual corruption. We are in the presence, not of Swift, but of Timon of Athens. One of the few uses of Scripture which rings really true in *Common Sense*—perhaps because it is not buttressed with politic quotation of text—is Paine's likening of the acceptance of hereditary monarchical succession to the fall of Man by Adam's original sin, and the statement that "our innocence was lost" there makes chilling reading in conjunction with the passages quoted previously.

Swift's was not "a heart burning with hatred against the whole human race." But Paine's?

Charles M. Schultz in late 1959 concluded one of his *Peanuts* daily comic strips with Linus van Pelt shouting at his sister "*I* love mankind . . . it's people I can't stand!!" Thomas Paine, "friend of mankind," as more than one biographer has styled him, found people easy to hate, whether Howe, in *The Crisis*, or Burke, in *The Rights of Man*, or Washington in the 1790s, to whom he wrote: "As to you, Sir, treacherous in private friendship . . . and hypocrite in public life, the world will be puzzled to decide, whether you are an apostate or an impostor, whether you have abandoned good principles, or whether you ever had any." Albert Jay Nock felicitously remarked of the effect of this on Washington that it "merely wounded his sensibilities without ever reaching his understanding." Nock hardly meant it, but the mystery eludes far more profound minds than Washington's. *Common*

Sense Professor Bailyn has termed

the most brilliant pamphlet written during the American Revolution, and one of the most brilliant pamphlets ever written in the English language. How it could have been produced by the bankrupt Quaker corsetmaker, the sometime teacher, preacher and grocer, and twice-dismissed excise officer . . . who arrived in America only 14 months before *Common Sense* was published is nothing one can explain without explaining genius itself.

Where had the cosmic alienation come from? On his arrival in colonial America, Paine turned his first polemical attention against black slavery— an interesting irony against the argument that the Revolution increased anti-slavery sentiment, for the enlistment of Paine in the cause of the Revolution certainly killed a fine abolitionist. The speed with which that preoccupation was taken up and laid down, the further speed with which the Englishman of yesterday proclaimed an Americanism more total than any but a handful of natives would concede, will not bear the charge of self-interest. Paine's whole career gives the lie to that. But the idea that slavery, and American disaffection, and French revolution, gave him a platform on which to express this hatred of his world, offers a unity of explanation. So, too, do the strange friendships, superficial and illusory, symbolized by the letter to Burke after the French Revolution had broken out in which Paine, in extraordinary detail, rhapsodized the new dawn with a certainty of Burke's agreement. He was inevitably to be betrayed by the Burke he had created, the Washington he had created, the Jefferson he had created, and his failure to come to terms with the reality of any of them invites the thought that, subconsciously, the creations were intended to prove their unworthiness. Even the most superficial acquaintance with their statements and writings would have respectively discovered to an observer the traditionalist philosopher, the gentleman freeholder, the closet deist. In one sense Linus's cry is more true of Jefferson than of Paine: Jefferson really disliked meeting people, whereas Paine scarcely knew them to exist until, inevitably, they qualified for inclusion in his commination service.

There is a passage in a remarkable short story by Graham Greene, "The Hint of an Explanation," which goes:

Then something happened which seems to me now more terrible than his desire to corrupt or my thoughtless act: he began to weep—the tears ran lopsidedly out of the one good eye and his shoulders shook. I only saw his face for a moment before he bent his head and strode off, the bald turnip head shaking, into the dark. When I think of it now, it's almost as if I had seen that Thing weeping for its inevitable defeat. It had tried to use me as a weapon, and now I had broken in its hands and it wept its hopeless tears through one of Blacker's eyes.

And this is the most terrible vision among the writers of the American Revolution. His name was a pun, a hideous pun. And from that pain, against the universe, a man was crying.

> Unendowed with wealth or pity,
> Little birds with scarlet legs,
> Sitting on their speckled eggs,
> Eye each flu-infected city.

Thomas Paine became thirty-nine in 1776; John Adams became forty-one; Jefferson became thirty-three; Franklin became seventy. Alexander Hamilton reached the age of twenty-one in that year, and until recently was assumed to have been two years younger than that. He was a student at King's College in New York (later Columbia University). That he was precocious is universally agreed. What must also be remembered is that he was still extraordinarily young when he took his place among the writers of the American Revolution. We are dealing, in fact, with a student radical.

It is a singular fact that our five writers, the best-known five of the Revolution, should only include two men of purely indigenous origin. Franklin's "road to revolution," as Dr. Cecil Currey stresses in his useful monograph of that title, had its critical ten years in the British Isles; Paine did not know America until 1774, and Hamilton, not until 1772. Alone among the five Hamilton had a lengthy, if childhood, experience of non-British rule, on the Danish West Indian island of St. Croix. In America, he lived in Boston, in Elizabethtown, New Jersey, and in New York City, easily making good and helpful friends and carrying no noticeable chip on his shoulder from his alien background and illegitimate birth. He probably entered King's College in 1773 (I follow the invaluable biography by Professor Broadus Mitchell here as elsewhere, and hence his judicious choices amid the forest of disputed chronology in Hamilton's early life). He seems to have liked the high-living President Myles Cooper, but how far his free-and-easy West Indian background fashioned him for the Oxonian style in which Cooper administered King's is open to speculation.

Appropriately for a student radical, Hamilton's participation in the American revolutionary cause began with an unscheduled speech to an audience in City Hall Park, where he harangued a friendly crowd on the need for colonial solidarity against the Boston Port Act and unjust parliamentary taxation. As Professor Mitchell stresses, from the first he took a "national" view, despite his origin in small islands: he could indeed have said "because" of it. Hamilton's detachment in origin enabled him from the first to view his new homeland among the continental colonies as a totality, and the Odyssey since his Boston landfall maintained an identification with America rather than with any single colony.

The Continental Congress was the clear and visible symbol of colonial unity, as well as of colonial resistance. Of its proceedings in 1774 Dr. Samuel

Seabury (D.D., Oxon.) penned his magisterial critique under the guise of a Westchester Farmer. This was less deception than convention; the ancient Roman virtues of agrarianism and simplicity received celebration from both sides of the controversy, John Dickinson's famous *Letters* against the Townshend Acts having claimed a comparable professional origin. But, as Professor Mitchell remarks, there is every evidence in Hamilton's reply, and in his subsequent rebuttal to Seabury's rejoinder, that the student knew perfectly well his target was indeed the learned theologian and, behind him, that circle of Loyalist friends of Myles Cooper who may well have inspired, and certainly encouraged, Seabury's barbs. Seabury no less than Leonard produced one of the most formidable cases on the Loyalist side. Hamilton in taking him on was playing David, but with Goliath rather than Jonathan in his sights.

Seabury, and his intimates, offered Hamilton the chance of adopting a maxim subsequently stated by Wilde: not to start at the bottom, but start at the top, and sit on it. The Continental Congress was vulnerable, and its session of 1774, in particular, left it open to serious charges of inconsistency and duplicity, notably with respect to the Quebec Act and its very different statements on Catholicism as addressed to London and to Quebec. Nor had New York's delegates been foremost among its leaders. Here, then, was a chance to come to the front in ranks not glutted with profound zealots, for a cause in urgent need of defense. Had Hamilton remained in Boston, his name would have been much less easy to make.

Moreover, there existed the question of student revolt. What Hamilton had—what indeed he shared with our other four, as well as with Benjamin Rush, James Wilson, and the rest of the remarkable if less well known intellectual leadership of the Revolution—was his conviction of his own intellect, and his refusal to allow English pretensions to dampen its glow. The most serious kind of student revolt is that in which Jack is brighter than his teacher, and intends to show it. The defense of authority in terms other than intellect, notably in an insistence on forms and ceremonial, exacerbates the vehemence of revolt. The emergence of Seabury's tract saved Hamilton from the frustrating internal bickering and factious activity such a role induces. On all grounds, he had every reason to thank the Westchester "farmer."

As if conscious of the fact that his years might betray his identity through immaturity of argument, his *Full Vindication of the Members of Congress* (15 December 1774) and his *The Farmer Refuted* (5 February 1775) are coldly unemotional. Adams, twice his age, was writing at the same time in a white heat: were it not for the fact that nobody could have accumulated the learning of *Novanglus* in twenty years, the novice uninstructed in authorship and chronology might ascribe to each scribe the age of the other. An opposition of Edmund Wilson's on Trotsky and Lenin might help us here: Adams identified the conflict with himself, Hamilton identified himself with the conflict. Professor Mitchell remarks that Hamilton did not produce information beyond what might be expected from his years; but to this it must be added that the cool discussion of economic dictates was remarkably unyouthful, and was indeed characteristic of Hamilton's objectivity on economic questions for all of his life. This is not to say that he would not hold, and did not then hold, to an economic view with passion; but he stood back from it while taking its measure.

Behind Hamilton's arguments lies the belief that economic self-interest dictates tough responses, if necessary with harsh effects on blameless individuals. If the measures of Congress should injure the economies of Britain and Ireland, it might induce pressure for change, it might cause social upheaval with ultimately similar effects, it might prompt emigration to a self-dependent America with need of a larger work force. He sought an equally austere realism about British conditions: industrialization in Britain, if set back by the American crisis, could not save itself by the relocation of its work force on the land, which could give no more employment than at present. In America, on the other hand, the abundance of land offered every chance of expansion. In one way Hamilton anticipated Turner's famous thesis in *The Farmer Refuted*; but his nature as well as his times dictated that he would be prophetic where Turner by his nature and situation was nostalgic. Hamilton had more positive uses for the past than had Paine, but his recourse to it was essentially pragmatic. The contrast is even more evident in their ideas on the future. Of course Hamilton in early 1775 stood by the link of kingship which Paine was to denounce in early 1776, but the logic of his economic arguments boded no good at all to the British connection.

Professor Mitchell accounts for Hamilton's revolt because of attachment to law, specifically civil rights. My own explanation rests on his evident desire to flex his intellect by challenging an establishment which would otherwise diminish its expression, save through the embarrassing support of patronage. He might have been taken up as a little Seabury, had he offered his talents to the Loyalist side; he would never have been more. But beyond either of these points lies his perception of the economic potentialities of America, and that was an argument for the opponents, not the supporters, of the British authorities and their economic suzerainty. At nineteen, the student radical was an economic statesman. He was not choosing what he took to be the winning side, but the side which he believed had the better economic case. This, too, foreshadowed his future.

But Professor Mitchell does well to stress his belief in rights, as the sequel proved. In May 1775 he played a critical part in rescuing Myles Cooper from a revolutionary mob. In 1776 he was captain of an artillery company. The beginning of January 1777 saw him engaged in the battle of Princeton. His cannon were brought to bear on Nassau Hall, the college building, and it is disappointing to learn from Professor Mitchell that no contemporary source bears out the story that his battery opened fire on it, sending a ball through a portrait of George II. Yet they still tell that story in Princeton, and if for a moment we may allow myth to superimpose itself on reality, it gives us a pleasing last glimpse of the foremost student radical in the American Revolution.

> Altogether elsewhere, vast
> Herds of reindeer move across
> Miles and miles of golden moss,
> Silently and very fast.

What did Auden mean by this verse? So far, I have been taking his "The Fall of Rome" as paradigm for the fall of another Rome, the First British Empire. But there is a decided possibility of identification between his subject and ours at this point. Is he speaking of the still unknown America at the time of Rome's fall, as a harbinger of greatness in the long-distant future when Rome's corruptions and contradictions would have receded into near oblivion?

Of all the five, Jefferson alone was an American in mind as well as in life. Adams, the only other one to bring a purely American background to his revolutionary writing, was animated by the Englishness of English law. He appealed from England drunk to England sober. Jefferson thought American. The story of Adams, the story of Massachusetts, worked itself out to the music of the ever-murmuring sea, and the sea was English. Massachusetts, even in revolt, thought of the other shore. The Blue Ridge Mountains of Virginia do not think of the sea. Jefferson regarded the view from the hill at Harpers Ferry, now outside his state, but not then, as more worthwhile than a journey across the Atlantic. His alleged Francophilia of the 1790s was much more Anglophobia, coupled with optimistic views about the Americanization of France. His presidency marks the real turning away of the United States from European preoccupations.

He was a most appropriate person to have written the Declaration of Independence.

The Declaration of Independence had two objects. Its diplomatic intent was to persuade European powers that the Americans were serious in their revolt, would not—indeed, because of the violence of their language, could not—wipe the slate clean with Britain and start afresh, were to be trusted in an alliance, and would fight to the end In this it failed. The French, for whom it was primarily intended, declined to risk their diplomatic necks for a document, and the longed-for alliance was only made possible by the much more concrete evidence of Saratoga.

The other object was political. By asserting that the country was independent, it hoped to convince the reluctant majority of Americans that it ought to be. To achieve this, it had to be an act of exorcism. John Adams, forty years later, defined the American Revolution as the moment when Americans ceased to pray for King George. His narrative on the point might suggest that this event predated the Declaration by several months, but in fact, of course, it certainly did not. No doubt well before 4 July 1776 John Adams had ceased to pray for the King, and Jefferson had probably ceased to pray for anyone, left to himself, but the American identity, the enlarged ego of the average American, had long expressed itself by reference to the King, and it was going to take much to alter this. The American swore by his King, litigated by his King, prayed for his King, fought for his King, and died for his King. The loneliness of his life and his own minuteness against the forces of nature were triumphantly offset by the contemplation of his place in a mighty organization, whose imperfections could be forgotten by absorption in the symbol of the King. His life was the richer, his death the sweeter, by the knowledge that he represented the King. Well might Paine go to war against all history in his attack on monarchy; the King was very old magic indeed, all the stronger because the English King had taken on himself many of the attributes of the Pope. In specifically religious terms these attributes might cut as little ice among anticlerical Virginians as among Massachusetts Congregationalists. But the magic far transcended religious specifics. The King might not rule America, but the King still was America. Even the most embittered pamphleteer, Paine alone excepted, even the soldier in arms against British forces, stopped short of attacking the King directly. The embattled farmers of 1775 were still King's men. American identity remained overshadowed by the King.

The King must die.

It is only thus that we can account for the most obvious fact about the content of the Declaration of Independence: its appalling unfairness. Even if George III had wanted to do all the things he was charged with in its clauses, he could not have done them. The point was not one of entering a reasonable plea. It was to curse the King, to write a blasphemous litany against him, to blot out his name under every conceivable charge. The legalistic proofs of John Adams and James Wilson, the historical arguments of John Dickinson, the economic reasoning of Alexander Hamilton, the fertile contrivances of Benjamin Franklin, the dubious logic of Thomas Paine, were not wanted here. Language was at last supreme. Assertion, denunciation, repetition were what was wanted and what was given. Prayer for the King had been, at bottom, an act of faith. Then let there be an antiprayer to demolish that faith.

Whatever the private beliefs of its author, the antiprayer had no intention of questioning the fitness of the original recipient of prayer. More economically than Paine, Jefferson was quick to include God on his side. Independence was declared against the King, not against God. The religious-minded waverers were too numerous for any indulgence in secular feeling. The Constitution, here as in other respects more revolutionary than the Declaration, excluded God. But God was not needed to carry the Constitution. He was needed to carry the Declaration. He was needed to help kill the King.

Dr. Cecilia Kenyon, in the same lecture series whence I have already cited Professor Bailyn, draws attention to the Declaration's debts to the Putney Debates of Cromwell's army in October 1647. In nature if not content it seems to me to be much more sharply aware of another document from that period and, to some extent, from those ranks: the death warrant of Charles I. The most obvious point lies in the putative fate of the signatories. The regicides had been exempted from Charles II's judicious mercy at his Restoration. A few escaped by ignominious contrivance; a few were safe in exile, as the folk memories of New Haven well knew; several were dead, of whom Cromwell, Ireton, and Bradshaw were exhumed to be hanged. The rest were put to death with revolting cruelty. The modern eye glides rapidly over the Declaration's closing words, "we mutually pledge to each other our lives, our fortunes, and our sacred honor." Mencken's "translation" into modern American rightly terminates by the acknowledgment that the signatories may be "hung for it." As Professor Murphy implies elsewhere in this volume, the great signature of the president of Congress, John Hancock, boldly asserted a readiness to face the decided possibility that this might be his own death warrant. "We must all hang together," smiled Franklin grimly, "or assuredly we shall all hang separately." But as he saw very clearly, they might hang together in his second sense. The King could only be killed by his executioners' showing their own readiness to die.

The document has seventeenth-century origins. In tone it is severely derivative of the eighteenth-century Enlightenment, as firm a proof as one needs that the American Enlightenment can only be assessed by study of the American Revolution. But in another respect it harks back to ages before the dawn of recorded history. Jefferson was far too shrewd to leave it to the Enlightenment to do his work for him. It might be the age of the Enlightenment, but the Enlightenment was elitist, and he had to win a reading and a listening public far beyond its confines. The Enlightenment is not rejected: its children could devour the Declaration without any sense of wallowing in rejected superstition. Even God—"nature's God"—is made to sit easily enough with the Enlightenment, far more than does the God of *Common Sense*. The preamble moves with the utmost elegance between its theocratic and its Enlightened audiences: the former could take comfort in endowment by all men's creator, the latter by what all men were endowed with, to wit certain unalienable rights. But behind this maneuvering, and beyond the preamble, the Declaration moves into a mood which makes it part of ancient ritual.

I had thought that my sense of the magic of this document was peculiar to me, but Professor Merrill Peterson, the great historian of Jefferson's posthumous image, brought a professional lifetime's work on Jefferson's writing to the conclusion in his *Thomas Jefferson and the New Nation* that "its ideas could not be developed, nor even stated; they could only be conjured up by magical words and phrases in trim array." The conjuring activity and the deployment of magic had of course to be a matter of extraordinary precision. Not only had the idea of ritual king sacrifice to be presented as a holy act, but the victim had to be shorn of any possible sympathy. Here the immediate precedent supplied its own warning. Cromwell had set the stage for the killing of Charles, but Charles won back for the institution of kingship by his death what he had lost for it by his life. As Andrew Marvell's generous lines acknowledge, it was a sacred drama; but it was one in which the director ultimately failed to control the star. Fortunately George III was not visible, and his verbal death could obliterate sympathy as his physical death could not have done. It was also true that while George III and Lord North were far more admirable and honorable men than Charles I, neither embodied the dignity with which Charles turned the tables on his adversaries. Jefferson could be certain that if he ascended the heights of awesome majesty, no ground could be taken from him by pompous royal proclamations. There is a great advantage in dealing with martyrs who are unaware of their martyrdom.

The King must die, that the nation could be born. The daggers of each count in the indictment speed sharp and true, deadly in their brevity, yet deadly also in the occasional interruptions of their fixed pattern. Twelve counts ring like drum rolls in succession, introduced by the staccato double beat "He has. . . ." Then follows a change of tempo: a long drum roll comes, but below its length, so stongly contrasting with the shortmess of the earlier counts, are what prove nine subcounts on the "jurisdiction foreigh to our constitutions" and the "acts of pretended legislation" under it, again with the common introduction, this time "for. . . ." Its effect is that of a flight of arrows which in the distance seem like one, and prove nearer to be many. Five more major counts follow (though Jefferson had seven): the pace is now so fast that Jefferson can afford to vary "He was . . ." by "He is . . . ," while his content moves from the constitutional to the horrific: "plundered our seas, ravaged our coasts, burnt our towns, and destroyed the lives of our people . . . works of death, desolation and tyranny . . . cruelty and perfidy . . . executioners of their friends and brethren . . . merciless Indian savages . . . destruction of all ages, sexes and conditions. . . ." The academic work of constitutional grievance at the outset is subordinated to an extraordinary control of rhythms and groupings; once the content begins to charge the King with murder against the Americans, the rhythms and numbers are broken. As killing becomes the theme, the counts become deathblows. The *coup de grace* was written by Jefferson as "A prince whose character is thus marked by every act which may define a tyrant is unfit to be the ruler of a people who mean to be free," with an additional somewhat hollow sentence on the incredible nature of George's actions, but Congress wisely struck the latter out and, since the instrument asserted American independence, wrote "ruler of a free people."

The next passage, deliberately minor in key, says its word on the breach with the British "brethren." The quieter tone is essential: this is but a foot-note to the work just done, and Congress wisely tightened the diffuseness which now overtook Jefferson. Then follows the moment of life, to answer the act of death: the united colonies—Jefferson, significantly for the ideology of his middle years, did not originally include the word "united"—were "free and independent states." The pledge of common solidarity concluded the whole.

In this sense, Jefferson is the witch doctor of the American Revolution. The orchestration is all the more extraordinary when one looks at his other writing. To say that he never wrote anything comparable to it is to say nothing: he never had the opportunity, let alone the capacity. With all due respect for Congress's improvements—and, when one considers deletions such as the clause on slavery, its pusillanimities—Jefferson's own control of his material in the draft is phenomenal in anyone, but even more so in him. "He was curiously vulnerable," wrote Henry Adams in his *History*, "for he seldom wrote a page without exposing himself to attack. . . . Ridicule of his opinions and of himself was an easy task . . . for his English was often confused, his assertions inaccurate. . . ." And Gore Vidal's *Burr* does little violence to the probabilities in picturing Hamilton and Burr grinning over the unintentional absurdities of Jefferson's second Message to Congress. But in the Declaration inaccuracy was his servant and English his pliant tool. Perhaps, in a way, the care of the author cannot alone account for it. Perhaps the magic also transformed the magician.

FOR FURTHER READING

The literature is voluminous, and only certain highlights can be noted. For texts of the works involved, the following are standard editions: J. P. Boyd, ed., *The Papers of Thomas Jefferson*, 18 vols. (1950–72), and Paul L. Ford, ed., *Writings of Thomas Jefferson*, 10 vols. (1892–99); H. C. Syrett, ed., *The Papers of Alexander Hamilton*, 25 vols. (1962–); William T. Hutchinson, ed., *The Papers of James Madison*, 10 vols. (1962); Leonard W. Labarré and W. B. Willcox, eds., *The Papers of Benjamin Franklin*, 20 vols. (1959–76); John C. Fitzpatrick, ed., *The Works of George Washington*, 39 vols. (1931–44, reprinted 1968); Philip Foner, ed., *The Writings of Thomas Paine*, 2 vols. (1945); L. N. Butterfield, ed., *Diary and Autobiography of John Adams*, 4 vols. (1961); Lester Cappon, ed., *The Adams-Jefferson Letters*, 2 vols. (1959); Charles F. Adams, *The Works of John Adams*, 10 vols. (1850–56). Of these, the Franklin papers have so far reached only the beginning of the revolutionary period, and the Jefferson and Madison series are also far from complete. Gaillard Hunt, *The Writings of James Madison*, 9 vols. (1900–1910), and A. H. Smyth, *Writings of Benjamin Franklin*, 10 vols. (1905–7), together with the Ford edition of Jefferson, provide the most important revolutionary era papers and publications still unpublished in the new editions, as does H. A. Cushing, *Writings of Samuel Adams*, 4 vols. (1904–8).

Writings upon the writers range from the studiously biographical to the broadly interpretive. Among the most important of the latter are Bernard Bailyn, *The Ideo-*

logical Origins of the American Revolution (1967); Daniel Boorstin, *The Lost World of Thomas Jefferson* (1948); Adrienne Koch, *Power, Morals and the Founding Fathers* (1961); John R. Howe, *The Changing Political Thought of John Adams* (1966); Paul Connor, *Poor Richard's Politicks* (1965); Clinton Rossiter, *Seedtime of the Republic* (1953); Gordon S. Wood, "Rhetoric and Reality in the American Revolution," *William and Mary Quarterly*, 3rd ser., 23 (1966): 3–32. Somewhat differing interpretations than those presented herein can also be found in individual biographies, notably Eric Foner, *Tom Paine and the American Revolution* (1976), and David F. Hawke, *Paine* (1974); Merrill D. Peterson, *Thomas Jefferson and the New Nation* (1970); A. Oliver, *Portrait of John and Abigail Adams* (1967); James Flexner, *George Washington*, 4 vols. (1968–); John C. Miller, *Samuel Adams* (1936); Carl Becker, *Benjamin Franklin* (1946). Likewise broad intellectual contexts shed complementary light, notably Henry F. May, *The Enlightenment in America* (1976); H. Trevor Colbourn, *The Lamp of Experience* (1965); and Alan Heimert, *Religion and the American Mind* (1966).

THE
AMERICAN
EXILE
ROBIN W. WINKS

Exile is a common theme in the history and hence the literature of all immigrant societies. The theme is especially strong in those cultures that, in their colonial periods, saw themselves as (to use Louis Hartz's term) fragments of a European tradition. One should not be surprised, therefore, to find the idea of exile both real and also romantically attractive to writers, including historians, from Canada, the United States, Australia, New Zealand, South Africa, Brazil, Argentina, or Mexico. Exile is also a common theme in those societies that gave forth of the emigrant, and perhaps no body of transplanted Europeans (if one may be permitted the term) has reflected so poignantly on this theme as have the Irish. Since so many from Ireland came to North America, they reinforced the theme doubly and more.

Nowhere is the sense of separation so well expressed as in Rudyard Kipling's "Song of the Cities" when, after carrying his reader through fifteen outposts of the British Empire, the poet of Rottingdean gives us something of himself as he reaches New Zealand, where Auckland is "Last, loneliest, loveliest, exquisite, apart"; a line New Zealanders alter to "Last, loneliest, least." Indeed, the central theme of New Zealand's literature is that of "the Man Alone"—the title of John Mulgan's famous novel about "the bit in between," meaning the interwar years—and it is a theme which recurs in the most representative of New Zealand poets, such as Denis Glover and Allen Curnow. Johnson, the protagonist of *Man Alone*, is solitary, asocial, reticent, self-sufficient, tough. He is alienated man, the ultimate exile, turning away from the traditions of European culture and away from his own society as well. The exile as seen in this kind of literature is (or was until Sylvia Ashton-Warner wrote *Spinster*) male, and the notion of exile is given an essential male*ness* by virtually all of New Zealand's writers.

By most of Canada's too, at least until Margaret Atwood wrote *Surfacing* in 1970. To be sure, the exile also plays an important role in the work of that other Canadian, Margaret Laurence, and no one who has read *The Fire-Dwellers* can make exile and its accompanying ambivalence an exclusively male preserve. Even so, as the New Zealand poets address themselves to their native scenery, they more than most appear to be exploring the idea of exile constituting the making of a new nation. It is not in *Exiles*, however, so much as in *Ulysses* that James Joyce best captured the inarticulate nature of the notion:

But do you know what a nation means? says John Wise

Yes, says Bloom.

What is it? says John Wise.

A nation? says Bloom. A nation is the same people living in the same place.

By God, then, says Ned, laughing, if that's so I'm a nation, for I'm living in the same place for the past five years.

So of course everyone had a laugh at Bloom and says he, to muck out of it:

Or also living in different places.

That covers my case, says Joe.

It covers the case of the North American norm, in fact, where a person must carry his sense of identity with him, for he is unlikely to grasp it from the landscape, changing his place of mental and sometimes physical residence with the frequency North Americans typically have done. Harold Bloom as literary critic has it right if one may, in his *Kabbalah and Criticism*, substitute "travel" for "reading" in his sentence, "Reading is defensive warfare, however generously or joyously we read, and with whatever degree of love, for in such love or such pleasure there is more-than-usual acute ambivalence." Exile, then, is a state of mind, and especially so for the North American.

The Irish poet Frances Gwynn suggests that the exile owns a "sting of memory." True enough. If one consults the card catalog of most libraries, one will find "exile" cross-referenced to "expatriation," "deportation," "penal colonies," "refugees, political," and "Siberia—exiles"—all references well calculated to invoke that sting. But exile also constitutes a form of survival. This is the (perhaps too simple) thematic guide to Canadian literature provided to us by Margaret Atwood—*Survival* (1972). In this tour de force, Atwood analyzes, among much else, "failed sacrifices"; that is, the reluctant immigrant. She does so under the aphorism of John Marlyn in *Under the Ribs of Death*—"It is meaningless to call anyone a foreigner in this country. We are all foreigners here." To see the whole of the Canadian identity as enveloped in a sense of failure and all Canadians as victims is a silly idea and not worthy of Margaret Atwood, but to see it as a land of spiritual exiles, fed from an eternal spring of renewed exile, is not far off the mark, provided we remember the ambivalent note of affirmation that may be present in all celebrations of exile: "Each day we can watch the paper boy wonder why / instead of a wreath you have tacked a new list to the door."

There is no journey if there is no destination. This may be the ultimate problem of the exile as seen in the literature of Canada or New Zealand. So often Canada has been the physical destination of exiles from the United States: it has had to play a special moral role in changing American perceptions of what constitutes the desirable life. *That*, surely, is the destination, and so long as Americans consciously sought out, or still may seek out, Canada as the end of a journey toward the defined "desirable life," it will not be a nation of mere survivors. In this sense, exile to Canada often has been a positive act for Americans, and the historical facts make foolishness of the overly precious observations of those who find a perverse romanticism in the persistent notion of the exile as failure, of Canada as the recipient of failures. Surely the *Sunday Times* of London was wrong in spirit if right in historical fact when it proposed to call its bicentennial exhibition on the British after the American Revolution "The Losers." In "September 1913" Yeats's irony also has its affirmative note:

> Yet could we turn the years again,
> And call those exiles as they were
> In all their loneliness and pain,
> You'd cry, "Some woman's yellow hair
> Has maddened every mother's son:"
> They weighed so lightly what they gave.
> But let them be, they're dead and gone,
> They're with O'Leary in the grave.

By 1972 a group of writers, symbolically giving their new Canadian journal the title of *Exile*, declared that "The imaginative writer . . . is . . . in exile now." *There* is a bit of self-romanticizing to contrast with Yeats, state of mind though both may be.

There is a point to all this maundering, indeed several points. There invariably is a large element of melancholia and nostalgia attached to the exile, or the expatriate (not precisely the same thing) experience. There is a good bad poem which shows these feelings clearly: "The Exile's Lay," by an unknown border minstrel, which for all its banality suggests the exile point of view as one perceived from persistent enemy territory:

> And thou, smiling cottage, the place of my birth,
> No more wilt thou witness my sorrow or mirth:
> Where the brook sweetly warbles a soft, chiding tune,
> No more shall I stray, by the light of the moon!
> Adieu, to thy daughters, so bright eyed and fair,
> (How oft have I roamed with them, free from all care,
> When the landscape look'd gay, under bright summer skies,
> 'Neath the light of the stars, and the glance of their eyes!)

> Nor again where of yore, (tho' I scarcely knew how,)
> With delight strike my lyre, as I followed the plough:—
> My companions the lark, with his sweet gushing sound,
> The robin, and sometimes, the muse hov'ring round,
> Never more tending gaily thy flocks and thy herds,
> Nor listen again to the songs of thy birds!
> Farwell [sic] early friends! do you e'er think of me?
> Adieu to my kindred, left beyond the dark sea!

Dreadful as all this is, one can detect within it all too clearly the reasons why the exile so often was thought to be an unhappy creature. When the American Loyalists left for Canada, they should have known that snow and adultery were not their only choices. Somehow the American who went a-Westering thought of his new-found-land as a land of beginning again, as Emerson's land of the eternal return; why then, one might ask, did those Americans who hied themselves off to another country (in James Baldwin's words) not see that other country as the land of opportunity?

One reason may be that, on the whole, individual Americans, whether abroad as exiles, expatriates, or merely as travelers, do not see themselves as repositories of their culture, perhaps because they are never certain of what their culture is. Sharing a language with many other countries, carrying (black Americans aside) no particular badges of identity that mark them instantly, provided they do not speak, they may merge with the culture to which they have gone. Nor need the American variant of English mark them off for long as foreigners if they choose their exile well. The great majority of both exiles and expatriates from America, the colorfulness of those who sought out France or Italy notwithstanding, have gone to England, Canada, or increasingly today to Australia, that is to other fragments of the same lingua franca.

Then, too, Americans have been greedy for experience. They have roamed the world like the avaricious jackdaws they are; they have not denied nor forgotten their past experiences, even though they may have renounced them; they have seldom slipped silently into their new countryside like the good exiles some were meant to be but have, rather, surfaced quickly not only as survivors but as leaders in the new societies to which they have gone. In modern times, they have been able to entertain the idea of an eventual return, seeing exile as a temporary condition, and their immigration laws (and from these, their laws of citizenship, including the resumption of citizenship) have been relatively generous, despite the stereotype of a nation said to be xenophobic, frightened of foreigners, certain that its citizens, if overseas for long periods of time, would come back subversive of American goals. The nation has, in general, welcomed its exiles back, quietly absorbing them into a nation which may have caught up with them.

Most important perhaps is the simple fact that, because of the size of the United States, and because of the vitality of retained regional cultures within its borders, many Americans already have experienced an exile mentality without leaving the country. Adjustment to an unwanted move from the sun of California to the snow of New England, like adjustment from the pine barrens of the Carolina uplands to the short grass plains of Nebraska, has inured the American to confrontations with new environments. The shift from Donegal to the coasts of New England is in some ways less great, national borders and great oceans to the contrary. Americans, it may be, are unique because they *can* go home again, within their own borders, but the shock of exile is no less great at the time it occurs for taking place within the borders of the nation.

In truth, a period of expatriation from the scenes of childhood sojourn seems essential to many Americans. Consider these works of American literature: "The Legend of Sleepy Hollow," *Washington Square*, *The Bostonians*, *The Damnation of Theron Ware*, *The Age of Innocence*, *The Great Gatsby*, *Babbitt*. Do these sound like works of nostalgia, of lessened perception? All were written by their authors while expatriates from America. Distance clearly gave strength to their sense of identity as Americans. Even Ishmael Reed has shown us, in *Flight to Canada* (1976), a contemporary black author's perception of the fugitive slave experience in Canada, that the group of American exiles who most assiduously sought to escape to another land ultimately chose to return to the land from which they had escaped.

Reed is speaking of a fact, and we shall turn to that fact in a moment. Let us dwell on Reed's more important point, however: that Canada has both literal and metaphorical meaning to the American exile. It is a place of real experience and it is a place of anticipated experience which provides the American writer with a mirror image. There was a time, in the 1840s, when a casual stroll down an Ohio small-town street might reveal a half-dozen shop windows shuttered, showing a sign that read "G.T.T."—Gone to Texas. The interest in Canada was never so sharply focused, so intense, but it has been a consistent goal for the American exile, and Canadians have especially felt this to be so, entertaining notions of a moral superiority to the ways of the Republic that would ultimately assure a steady northward flow of the more intelligent and sensitive. Time and again American literature reflects this theme: two obvious examples are Theodore Dreiser's *Sister Carrie*, in which Carrie Meeber, "a waif amid forces," flees with Hurstwood to Montreal from Chicago, and William Dean Howells's honeymooning couple who seek out Niagara, Montreal, and Quebec on *Their Wedding Journey* as they come to their own discovery of their mutual exiles. Interestingly enough, each novel was its author's first, and each author seized upon Canada as the locale in which he could best reflect upon what being American meant. The tradition has continued in the literature of the United States, in Saul Bellow, even in Ken Kesey's *One Flew Over the Cuckoo's Nest*. Canada is escape; it does not provide satisfaction; it becomes the focus for exile.

This vision is historically valid enough, of course. Canada often has been the goal of the exile American and particularly so in times of war. It is a cliché of Canadian history (no less true for that) that New Brunswick, the Eastern Townships of Quebec, and the lands along the Niagara Frontier were first effectively settled by Loyalists, and that much of the early anti-Americanism in Canada is to be attributed to their influence. To be sure, Loyalists at the end of the American Revolution also poured into the Bahamas, and many went to England, but clearly the British North American Provinces absorbed the most. They came in two waves, white, and in two waves, black: those who in 1783 departed for Canada; those who a few years later saw that there was little chance of reconciliation between the former mother country and the new Republic and, belatedly, made their way north, to be greeted as "Late Loyalists"; the black Loyalists who, having fought with the British during the Revolution, sailed from New York harbor in 1783 and expected to acquire plots of land in Nova Scotia; and the even later black pioneers who, seeking refuge behind British lines or on British vessels during the War of 1812, were transported to Nova Scotia in 1813–15, perhaps the last group to arrive in Canada that might be thought of in the Loyalist context. Let us look at each of these groups in turn.

Quite possibly the most representative Loyalist was Jonathan Sewall. Born to a distinguished Massachusetts family in 1728, Sewall's interest in the law led him—despite a diametrically opposed personality—into a lively correspondence with John Adams. Deeply involved in colonial politics, Sewall came to his own conclusions about liberty as an abstraction, conclusions which were remarkably like those of Edmund Burke. Even so, when the Revolution burst upon him, Sewall did not—as Burke did—defend the colonial position, for his definition of liberty had become not only conservative but virtually inert. In 1775, even though attorney general, he left Massachusetts for England, there to remain throughout the Revolution a loyal servant of the Crown.

Sewall soon found himself intensely homesick for Massachusetts, whether in rebel hands or not. He wanted American fish, newton pippins, cranberries. His sense of loss of place was enormous—not alone of social standing but of actual environment. He was the American exile *par excellence*, not admitting to himself until the spring of 1778 that his English residence was likely to be a protracted one. Finally, facing reality, he settled in Bristol to wait to see what the war would bring. The "damned fanatical, republican, New England, rebellious, ungenerous, ungrateful sons of bitches" were, he thought, behind him.

Sewall's most consistent argument against the war was that it was stupid and senseless. This would be a note struck again and again by American exiles from America's wars. A land so soiled by so heinous crimes against humanity could no longer be his own. Reason no longer played a role in American decision making. As his most perceptive biographer has written,

Sewall "saw nothing and searched for nothing in his own political behavior in Massachusetts to warrant exile, or even opprobrium." The recognition of the independence of the United States suggested that Britain now saw loyalty as "a crime and an attachment to government the source of disgrace. . . ."

Sewall was now but one of many Loyalist exiles in England who were seeking reimbursement for their lost property and furnishings, whether destroyed or confiscated by the Americans. Many lived near each other, along the Brompton Road, feeding on each other's grievances. From 1785 on, claims become more difficult to press, as key witnesses left for Nova Scotia, Scotland, or Ireland. Increasingly they felt themselves to be among strangers, unwanted; as adjudications proceeded, the results were less than happy; after settlement, employment often was hard to come by. In 1787 Sewall joined the exodus to Canada, following his friend Ward Chipman to New Brunswick, and brooded his way to death in 1796.

Here, then, were the first exiles. How many? How influential? The new school of Loyalist historians is providing answers to these questions. Mary Beth Norton estimates that upward of 80,000 fled America, most expecting to return shortly, with little to do and much time to do it in. Some 1,440 heads of families migrated to Britain—perhaps 8,000 people in all—where they appealed for pensions, aid, and compensation. But they were dispersed by 1789, and the great majority no doubt did not go to Britain in the first instance. Wallace Brown suggests there were 100,000 Loyalist exiles, a figure taken from a contemporary British consul, Phineas Bond, and argues that if one may assume that perhaps half the Loyalists went into exile, the actual Loyalist population may have been anywhere between 160,000 and 384,000. (Robert Palmer has also made the important point that, even allowing for possibly substantial errors in these estimates, the American Revolution produced nearly five times as many émigrés as the French Revolution did.) Arthur R. M. Lower concluded that perhaps 35,000 Loyalists actually came to Canada. These figures do not account for those who returned to the United States, finding that they were more attracted to an environment than to an ideology. The ultimate influence of those who remained in Canada seems, on a per capita basis, to have outweighed the influence of any one of the shards of the one true cross.

This is not the place, nor is there any need, for a rehearsal of the history of Loyalism, early or late. No more so need this author recite at any length the fate of the black Loyalists, for he and others have done so elsewhere. Sewall's friend Ward Chipman, as solicitor general of New Brunswick, was responsible for the effective end to slavery in that colony in 1800. By then the black Loyalists had, in large measure, moved from the Nova Scotia in which they had found scant welcome to Sierra Leone in West Africa, exiles twice removed. In Nova Scotia they had proved unable to depart from the methods of agriculture they had learned in the "American" environment to the south, and in Sierra Leone they would become the nucleus for a group of Africans who would hold to North American ways. They would be followed by other groups, just as the refugee blacks would follow them from the Chesapeake Bay into Nova Scotia, again to think of themselves as exiles.

The black Loyalists were not so pro-British as they were pro-black; they sought less protection under the British flag than they sought a place where they might thrive together. Thus when they obtained freedom by fleeing from their owners to the British lines, they were making a personal affirmation, not an ideological one. It is in this sense, as with subsequent groups of American exiles in Canada, that one sees them as carrying their sense of identity with them—hence, unlike the white Loyalists of the Revolution, their feeling of exile with its negative connotations was less acute. Nonetheless, they rightly saw themselves as Loyalists, fully as loyal (if not more so by virtue of military service on the part of many) as those who later saw themselves as the scions of the United Empire Loyalists, and hence entitled to the same rewards. That they did not receive those rewards, at least in equal measure, is by now a well-recorded part of Nova Scotian history. They were not runaway slaves. They were Loyalists in the best sense of the word, remaining with the Crown because they were convinced that such a course would lead to black liberation. As Loyalists they were no more and no less self-interested than white Loyalists; as exiles, they were far more adaptable over the long run, for their goal was a different one.

A second such group of black exiles would reach the Maritime Provinces of Canada during the War of 1812. Beginning in 1813 and running well into 1815, the British navy brought escaped slaves who had sought refuge behind the British lines into Halifax harbor, where they were slowly filtered through a cumbersome receiving system and onto the land. Unlike the black Loyalists, many of the refugees were fleeing from slavery but not toward any clear goal, and their lack of cohesion and preparation soon showed. They were unable to contend with the harsh Canadian winters, remained on a form of the dole for many years to come, and saw themselves as exiles from a land they remembered with pleasure and a government which they continued to fear.

Interestingly, by the end of the nineteenth century the white population of the Maritime Provinces of Canada had confused the descendants of slaves, Loyalists, and refugees with each other. Separate exile experiences were conflated into one experience by the dominant society. As a result, Canadians came to praise themselves as the land of freedom where blacks had sought security "under the lion's paw." That the blacks saw themselves as exiles was accepted only in the sense that many observers thought Canada too cold a climate for Africans; little thought was given to them as exile *Americans* and very little more as Canadians in exile within their own new found land.

It often is argued that the American Revolution produced another set of exiles: the revolutionary Irish. Certainly this is so in the sense that the revolution did much to stimulate revolution in Ireland. The parallel between English attitudes toward the colonists and English attitudes toward the Irish, as shown by Perry Curtis and others, is too obvious to repeat here. For this reason as much as any other Americans sensed that, perhaps alone among their forebears, the Irish did not look down upon them. Britain had entertained a domino theory about the American Revolution as shown by George III's fear, explicitly expressed in 1779, that if America succeeded in its purpose, the West Indies, then Canada, then Ireland would follow. Queen Victoria would invoke a similar theory during President Grover Cleveland's first term, writing to Lord Salisbury that if Americans were to be allowed to declare Cuba independent, such a precedent ought to be protested against. "They might just as soon declare Ireland independent!" she wrote.

Benjamin Franklin's quite possibly apocryphal letter "To the Good People of Ireland," as printed in the *Hibernian Journal* on November 4, 1778, nonetheless expressed widely held sentiments. The Irish would play, as soldiers, as Loyalists, as patriots, as exiles, a considerable role in the Revolution, just as the Revolution would play a considerable role in their lives. Exile Irishmen in America would thereafter play a vital role in Irish politics; as Conor Cruise O'Brien noted in his study of Parnell, Parnell could never have survived without American power. Indeed, Lawrence McCaffrey credits Lloyd George's decision to summon the Irish Convention of July 1917 almost entirely to his need to satisfy American opinion.

The interconnection between the two sets of exiles may be overemphasized, of course. Some have felt that the United States spent too much time bleeding for Ireland and not enough for "their own Ireland," as the *Nation* called Haiti–Santo Domingo in 1920. When eighty-eight congressmen sent a telegram to Lloyd George urging him to avoid warlike acts in Ireland, the *Black American* urged the congressmen to protest equally on behalf of Hispaniola. They were, they felt, exiles in their own land, whereas the Irish were showing divided loyalties.

Divided loyalties are of the essence of exile, of course, and although many who might have supported Fenian designs also scorned the Fenians as hyphenated Americans who were prepared to embroil their newly adopted country in war with Britain to help the country they had abandoned, others did not see exile (or immigration) in quite so polarized a way. One could be an exile and loyal nonetheless. Few Americans, after all, went to Ireland, so the experience ran in one direction. And what happens when one looks, in fact, at the accomplishments of the Fenians of the nineteenth century? There is little significant evidence that the United States, as a government, ever gave thought to intervention on behalf of Ireland at any time. Indeed, the Fenians gave rise to much anti-Irish feeling, for they appeared unable to put the country they had left out of their minds as they should put its language out of their hearts. William Roger Louis and Ronald Robinson, in their as yet unpublished study of the United States and the liquidation of the British Empire, in which they seek well back in time for serious presidential or cabinet-level rhetoric on the question of anti-imperialism, find repeated references to India, none at all to Ireland. Irish Americans may well have fought for Irish independence but they did not learn to do so in the American revolution, and the American government—which except in election year did relatively little other than passively allowing its citizens to act on behalf of Ireland—sped the independence of Asia and Africa. In the long run the black Americans, once exiles themselves, would count more heavily than other exile groups in the shaping of American policy.

But these reflections carry us ahead of our story, in which we must return to three other groups of exile Americans who, as it happens, also largely involve Canada. (The inability to separate Canadian history from American history is a theme I have sought to develop elsewhere.) Perhaps Canada was above all the haven of American exiles in the decade before the American Civil War. Canadian legend has come to claim that at least 60,000 fugitive slaves came to Canada West (present-day Ontario) alone by 1860. The figure represents a substantial inflation, confusion over what a fugitive slave was, and an amalgamation of all Canadian provinces into one. That a legend grew to the point that Canadians firmly believed they had provided succor to a majority of all fugitive slaves suggests that the fugitives filled an important need in Canadian mythology. The total number of fugitives was substantially lower. They did tend to see themselves as exiles. With the outbreak of the Civil War they looked forward to their eventual return to the United States. In 1861 the reported black population of Canada West, on the official census, was 13,566; by 1871 the black population had fallen very little; but by 1901 the population was 8,935.

Once again, this is not the place to investigate an extremely complex story, especially given its investigation elsewhere. Rather, there is a point to be made: fugitive slaves were fugitives from slavery, not from America as such. Many saw slavery and America as synonymous, to be sure; yet, with the removal of slavery, they began to return to the United States. They had not sought Canada so much for its positive attractions as from the negative propulsion which the desire to escape from slavery represented. This is, surely, exile in its purest form.

Two other bodies of American exiles in Canada also came for essentially negative reasons: those who sought to escape from the draft, or from militarism, during the two world wars and after. There was an essential difference between Canada's response to the self-exiles, however, for during World War I the Dominion sought to exclude draft dodgers and deserters whereas in the post–World War II period they were welcomed. The press and the churches of Canada also mirrored these differences.

There was a more significant difference upon which historians have not remarked. Those who sought refuge in Canada during World War I and in

1919 were largely Hutterites and Mennonites—that is, they had not seen America as home except in the sense of a place of temporary habitude so long as it tolerated their practices with respect to militarism. In World War II, and far more importantly, during the war in Vietnam, many Americans who sought refuge in Canada felt they were doing so precisely *as* Americans and precisely in order to uphold what they believed to be American ideals which were being trampled upon by an unthinking, even mad administration. They shared, at least at first, some of the emotional responses of Jonathan Sewall, responses which set them apart from those who sought refuge and thus exile in Canada at the height of Canada's own anti-immigrant sentiments of 1919 and the 1920s.

The path of the conscientious objector often has been exile, and reasonably enough the place of exile, at least initially, has been chosen for its similarities to their home and for its proximity. When ideological considerations color the moral ones, objectors may seek a society they perceive to be quite different, as when many of those who protested against the war in Vietnam went to Sweden, but in general proximity and similarity have been the chief criteria —hence the persistence of Canada in the story of the exile American. During and immediately after World War I, the Mennonites who had taken conscientious-objector status often suffered from the stigma of "Germanism"; further, they tended to reside in (and be imprisoned in) Oklahoma, Ohio, Iowa, Kansas, Illinois, and Montana, all states with relatively ready access to Canada. (At roughly the same time, beginning in 1909, black Americans from Oklahoma and Kansas would be seeking to start new lives in Saskatchewan and Alberta.) Canada had been advertising for new settlers especially heavily in these states, for the ministers of immigration contended that Canada needed strong-armed yeoman farmers and that these were most likely to be found in assimilable quantities in the prairie states of America. They had not counted on the Mennonite farmers any more than they had thought of the black farmers. The lack of warmth in the welcome given to both groups no doubt intensified their sense of being unwelcome everywhere, but there is little evidence as to how such exiles saw themselves, if they thought of themselves as exiles at all. The Mennonites, at least, were present in Canada under an arrangement made with the Canadian government in 1899, an arrangement the government promised early in 1918 to honor, and possibly had they moved onto the prairie lands east of the Rockies they might have attracted little attention. The decision to settle in British Columbia, a province to which few Mennonites had gone before, assured that their experience in Canada would be at once isolated and the subject of intense focus.

Public opinion in Canada was strongly against the exiles, and the government in Ottawa soon found that it had to appease those who had accepted prejudicial views about the Mennonites and blacks. Mennonite preachers were barred at the border, German Mennonite papers were ordered to cease, those who had entered Canada as conscientious objectors were informed that they would not be given access to the franchise even should they become citizens, and religious groups spoke out against allowing Mennonites the privilege of starting schools in which German was the language of instruction. After the return of Canadian war veterans, who felt strongly about doing one's duty for national defense, the Canadian Parliament moved, in the spring of 1919, to amend the Immigration Act of 1910 in such a way as to restrict the entry of Mennonites, Hutterites, Dou-kobors, Chinese, Japanese, and blacks. For those who had already gained admission, a sense of internal exile settled heavily upon them.

Admission came far more easily to the exiles from the war in Vietnam. Many Canadians also opposed the war and saw themselves offering succor in the manner in which they had aided the fugitive slaves of the 1850s. Others recognized that the self-selected exiles from the war often were college students who brought education, and perhaps skills, to Canada. Conscious of the dependent nature of the Canadian economy, Canadians were happy to embrace those who might, at least in theory, help make the economy less dependent: "Send me your skilled and educated men yearning to breathe free" is representative of that frequent combination of piety and practicality that one finds under such circumstances. The several refugee aid groups that sprang up in Canada spoke for both motivations, although they were careful to emphasize the fugitive-in-exile aura in their literature.

How many exiles? The U.S. government admitted to 240,500 Americans living in Canada in 1971, most of whom one can presume were not among the fugitives. The Canadian National Council of Churches suggested that there were 150,000 American exiles living in Canada, a figure which suggests —assuming the total figure submitted by the American census to be accurate—that only 90,000 Americans were living in Canada voluntarily— not a credible thought. Nonetheless, there are nearly a quarter-million Americans living within the Dominion for one reason or another, and in a population as small and attenuated as Canada's, they tend to rank as well as to rankle in a variety of contexts. The media in Canada, preoccupied with bolstering Canada's sense of moral superiority, naturally searched out those who would say that the United States had become a sick society.

But often the young exiles did not wish to be used in this way. They did not feel that they had irrevocably turned their backs upon the United States; rather, they had left in protest to a particular administration and in the context of a temporal set of circumstances. Further, older Canadians often appeared to fear the youth who had been implanted in their midst, since by self-definition they were not respecters of authority, and Canadians on the whole—if one is to accept Seymour Martin Lipset's comparative analyses— were more conservative than were Americans. Sadly, Canada showed no consistent ability to adjust to the temporary surge of young Americans who, rightly or wrongly, attempted to seek out some means of not participating in a system with which they profoundly disagreed, and the Canadian reaction became confused, and particularly so in academic circles.

The exile American who hoped to find a place within the traditionally liberal academic community came to find, to his surprise, that he was not always welcome. Led by the voice of Robin Mathews, some Canadian universities began to apply quotas to the number of Americans who might be employed by them. In the late 1960s and early 1970s Robin Mathews and company sounded a representative Canadian trumpet from the right wing, in the sense that Charles Reich, in *The Greening of America*, ultimately also was well to the right. Draft dodgers, among others, were Americans; they were unconscious polluters; even if they might regale against American imperialism, they nonetheless represented the American way of life. They knew little of Canada and made few efforts to diminish their ignorance. The American way of life was and is, the argument ran, intensely contaminating, for it leads to Americanization (for which read industrialization). If one asked, does a quota on Americans today mean a quota on Englishmen or Dutchmen tomorrow, the reply was that only Americans constituted a real threat to the Canadian way of life. This was so even if they took out Canadian citizenship (which most did not); in time, those who feared the presence of Americans in Canadian academia would argue that even an advanced degree from a university in the United States was indicative of a certain lack of commitment to Canadian values. The American could never cease being an American in the eyes of such people; a moral indefeasibility of allegiance applied. With little sense of irony the anti-American group of Canadian academicians embraced that most colonialist of weapons, the notion that the tiger cannot change its stripes. The United States had become the Republic of Junk and those it had once nurtured, however many American flags they might burn in expiation for the accident of birth, were contaminated for all time.

When the exile, or the expatriate, is reduced to a symbol—when he becomes Camus's *Exile*—he may as well come home. For Robin Mathews was right. There is a unique American identity, and it is carried with one as one goes overseas, seldom discharged, never forgotten. The American does not put down roots, he takes them with him. Yet this also was to strengthen the adaptation of those Americans who elected to remain in Canada, for they could become Canadian citizens while enjoying a commonly shared North American standard of living. The U.S. offer of amnesty to the draft evaders met with little response, in part because the offer was not without its objectionable qualifications, but also because the American exile in Canada was not fully an exile—Canada had become his halfway house. One could have one's identity and consume it too. Those who found employment in Canada often found that their employment was with a branch of one of the great predominantly American multinational corporations; thus they were channeled back into the North American capitalist system.

Many of the new exiles resisted such complicity in the system from which they had fled. As one argued, "As new Canadians who have gone through the American experience, we are perhaps in a unique position to comprehend the positive aspects of Canadian culture and to helpfully join the new Canadian nationalist movement in affirming them." Perhaps they might yet bring change, even liberation, to the land they had left behind. Perhaps it was still uppermost in their minds. Those young Americans who joined in the call for an independent Canada were exiles in the fullest, and perhaps the most positive, sense of the word.

If this is so, then so too were the exiles from Ireland who sought to use the United States as a base for the transformation of the land they had left behind equally conscious of the basic fact of exile: it may be a positive statement about a future devoutly wished; it need not be the negative, slow running of one's life out into the sands of bitterness and futility embraced so perversely by Jonathan Sewall. Men in exile feed on dreams. The exile experience has bound Ireland and America together in a double irony, for as Stephen Vincent Benét wrote,

> Remember that when you say
> "I will have none of this exile and this stranger
> For his face is not like my face and his speech is strange,"
> You have denied America with that word.

But then, perhaps the exiles of other lands have come to the more bitter end. Was it not Deirdre, in *The Exile of the Sons of Usneach*, who leaned out from a chariot and let her head be smashed against a high block of stone that jutted out into the road, and died?

THE
AMERICAN
IDEA

ALASDAIR MacINTYRE

Rhetoric about the United States is in this bicentennial era suffering from a crisis of overproduction; everyone must by now have consumed almost as many sentences as they can bear. Just one more platitude, one last cliché and perhaps the population of the United States will rush screaming into the oceans and the Great Lakes. It is at this tense moment of surfeit that I choose to open my mouth about the American Idea, an enterprise so rash that I can perhaps hope for an immediate reaction at least of astonishment, if not of sympathy. And since I have been so foolhardy as to speak at all, I may as well continue in the same vein with a harsh judgment on all that preceding outflow of self-congratulation. It is that conventional praise is apt to conceal rather than reveal the American idea, while the best clue to its true nature is to be found in anti-Americanism. For anti-Americanism is itself a peculiarly American phenomenon, felt in genuine form only by Americans.

What do I mean by anti-Americanism? I do not mean mere dislike or even hatred of Americans or of the United States. Those are clearly universally available emotions. But when Asians are napalmed by Americans and consequently hate Americans, they are not being anti-American in the sense that I intend; for they would hate anyone who napalmed them in precisely the same way. And when delicately brought up English lecturers in the United States are disgusted by exhibitions of bubble gum among their audiences, they too are not being anti-American in the sense that I intend; for they would hate anyone who bubble-gummed them in precisely the same way. But a very large number of Americans *are* anti-American in a quite distinctive mode. Let us take as a starting point the way in which Americans attacked each other over and during the Vietnam War. Whatever side they were on, their peculiar bitterness and intensity were perhaps only to be explained by the theory that each controversialist was engaged in attacking part of him or herself as much as the other. For those who attacked that war could recognize in the manner and matter of that appalling enterprise a good deal of themselves; and those who defended it could not fail to see in the attitudes of those who attacked them an embodiment of the very same principles which they themselves professed. "What are *we* doing in Vietnam?" was a shared question. Irishmen, West Germans, Frenchmen, Englishmen do not find it too difficult to disown their governments totally, to abstract themselves from the political nation and depart rejoicing. Americans seem to find it far harder to disengage the political self without disrupting the cultural self. I think of those American expatriates of the 1920s who wrote home regularly cursing their origins, but treating them as a curse to which inexorably they had to return. How different from James Joyce, who remained obsessed with Ireland, but an Ireland of the past. His Dublin was never allowed to progress beyond 1904. And to note this is to note that this phenomenon of the divided American self goes back beyond the immediate past. How far back?

Ever since Charles Beard historians of the revolutionary period have been fascinated by and have quarreled about the relationship between the apparently radical political principles of the Founding Fathers and the apparently conservative attitudes informing their social and economic stances. From one aspect they look like rebels and revolutionaries; from another like characteristically self-protective men of landed and mercantile property. On how these two aspects relate almost every possible position has been taken from that which naïvely takes their revolutionary professions entirely at face value to that which equally naïvely treats those professions as a mere ideological Whig mask worn by nascent capitalists. To the latter we need to point out that after 1660 no other group of English landed and mercantile gentlemen ever approached even the revolutionary principles, let alone the practice of 1776. For 1776 was *not—pace* Burke—1688, and there were no conventional Whigs in Washington's winter quarters at Valley Forge; but there was Tom Paine, as genuine a revolutionary as could be found. To the former we nevertheless need to point out as forcefully that deep contradictions were indeed embodied in the principles and practice of the Constitution makers. Nobody recognized this more clearly than the members of the first Confederate congress at Montgomery, Alabama, eighty-five years after the Declaration of Independence. They rightly and clearly saw the most flagrant contradiction between the declaration of the inalienable and equal right of every man to live, to be free, and to pursue happiness, and the institution of slavery. But this contradiction in the 1770s and 1780s was neither mere rhetorical carelessness nor just a symptom of hypocrisy, although doubtless there was an element of both in the Continental Congress and in the Constitutional Convention. Rather this contradiction represented a conflict already so deeply embodied in the American character that no care for a surface appearance of consistency or a superficial disguise for hypocrisy could have got rid of it. It is the contradiction between a profound commitment to the principles of equal rights and liberty on the one hand and an equally profound commitment to individualistic practices which generate inequality and unfreedom on the other. American history is the tragic working out of this internalized contradiction. But why do I call this history tragic?

It will help to answer this question by considering first three of the key features of the milieu in which the American Idea has had to be realized. The first is that form of property which has most signally disfigured American aspirations to equality of right: slavery. It took the briefest space of time, the least burdensome of devices to introduce slavery to the Americans; its abolition has already taken over a hundred years and is not yet completed. For the state of being a slave owner, even heir to slave owners, turns out to be extremely difficult to eradicate, much harder than the state of being a slave. "But," say many contemporary Americans, "*we* were *never* slave owners. That was someone else, elsewhere, long ago." But this kind of attempt to deny one's historical identity, one's historical solidarities, is itself in part a symptom of the slave-owning consciousness. For it is of the essence of the slave-owning consciousness to deny that slave owning is anything but an external, an accidental attribute of any human being. The slave owner likes to think, has to think, that he is a man like any other men—except of course his slaves. He merely happens to own slaves as a man might happen to own racehorses or mousetraps. But in believing this he both deceives and does violence to himself; for to be a slave owner is to disown part of one's common humanity. It is to refuse to recognize parts of oneself. It is for Americans specifically an inability to recognize themselves as having been cast for a role in black history, a role such that without being at one in a community with black Americans white Americans cannot be at one with themselves. Thus white American liberalism has been profoundly mistaken when it has defined its political tasks in terms of a contrast between white power and benevolence on the one hand and black deprivation on the other. Not white power and benevolence but forms of white deprivation are at the root of the problem of black liberation into equal rights.

The second defining feature of the milieu in which the contradictions of the American Idea have to be worked out is money, money whose power as symbol extends its power as reality. It is no accident that the game of *Monopoly* was invented in America; for *Monopoly* mimics our deep social agreement to pretend that pieces of engraved paper and lumps of shaped metal signify something else. And because we all connive at that pretense it becomes true. Money is a myth of which we are all eager narrators and nobody more so than Americans. Money thus ceases to be a mere means of exchange; it becomes a measure of worth. A market economy turns the question "How much do I want such-and-such?" into the question "How much am I prepared to spend on such-and-such?" and the question "What weight should *my* desires be given as against *yours*?" into the question "How much money have I and how much money have you?" There were and are rich men in precapitalist societies; of them what Hemingway said to Fitzgerald is true—the difference between them and us is just that "they have more money." But in capitalist America the rich man aspires to be the measure of worth; he is, as Fitzgerald shows us, a work of art, a dazzling fiction, who seeks to make his own unreality prevail over our reality. I therefore take riches to be a form of aesthetic vice, money to be a medium of corruption. Of course not all rich men are vicious, just as not all heroin takers succumb; of course money is indispensable and I like it too. But the gospels and the rabbis made it clear long ago that the coexistence of riches and poverty deforms both the rich and the poor and America is one more parable.

The third essential defining feature of the American milieu is of course technical invention. I think here of the Remington family. Eliphalet Remington, Sr., was a mechanic who established himself around 1800 in rural New York State as a manufacturer of agricultural tools, as well as in horseshoeing and repairs for farmers. Eliphalet Remington, Jr., his son, went into the rifle business and became one of the founders of the mass manufacture of repeating rifles. His son, Philo Remington, diversified into typewriters and other electrical appliances before the plants were taken over by others in the 1880s. Thus we have in one family major contributions to the technological base for the creation of the modern American widow—through the Lee Remington rifle in its mass slaughter, Civil War version—and the even more modern American divorcee—able to support herself through office work of a kind made possible by the Remington Rand and other typewriters.

Slavery, money, and continually growing technical power with continuously unpredictable social consequences—for the Remingtons scarcely set out to manufacture widows and divorcees—these have all effectively shaped the scene in which the American drama has had to be enacted. And slavery, money, and technical power—and their various social consequences—all tend continuously to generate inequality. But more than this: in a social milieu with such defining characteristics it is the exercise of the freedom assured by rights, it is the release of human energy and potentiality provided by political freedom, which embodies itself in social, financial, and technical inequality. Hence the tragic character of American history: right conflicts with right, right frustrates right. Nowhere is this clearer than in the Jacksonian period. For it is Andrew Jackson whose Bank veto, proclaimed to uphold radical democracy in the very same activity, unleashed the power of money upon that democracy. And it is in Jackson's period that James Fenimore Cooper could see what he took to be the first great period of the American republic gradually overwhelmed by the forces of money. "Here the democrat is the conservative, and, thank God, he has something worth preserving." There is thus a continuity in conflict to be traced in American history in which "America" is simultaneously claimed as the name of an aspiration to liberty and equality of right, and the name of the very power that stands in the way of that aspiration. Consequently the American is characteristically at war not only with other Americans but with himself. Citizens of other nations are free to measure what their government and society does by *external* standards of liberty and right and can choose between their loyalty to these absolutes and their loyalty to their own nature; but the American finds that these absolutes *are* his constitution, that he cannot disown his national allegiance without disowning these moral absolutes or vice versa.

America is thus not just a country, but a metaphysical entity, an intangible abstraction always imperfectly embodied in natural reality. It is always *not yet*, it is always radically incomplete; and, because the values it aspires to incarnate were from the first seen as *the* essential human values, anyone and everyone may be summoned to take part in that completion. Hence the American idea can never be just what the Founding Fathers said it was or what any particular later native generation has made of its variety and contradictions; it waits also on what the immigrant has to say about it. Different as immigrant generations have been, they have shared a contrast between what they took to be the particularity of their own earlier circumstances, of the barriers and frustration that held them back at home, and the universality of what they took to be the release from those frustrations awaiting them in the United States. Anyone—a Pole, an Irishman, a Japanese—can be an American, because to be American is no different from being *man as such*. Hence to be an Irish American or a Japanese American is not to weld together two or more ethnic particularities from this point of view; it is to merge ethnic particularity with something else. This is one-half of the immigrant contribution to the American idea.

The other lies in the confirmation and extension of part of the idea which goes back to those earlier immigrants, the Pilgrim Fathers. It is the belief that a genuine break with the past is possible, that new identities can be forced, that a new Zion can be built. Not only is the future open, but in that future there are no ultimate limits to possibility. This is the belief which was continually reinforced by the continuous expansion across the western frontier and later by the continuous expansion of that other frontier, the Dow Jones average. Both types of frontier strengthened the belief that anyone can perhaps become anything. Many different kinds of talisman have been carried on these journeys into the open future: the Puritan faith in the God of the Old Testament, Benjamin Franklin's preachment of thrift, industry, chastity, orderliness, and punctuality, Horatio Alger's faith in hard work, the numbers game's tribute to sheer luck.

The elements in the American Idea as I have characterized it so far are many, disparate, and complex. They stand in a variety of complementary and conflicting relationships with each other. The American Idea is not single, unitary, and consistent but presents very different aspects from different points of view. Having understood this it is important to understand also that in its historical embodiments the American Idea has appeared in many different guises, each representing an attempt to impose some order and coherence into this intractable material. I therefore venture to examine four different versions of the Idea, each with a historical life of its own. The first two of these at least involve characteristic forms of blindness to certain aspects of American reality; they supply coherence at the cost of self-deception, but their forms of self-deception are themselves peculiarly American.

I have suggested that the reality of American historical experience is tragic, and I have also suggested that Americans are apt to discard their sense of the past and with it any sense of their own historical identity or of its tragic character. When this awareness of their historical particularities vanishes, there tends to vanish also any sense of historical limitations and there appears on stage a self-consciously American parody of the American Idea. For this type of American, complexity, contradiction, and tragedy are completely alien ideas. Sin has not yet come into his world and he sees money and technical power as mere instruments of his own goodwill. The social world—both American and foreign—is a milieu for the embodiment of his virtuous intentions. Lacking a historical culture himself, he is not only reduced to gross moral simplifications but he cannot perceive the historical culture of other peoples either. His own impoverished consciousness makes him impatient of moral complexity. His mode of thought is that of technology: Every situation presents a problem for which more or less efficient solutions are available. Such an American is what he does; when he is not acting, he is nothing. When he is alone in his hotel room in a foreign country at night, the room is empty.

For such Americans of course things are always going wrong; lacking any ability to interpret the actions of others, lacking indeed the concept of interpretation—it is no accident that such Americans often find it impossible to learn foreign languages adequately—they are continuously surprised by the failure of their own predictions. When it is their personal lives in which havoc appears as if from nowhere—their marriages, their children, or their psyches—they at once invoke all the resources of technique: counseling and "How to do it" manuals stand to sex, marriage, and child care as auto mechanics stand to automobiles. And if it is pointed out that tenderness, compassion, and insight are left out, these are promptly labeled "the problem of values" and become one more set of variables for technical manipulation. But it is not of course only his own self that such an American seeks to to remold in this way. It is also the external social world and not only in America. It was also in Asia.

Only historical accident can explain why Asia—first of all China, to some degree India, and worst of all Southeast Asia—originally became the chosen victim of this type of American benevolence. It began with Protestant missionaries and it ended—we perhaps have some grounds for hoping that it may now have finally ended—with marines. It is of course true that a large part of the intervening history was defined by most Americans in terms of anticommunist politics and therefore to ascribe the ruin caused in Asia to aspects of American culture and personality may seem at first sight almost willfully misleading. But why did anticommunism—another aspect of which was and is the legitimate and even generous commitment to oppose the imperialist designs first of Stalin's regime and then of that collective czar who has inherited his tyranny—become the crude, imperceptive, destructive force which it has been? A key part of the story is that of how it became the political mask worn by this kind of deprived American personality whose benevolence is more terrifying, as the Vietnamese well know, than the malice of many other people.

The writer Paul Theroux asked an ARVN colonel in 1972 what the general feeling in Vietnam was toward Americans after so much war, disruption, and death. Colonel Tuan chose his words carefully. "We think the Americans are well-disciplined . . . and generous. But we also think that they are people without culture—none at all, none that we have seen!" I take it that this view of Americans by the Vietnamese resulted precisely from the dominance of that pathological American type that I have been describing. The American is perceived as being without any specific culture because he approaches the Vietnamese as though they were a people without culture and without a historical identity. And when he is told that the Vietnamese are unintelligible without a knowledge of their culture and their history, this too becomes part of "the problems of values" and social and political scientists are called in to identify the appropriate set of manipulable variables. And with the aid of technical power and money another culture is devastated before it is even perceived.

These are necessarily harsh words; for the American Idea has its pathological exemplifications as well as its normal ones. I began the characterization of this type of incarnation of the American Idea by speaking of its ability to reject all historical consciousness and to turn every stage set for action into an egocentric present. One consequence of this determination to live in the present is an ability to forget even the very recent past almost instantly, to manufacture a form of consciousness from which traumatic history has apparently been expelled. No instance of this is more striking than that which has led to the almost complete disappearance from the immediately contemporary American consciousness of the Vietnam War. It was after all a war in which thousands of Americans died as well as nearly a million Asians; it was a war in which not only was the greatest military power on earth humiliatingly defeated, but in which at the last it dishonorably deserted those who had trusted it; it has been the occasion of a major crisis in the morale of the American officer class; every major presidential candidate in 1966 supported it strongly until desperately late in its course. And yet in American politics and culture now from the Left to the Right there is almost total silence; it is as if that war had never happened and it is certainly as if there has been a tacit social agreement to behave as if it had never happened. But so widespread is this that it cannot be treated simply as part of the pathology of any one type of American. Consider two very different types from that which I have just been describing.

The first is that exemplified in a certain kind of recurrent radicalism. I argued initially that at the heart of the American Idea there is a contradiction between ideals of liberty and equality on the one hand and a commitment to forms of power that generate inequality and unfreedom on the other and that this contradiction has a highly specific history which is part of its definition. The type of attitude which I have just described cuts itself off so far as possible from any consciousness of this history and this contradiction. The type of American radicalism which is its counterpart seizes upon the contradiction while ignoring its historical character. So it begins with a very simple contrast between what is right and what is, between the ideals of liberty and equality and the inequalities and unfreedom of America at any one time. Its primitive expectation is that it will only require the announcement in suitably dramatic terms of the abject failure of the real to accord with the ideal to secure immediate national repentance and reform; when this primitive expectation is disappointed, as it always is, the abstract moralism of this approach responds by dividing the social world into the good and the evil; it is because of some conspiracy of evil people that the real and the ideal remain apart. The politics of this type of radicalism consists therefore of a series of preachings against evil; it relies on arousing a peculiarly American capacity for instant moral indignation, a capacity which itself depends on seeing all evils, sufferings, unfreedoms, and inequalities as *something that someone ought to have done something about by now*. Such a radicalism is by no means the prerogative of the American Left; it has its right-wing versions too. But when it does appear on the Left, its abstract moralism distances it not only from European Marxism with its strong sense of history and its inheritance from Marx himself of a suspicion of all moralizing, but even more from the concrete and practical concerns of the American labor movement. The abstractions of such radicalism derive from the fact that its moralism has no historical roots; it aspires to absolute judgments, independent of time and place. It sees nothing specific in American culture, and it does not see itself therefore as an expression of the very way of life which it aspires to disown. It is therefore rootless and although—like the great Protestant revival movements of which it is the heir—it often has great drawing power when it first appears—for it does after all appeal to parts of the cultural self that it does not acknowledge—it is apt to disappear with equally surprising rapidity.

What I want to stress about this radicalism is its mirror-image quality, how much it shares with the type of American who most appalls it. Both are insensitive to culture and history, to the presence of the past in the present; both caricature themselves as well as others by their moral impoverishment; both are unable to face the complexity and contradiction, the enormous difficulty of the American idea. And both therefore substitute for that real complexity an unreal simplicity. Both take the part for the whole. It is not surprising that often, quite literally, the one type is father of the other. Between them they have sometimes usurped the image of America, and when they do they help to evoke a third type of partial response to American complexity.

Both the politics which results from the manipulative benevolence of the technological American and the politics which springs from the moralistic benevolence of the radical American are instances of what Quentin Anderson has called "Our persisting habit of stretching the moral imperatives of individual conduct to cover the aims of the nation-state. . . ." Those who have seen clearly how inappropriate this is and who have reacted with disgust to the consequent vulgarities have all too often responded by supposing that individual conduct is all, that it is within the moral sphere of the individual consciousness that everything of worth is achieved or fails to be achieved. This proclamation of the self as coextensive with the moral universe has appeared in very different guises at different stages of American history. With Emerson in the 1820s and 1830s it is still possible to try to annex America to the self, to see America as at least potentially nothing but the outward expression of the timeless, transcendental consciousness of each individual soul. But outward American reality proved exceptionally intractable; the gap between the purity which the individual soul might achieve and the external deeds of politics, commerce, and war was not to be closed. Hence instead of assimilating and annexing the external universe to the moral self, the historical to the timeless, the protagonist of the imperialism of the self turns to rejection. After the Emerson of the twenties comes the Thoreau of the forties. Thoreau can still accept America as nature; his moral consciousness finds on the sands of Cape Cod or on the Merrimac River the natural milieu for righteousness. But America as nature is now where you retreat from America as society or as government. The self in its necessarily lonely righteousness—and for such a self, righteousnes is self-righteousness—retreats from the contaminated worldliness of Concord to Walden Pond. But in the next decades the external vulgarities of society become overwhelming; the self can only protect itself from the invasion of the American culture it rejects by such more thoroughgoing strategies as emigration and the acquisition of a new secondary protective culture as a weapon against America. So the Thoreau of the forties is succeeded by the Henry James of the eighties; and within James's own progress the self retreats from the externalities of *The American* and *The Princess Casamassima* to that final enclosed finely wrought universe of the moral self equating itself with everything, *The*

Golden Bowl. And it is part of James's greatness that along this road there is nowhere further to travel. So that later exponents of the imperialism of the self, such as Allen Ginsberg in our own time, turn out to be minor reeditions of Emerson or Thoreau, not only versions of retreat, but infantile regressive versions.

Yet it turns out that what all these variant versions of American response to America exhibit are the vices which are the counterface of American virtues. And it is part of the cunning of American history that often enough those very attributes which lead others to condemn Americans and Americans to condemn themselves have been put at the service of American virtues and ideals. Without the founding constitutional ideals the American Civil War could not have been turned into a war for the abolition of slavery; without the technologizing consciousness it would not have been won; without the sectarian moralizing of the abolitionists the cause of antislavery would not have been there to be embraced. The whole was greater than the parts. If therefore we from time to time despair of the vulgarity of the technologizing consciousness or of the abstract self-righteousness of radicalism or of the mandarin rejection and withdrawal into high culture, we do not therefore have to despair of America itself and still less of the American Idea.

But it is important to notice such distortions of the Idea because they too are part of the whole; and they are distortions precisely because those who embodied them were unwilling to acknowledge that fact, were unable to tolerate the complexity, the ambiguity, and the contradiction of the whole. It is in seeing the whole, the dark as well as the light, the confusions and flaws as well as the clarities, that ground appears for hope. For at its best the American Idea does not involve a rejection of the past in the name of the future or rather in the name of an ahistorical present. America rather is an attempt at one specific way of connecting the past to the future and a way that was new in human history; it was and is an attempt to found a historical tradition that would move continuously from a particular past to a universal future, a tradition that in becoming genuinely universal could find a place within itself for all other particularities so that the Irishman or the Jew or the Japanese in becoming an American did not cease thereby to be something of an Irishman or a Jew or a Japanese. In assuming the burden of this task America took into itself a genuinely Utopian quality, the quality of an attempt to transcend the limits of secular possibility. America's failures are intimately connected with this grasping after impossibility; but so are its successes.

Consider some of them: in 1950 one American in every three over age twenty-five had a high school diploma; in 1975 it was two out of three. In 1975 there were five times the proportion of black adults who had high school diplomas compared with 1950, and the proportion of black college graduates in the black population had risen from 2 percent to 10 percent.

With whites it had risen from 6 percent to 14 percent. In 1964 there was a large gap between the frequency of visits to physicians and of hospital treatment both between Britain and the United States and between rich and poor in the United States; ten years later both gaps had largely been closed. Prosaic statistics of this kind have a good deal of importance in themselves, but even more as signs of the persistence of an ideal the poet Randall Jarrell described by saying that "One of the oldest, deepest and most nearly conclusive attractions of democracy is manifested in our feeling that through it not only material, but also spiritual goods can be shared; that in democracy bread and justice, education and art will be accessible to everybody." Another poet, Stephen Spender, reacted to this by saying "Needless to say this conception of democracy is utterly different from the English. . . . To any Englishman with common sense, it is perfectly obvious that spiritual goods are graded and only shared in the sense that one public gets the top grade, another the inferior." What Spender calls the English view is of course powerful in America too, but in America it has had to fight the notion that if excellence has a claim at all, it has a universal claim on man as such and that what were the preoccupations of an eighteenth-century English elite ought to become the preoccupations of us all. There is nobody so deprived that he ought not to try to become Thomas Jefferson; and at the heart of trying to become Thomas Jefferson there has to be the knowledge of all that historically both separates and unites him or her from Jefferson, of that identity of contradiction and complexity which they share.

When Jefferson in later life was asked from where he had taken the ideas of the Declaration of Independence, he replied "From the commonplaces of my own age and from Aristotle, Cicero, Locke and Sidney." Some scholars have tried to build very elaborate, minute structures on this kind of slender evidence; but I take it that the point of such utterances by Jefferson was to assert that the ideas on which America was founded were simply the best ideas that human history from the Greeks to his own day had put forward, that being an American is simply an attempt at the best possible way of being a man in the modern world—an attempt perhaps botched, dangerous, and often one-sided, but still an attempt at nothing less than that. And all the features which are centrally defining to America turn out after all to be features of the modern world as such: money, technical power, racism, the imperfect and conflict-ridden assimilation of peoples, freedom and oppression, equality and inequality.

What ought then finally to impress us are not the distorted, partial versions of the American Idea, necessary as it is to notice these, but the ability of America when it faces up to its own full, often horrifying, and yet always hopeful reality, to move beyond limitations and frustrations and continually to revive in its own people and in others the task of achieving a future at once compelling and impossible. America's worst danger is to forget how conflict and contradiction are central to its historical identity; but Americans ought also to remember that this is so because theirs is the representative historical identity of the modern world, because it is in America that Europe undertook what it could not achieve at home.

There is therefore a kind of anti-Americanism, quite different from that of which I spoke at the beginning of this paper, which we ought unequivocally to repudiate. This is the kind of anti-Americanism which seeks to make the United States the scapegoat for the sins of Western modernity, the kind of anti-Americanism which being unable to discharge the tasks of modernity itself leaves them to the United States and then with passionate complacency blames the United States for everything that goes wrong. This kind of anti-Americanism is one of the luxuries of certain kinds of European politicians —it has flourished among certain types of French Gaullist, among the right wing of the British Conservative party and the left wing of the British Labour party—and among many nonpolitical people too. When it appears, it is always a sign of a failure to recognize that in the democracies of the West you cannot reject America because in the end, if you are honest, America is you. Every American has two nationalities, his own and that from which his or her ancestors originally sprang, whether in Europe, Asia, Africa, or in North America itself. But the counterpart to this is that free persons anywhere also have two nations, whether they like it or not—their own and the United States.

THE
AMERICAN
IMAGINATION

DENIS DONOGHUE

I shall take the imagination to mean the mind in the aspect of its freedom; and assume that the question of the imagination is the nature of that freedom, and its exercise.

In 1828 James Fenimore Cooper published in London a book called *Notions of the Americans: Picked Up by a Travelling Bachelor*. The bachelor was an aristocrat and therefore European. Cooper sent him traveling in the United States to discover the difference between the two civilizations, Europe and America, and he gave him an American companion to make the differences explicit. At one point the European comments upon the view from a height some fifty miles west of Albany, New York, and he tells his American companion that the scene "only wants the recollections and monuments of antiquity to give it the deepest interest." He means that the scene would have the deepest interest if in addition to its obvious merits it had the advantage of being set in Europe; it would then have the romance of antiquity, a certain depth of character that American landscape could not be expected to provide. The American scene gratifies and often astonishes the eye, but leaves the sense of human reverberation unfulfilled. The point is well taken. If we set aside the landscape of New Mexico and the Southwest, we find that the historical sense is unappeased by American landscape, finds it thin and bare, impoverished in its human meaning by comparison with the density of European scenes. It would require a geologist's eye and imagination to make the American landscape disclose its density, and then it would yield only the density of natural forms, an unpeopled plenitude. The European mind values in a landscape only evidence that the scene has become human; has been human now for a thousand years. The historical sense in which Europeans take such unearned pride is chiefly memory, a sense of kinship and recognition, evidence of human action and suffering over centuries. Interest is "deep" in terms of time, human feeling, generations of blood.

Cooper allows the European aristocrat to make his point, but it is answered at once by the American, who tells the European that "the moral feeling with which a man of sentiment and knowledge looks upon the plains of your hemisphere is connected with his recollections; here it should be mingled with his hopes." The scene promises "all that reason allows may be hoped for in behalf of man," and those who live there "live in the excitement of a rapid and constantly progressive condition." The view west of Albany seems impressive but finally thin to the European, but to the American its penury of historical event becomes a valued image of possibility and hope. Instead of the burden of gone times, the American feels the surge of a future, and finds promise in the bareness of the scene. Hope is one name for this feeling; it is the silent grammar of prophecy.

I have recited this little episode in Cooper's book because it embodies a fundamental attribute of American feeling, the New World's indifference toward the mere past and a correspondingly intense exaltation in a vision of the future. Many Americans interest themselves in the past and cultivate the predilection of an antiquary, but it is a commonplace that Americans generally take the past lightly and refuse to be intimidated by it. Emerson called himself "an endless seeker with no Past at my back." Henry James remarked in *The American Scene* that his fellow Americans relegated "the previous" to the lowest category of their interest; they blithely burned their bridges behind them. This habit has often been taken to mean that Americans are superficial in their sense of life, and barbarous in their indifference to the past. The conclusion is premature as well as rude. The truth is that Americans are inordinate in the value they ascribe to "the unconditioned," in Quentin Anderson's phrase, to everything whose existence is absolute. But we ought to remind ourselves, as Europeans, that there is no moral advantage in following an antique drum or assuming that we are in full possession of our historical experience. V. S. Pritchett has referred to Americans "whose energies and wealth have never been wasted in living down their fate or their errors; who are adept at forgetting and at going on, constantly in touch with the *zeitgeist*." That last phrase has an ironic note, a suggestion that Americans identify their morality with the spirit of the age and think their energy well occupied in keeping up with it. But Pritchett also meant that the act of forgetting and going on has its own moral force, and that it calls for courage; it need not be crass. I shall put the point crudely by saying that the European mind defines itself chiefly in relation to the past as an anthology of gone occasions, or perhaps to a general impression of those events as burden and responsibility, voices calling for response. The American mind takes that burden more casually, and turns its vitality toward a future which it construes as possibility. To the European, mistakes are definitive; to the American, mistakes are regrettable but not fatal—there is always a second chance. The American mind thinks itself a pioneer, and its best morality a matter of trials and errors. Evidence from the past is not considered conclusive; evidence from present structures of possibility is considered more persuasive. Thus a poet of Marianne Moore's disposition is willing to deprive a word of its history so as to increase its mobility: a style may be regarded as an achievement of speed rather than density, a rapid-transit system rather than a device to remind readers of the experience behind them. Landscape is crucial to the American imagination precisely because its story, as a human enterprise, is still incomplete, free from an end already inscribed.

There are exceptions to these rough generalizations. The writers of the American South have set themselves against the amnesia which they associate with New York and New England; they have made the most of their past, the historical drama of their region, and they have tried to extend that past into the Old Europe through rhetoric, law, and the Latin authors. The mythology of the Old South, as mediated through writers such as Ransom, Tate, Faulkner, Welty, and Lytle, finds its force in the past, old wounds, burdened memories. More recently, writers of black America have emphasized "the Africa within" in the hope of giving present bitterness the weight and dignity of a known past. But in both cases the past is the sought past, rather than—as in many European countries—a burden to be borne. In Ireland, for instance, the past is that which cannot be forgotten; it is unfinished business with ourselves. We are imprisoned in history as others are imprisoned in circumstances and conditions; so deeply imprisoned that we commit the extravagance of identifying our history with our nature. We do not feel that we have a mission in the world, a gospel to preach, a future to unfold. We embody our history not to fulfill a prophetic role but to enact a fate. When an Irish writer feels ill at ease in his work, it is usually, I suggest, because he feels inadequate to the experience he has been given, to his past as an Irishman, or because he feels that he has been disloyal to his true gods, speaking of experience not entirely his own in a language not at all his own. The one thing he cannot be for long is nonchalant, free and easy, and he envies the American writer the grace of this freedom.

Historians of American feeling generally agree that the American attitude to the past arises from a sense that it has other promises to keep. The American mind is committed to the idea of forming in America a new society and a new kind of man. Increase Mather called his country "our Israel," and the phrase carries a note of missionary zeal audible even now. The crucial tense is the future, according to an optimistic, Protestant vision of the City of God becoming the City of Man; a redeemed man. This vision is sustained not only by a Puritan theology of election but by a politics of idealism, responsibility, and freedom. America is deemed to be the country in which it is possible to forgive oneself: a plural society determined to set aside the past, its ancient wounds, the dreary accumulation of crimes and corruptions which constitutes the history of Europe. The note of wonder and exaltation which sounds naïve to European ears is the real American note because it assumes that the true story is an internal narrative of feeling, and that the story can still be changed. Fate is a Providence still to be wooed, rather than a doom already determined. To the American, the only story he believes is a story without end; the only history is a provisional sketch; Act Five is not determined entirely by the logic of Act One.

I am already speaking of the American imagination as if it were exceptional, a special case, an exception to a rule deemed to be European. It is common to do so. Until very recently it was standard practice to insist upon the exceptional nature of American experience: this practice was in keeping with a nation which saw itself as having a "manifest destiny" to be unique, not only uniquely strong but uniquely true to its vision of a new humanity. Life on the American continent was to reveal a new Book of Revelation, promising a secular apocalypse. The millennial sense of life ascribes to America the role of the "redeemer nation," where the New World's innocence dissolves Old World's corruption. History and Providence are to coincide in favor of Americans as the chosen people. Nearly every description of American civilization is animated by this sense of special destiny. But in the past year or two this mood has receded. The emergence of Russia and China as major powers, and the humiliation of national pride as a result of the Vietnam War and the Watergate disclosures have forced Americans to reconsider the evidence of manifest destiny. It is now common for American scholars to emphasize not the exceptional nature of American experience but the features it shares with that of other people. Robert Penn Warren and Cleanth Brooks have agreed in a recent conversation that addiction to millenarian feelings is one of the worst factors in the American tradition, a facile assumption that to Americans all things are possible. It is too soon to say whether this mood of humility is more than a passing phase in American feeling.

At the same time it is clear that American experience is at least distinguishable if not unique, and it is plausible to hear a distinct tone in the imaginative response to that experience. When we read three classic works in American fiction, *Moby Dick*, *The Scarlet Letter*, and *The Adventures of Huckleberry Finn*, we find it natural to construe them as issuing from feelings and imaginations so typically American that we cannot conceive of any other source for them. It is not simply a question of the size of the country, the variety and differentiation of its experience. *The Scarlet Letter* does not invoke any unusual latitude of experience; its origin is local, a place, an occasion, a particular chain of sins and expiations. The size of America is indeed important in any account of the imagination which responds to it; it makes for diversity of feeling, and therefore offers as a question the predicament which Henry James named as "the complex fate of being an American." But it becomes a crucial factor in the history of the American imagination only when it is taken to suggest that the American imagination is called upon to encompass an entire continent. The scale of the country presents as a basic problem of mind the assimilation of a vast range of experience. The

American cast of mind may indeed be optimistic, as a general inclination, but it also feels itself incomplete, not yet fully formed in its humanity. This sense of incompleteness is embodied in the individual mind's relation to the American continent. Space becomes a moral as well as an aesthetic problem because it incites a mighty effort of the imagination to engage it. Charles Olson declares in *Call Me Ishmael* : "I take SPACE to be the central fact to man born in America, from Folsom cave to now." Geography assumes the force of history, and although the American frontier may be deemed to have closed in 1893, the sense of frontier has not closed, and it endows with symbolic radiance the motifs of space and movement, the transfer of energy from origin to mind, the question of possibilities and limits.

"What manner of building shall we build?" Wallace Stevens asks. The question is American in its note of potentiality, but it presents as a problem of morality and sensibility the relation between nature and mind. We often think that the typical American attitude is a certain openness to experience, a boyish sense of possibility, perhaps naïve but charming in its naïveté, an easy assumption that the world is the American's oyster. But the same circumstances often provoke a stranger attribute of American feeling, the suspicion that the domestication of landscape and frontier will leave the essential desire baffled and unappeased. The American imagination, as Henry James said of one of his characters, makes a good thing of the hour and keeps the actual very actual; but it does not believe that its freedom will really be fulfilled in time and place. The American vision is crucial to Americans because of the quality of its passion, the particular structure of feeling which it embodies, but there is always a suspicion that the passion is bound to be disproportionate to its practical fulfillment. The euphemistic version of this is that, in Irving Howe's formula, "you need not suppose civilization your necessary home," you can leap beyond society with the same verve which prompted you to leap beyond history. You can make your own society. But the sinister version is the suspicion that whatever society you make will somehow fail to be your own or precisely adequate to your vision.

With this predicament in mind we distinguish between American and European fiction by remarking that European novelists take for granted a valid relation between man and society, the feeling and its institutions. American writers often write about environments, places, and people, and some of them (from Wharton to Auchincloss) take society seriously, but they rarely present individual feeling realizing itself in a relation to a society or an environment: it is far more typical of them to imply that the real feelings in the case are those which cannot find a home for themselves. The density of American fiction is therefore rarely social; we do not find in American novels the European confidence in the moral significance of family, land, money, tradition, class, marriage, or in the syntax of a society which these forces provoke. American writers often envy—or pretend to envy—their European colleagues the density of their reference, their opportunities to show characters immersed in the plenitude of relationships, surrounded on all sides by a world against which they can define themselves. The American writer longs for a world of true mediations, but he does not believe in the possibility of such a thing. American writers feel their world, the given world, as somehow incapable of receiving human feeling or defining a person's character. The classic expression of this complaint is the passage in Henry James's monograph on Hawthorne in which he reflects upon the lack of depth, ramification, and complexity in the life Hawthorne had to deal with. Society does not provide structures or textures sufficiently authoritative to define American feeling: the life ostensibly mediated by forms, conventions, rituals, and institutions is not sufficiently "present" to make a difference. Or the mediation is felt to be bogus. So the enormous effort of American writers is to make language itself do not only its normal work but the work done in European literature by allusions to nature, society, and history. I am not raising the current question about such institutions, the extent to which they depend upon language and are inconceivable apart from language. It does not affect the case: even if they are deemed to be linguistic structures, they exist as such and do not need to be invented again. Allusions to them are easy, casual in European literature, but not in American literature: the difference is the degree of confidence in structures which are by definition conditioned.

Richard Poirier has argued in *A World Elsewhere* that "the great works of American literature are alive with the effort to stabilize certain feelings and attitudes that have no place in the world, no place at all except where a writer's style can give them one." This is not merely the inevitable gap between consciousness and experience: it points to a distinctively American Platonism which arises when a desire can realize itself only as an idea. Poirier is referring to the American desire to find a world in which consciousness is free to explore its powers and possibilities, and to the inevitable American discovery that no such place exists. What exists is a place, indeed, a structure of laws, conventions, and relationships, mostly economic, social, and sexual: this structure the American mind finds good enough or "real" enough to appeases his daily feeling, but not his deepest feeling. The deepest feeling, which the American identifies with the truest, is what is homeless, running wild beyond every form offered for its definition and domestication. Where can it go to find itself? American novelists regularly send their heroes "on the road," traveling loose and easy, but only to discover that there is no public road for their freedom. In *The Adventures of Augie March* Saul Bellow sends his hero rushing off from Chicago to Mexico, but with no hope of finding a place in which his consciousness may freely live. Chicago exists, and it is taken seriously but it is not deemed to provide a setting for Augie's freedom, a home for his consciousness; Augie is free only "in principle" and according to figures totally linguistic and rhetorical: he is free in his book, the possibilities of his language. The conditions of his freedom are linguistic, the possibilities of his diction and syntax, not the verve with which he runs up and down and all around the town. And the same principle applies to novels as different otherwise as *One Flew Over the Cuckoo's Nest* and *Gravity's Rainbow*. These books are dramatic precisely because of the tension they set astir between their language and their ostensible subjects—life in a psychiatric hospital, or whatever. The official subject matter is merely ostensible, an excuse, a bone thrown to the dog while the novelist runs away with the loot: the loot is that freedom of feeling and consciousness that is possible in language, according to the American imagination, and nowhere else. So when Poirier speaks of "a place," he means an alternative to "the book," a world correlative to language but somehow distinguishable from language. The American writer knows no such world. Place, in his work, is a trope, a linguistic figure, nothing more or less. It follows that his concern with language and style is peculiarly intense because he feels that they must do everthing, must not merely refer to relationships as if they existed beyond the book, but must somehow constitute them, making up in the book for everything missing from the world.

Do I contradict myself? I started by saying that the American imagination stands between present and future tenses and thinks everything possible. Now I am saying that everything is indeed possible, but not here and not now, and strictly speaking not anywhere, except in language. There is no contradiction, so far. But I have also said that what is free and true, to the American imagination, is what escapes from structures and environments and rushes off into language. And does this not contradict the common assumption that reality, to Americans, is simple, direct, and blunt?

The question is too important to brush aside. It is indeed commonly assumed, and often by Americans themselves, that reality consists in what Lionel Trilling called in *The Liberal Imagination* "a lively sense of the practical world, the welter of ordinary undistinguished things and people, the tangible, quirky, unrefined elements of life." There is a democratic sense of reality which expresses itself in these terms: it takes for granted that "there is a thing called reality; it is one and immutable, it is wholly external, it is irreducible." Trilling goes on to explain this attitude in terms of the common, middle-class American belief that there exists "an opposition between reality and mind and that one must enlist oneself in the party of reality." What he has in view is the common American assumption that the constituents of reality do not include the individual mind, and that the mind can only deal with reality by bringing practical skills to bear upon it. This is the American pragmatism of supermarkets and highways. But there is no contradiction. Indeed, the point is endorsed rather than weakened by the separation of reality and mind. If reality and mind are deemed to be independent and opposed, one to the other, the common middle-class American votes for reality, and the imaginative writer votes for mind. They agree in taking reality and mind as distinguishable and opposed; they disagree only in the scale of preference which each employs. The middle-class John Doe thinks that since you cannot beat reality, you had better join it, keep up with its irresistible spirit. The artist thinks that reality, in that crude sense, is not real at all, that it is merely a public nuisance, and that the only true reality is his own imagination. What else could the artist think, given that the two terms are opposed? The artist believes that genuine moral authority does not reside in "reality" or society, and that he is better employed trusting his own aesthetic instinct, committing himself to his imagination. What the imagination sees must be true, all the truer if its truth is denied in the supermarket.

Am I saying, then, that American literature is not pragmatic, naturalistic, materialistic, all those things it is widely suposed to be? Yes—in fact, American literature is Platonic, in the sense that it presumes "the real" to exist behind and beyond appearance. The true reality is identified not with automobiles but with dreams, visions, and styles. A sense of reality is not taken to mean a feeling for the way things are, but a feeling for the true way beyond the way things are; a way invisible except in the work of art, inaudible except in language, inexpressible except in style. There are indeed American writers such as Theodore Dreiser and James T. Farrell who judge the opposition of reality and mind so much in reality's favor that they cannot regard the mind as strong enough to count: in their books mind hardly makes a difference, and matter is accorded the power of fate. But the greater American writers have voted for mind, at whatever cost.

There is another way of putting the same point; it is Wallace Stevens's way, when he speaks of reality "changing into the imagination (under one's very eyes) as one experiences it, by reason of one's feelings about it." Many American books are designed to effect this change, and it would not make much difference if we spoke of reality changing into language under one's very eyes, by reason of one's feelings about it; because it is the feelings which make the difference; the feelings, and then the language. Stevens presented the imagination as a man with a blue guitar, so that he could say that "things as they are" are changed when played upon the blue guitar, as we might say that "things as they are" are changed by the imagination, which registers not only the things but our feelings about them. In a late poem Stevens refers to something that is "not to be seen beneath the appearances that tell of it." American writers are peculiarly sensitive to the invisible thing that exists beneath or beyond the appearances that tell of it; and they value the appearances only as signs to be surpassed. We say of Henry James, for example, that he is remarkably responsive to the ways in which reality offers itself, to the pleasures which the moral sensibility finds in places, people, and relationships. We also say that more than most writers he trusted his imagination and valued the movement of energy between reality and imagination. This is true. But it is worth emphasizing that he never allowed reality to evade the imagination or to overwhelm its formal ministry; and he did not think that reality set an outer limit upon the imagination. The imagination inscribed circles beyond any circles given to its attention. In the ideal Jamesian fiction reality and imagination are equal in authority, and the imagination is superior to reality only by virtue of the more exacting fineness of its composition; but that single virtue is enough to make the difference. It is the imagination that tells us that there is a life beneath and beyond the life we know: it is James's imagination that tells us that art stands for everything worth living in a free life—which is not the same thing as saying that art is itself the best thing in such a life; it merely stands for the best, and represents it in default of another representation.

Stevens's formula, his sense of reality changing into imagination as one experiences it, by reason of one's feelings about it, has only this limitation, that the reason given for the change is psychological and there is no reference to the means at hand. In reading William Faulkner we often remark his rhetorical movement and flow, but these are nothing apart from his determination to make the mere facts of the case change into imagination under the pressure of a demanding language. Language is the process and the force by which the imagination drives beyond fact, not merely to leave fact behind but to surround fact with a gleaming halo, its meaning identified with its radiance. We often think, reading Faulkner, that the facts are invoked only as useful obstacles, like a net in tennis, to incite the imagination to transcend them and to ensure that the transcendence is properly earned. My argument is, of course, that American feeling is characteristically above or below or aslant its ostensible subject. Whatever the imagination receives from nature or society as the available substance must be changed in some way, its rhetoric deflected, before it can be accepted for a serious purpose. Stevens says: "The world imagined is the ultimate good," but it is always a question of the transforming force contained in that imagination: in any case the world without imagination is deemed a poor thing.

There is a moment in *The Great Gatsby* in which many of the motives I have been describing come together: it is one of the classic occasions in American literature. Scott Fitzgerald's narrator, Nick Carroway, is going home, leaving West Egg, now that the whole garish party is over; and on the last night Carroway goes to Gatsby's deserted house and then down to the beach:

Most of the big shore places were closed now and there were hardly any lights except the shadowy, moving glow of a ferryboat across the Sound. And as the moon rose higher the inessential houses began to melt away until gradually I became aware of the old island here that flowered once for Dutch sailors' eyes—a fresh, green breast of the new world. Its vanished trees, the trees that had made way for Gatsby's house, had once pandered in whispers to the last and greatest of all human dreams; for a transitory enchanted moment man must have held his breath in the presence of this continent, compelled into an aesthetic contemplation he neither understood nor desired, face to face for the last time in history with something commensurate to his capacity for wonder.

What is present and active here is not Nick Carroway's historical sense, or even Fitzgerald's. History is not felt as the pressure of significant acts and events. Reality is not construed as that which resists the mind. The Dutch sailors do not offer Carroway's mind any more resistance than the inessential houses melting away before his eyes. Carroway's American desire is not appeased by anything the Dutch sailors saw, because his desire only hovers upon the vision long enough to know that it is transitory and provisional: no resting place is invoked. The object of attention is already receding: while it lasts, it is a momentary conjunction of fact and romance, making not history but mythology, a mythology of self. The capacity for wonder, which Carroway invokes, is best understood if we distinguish it from the capacity for analysis: a distinction which Tony Tanner has made and applied to American fiction in his *The Sense of Wonder*. The analytical passion examines the object in its internal relations, rejecting hallucination and romance: it stops with the object even at the risk of dissolving it and leaving a void instead. Wonder always runs ahead of the object it sees, or stretches beyond it in an air of joy and praise. What the Dutch sailors saw in the fresh, green breast of the new world was not only novelty but promise. What Nick Carroway sees is not an object or a world or a place at all: what he feels is the rush of his desire beyond every object in the given world.

PART TWO
THE IRISH
PRESENCE

A PROFILE
OF IRISH
AMERICA

LAWRENCE J. McCAFFREY

Proportionate to its size and numbers, Ireland contributed more people to the United States than any other European country. From 1820 to the present, about 5 million Irish entered the United States, the vast majority of them Catholic. The years 1840 to 1880 were the peak period of Irish immigration. During that forty-year span, close to 2.5 million, an annual average of around 62,500, arrived in America.

Anglo-American Protestants did not welcome the early waves of Irish Catholic immigrants, whose cultural and technological poverty encouraged prejudice against them. Unequipped to cope with the challenges of large-scale American farming and unwilling to confront the isolation of existence in the vastness of rural America, most Irish immigrants preferred to congregate in cities as the pioneers of the American urban ghetto. Their poverty, loneliness, and psychological insecurity bred alcoholism, crime, violence, and mental disorders. Anglo-Americans turned their wrath on the Irish who converted their cities into unsafe pestholes, forcing tax assessments and large expenditures of public funds to contend with the nation's first major urban social problem. Protestants with Ulster Nonconformist origins, the people who dominated Irish emigration to North America from 1715 to 1822, started to describe themselves as Scotch-Irish to avoid the penalties of anti–Irish-American prejudice, and they gradually melded into the Anglo-American Protestant cultural community.

Irish poverty, vice, and crime inadequately explain the strong anti-Irish mood of nineteenth-century America. Even if most Irish Catholics would have entered the United States as literate, skilled farmers or craftsmen rather than refugees from indigency and hunger, they would not have received a warm hello. Rooted in English no-popery, American nativism defined itself in terms of conflict between Anglo-Saxon Protestants and Roman Catholics. Ancestors of Anglo-Americans, particularly New England

Puritans, had been intense enemies of Romanism. They had left England to escape homage to an established Protestant church tainted with popery. More than English, Scots, or Welsh foes of Catholicism, Americans were convinced that the church of Rome represented idolatry, ignorance, superstition, and tyranny. They viewed the swarming masses of Irish Catholic immigrants infesting their cities as agents of popery and European despotism, endangering Anglo-Saxon Protestant culture and liberty.

Although wearing the Catholic label added to Irish liabilities in the United States, Catholicism provided them with a touch of beauty, spiritual comfort, and psychological security in ugly ghetto situations. Combined with nativist pressures, Catholicism also brought cohesion to Irish America. Loyalty to the Catholic identity superseded the parish, county, and province associations that the Irish carried with them from the old country. Catholic schools educated the children of transplanted peasants so that they could function in urban America. Not only did the Catholic educational system diminish Irish cultural and technological inadequacies, it also trained the teachers, lawyers, politicians, doctors, priests, and businessmen who provided leadership and a great deal of self-sufficiency to Irish-American communities.

Culturally and historically Catholicism linked Ireland and Irish America. During the sixteenth and seventeenth centuries' resistance to British political and cultural imperialisms, Catholicism emerged as a fusing symbol of the Gaelic and Old English nation whereas Protestantism represented the cause of the newer Anglo-Saxon invaders. With the defeat of the clan chiefs, the Gaelic life-style faded while Catholicism survived and became the leading cultural dimension of Irishness. Protestant Ascendancy in Ireland allied to no-popery in Britain solidified the ties between religious and cultural allegiances. In the United States, the Protestant crusade against Catholicism reinforced the Irish and Catholic connection.

Catholicism as a banner of Irishness strengthened Roman influences in Ireland. Once the most independent and individualistic Catholics in western Europe, the Irish became the most loyal subjects of the Pope. Romanization was slow and as Emmet Larkin has shown in his essay "The Devotional Revolution in Ireland, 1850–1875" (*American Historical Review*, June 1972), the process was not complete until the second half of the nineteenth century. As an emissary of his friend Pius IX, Paul Cardinal Cullen completely subordinated Irish Catholicism to the pietism and authority of Rome. Following in the wake of the church in Ireland, Irish-captained American Catholicism sailed into the Roman harbor. Catholicism united urban Irish Americans with the rural Irish in Ireland in one fellowship of values, attitudes, and religious allegiance.

In addition to establishing an Irish spiritual empire throughout the English-speaking world, Catholicism played an important role in shaping the famous but hard-to-define Irish political style. But Irish politics owes as much to the English as the Roman influence. Although there is a dichotomy between the conservative Roman and liberal British political traditions, the Irish have managed to blend the contradictions into a unique political personality.

In agitating for Catholic Emancipation, political and economic reforms, and repeal of the Union, Irish nationalists articulated their grievances and demands in the language of British Whiggery, Radicalism, and Liberalism, and they cleverly manipulated the levers of the British constitutional system to achieve their objectives. Daniel O'Connell deeply and permanently planted a commitment to the principles of liberal democracy in the soil of Irish nationalism. This commitment helps explain the relative success of the Irish nation-state in the twentieth century when other nations emerged from the throes of imperialism to descend into conditions of chaos and then military dictatorship.

Because of their participation in Anglo-Saxon politics, Irish immigrants were prepared to take part in the American political process. Their hatred of Tory aristocracy and preference for democracy, and the nativist orientation of the Federalist, Whig, and Republican parties drove the Irish into the Democratic fold, the party of Thomas Jefferson and Andrew Jackson. Although they began their American political experience as an army of voters, by the 1890s they had become, to the consternation of nativists, the masters of urban America. In 1916, Sir Cecil Spring Rice, the British ambassador to the United States, described Irish Americans as the "best politicians in the country" and marveled at their organizational abilities. After World War I, Irish Americans extended their political influence beyond city halls into statehouses and governors' mansions, then to the Congress of the United States, and finally into the White House. At the present time, the majority leaders of the House of Representatives and the Senate are Irish-American Catholics, and the American Irish may produce future presidents. If Jerry Brown's star is fading in the west, Ted Kennedy's is rising in the east.

Despite the similarities in language, principles, objectives, and procedures, Irish politics is different from the Anglo-Saxon and Anglo-American varieties. As Catholics they never have accepted the natural goodness of man, the perfectability of human nature, or the Enlightenment sources of Anglo-Saxon liberalism. Irish liberalism is real but more pragmatic than ideological, geared toward improvement rather than perfection. And because it is more practical in judgments and goals, it has achieved more reform in the United States than the ivory-towered liberalism of Anglo-Americans. As Catholics, the Irish have been more communal-minded in their politics than individualistic Anglo-American Protestants.

Many critics of Irish-American politics, including Daniel Patrick Moynihan in his essay "The Irish" in *Beyond the Melting Pot* (1963), have described the Irish political style with its Catholic peasant mentality as a conservative, negative force. Moynihan claims that although the Irish know how to acquire power, they do not know how to use it for constructive social purposes. He argues that Irish control over American city governments has led to social stagnation. His thesis is more clever than accurate. In fact, it has been Anglo-Americans who have resisted social welfare reform programs with laissez-faire economics and Darwinist sociology. In contrast, Irish political machines and their bosses sketched the outlines of the American welfare state. They were the nucleus of the coalitions that made possible the social legislation of the New Deal, Fair Deal, New Frontier, and Great Society.

In general, the American Irish are more liberal than their kindred in Ireland. American pluralism and the increasing sophistication and intellectualism of the Catholic laity have restrained the authoritarianism and dogmatism of the hierarchy. Irish Americans seem to be more determined to maintain a separation of church and state than the Irish in Ireland. In his 1960 address to Protestant clergymen in Houston, Texas, John F. Kennedy spoke for most Irish Americans when he said

I believe in an America where the separation of Church and State is absolute—where no Catholic prelate would tell the President (should he be a Catholic) how to act. . . . If my church attempted to influence me in a way which was improper or which affected adversely my responsibilities as a public servant, sworn to uphold the Constitution, then I would reply to them that this was an improper action on their part, that it was one to which I could not subscribe, that I was opposed to it, and that it would be an unfortunate breach—an interference with the American political system. I am confident there would be no such interference.

According to Reverend Andrew M. Greeley of the National Opinion Research Center, University of Chicago, and the findings of other public-opinion experts, next to Jews, the Irish are the most liberal group in the United States when it comes to civil rights, peace, and social justice. Abortion is one issue on which the American Irish and other liberals part company. Irish-American Catholic lay people are not as rigid as their hierarchy on right to life—a majority would allow abortion to protect the mental and physical health of mothers or in cases of rape—but they are opposed to abortion on demand. History has yet to judge whether the friends or enemies of abortion are doing the most to preserve the dignity of the individual. In connection with the advanced social views of Irish Americans, it is important to note that Father Greeley discovered that, like other American Catholics, the Irish who have been educated in parochial schools are more liberal than their coethnics who have attended public educational institutions.

Many Catholic intellectuals, including some with Irish names, have lamented Irish predominance over the American church. They have argued that French, Italian, or German leadership would probably have brought about a more sophisticated and intellectual American Catholicism. Not only does this thesis exaggerate the intellectual quality and sophistication of nineteenth-century Continental Catholicism, it underestimates the progressive influence the Irish have had on American Catholicism. As Philip Gleason has said in "Thanks to the Irish" (*America*, May 14, 1966), it was most fortunate for American Catholicism that the Irish arrived in urban America before the Germans, Italians, or Poles and took control of church affairs. Their familiarity with and participation in the two contrasting cultures—Anglo-Saxon Protestant and Roman Catholic—placed them in a position where they were able to solidify Catholic ethnics in an inclusive religious community. And because of their essentially liberal political persuasion, the Irish were the only Catholic ethnics who could have led the American church with its diverse European immigrant constituency into an accommodation with the dominant Anglo-American Protestant culture. Irish liberalization of the church has prevented the triumph of clericalism in American Catholicism and the construction of permanent walls of hostility and suspicion between Catholics and other Americans. If Continental Catholics from authoritarian, union of church and state political traditions would have taken the helm of American Catholicism, the church might have resisted rather than adjusted to the American environment. If so, Catholics would still be huddled in the ghettos of place and mind, nursing paranoia rather than hope.

In discussing the associations between Ireland and Irish America, this paper has been emphasizing the impact of the former on the latter but the relationship has been reciprocal. Irish emigration has changed Ireland as much as it has altered America. Although it has meant the loss of energetic and ambitious young people, it has relieved pressures on a primitive, inflexible agrarian economy. Emigrants not only raised the standard of living by leaving, they also sent a steady stream of dollars back to Ireland to support their parents, finance the emigration of relatives, and to sustain Irish nationalism.

Irish Americans invested more than dollars in the Irish freedom cause. As a group they were more passionate about liberating Ireland than were the Irish in Ireland. Their enthusiasm for a free Ireland expressed a number of motives and interests. Many of them despised Britain as the source of their exile from a romanticized Ireland to a coldhearted, competitive urban America where they suffered from discrimination. Other manifestations of Irish-American nationalism were less bitter and paranoid. Some of the American Irish embraced Irish nationalism as an identity shield to protect their egos against the assaults of Anglo-American religious and racial prejudices. And there were those who supported Irish nationalism as a route to respectability in the United States.

In *Irish-American Nationalism* (1966), Thomas N. Brown has emphasized that some Irish Americans believed that they were not well thought of in the United States because their homeland was in bondage. They decided that an Irish nation-state would confer dignity on its exiled children. Other ethnics and racial minorities who followed the Irish into urban America accepted this logic which linked success in the United States with the independence and prestige of the mother country. That is one reason the American Jews are so devoted to Israel, American Slavs so concerned about countries in Communist eastern Europe, and American blacks so enthused over the emerging nations of Africa.

Irish-American participation in Irish nationalism started with the Repeal movement of the 1840s, but Fenianism best represented the American spirit in the Irish freedom effort. After the decline of the Fenians in the late 1860s, Irish Americans and Clan na Gaelers, John Devoy and Patrick Ford authored the New Departure and the American Irish furnished most of the money behind the Land League and the Irish Parliamentary party. During the Anglo-Irish war, Irish Americans purchased many of the weapons used by the Irish Republican army and made a substantial contribution to the world opinion that coerced the politicians at Westminster into offering dominion status to twenty-six Irish counties.

Much of the Irish-American ingredient in Irish nationalism is very difficult to evaluate. On the positive side, the American connection must have strengthened the liberal, democratic content of Irish nationalism. And the republican flavor and goal of the physical-force wing probably owed more to the American inspiration than it did to any memories of the United Irishmen. On the negative side, perhaps American violence passed through the veins of Irish nationalism into the mainstream of Irish life.

Throughout the nineteenth century the Irish in Ireland and the American Irish acknowledged that they were members of a common cultural community. Nationalist politicians visited American cities to collect money for various causes or to attend Irish race conventions. American bishops recruited Irish priests, nuns, and brothers to serve the needs of American Catholicism. Because the Anglo-American political establishment was culturally British and Britain began to play the role of the most dependable ally of the United States in international disputes, Irish-American political and nationalist pressures had less influence on the direction of American foreign policy than present-day efforts by American Greeks and Jews who are following Irish precedents, but the existence of a politically potent Irish America certainly forced the British government to make numerous concessions to Irish agitation. And as Emmet Larkin has shown in his *The Roman Catholic Church and the Creation of the Modern Irish State 1878–1886* (1975), the significance of an Irish Catholic church that extended throughout the English-speaking world into mission territories restricted papal tendencies to court British favor at the expense of Irish interests.

Since 1921, the links between the Irish in Ireland and the American Irish have become tenuous. The disintegration of the Irish cultural empire is the result of (1) the decline in Irish emigration to the United States, (2) the economic and social mobility of Irish Americans, (3) the fallout from the Civil War in Ireland, (4) a change in the character of Irish nationalism, and (5) a fading Irish identity in the United States.

Beginning in the 1920s, a variety of factors, including immigration laws and economic considerations, diverted the main flow of Irish emigration from the United States to Britain. This decline in the numbers of Irish people entering the United States diluted the Irish dimension of the Irish-American personality and weakened the contacts between Ireland and America. Most of the recent immigrants do not mix well with the American Irish. Except for the notable exception of the Boston Irish and some others in New England, who seem to be victims of a frozen historical experience, Irish Americans are a prosperous, well-educated, influential segment of American society. Although some physicians, academics, and other university-educated professionals emigrate to the United States, most of the Irish coming over are unskilled working-class people who have little in common with the middle-class American-born Irish. Many tend to isolate themselves and express their resentment against failure both in Ireland and the United States by contributing money to Provisional IRA front groups.

As Irish Americans evolved from unskilled working to affluent middle class, they abandoned their dependence on and interest in Irish nationalism as an identity badge and pathway to respectability. As they began to participate in the richness and variety of American life, they became less interested in what was happening in Ireland, particularly after the Irish Civil War. The conflict between Free Staters and Republicans puzzled and disgusted them. As political pragmatists, most Irish Americans agreed with Michael Collins that dominion status was a considerable concession to Irish freedom demands, one that promised further extensions of sovereignty. They could not understand why the treaty could provoke fratricide over issues that seemed more theological than political.

Leaders of the Irish nation-state that emerged from the Anglo-Irish war were committed ideologically to an Ireland Gaelic as well as free. Irish-Ireland idealism may have clarified identity and purified nationalism in Ireland, but its rural and narrowly Catholic content and image excluded the Irish of the Diaspora who were shaping their destinies in urban, pluralistic, and English-speaking situations. Rightly or wrongly, they considered Irish Ireland a provincial, reactionary, anachronism, a retreat into a world of myth and legend, a rejection of an increasingly important Irish international community respected for its political and literary genius.

At the same time that Irish Irelanders were excommunicating the Diaspora from the Irish cultural fold by defining nationalism in an exclusive manner, Catholic educators in the United States were completing the process of Anglicizing and Romanizing their students. Ashamed of their Irish peasant origins, unaware of any merit in Irish culture, and in their attempt to create an inclusive American Catholicism, they purged Catholic education of "divisive" ethnicity, emphasizing a political allegiance to the American constitutional system and loyalty to the pope as monarch of a supranational religious empire. Students in Catholic schools—elementary through university—became familiar with English and Continental European history and literature but knew nothing about Ireland or their Irish-American backgrounds.

By the 1950s all that remained of Irish identity in the United States was its Catholic associations and the solidarity of predominantly Irish-American neighborhoods. Then in the mid-1950s these neighborhoods began to vanish. Irish-American social and economic success plus the influx of blacks into the cities of the East and Midwest encouraged an Irish exodus to the suburbs. The contradictions between the secular values of suburban melting pots, and the reactionary and illogical positions of the papacy, particularly on the subjects of authority and sexuality, alienated many middle-class Irish Americans from organized Catholicism.

Post–Vatican II changes in the spirit and liturgy of the American church meant the end of Irish-style Catholicism in the United States. The private-conscience, free-spirited, hymn-singing, shake-hands-with-your-neighbor contemporary American Catholicism may have some attraction to young de-ethnicized Catholics, but to those with residual Irish instincts it seems an alien, uncomfortable, somewhat Protestant religious expression. Until quite recently, American Catholics boasted of their full churches at Sunday masses and the long lines outside the confessionals on Saturday afternoons and evenings. Now the churches are half empty on Sunday mornings and few people confess their sins. Since Irish Americans, along with Poles, were the most diligent in practicing their religion and contributing to its support, they are the ones obviously defecting as far as formal practice is concerned —Poles are still devout. Well-educated, prosperous Irish Americans are sending a message to the leaders of American Catholicism. They are saying that if it is no longer important to be Irish it may not be meaningful to be Catholic. They are warning Catholic educators that the loss of ethnicity means a decline in Catholic fervor.

In this age of fashionable ethnicity, many voices insist that Irish America is close to extinction. Government and privately endowed research agencies are not keen on financing scholarly investigation of the American Irish. Their reluctance suggests that they think that the Irish have become so much a part of the American mainstream that they do not deserve special attention. Doubts about the validity of Irish ethnicity have spread beyond the groves of academe. In his popular book on Latin and Slavic American Catholics, *The Rise of the Unmeltable Ethnics* (1973), Michael Novak claims that Anglicization has compromised Irish separateness.

Many intelligent Americans, including substantial numbers of the Irish variety, are pleased with Irish assimilation. Sharing Woodrow Wilson's distaste for hyphenated Americanism, they think it is an appropriate time to

ring down the curtain on Irish America. After all, they say, people left
Europe for America to earn wealth, acquire property, and achieve respectability and the Irish have done these things. To them, the Irish success
story confirms the American dream. The Irish have shown othe ethnic and
racial minorities that America is indeed the land of opportunity.

But what happened to the Irish in America might be a warning to others
as well as a promise. Perhaps the journey from urban ethnic neighborhoods
to suburban melting pots has been a trip from someplace to no place? Americanization is such a nebulous term. There is certainly an American political
identity related to Anglo-Saxon political and legal principles. They have
fostered political unity and consensus. On the cultural level, Americanism
signifies ethnic, racial, regional, and religious diversity. Pluralism makes
the United States the most interesting, exciting, and dynamic nation in the
world. By seeking assimilation, the Irish have rejected pluralism to become
satellites of the Anglo-American Protestant community. They chose imita-
tion rather than uniqueness and creativity. The so-called Irish success story
has meant social and economic progress but cultural retrogression.

FOR FURTHER READING

GENERAL INTERPRETATIONS OF IRISH AMERICA

Recently these have multiplied. Taken together, they are stimulating and diverse.
Yet none of them claims to be a definitive synthesis of the burgeoning specific
literature, to which they offer a guide to the issues, rather than complete summaries
of findings: John B. Duff, *The Irish in the United States* (Belmont, Calif., 1971);
Oscar Handlin, *The Uprooted* (Boston, 1951); Maldwyn A. Jones, *American Immigra-
tion* (Chicago, 1960); Edward M. Levine, *The Irish and Irish Politicians* (Notre Dame,
1966); Daniel Patrick Moynihan, "The Irish," in Nathan Glazer and D. P. Moynihan,
Beyond the Melting Pot (Cambridge, Mass., 1963), pp. 217–87; William V. Shannon,
The American Irish, rev. ed. (New York, 1966). Two contributors to this volume
develop their ideas more fully in Andrew Greeley, *The Most Distressful Nation: The
Taming of the American Irish* (Chicago, 1972), and Lawrence J. McCaffrey, *The
Irish Diaspora in America* (Bloomington, Ind., 1976). Another recent overview is
Joseph P. O'Grady, *How the Irish Became Americans* (New York, 1973). Philip
Taylor, *The Distant Magnet* (London, 1971), is the best study of Irish migration amid
the general transatlantic flow.

SPECIFIC PERIODS AND LOCATIONS

Irish-American studies have been more fully, if less imaginatively and holistically,
served in their more specific aspects. The earlier period of Ulster Irish settlement and
early Catholic arrivals as indentured servants, culminating in the revolutionary
period, and their participation in it, finds treatment in R. J. Dickson, *Ulster Emigration to Colonial America, 1718–1775* (London, 1966); David N. Doyle, *Ireland, Irish-*

men and Revolutionary America, 1760–1820 (Dublin: 1980); Wayland F. Dunaway, *The Scotch-Irish of Colonial Pennsylvania* (Chapel Hill, N.C., 1944); Owen D. Edwards, "The Impact of the American Revolution on Ireland," in R. R. Palmer, ed., *The Impact of the American Revolution Abroad* (Washington, D.C., 1976); E. R. R. Green, ed., *Essays in Scotch-Irish History* (London, 1969); Guy Klett, *Presbyterians in Colonial Pennsylvania* (Philadelphia, 1937); James G. Leyburn, *The Scotch-Irish* (Chapel Hill, N.C., 1962); Audrey Lockhart, *Some Aspects of Emigration from Ireland to the North American Colonies Between 1660–1775* (New York, 1976); Francis G. James, *Ireland in the Empire, 1688–1770* (Cambridge, Mass, 1973); Charles Metzger, *Catholics and the American Revolution* (Chicago, 1962); and Abbot E. Smith, *Colonists in Bondage, 1607–1776* (Chapel Hill, N.C., 1947); the works of Dickson and Doyle have the fullest further references.

For the early nineteenth century, George Potter, *To the Golden Door* (Boston, 1960), published posthumously—Potter died before he had assembled his documentation—is recognized as comprehensive and fully reliable. Also see W. F. Adams, *Ireland and Irish Emigration to the new World* (New Haven, Conn., 1932); Marcus Hansen, *The Atlantic Migration, 1607–1860* (Cambridge, Mass., 1940), pp. 69–225; Oliver Mac-Donagh, "Irish Famine Emigration to the U.S.," *Perspectives in American History* 10 (1976): 357–446; John F. Maguire, *The Irish in America* (London, 1968; New York, 1969), and the final sections in the works by Green and Doyle cited previously. For all of the nineteenth century, Carl Wittke, *The Irish in America* (Baton Rouge, La., 1956), remains solid and unreplaced, but the context has been decisively transformed by David Ward, *Cities and Immigrants* (New York, 1971). Studies of the later part of the nineteenth century are exceptional, but see Thomas N. Brown, *Irish-American Nationalism, 1870–1890* (New York, 1966), Robert D. Cross, *The Emergence of Liberal Catholicism in America* (Cambridge, Mass., 1958), David N. Doyle, *Irish Americans, Native Rights and National Empires, 1890–1901* (New York, 1976), and Arnold Schrier, *Ireland and the American Emigration, 1850–1900* (Minneapolis, 1958), all of which range more broadly than their titles in the absence of usable syntheses. John D. Buenker, *Urban Liberalism and Progressive Reform* (New York, 1973), and Daniel Callahan, *The Mind of the Catholic Layman* (New York, 1963), are so disproportionately about the Irish as to be valuable interpretations about them alone in the period before 1920.

Local studies proliferate by the year, and among the best are the following: Dennis J. Clark, *The Irish in Philadelphia* (Philadelphia, 1974); Robert Ernst, *Immigrant Life in New York City, 1825–1863* (New York, 1949); Howard M. Gitelman, *Workingmen of Waltham* (Baltimore, 1974); Constance M. Green, *Holyoke, Massachussetts* (New Haven, Conn., 1939); Oscar Handlin, *Boston's Immigrants, 1790–1889*, rev. ed. (Cambridge, Mass., 1959); Peter Knights, *The Plain People of Boston, 1830–1860* (New York, 1971); Grace McDonald, *History of the Irish in Wisconsin* (New York, 1976); Earl F. Niehaus, *The Irish in New Orleans, 1800–1860* (Baton Rouge, La., 1965), James P. Shannon, *Catholic Colonization on the Western Frontier* (Yale, 1957); Douglas V. Shaw, *The Making of an Immigrant City: Jersey City, 1850–1877* (New York, 1976); Stephan Thernstrom, *Poverty and Progress* (Cambridge, Mass., 1964), and *The Other Bostonians, 1880–1970* (Cambridge, Mass., 1973); and JoEllen Vinyard, *The Irish on the Urban Frontier: Nineteenth Century Detroit, 1850–1880* (New York, 1976).

AMERICANS AND THE IRISH

The literature here is rich, but imbalanced. Contrasted with the reception of the Irish in nineteenth-century Scotland, England, or even sections of Australia, America was a haven of tolerance and acceptance ; even when contrasted with the reception of migratory workers in much of contemporary Europe. Apart from colonial America and the 1790s, no effort was made before the 1920s to restrict Irish entry, and no efforts were ever made to circumscribe their religious and organizational life, except in informal, local ways. The policy change of the 1920s was not aimed at the Irish, and was supported by many Irish Americans. For positive images see Dale T. Knobel, "Paddy and the Republic: Popular Images of the American Irish, 1820–60," Ph.D., Northwestern University, 1976; Owen D. Edwards, "The American Image of Ireland: A Study of Its Early Phases," *Perspectives in American History* 4 (1970): 214–41, and Ruth M. Elson, *Guardians of Tradition* (Lincoln, Neb., 1964). Yet anti-Irish and anti-Catholic prejudice and its manifestations were pervasive, and have evoked a large literature, notably, M. A. Ray, *American Opinion of Roman Catholicism* (New York, 1936); Ray Allen Billington, *The Protestant Crusade, 1800–1860* (New York, 1938); John Higham, *Strangers in the Land, 1860–1925* (New York, 1963); Donald Kinzer, *Episode in Anti-Catholicism* (Seattle, 1964); and Kenneth Jackson, *The Ku Klux Klan in the City, 1915–1930* (New York, 1967). It could be argued, as did Dietmar Rothermund, *The Layman's Progress* (Philadelphia, 1962) for immigrant groups in colonial Pennsylvania, that the readiness of later Americans to contain their prejudice against the Irish, and express it in a political game, bounded by fundamental rights, in which the Irish were allowed participate, was an expression of this essential toleration, as the works listed under politics and christian churches would imply. Since this book was completed, further work has continued full study of these matters: Francis M. Carroll, *American Opinion and the Irish Question, 1910–1923* (Dublin and New York, 1978); although Edward Cuddy," 'Are the Bolsheviks Any Worse Than the Irish': Ethno-Religious Conflict in America During the 1920s," *Eire-Ireland*, 11 (1976): 13–32; John Duffy Ibson, "Will the World Break Your Heart: A Historical Analysis of the Dimensions and Consequences of Irish American Assimilation," Ph.D., Walthan, Mass.: Brandeis University, 1976; and Richard Stivers, *A Hair of the Dog: Irish Drinking and American Stereotype* (University Park, Pa., 1976), each tend to overstress negative aspects, unlike Knobel, Edwards and Carroll.

IRISH EMIGRATION TO THE UNITED STATES IN THE NINETEENTH CENTURY

CORMAC Ó GRÁDA

"If we only had old Ireland over here," runs the refrain of one of the best-known of Australian-Irish emigrant ballads. However, for some decades after the middle of the past century, so large was the outflow from Ireland to America that some observers saw this sentiment as a wish come true in the case of that country. In the late 1860s Frederick Engels complained, "it this [emigration] goes on for another thirty years, there will be Irishmen only in America." Forty years later the French writer Louis Paul-Dubois warned that "emigration will soon cause it to be said that Ireland is no longer where flows the Shannon, but rather besides the banks of the Hudson River and in that 'Greater Ireland' whose home is in the American Republic." The exaggeration is perhaps understandable, given that between 1851 and 1891 Irish-born persons living in America as a proportion of those living at home rose from less than 15 percent to over 40 percent, though the proportion declined thereafter.

The emigration statistics provided the raw material for melodrama, and for nationalist outrage too. To the *Nation* newspaper they were simply a reflection of "the peasant-exterminating and farm-consolidating policy of Irish landlordism"; later, to more moderate Home Rulers they underlined the necessity for a domestic industrial and commercial policy, just as to recent generations the heavy emigration of the 1920s and 1950s has often been taken as evidence of "bad" domestic economic policy. In any event, the statistics suggest a total emigration from Ireland to all areas of around 4.2 million between 1852 and 1921. And there are good reasons, too involved and tedious to repeat here, for suspecting that even this is an underestimate of the true level for these years. Much emigration, particularly to Great Britain—internal migration within the United Kingdom at that time, remember—seems to have gone unrecorded, so that a total of 5 million may be nearer the mark. The data are less complete and less reliable for the years before 1852, but at a rough guess gross emigration from Ireland between 1815 and the treaty was about 8 million. The lion's share of this movement was destined for the United States, certainly two-thirds of it. Irish emigration in turn contributed significantly for decades to the total U.S. inflow. Between 1820 and the early 1850s—when German immigration began to outpace it —Ireland was the greatest single exporter of humans to the States in every year but two, and in the 1870s and 1880s still accounted for a seventh of the total. The proportion fell back to about a thirtieth by the late 1900s, and in absolute terms was only a trickle after 1930. I may be forgiven, then, for concentrating largely on some aspects of the nineteenth-century Irish emigration to America, though I shall refer here and there to other movements and other periods.

I

First of all, what kind of people left? We know that the emigrants were mostly young people—though not as young as postwar Irish emigrants to Britain—that as a rule they traveled individually or with neighbors, rather than as members of a family group, and that males and females left in roughly the same proportions. But there are little firm data on the regional and county origins of the emigrants to America or elsewhere, nor indeed of their socioeconomic backgrounds. In the absence of concrete evidence, there are a number of competing theories. We might expect, for example, emigration to have been heaviest throughout from the west, then as now the area with the lowest income per capita. But it is countered that before the 1870s or even the 1880s, the west of the country was too impoverished and too traditional to supply an appreciable emigrant labor force to labor markets as distant as America, and that people from Connacht or Donegal were relatively few in the States before 1880 or so for that reason. This, it is suggested, was due to a combination of factors: the prohibitive cost of the passage abroad, and the weak presence of "civilizing" influences such as literacy, production for the market, and a credit market. Such an interpretation does not explain, however, why emigration from the west should have "taken off" in the late seventies. Surely if the west was too backward to begin with, increasing population pressure there—in the absence of sharp domestic demographic adjustment (for which we do not have the evidence) —must have made emigration a more difficult proposition as the years passed by.

Another, more optimistic, hypothesis—really an assertion—finds expression in an editorial in the *Freeman's Journal* of September 18, 1859:

We rejoice in the progressive prosperity of our countrymen. Prosperous they are, and more so they are likely to be. They no longer have occasion to break up traditional ties and rush anywhere out of Ireland. The farmer is well off, so is the mechanic and the agricultural labourer. Prices are good, and so are wages. In reply to the statement that the want of means was the only reason why a greater number did not abandon this country thus last year, there is the nut very difficult to be cracked that the amount remitted or employed in the pre-payment of passages reached half a million sterling. Now the whole emigration of last year was only 33,636, and as the expense of emigration could scarcely have exceeded £3. a head, the total expended on emigration was not one-half of the remittances.

This, typical *Freeman's* fare, seems somewhat too sweeping, besides being singularly inappropriate in retrospect, since the autumn of 1859 saw the beginning of one of the most severe economic slumps in nineteenth-century Ireland. After all, the recorded emigration statistics do imply that emigration from the west, by common consent the most poorly endowed region, was much lower than from other parts of Ireland. They report an annual rate of only 13.8 per thousand from Connacht during the 1850s and 1860s, compared with a Munster average of 24.5 per thousand. So what to make of such seemingly contradictory evidence? The following reconciliatory interpretation is offered. There was considerable *unrecorded* emigration from the west to England and Scotland, particularly in the immediate post-Famine decades, but in the 1870s emigration to the New World on a much larger scale began to replace the traditional outflow. Now it is worth remembering that for a century or more before the Famine seasonal migration to Britain had been a feature of the western economy, work being plentiful for harvestmen and the passage costing only a few shillings. It is easy to envisage some of that seasonal migration becoming permanent with increasing industrial employment opportunities in Britain in the post-Famine period. So far this is but a hypothesis; only a thorough study of the county origins of Irish emigrants to Britain and the United States can tell whether it stands up.

As for the socioeconomic background of emigrants, the high cost of emigration to the States in the pre-Famine period suggests that it was primarily the families of the more well-to-do who were most likely to leave. So argued William Forbes Adams in his standard work published over forty years ago, and so implies the bulk of the evidence collected by the Assistant Poor Inquiry Commissioners in the mid-1830s. Thus:

Few labourers are to be found among the emigrants; they are unable to pay the passage; their earnings hardly suffice for their daily maintenance, they cannot save . . . [Dromahair, County Leitrim].
The Clonbrock labourers have told me that they would start immediately if they had but £5 [Kilconnell, County Galway].
If a free passage to America were offered, almost all the labourers would go—old, young, married and single [Maryborough, Queen's County—now Portlaoise, County Laois].

This is only a sampling, but taken together the Poor Inquiry evidence seems conclusive enough. Let us mention briefly, though, one less impressionistic source, the surviving enumerators' records for Killeshandra Parish, in County Cavan, from the population census of 1841. These records, quite by accident, contain information on over 300 recent emigrants to America from the area. The information appears under the following heading: "Return of members of this family now alive, and whose home is in this house, but who are absent on this night of Sunday, the 6th June, 1841." Now, strictly speaking, of course, emigrants should not have been included under this heading, but it is our luck that so many were. The data also indicate disproportionate representation among the more comfortably off in the emigrant ranks: almost 60 percent of the emigrants came from seemingly well-to-do homes, though such homes accounted for only 43 percent of the total in the area. Killeshandra was hardly typical of the country as a whole. If anything the poor in Killeshandra were better off than elsewhere, but the conclusions of the Poor Inquiry and Forbes Adams must hold *a fortiori* for that reason. Surely, were there data extant for pre-Famine Clare or Galway, the contrast between the mobility of the "rich" and the "poor" would be greater. The Famine emigration, on the other hand, was largely an exodus of the poor and the starving: lucky for them that there was an America to receive them, however grudgingly. The post-Famine emigration seems to have been disproportionately from the ranks of the cottiers and farm laborers, whose number declined dramatically. Emigration of farmers' sons and daughters was common too, but enough remained at home to keep up numbers. Thus the number of farm holdings of fifteen acres and over showed little change between 1851 and 1920, while the numbers of farm workers and really small farmers declined steadily.

An mac is sinne in ait an athar ("the eldest son to replace the father"), so goes an old south Kerry saying. If this was in fact the general tradition, then emigration to America would have been supportive of a system of primogeniture, and the male emigrants from a farming background would have been mainly the younger sons. In fact, however, it seems that primogeniture was more an aspiration than the common practice. The novelist William Carleton's short story "The Party Fight" noted the opposite tendency at work in the pre-Famine period, as did activist and writer Peadar O'Donnell in the more recent past. According to O'Donnell, "small farmer areas are the great source of emigrants. It is indeed a good thing that the young people there leave home as soon as they grow up, so that leaves the floor free for the youngest son, on whom the task of looking after the parent falls, to marry early." Evidence on this problem is hard to come by for the nineteenth century, but the following hypothesis seems plausible: the smaller the farm and the younger the father, the more likely was the eldest son to pack his bags and leave.

II

Since the immigrant experience in America is discussed in several other contributions to this volume, it is dealt with briefly here, and with the main emphasis on the results of some recent work by economic historians in the area. There is, for example, the frequently urged claim that the Irish, unlike other immigrant groups, unwisely stuck to the towns and cities on arrival. Thus John Francis Maguire, M.P. for Cork, wrote colorfully and at some length in 1869 about "the evil consequences of the unhappy tendency of the Irish to congregate in the large towns of America." Maguire was worried about the moral dangers, but the point is often made that immigrants would have fared better economically inland or in rural areas some distance from the overcrowded northeastern seaboard. This urban bias was sometimes attributed to the high cost of moving to work locations "best suited to the knowledge and capacity" of the Irish. The argument may sound plausible for recently arrived immigrants, but what of those who had already spent some time in America? Maguire falls back on what economists would term "money illusion" and "psychic income" arguments to explain subsequent reluctance to move:

So splendid seemed the result of (city) employment, even of the rudest and most laborious kind, as compared with what they were able to earn in the old country, that it all at once predisposed them in favour of a city life. . . . Then there were old friends and former companions or acquaintances to be met at every street corner; and there was news to give and news to receive. . . .

Such considerations were sufficient to satisfy Maguire. Recently, though this interpretation has been questioned, notably by Lowell Gallaway and Richard Vedder, who have maintained instead that the Irish (like other immigrant groups) were in fact quite sensitive in their settlement patterns to interregional income differences, and that their spread across the United States at different points in time reflects this. Gallaway's and Vedder's approach is to regress the proportions of Irish settling in different states on state income per capita, and a number of other potentially relevant variables, such as aversion to the South, distance from port of entry, and density of population. Although the results may be interpreted as lending support to the traditional interpretation for 1850, they suggest high mobility on the part of the American Irish in response to income differentials in subsequent periods. The Gallaway-Vedder results are consistent with Irish nineteenth-century immigration, like that of other nationalities, being a two-stage process, "the migrants first took jobs . . . in Eastern cities. . . . Having accumulated a minimum competence, only then could they move on both geographically and economically."

Another view increasingly under attack is that the Irish immigrants were upwardly immobile on the socioeconomic scale, their wages being too low in Oscar Handlin's words "to permit a man to accumulate the stakes of a fresh start." Recent research by Stefan Thernstrom, David Doyle, and others has refuted this: but why the sons and daughters of the immigrants, the Irish Americans, subsequently performed less well in the economic-success league than, say, the Jews or the Germans, is a separate, tricky question. Economic research would question too Handlin's claim that the Irish laborer was exploited, in the technical, neoclassical sense that he was paid less than his marginal product. According to the latest research in the area, if immigrants were lowly paid, this was due to their lacking in skills, not to discrimination on the part of bosses. Competition between employers, it is argued, was too intense for such discrimination to persist. At any rate, a recent study by Peter Hill, using numerous wage studies from several industries, concludes that "the immigrants did not differ markedly in any economic sense from the native born . . . and probably adjusted quite rapidly to economic opportunities in the United States." And what of another alleged trait of the Irish in America, that they failed to avail of the opportunities opening up to them on American land? This problem awaits proper analysis, but two points need stressing. Firstly, a rural background in Ireland was no guarantee of the human capital or skills required for farm management. As mentioned earlier, the bulk of post-Famine emigration consisted of laborers and cottiers rather than farmers. Secondly, home-steading in nineteenth-century America, despite a generous land policy, required considerable capital, which the Irish on arrival may not have possessed. But if Gallaway and Vedder are correct, these considerations are really not all that relevant. Thus the advice "not to linger a moment longer than necessary in a city lodging-house" may not have been to the point.

III

Irish emigration to America was overwhelmingly economically motivated from the start. The stories about Northern Presbyterians and Southern Catholics fleeing from persecution to "the land of the free" are exaggerated, however appealing to some in bicentennial year. The economic motivation is clear from surviving ballads and emigrant letters—where reference to bailiffs are few and to dollars and wages plentiful. It is also clear from a cursory glance at the figures: emigration rose and fell with economic conditions, and the share of total emigration bound for particular countries reflected their relative economic prosperity. Thus the United States was avoided by many prospective emigrants in the "panic" periods of the late 1850s and 1870s, while emigration to Australia and New Zealand, which amounted to over a fifth of emigration to the States during 1874–80, fell back to less than 3 percent of the U.S. flow during the 1890s.

In recent years economic historians with a quantitative bent have dwelt at some length on the old question whether nineteenth-century European emigration was due more to "pull" or to "push" factors, and have attempted to measure prospective emigrants' responsiveness to relative wage and income shifts. The literature, which is often both difficult and confusing, has not yet dealt with Irish emigration because of the unavailability of the requisite wage and national income data. Thus the Irish literature on "push" and "pull" is at a more impressionistic level, as witness the following summary account from Arnold Schrier:

> The endless movement from Irish farm to American city led many an anxious contemporary into a fruitless discussion as to the principal cause of the phenomenon. They wanted to know whether the "pull" of American opportunity was more important than the "push" of Irish distress, an argument that has not yet lost its interest. All agreed that in the famine years there could be no doubt that the failure of the potato crop was the most important initial impulse to the vast emigration of that period. But in explaining the continuing drain, long after the Famine had passed, there was no such unanimity. In 1869 the emigration commissioners strongly implied that emigration was regulated by conditions at home, while a generation later the Registrar General had reversed himself and under persistent questioning by the Financial Relations Commission he admitted that repellent conditions in Ireland were relatively less important than the attractions of America. . . . So recently as 1935 the current chief of the Central Statistics Office insisted that since the Famine, "emigration has been due more to attraction from abroad than repulsion from within. . . ."

What is at issue is whether expansions and contractions in American or Irish living conditions explain most of the outflow. Seen in this way the Famine exodus of 1846–52 may be obviously largely attributed to "push." "The emigrants of this year are not like those of former years," said the *Cork Examiner* of those of 1847; "They are now actually running away from fever, and disease and hunger, with money scarcely sufficient to pay passage for and find food for the voyage." Subsequent emigration is more problematic, though arguably most of it must be explained in "pull" terms, as urged by Dr. Roy Geary, late of the Central Statistics Office, in the preceding passage. This may be seen as follows. Had economic conditions in Ireland remained at their level of the 1850s during subsequent decades, emigration to the States would almost certainly have been greater than was in fact the case. But conditions in fact improved, so that domestic or "push" factors served over time to reduce rather than increase emigration. Clearly, bad harvests after mid-century continued to "push" emigrants to America in isolated years, for example, in the early 1860s and 1880s, but to borrow from Professor Jeffrey Williamson, "the total impact on [American] immigration was not sufficiently important to produce net "push" effects over longer periods of time." Williamson, through clever manipulation of scarce data, has been able to arrive at estimates of the share of the transatlantic flow from several countries, not including Ireland, between 1870 and 1910 attributable to "push" and "pull." He concludes: ". . . had European employment and living standards remained at their 1870 levels, America would have had a stock of immigrants twenty per cent larger than was in fact the case." For that period the total immigration was 8.3 million, but the "pull" effect accounted for almost 10 million, so that "push" kept at home 1.6 million that would otherwise have left. As for post-Famine Ireland, it must not be forgotten that no matter how poor people were, living standards were rising, so that other things being equal there was less incentive to move. The rise in wages and farm incomes in the three decades after the Famine has often been stressed in the literature. The 1880s were tough years, but there was no real protracted agricultural depression in Ireland like that which affected parts of Britain between the late 1870s and the mid-1900s. Thus the period between the Famine and the Great War may be characterized as one of steady improvement in bread-and-butter terms. And, indeed, the recorded emigration rate to America decreased during it. One should not confuse the heartbreak of families splitting up with "push" alone: such trauma is part and parcel of nearly all emigration, whether due to "push" or "pull."

One of the saddest chapters in Muiris O Suilleabhain's *Fiche Blian ag Fas* (translated later into English under the title *Twenty Years a-Growing*) deals with his sister's emigration to America at the turn of the century, and yet there is no doubt but that it is the attraction of America that prompted Maire and her friend Cait Pheig to leave. *"Leimidh laithreach,"* prodded an enthusiastic father, *"seo libh sall agus beidh an t-or le fail ar na sraideanna agaibh"*("Jump now: off with you over there and you will find gold on the streets").

The point is that, despite improving incomes, young people did not take the same "great delight in their own country" as did Arthur McBride of the popular ballad. They left despite efforts "to coax them to stay at home by appeals to their patriotism, or to distant prospects, formed on theories ever so plausible." Nor did they return in substantial numbers—to be expected if the problem was mainly "push."

One counter to this line of argument might be that it took less to "push" an emigrant in, say, the year 1900 than it did in 1850 because of rising expectations. The argument has appeal, but there are at least two counter-arguments. One is purely negative: to introduce such considerations makes "push" somewhat of an unmeasurable will-o'-the-wisp. The second, more substantive, counter is that rising expectations themselves are the result of "pull." Emigrants' letters, it is often urged, enticed away many with their prosaic accounts of wages "on the other side" and heightened the resolution of parents to send several of their children: but such demonstration effects are "pull."

Perhaps a more troublesome riposte to the claim that "pull" was more important is that though conditions economically were improving, the quality of life at home was not. There have been efforts in recent years to idealize nineteenth-century Irish country life—one has only to think of *Siamsa Tire*—but in truth it was a time of increasing Jansenism and puritanical discipline. This side of the coin has been studied but little. However, I suspect that it was of secondary importance: after all the Irish settled out of choice into highly clerical communities on the other side, and largely kept the faith.

IV

The impact of emigration on the nineteenth-century Irish economy was marked. The importance of emigrants' remittances has been shown by Schrier, whose figures suggest that they may have amounted to as much as 1 to 2 percent of Irish national income in the 1880s. More significant was the increase in average incomes at home. The rapid rise in wages after 1850, admittedly sometimes exaggerated, was in the main due to emigration. The other symptoms are well known: housing conditions improved, and there was a marked consumption of tea, sugar, and tobacco, items with a high-income elasticity of demand then. Not all the improvement was due to emigration, needless to say, but my guess is that much of it was. Emigration also contributed mightily to the decline of the Irish language. The prospect of a better living in an English-speaking area was probably more crucial than the mere commercialization of production of British policy or attitudes. For many of the early emigrants illiteracy may not have been such a drawback in the mills and factories of Lancashire or New England, but ignorance of English must have been a real nuisance. Thus the "pull" of America was a major factor in the Anglicization of Irish-speaking areas. Monoglot parents made sure their children learned English. It was they, not the school system, which ensured the success of the notorious *bata scóir* or tally stick. English was indispensable for the ambitious emigrant, and more easily acquired by the Irish than by other European emigrants at the time. Emigrants' letters, even to purely Irish-speaking parents, were always in English. According to a Kerry folklore collector:

My grandmother, who did not know any English, when a letter arrived from her son or daughter and after it was read aloud to her by some member of the family, used to remark in Gaelic: *"N'fheadar cad tá ann, a dhaltha, ach tá's agam go bhuil* dear Mother *agus* pleasure *ann go háirithe"* (I don't know what's there, darling, but I realise that "dear Mother" and "pleasure" are there at any rate). The letters of the time had the usual salutation: "Dear Mother, I now take the pleasure of writing you this letter, hoping it shall find you in a good estate of health as it leaves me at present etc."

There was no contemporary consensus on the merits and demerits of emigration. "We can understand," wrote a contributor to the London *Economist* in 1863, "that the Irish poet whose fancy is stronger than his reason, should lament over shiploads of Celts leaving their native land." The poets were plentiful. But economists such as Nassau Senior and Neilson Hancock, little concerned with poets or patriots or the old people left behind, argued that emigration from a low-wage to a high-wage area benefited those who left and those who staryed. *"Go bhfóire Dia ar na Sean daoine, ní fhanfaidh éinne len iad a chur ar an bhfuadar atá fen saol"* (God help the old folk, there will be nobody left to bury them, with all this restlessness), complained Muiris O Suilleabhain's father in *Fiche Blian ag Fas*. But economists have always been a rather unsentimental bunch, and the disagreement is in part one of sentiment. In retrospect, though, the emigration must be seen as inevitable, Famine or no Famine, a by-product of the Industrial Revolution and the breaking up of the "antiquated system of society," rather than the result of a deliberate British policy of extermination. As Karl Marx put it in one of his contributions to the New York *Tribune*: "Society is undergoing a silent revolution, which must be submitted to. . . . [T]he classes and the races, too weak to master the new conditions of life, must give way." The same was happening in rural areas throughout Europe, and nearer home in parts of Scotland and Wales, places removed from the raw material sources linked with modern industry. The availability of the temperate zones for emigration made the adjustment of labor supply to demand much easier in the nineteenth century. Not without trauma, to be sure, but compare present-day labor surplus economies!

FOR FURTHER READING

Among works cited in the previous selection, R. J. Dickson, *Ulster Emigration to Colonial America*, and W. F. Adams, *Ireland and Irish Emigration to the New World*, are important on the earlier period, and Oliver MacDonagh, "Irish Famine Emigration to the U.S.," *Perspectives in American History* 10 (1976): 357–446, together with his earlier "Irish Overseas Emigration During the Great Famine," in R. D. Edwards and T. D. Williams, eds., *The Great Famine* (New York, 1956), pp. 319–88, succinctly survey the later flow. More specific studies include Robert E. Kennedy, Jr., *The Irish: Emigration, Marriage and Fertility* (London, 1973); Arnold Schrier, *Ireland and the American Emigration, 1850–1900* (Minneapolis, 1958); the Ph.D. dissertations of Michael F. Dillon, "Irish Emigration, 1840–1955" (Los Angeles: University of California, 1940); George R. C. Keep, "Irish Migration to North America in the Second Half of the Nineteenth Century" (Dublin: Trinity College, 1951); Kerby A. Miller, "Emigrants and Exiles" (Berkeley: University of California, 1976); and Nicholas Nolan, "The Irish

Emigration: A Study in Demography" (Dublin: University College, 1935). The wider context is provided in Brinley Thomas, *Migration and Urban Development* (London, 1972), and *Migration and Economic Growth*, 2nd ed. (London, 1973), with a counter-interpretation in Jeffrey G. Williamson, *Late Nineteenth-Century American Development* (London, 1974), pp. 221–49; and these trends (and countertrends) are applied more specifically to the Irish in David Ward, *Cities and Immigrants* (New York, 1971), R. K. Vedder and L. E. Gallaway, "The Geographic Distribution of British and Irish Emigrants to the U.S. After 1800," *Scottish Journal of Political Economy* 19 (1972): 19–35, and Joseph Schachter, "Capital Value and Relative Wage Effects of Immigration into the United States, 1870–1930," Ph.D. (City University of New York, 1969). Analysis of the regional breakdown of Irish emigration is revealing much more of its characteristics: See particularly the series of articles by S. H. Cousens, "Regional Pattern of Emigration During the Great Famine, 1846–1851," Institute of British Geographers, *Transactions and Papers* 28 (1960): 126–29; "Emigration and Demographic Change in Ireland, 1851–1861," *Economic History Revies*, 2nd ser., 16 (1961–62): 275–88, and "Regional Variation in Population Changes in Ireland, 1861–1881," *Economic History Review*, 17 (1964–65): 301–21. Forthcoming series of Thomas Davis lectures, on emigration, edited by Joseph Lee, and on women in Ireland, edited by D. Ó Corráin and Margaret MacCurtain, will illuminate further the relations of migration and sex role relations, as does Lynn Lees, "Mid-Victorian Migration and the Irish Family Economy," *Victorian Studies* 20 (1976): 25–43, and L. Lees and John Modell, "The Irish Countryman Urbanized: A Comparative Perspective on Famine Migration," *Journal of Urban History*, 3(1977), 391-408. For recent overviews of statistical and general demographic problems, see Cormac 'O Gráda, "A Note on Nineteenth Century Irish Emigration Statistics," *Population Studies* 29 (1975): 143–49, and "The Population of Ireland, 1700–1900: A Survey," in *Annales de Démographie Historique* (1978). Official British and Irish statistics of the emigration, by county, sex, and year, are conveniently collected in W. E. Vaughan and A. J. Fitzpatrick, *Irish Historical Statistics: Population, 1821–1971*(Dublin, 1978): 259–353, although Ó Gráda points out their weaknesses in the aforecited papers. Official American statistics contained in the various editions of *Historical Statistics of the United States* lack county and sex breakdowns, but are broadly more accurate. Their defects are traced in E. P. Hutchinson, "Notes on Immigration Statistics of the United States," *Journal of the American Statistical Association*, 53 (1958): 963–1025. The view that Irish workers earned as much as their skills could sustain is presented by Peter Hill, "Relative Skill and Income Levels of Native Born and Foreign Born Workers in the United States," *Explorations in Economic History*, 12 (1975): 47–60, but some counter evidence for the views of Andrew Greeley and Lawrence McCaffrey on persisting prejudice is presented in Paul F. McGouldrick and Michael B. Tanner, "Did American Manufacturers Discriminate Against Immigrants Before 1914?" *Journal of Economic History*, 37 (1977): 723–46.

THE INFLUENCE
OF AMERICA
ON IRISH
NATIONALISM

JOHN A. MURPHY

The public commemoration of historical events is a mixed blessing. Scholars are stimulated to attempt those fresh assessments which are central to the activity of being a historian, since no historical case can ever be marked "closed." At the same time, certain aspects of the event being commemorated can all too easily take on a disproportionate or exaggerated significance. We Irish are prone to do that in any case. It may be a harmless, indeed healthy, piece of insular vanity to imagine that, like the *Skibbereen Eagle*, we have our eye on the doings of the great in faraway places or, like Eamon de Valera at the time of the Anglo-Irish Treaty debates, to think that the eyes of the outside world are riveted on us in fascination. In the present context, the greater part of this book is devoted to discussing the contribution of Ireland to the making of America, a contribution which, we all agree, has been substantial. I am far from sure that the American role in shaping modern Ireland has been equally important.

I should like, at the outset, to say a word about my terms of reference. American influence on the Irish economy and on Irish society generally has been significant. Without emigration to the United States, the extraordinary economic, social, and demographic changes in late nineteenth-century Ireland would be difficult to imagine. Emigrant remittances played no small role in the nineteenth-century rural economy. And, in different ways, the American influence is still very considerable, though perhaps less so, since Irish eyes have come to peer myopically at Brussels. I must, however, restrict my paper to the American influence on Irish *nationalism* and, to obviate the usual endless discussion on what that means, let me offer by way of definition a splendid phrase in Nicholas Mansergh's *The Irish Question* —"a slowly maturing and finally indestructible conviction that Ireland should and would be free." This has the advantage of embracing both the physical force and constitutional streams, the distinction between which is, in any case, not as clear-cut as is popularly supposed.

But let us look, first of all, at the impact of the American Revolution on late eighteenth-century Ireland. It has been commonly assumed that the legislative changes in Dublin between 1779 and 1783 were strongly influenced by the course of events in America and that they constituted Ireland's "American revolution." "All Ireland," said Benjamin Franklin as early as 1769, "is strongly in favour of the American cause. They have reason to sympathise with us." And Horace Walpole observed that "all Ireland went America mad in 1776." What did "all Ireland" mean in this context? Primarily, one might suppose, the "patriots" and progressives of the Protestant nation. The attitude of Irish Roman Catholics to the American Revolution raises a much more complicated and, as yet, relatively uninvestigated historical question. That individual Catholic Irishmen like Stephen Moylan, brother of Bishop Francis Moylan of Cork, distinguished themselves in Washington's train is well known, as is the involvement in the American war of Irish officers in the French service. What is not so clear is how the American Revolution influenced Irish Catholics in general and whether we must distinguish in this respect between the middle class, lay and clerical, on the one hand and the lower orders, the *coitiantacht*, on the other. Modern scholars are beginning to query the wisdom received from Lecky through Beckett which is that politically aware Irish papists sided unequivocally with the Crown against the Americans and that the masses were too apolitical and too absorbed in their elemental concerns to evince any interest in momentous happenings across the Atlantic. Certainly, politically and socially aspiring Irish papists would have seen loyalty to the Crown as the *sine qua non* of further relief, as it had already proved to be the prerequisite of their survival. In 1775 and after, there was no shortage of Catholic addresses of loyalty and Lord Shelbourne spoke perceptively in September 1779 of the papists "avowing their dislike of a constitution here or in America in which they are not allowed to participate." Yet Catholic loyalty was more a prudent expression of distrust of their armed Protestant fellow countrymen than it was an explicit condemnation of either the Americans or the French.

Moreover, there is some evidence that prominent members of the Catholic Committee saw the possibilities of exploiting the American situation in the Catholic interest. In October 1777, Charles O'Conor of Balanagare suggested to Dr. John Curry that, following a British victory, they might petition the Crown to open areas of Maryland and Pennsylvania to emigration by Catholics, and use this in turn against the Anglo-Irish: " . . . most probably our Masters would rather repeal all Queen Anne's laws relative to us, than admit a general Emigration into that part of the world, where so much would be lost to this nation, and so much would be gained to the Crown. . . ."

In 1778, Sam Laffran of Kilkenny wrote in similar terms to O'Conor, promising the threat of mass Catholic emigration to America, if toleration, land, and civil rights were offered by the Americans and withheld by the Dublin government.

If, then, the alignment of the Catholic middle class is not as clear-cut as is commonly supposed, the attitude of the lower orders toward the American Revolution is even more a cause for developing debate among historians. Assumptions that the politically inarticulate are, by definition, politically uninterested have been shown to be unwarranted in the cases of eighteenth-century Russia and twentieth-century Mexico: further investigation of late eighteenth-century Ireland may well establish that the concerns of the Catholic masses went far beyond agrarian frustration and sectarian animosity. The intense agrarian agitation of 1785–86 was more than a little colored by the popular radicalism of the age. The propertyless Irish Catholic countryman had no incentive to share the prudence of his lay and ecclesiastical betters: he might not understand the details of the American cause, but he could rejoice in the discomfiture, across the ocean, of the ancient enemy. Although the impact of the French Revolution and of Napoleon on the Irish popular mind was to be attested in many popular ballads, both in Irish and in English, the American war did not go entirely unsung by Gaelic poets. Tómas O Miodhachain, an Ennis poet-schoolmaster, exulted in Washington's expulsion of Howe from Boston in March 1776. The event is made to fit in with the *aisling* convention, in that Louis XVI is expected to take advantage of the new war and this will be followed by the restoration of Ireland to Stuart rule. Another Gaelic poem follows the *aisling* pattern by having a visionary woman bring news of the defeat of "the English-speaking bears" by "Washington *beo*"—lively Washington.

It would appear, then, that Gaelic Ireland placed the American Revolution, as it was to place Bonaparte, in the context of its own anti-English tradition but much work remains to be done before we can say anything more definite on the subject.

As for the fortunes of the Protestant nation at the end of the eighteenth century, they were influenced less by the principles of the American Declaration of Independence than by the course of the revolutionary war and its economic and military side effects. There was, of course, considerable excitement over American events in 1775–76, and the Declaration was prominently featured in Dublin newspapers. But, as Dr. J. G. Simms has recently pointed out, the ideological influence had long been working the other way round. William Molyneux's seminal work, *The case of Ireland's being bound by acts of Parliament in England stated*, first published in 1698 as a rudimentary expression of the aspirations of an incipient Protestant "nation," influenced the fathers of the American Revolution and, significantly, one of the numerous editions appeared in 1776. In any case, it is a vulgar error to suppose that the concerns of the Protestant patriots in Ireland were identical with those of the American revolutionaries. Of course, the patriots did see a parallel, but they must have been aware that, even before the Revolution, the Americans already held power in representative bodies whereas they themselves, even after 1782, had failed to gain control of the Irish Parliament.

The Protestant nation was more interested in using the revolutionary war to embarrass Dublin Castle and the British Government than in giving its moral support to the cause of the American rebels. Indeed, the very qualified nature of that support (especially after the French entered the war) illustrates —significantly for the future—how the realities of politics in the British Isles and in western Europe took precedence over whatever links might exist between Ireland and America. As for the influence of contemporary American personalities on those Irishmen who were much more radical than the Protestant "patriots," it may be noted again that the United Irishmen took their cue from revolutionary France rather than from revolutionary America. On the other hand, Wolfe Tone observed America as well as France at firsthand, and could say that "in the glorious race of patriotism, I have pursued the path chalked out by Washington." Benjamin Franklin visited Ireland: Thomas Paine never carried out his threat to do so! Paine, whose influence with Irish radicals is in some dispute, had certainly the most popular image in Ireland, paradoxically so for an Englishman. Copies of his writings were widely found during the search-and-destroy operations of 1797–98. There was also a lighter side. In a popular Irish drinking song (then current and still fluent, so to speak) a verse to be heard in Dublin taverns nearly two centuries ago ran as follows:

> The mighty Thomas Paine
> Who reason did maintain
> And whose rights of man did herald a new dawn
> Was stupid as an ass
> Till first he took a glass
> Then truth sprang from his crúiscín lán [full jug].

A final comment may be made on the relationship between the American Revolution and the brief heyday of the Protestant nation. As has been said, the military and economic repercussions of the revolutionary war rather than its direct example led in Ireland to the concession of "free trade," in 1779, and to legislative independence, so-called, in 1782. Grattan's Parliament (which was certainly not controlled by Grattan!) came to be glamourized impossibly by nineteenth-century nationalist writers and politicians, as they looked back over the black barrier of the Union to what they fondly believed to have been a golden age. Today, the tendency of some historians, at least, is to assess that parliament was not only corrupt but bloody and oppressive and to see its abolition as an absolute prerequisite to reform in Ireland. Certainly, most will agree that it perished of cowardice, avarice, and pettiness of spirit, and in the end of sheer fright. With it died the Protestant nation and Ireland's "American revolution." The comparisons conventionally made between the political events on either side of the Atlantic are seen, under close analysis, to be not only odious but ludicrous. Where in College Green, even among the best-intentioned "patriots," was to be found a Franklin, a Jefferson, a Washington? Who among those timorous and pathetic posturers would have written John Hancock large?

Of the three great Irish nationalist leaders—O'Connell, Parnell, and de Valera—Daniel O'Connell was probably least involved in the American thing. In a sense, he was the beneficiary of an age "in which everything may be looked for." He was influenced by Paine and he admired Washington. And in a letter to the Dublin *Evening Post,*, 17 July 1828, he proclaimed:

Be it known to all whom it may concern that I was born on the 6th August 1775, the very year in which the stupid obstinacy of British oppression *forced* the reluctant People of America to seek for security in arms, and to commence that bloody struggle for national independence which has been in its results beneficial to England while it has shed Glory and conferred Liberty pure and sublime on America.

(His emphasis on *forced* is intended to convey his fundamental opposition to violence. He believed that if the political nonconformists had shared in English Government, the American Revolution need never have happened.) But it was the European Enlightenment and British radicalism rather than the American Revolution that really influenced O'Connell. The O'Connells of Derrynane looked to the Continent rather than across the Atlantic. The Liberator's political concerns had little to do with the United States.

But he held very firm views on one controversial American question. As a consistent liberal and reformer, the slavery issue stuck in his throat. At the height of the Repeal year of 1843, he launched a strong attack on Irish-American support for slavery. He divided letters of support from America into two classes—those from the "free" and "unfree" states, for he could never regard as "free" those states which condoned slavery. An appeal from areas such as St. Louis and Savannah to the God of Justice "fell on his ears like blasphemy."

What difference can it make in the eye of reason or of religion what the colour of a man's skin is. . . . It was shocking to any reasoning mind to hear such an appeal made. . . . It would be serving their interests . . . it would be advancing the cause of

Repeal of the Union if they suppressed their abhorrence of slavery, but they would not purchase support from any man by condescending for one moment to be an assenting party to the continuance in slavery of any human being.

He rejected an apology for slavery he had received from Irish Americans in Cincinnati, Ohio. He deplored the fact that, according to reliable evidence, the Irish in America "were the worst enemies to the people of colour."

As early as 1843 it was becoming clear that some Americans were prepared to play the Irish question for what it was politically worth. When, in that year, it appeared that Robert Tyler, the son of the U.S. president, was jumping on the Repeal bandwagon in America, James Haughton, the Dublin Quaker philanthropist, protested:

I believe in my soul that Robert Tyler is one of the greatest enemies of Irishmen and of Irish liberty on the face of the earth. He knows that our countrymen have much political power in America. He is anxious to gain their suffrages for his party; these are cheaply purchased by a few hollow-hearted and fiery speeches in favour of Irish independence, and by a willingness to contribute to our Repeal fund. I unite with the Liberator in repudiating all such unhallowed sympathy and assistance.

O'Connell's Young Ireland opponents took a different line on the slavery issue. An editorial in the *Nation* in January 1844 warned that no friends of Repeal should be antagonized: ". . . the men of the Southern states must not have their institutions interfered with, whether right or wrong . . . we might as well refuse English contributions because of the horrors of mill-slavery." More generally, though the wellsprings of Young Ireland nationalism were more European and English than American, the group as a whole was much more interested in the United States than O'Connell was (many of them were to live there later on). The United States was for them an inspirational source rather than an ideological model. Its very existence was living proof that the British lion was not after all invincible. Indeed this may well have been the principal influence of America on Irish nationalism throughout the nineteenth and early twentieth centuries.

"Now," said Sir William Harcourt, British Home Secretary in the early 1880s, "now there is an Irish nation in the United States, equally hostile, with plenty of money, absolutely beyond our reach and yet within ten days' sail of our shores."

The political implications of the great post-Famine exodus are immense. Students of Irish America are familiar with the T. N. Brown thesis that, essentially, the American Irish *needed* the cause of an unliberated homeland for the sake of their own identity: in a word, Irish nationalism for them was an ethnic assertion. Certainly, their nationalist perspective on Ireland helped to stiffen nationalist feelings at home. The Irish Americans had an image of the old country that was at once more nostalgic and more bleak than the reality. They concentrated on the worst aspects of British policy and on the bitter recollection of things past. They contrasted the land of the free with an island groaning, as they saw it, under English tyranny. Above all, they were unaware of factors back at home such as an improving economy from the 1850s to the late 1870s and the gathering momentum of reform during the nineteenth century which had the effect of gradually destroying the Ascendancy and undermining the Union.

It was the American Irish rather than the domestic Irish who increased the element of Anglophobia in Irish nationalism. By and large, they also supplied the vengeance factor and transmitted it to the "narrowbacks":

> Oh, father dear, that day will come when vengeance loud will call
> When Irishmen with feelings stern will rally one and all
> I'll be the man to lead the van beneath the flag of green
> When loud and high we'll raise a cry—"revenge for Skibbereen"

The political expression of all this was, of course, Fenianism, and the 1860s is, *par excellence, the* great decade of American influence on Irish nationalism (though there was to be another high point in a different context in the 1880s). Fenianism was the very heart of Irish separatism. It is a useful exercise to list the numerous ways in which a specifically Irish-American influence shaped subsequent Irish nationalism. First of all, the term "Fenian" itself was coined in America. It was the American Fenians who began the tradition of financial and moral support for the Irish liberation cause, and who raised high (but always dashed) the hopes of a transatlantic army of liberation. Commencing with the prolonged and spectacular obsequies of Terence Bellew MacManus, the Fenians introduced the necrolatrous element into modern Irish nationalism. Fenian activities in the United States inevitably provoked a reaction from Washington, D.C., and established that Anglo-American interests would always prevail over American sentiment toward Ireland: this was to become evident in the policies of a long line of presidents, stretching to Wilson and Roosevelt and perhaps beyond.

Paradoxically, the forging of the bond between the Irish on either side of the Atlantic was, from the beginning, accompanied by discord and misunderstanding—the problem of the piper and the tune, for example, was never solved. And to the domestic Irish, the political ramifications of Irish America grew ever more bewildering. Too frequently, there was bitter disappointment at home when the promised goods were not delivered: "What do our countrymen in America want?" asked Col. Thomas J. Kelly in the fateful year of 1867, "will they wait until the last man is slaughtered before sending aid?. . . if those scurvy Irish millionaires had done half their duty we would now be recognised as belligerents."

But the American Irish also made some positive contributions to the development of Irish nationalism. The leadership cult seems to be largely a domestic phenomenon for which the Irish Americans had a healthy disregard, as exemplified in their treatment of the egomaniacal James Stephens. American democratic attitudes, then, made their presence felt in this area. Again, Fenians in America were better placed than their comrades at home in the exercise of limiting clerical influence. In this connection there is a highly significant letter in the Fenian Papers in the Catholic University of America, written by John O'Mahony to Charles Kickham and dated 19 October 1863:

Becoming an American association and basing our right of action upon our privileges as *American citizens* and keeping within the laws of these states, we can place ultramontane plotters against human freedom in a very awkward predicament, and a very *unsafe one for them* if they presume to assail us. The pretext of "secret society" being taken from them they will be forced to assail us as a political organization. . . . We are free and sovereign citizens of the American Republic, and priests would be as much justified in attempting to control our votes as such, and of making us their political tools in the internal affairs of the Union, as in preventing us from taking whatever measures we deem right for the liberation of any oppressed nation under the sun. Were we to submit to their dictation in such a case, knownothingism would become a patriotic virtue and our American-born fellow citizens might justly declare us to be *unworthy* of copartnership in the national sovereignty.

Before we leave this question of American Fenian influence, one final point may be made. In the classical Fenian period the "republic" was very far from the cult, still less the mystique, it was to become in later Irish nationalism. Indeed, apart from individuals like Stephens and T. C. Luby, the average Fenian would find the connotations of "republic" distinctly uncongenial when considered in its European context—doctrinaire, socialistic, and antireligious. But the American brand of "republicanism" had none of these repellent associations. Rather did it suggest a political system where freedom was of the essence, where a man could practice his faith as a free citizen, and where, above all, no man was his social superior. It may well have been this large and flexible concept of "republicanism" which first made the republican idea attractive to nationalist Irishmen.

As we move into the closing decades of the nineteenth century, we are presented with two very different Irish-American influences working on Irish nationalism. One is the anarchist tradition of American-Irish Anglophobia expressing itself in the activities of the dynamiters ("not a cent for blatherskite, and every dollar for dynamite") and leaving a *damnosa hereditas* for our own day. The other influence is the constructive and pragmatic attitude of the bulk of Clan na Gael to the land question. Here we have the significant contribution of Patrick Ford and his *Irish World*, the attempt to work out the "new departure" and the making available of the vital financial sinews for the land struggle. But the outcome of that struggle, the establishment of peasant proprietorship, was very far removed from the dreams of Ford or Michael Davitt or Henry George. Thus again it was demonstrated that American influences could suffer the sea change of domestic Irish needs and ambitions.

It has been customary to make much of the American influences allegedly working on the political development of the young Charles Stewart Parnell. Recent scholarly studies, notably R. F. Foster's book on Parnell's family background and F. S. L. Lyons's masterly biography, have stressed the domestic roots of Parnell's political interests, and have suggested that the American maternal influence may have been very slight. Yet, dim as Parnell's historical perceptions were, he must have been aware that his American forebears did not find the British invincible and were not "worsted in the game." At any rate, he instituted the "American trip" tradition whereby Irish leaders visited the United States to enlist the financial and moral support of Irish Americans for the Irish cause. Like his successors, he found that sympathetic resolutions in Congress were of little avail against the indifference, not to say hostility, of the White House.

Once the dramatic days of the land struggle were over, political, social, and cultural developments in Ireland were very little influenced by America. The extension of the franchise, the democratization of local government, the continuation of land reform, the achievements of "constructive unionism," the partnership of church and party, the language revival, the literary renaissance and the new nationalism—all were set firmly in a domestic Irish or Anglo-Irish context. Perhaps the American Irish never really understood the course of these events, and the gap between the old country and Irish America continued to widen. Despite the elaborate liberation plans across the Atlantic, the 1916 rising took place in the end as a purely Irish thing. Indeed, in the period leading up to Easter Week, the confusion that prevailed between revolutionaries on either side of the Atlantic indicated a geographical and communications gap which had existed since the very beginning of Irish America. When Dail Eireann was set up, the constitutional and procedural model was, not surprisingly, Westminster rather than Washington (though the 1937 Constitution was to give forth some American echoes). So dominant, indeed, was British political culture that a tentative proposal in the First Dail to introduce the American committee system was rejected as being too revolutionary!

In 1919–21, the Irish Americans once more provided the sinews of war but once again official American recognition of Irish independence was not forthcoming. Eamon de Valera, himself a child of the Diaspora, was molded more by domestic Irish forces than by Irish-American ones. During his American tour in 1919–20, the differences between Irish and Irish-American nationalists were once more revealed. John Devoy and Judge Cohalan regarded de Valera as being too tepid in his attitudes to Britain. The divergence in interests became painfully obvious in Cohalan's reaction to de Valera's "Cuban" proposals.

"If Ireland," said Cohalan, "were to change her position and to seek a measure of self-government that would align her in the future with England as an ally, in what I regard as the inevitable struggle for freedom of the seas that must shortly come between America and England, every loyal American will, without hesitation, take a position unreservedly upon the side of America."

The Civil War of 1922–23 was a purely Irish event which the American Irish found bewildering. The republican emigrés of the period strengthened still further the intransigent Anglophobic strain in Irish-American nationalism. Meanwhile, Irish-American dollars continued to change direction: just as in 1914–15 they were diverted from the Redmondite to the Irish Volunteers, so in 1926–27 they flowed away from Sinn Fein and toward de Valera's new Fianna Fail party, and they further helped to make possible the launching of the *Irish Press* in 1931.

The experience of Irish statehood added a new dimension to Irish identity at home which was not always understood by our Irish-American cousins, who themselves, at the same time, were undergoing their own identity change in the United States. Irish neutrality was received with mixed feelings by the American Irish, and matters were not helped by the vexed relationship between the Roosevelt administration, egregiously represented in Dublin by David Gray, and de Valera's government. The nonalignment policy of Ireland at the United Nations from about 1957, and, in particular, Irish support for debating the admission of Communist China, angered and alienated many Irish Americans. On the other hand, the Irish visit of President John F. Kennedy in 1963 was joyfully symbolic of the bonds of kinship between the Irish of the Diaspora and those in the old country. Not only did Kennedy's address to the Oireachtas vindicate, in effect, Ireland's independent stance in foreign policy, but the rapturous reception he received from a normally undemonstrative people cannot be explained simply in terms of a glamorous occasion. In 1963, Ireland was experiencing an economic recovery and a national resurgence that ended pessimistic self-questionings about independence which were all too prevalent in the grey decade of the 1950s. In enthusiastically hailing the Irish American who, in his own person, represented the ultimate triumph of the emigrant Irish, the Irish at home were subconsciously acclaiming their own survival.

As this volume goes to press, there are welcome signs that influential Irish-American leaders have succeeded in persuading their people in the United States that violence is not the way to Irish unity, and that there are Protestant as well as Catholic elements in the Irish heritage (indeed, the latter is an educative exercise which is sadly uncompleted in Ireland itself). But much remains to be done in improving the climate of mutual understanding between ourselves and our Irish-American cousins. On both sides there is a need to recognize and respect different political and cultural experiences. Those of us who are privileged to visit the United States regularly must beware of assuming those attitudes of cultural condescension which rightly infuriate the American Irish. Let us at home resolve never again to sneer at the "Mother Machree" songs or the St. Patrick's Day extravaganzas, but rather to recognize that this Irish-American subculture is a valid and significant expression of a distinctive ethnic experience.

FOR FURTHER READING

Probably the most immediate gift of America to Ireland was its provision of a locale and an exemplary republic wherein some Irishmen could propagandize, plan, and finance the movement for Irish independence. This can be very differently assessed in its effects on the various movements in Ireland. It is usually forgotten that the vast majority of Irish Americans were constitutional nationalists in Irish matters, not revolutionaries:the glamour of the Clan na Gael and IRB minorities has obscured this, and awaits its full and unglamorous study. T. N. Brown, *Irish American Nationalism,* and Alan Ward, *Ireland and Anglo-American Relations, 1899-1921* (London, 1969), are the key works. See also Joseph E. Cuddy, *Irish-America and National Isolationism 1914-1920* (New York, 1976); John B. Duff, "The Irish," in Joseph P. O'Grady, ed., *The Immigrants' Influence on Wilson's Peace Policies* (Lexington, Ky. 1967); Michael Funchion, *Chicago's Irish Nationalists, 1881-1890* (New York, 1976); Joseph P. O'Grady, *Irish-Americans and Anglo-American Relations, 1880-1888* (New York, 1976); and, interpretively, Lawrence J. McCaffrey, ed., *Irish Nationalism and the American Contribution* (New York, 1976). The literature on Fenianism in America and Canada has grown enormous: examples include William D'Arcy, *The Fenian Movement in the United States, 1858-1886* (Washington, D.C., 1947); Brian Jenkins, *Fenians and Anglo-American Relations During Reconstruction* (Ithaca, N.Y., 1969); and W. S. Niedhardt, *Fenianism in North America* (London, 1975). Further items are listed in the bibliography to Ó Broin's article. On the impact of the American Revolution, see Doyle, *Ireland, Irishmen and Revolutionary America,* chapter 6. The assertions in this paper, however, rest ultimately upon a critical assessment of the whole stream of Irish history from 1775 to 1970: to this, the best guides are F. S. L. Lyons, *Ireland Since the Famine* (London, 1971), and Gearoid O' Tuathaigh, *Ireland Before the Famine, 1798-1848* (Dublin, 1972), which include extensive further book lists. More comprehensive will be the forthcoming volumes of the *New History of Ireland,* edited by F. J. Byrne, F. X. Martin, and T. W. Moody (Royal Irish Academy/Oxford University Press), volumes 5 through 8 on this period. On continuing connections, Donald H. Akenson, *The United States and Ireland* (Cambridge, Mass., 1973), despite its title, devotes only two chapters to them; T. Ryle Dwyer, *Irish Neutrality and the U.S.A., 1939-1947* (Dublin, 1977), is not exhaustive, but it is useful until further study is done. Dennis J. Clark, *Irish Blood: Northern Ireland the American Conscience* (Port Washington, N.Y., 1977), usefully demonstates how untypical of Irish America generally is the current IRA support network there, despite certain sincere misapprehensions of the author himself.

THE
FENIAN
BROTHERHOOD
LEÓN Ó BROIN

I

In a debate in the British House of Commons in the wake of the Great Famine and an abortive rising, Henry Grattan, Jr., deplored the government's law-and-order policy and cautioned his listeners not to excite feelings in the Irish people which it might be impossible to subdue. Rather more than a year before he had been in a seaport town, and had entered into conversation with a fellow Irishman who was on the point of embarking for America. He advised him to remain at home, in the hope of better times, but, the man replied, "No, sir: I will go to the land of liberty." "All right," said Grattan, "but consider your sons," to which the man answered, "Ah, they'll come back; and when they do come, it will be with rifles on their shoulders."

In the 1850s and 1860s, as maturing young men in the United States, those young fellows could well have become involved in a movement that aimed at doing precisely what their father had hinted at, namely, the re-conquest of their native land. The inspiration for the movement came principally from the farmer scholar John O'Mahony, who, after the Young Ireland fiasco of 1848, had worked with James Stephens in Paris in what A. M. Sullivan called the central training school of European revolutionism. About 1855, with Michael Doheny, another '48 man, he established in New York the Emmet Monument Association with the object of invading and liberating Ireland. This association had predecessors going back to 1848, among them the Emmet Club, the Irish Republican Union, various Irish Volunteer companies, and the Irish Emigrant Aid Society, and it was replaced in 1858 by the Phoenix Society, with O'Mahony as president and Doheny as one of his lieutenants. There were branches, a military organization —Phoenix Brigades and what not—and a Patriotic Defense Fund for the benefit of men who had been sent to prison in Ireland through membership of a parallel Phoenix organization which Stephens had tried to whip up but which had been stamped out by the government. Then the Fenian Brotherhood appeared as if the Phoenix Society had just changed its name. The synonymity of the terms "Phoenix" and "Fenian" was noticed in Dublin Castle, where no real distinction could be traced between the movement they had suppressed and the Fenian Conspiracy on both sides of the Atlantic which now occupied their attention. But "Fenian" was a term really only applicable to the American-based brotherhood, though like Sinn Fein in later times the term was widely, even officially, but incorrectly employed to denote the Irish Revolutionary, later Republican, Brotherhood or IRB. The separation of the two brotherhoods was always maintained. The pioneering Joseph Denieffe, in his *Personal Narrative of the Irish Revolutionary Brotherhood*, says, for example, that "we in Ireland were not Fenians . . . we were members of the I.R.B." The distinction is worth emphasizing, because the purposes of the two bodies were intended to be different, though complementary. The Fenian expert in Dublin Castle, and author of an official history of Fenianism, saw the IRB as a secret revolutionary society whose aim was to put an army in the field, whereas the Fenian Brotherhood was an auxiliary with the mission of providing "the sinews of war." They were to supply the IRB with arms and military stores, with officers, and conceivably with reinforcements of men (NLI Larcom MSS. 7517).

The Fenian Brotherhood developed slowly at first but, by the latter part of 1860, when O'Mahony came over to Ireland on a visit to the IRB, many circles had been formed and a spirit of optimism prevailed regarding the future. Indeed, at a meeting with Stephens in Dublin, an understanding was reached concerning the degree of American aid that would justify an Irish uprising. At least 5,000 disciplined men with competent officers would be required as a nucleus of an army of liberation, and at least 50,000 rifles or muskets for the insurgents. O'Mahony thought it possible that that amount of assistance could be obtained in the United States and was on his way back to the United States to organize for that purpose when the Civil War broke out. That changed the picture dramatically for the Fenian cause; and nothing was more depressing than the prospect of Fenians fighting each other instead of fighting the ancient enemy.

The idea then gained acceptance that combat experience would be valuable for an organization which consisted chiefly of well-drilled but entirely inexperienced state militia and volunteers. O'Mahony and Stephens, nevertheless, cannot have been happy to see branches of the Brotherhood disappear as the number of American regiments, staffed and manned by Fenians, increased. The situation was far from hopeless, however, and it was reversed, toward the end of the war, as the result of vigorous organizing in the Union armies by Thomas Clarke Luby and James Stephens. To Stephens's recruiting drives in particular can be attributed the fact that, after the war, the Fenian Brotherhood included among its members thousands of men who had fought through the entire campaign under the most distinguished generals, and that many of these who came to Ireland in 1865 had risen by their personal valor to important positions of command (NLI Larcom MSS. 7517).

The economic dislocation that followed the war played a part in the swelling of Fenian recruitment. By November of 1865 sometimes quarters of a million men had been demobilized and were thrown upon the labor market during a time of recess—when industries lost wartime contracts and the speculative boom collapsed. However, recruitment was to fall off later as the economy recovered, though other reasons also operated, as we shall see.

From the Roster of the Military Officers of the Fenian Brotherhood preserved in O'Mahony's Papers I quote, for the purpose of illustrating the continuity of the Irish-American revolutionary nexus, the career of Patrick J. Downing, a native of Skibbereen and one of four sons who served in the Union army. I do not know when Patrick went first to America, but he was back in Ireland in 1856 before the Emmet Monument Association became extinct, and commenced to organize and drill in anticipation of some form of physical intervention from the United States—an invasion perhaps. Under Jeremiah O'Donovan Rossa he helped to spread the Phoenix Society and when it merged in the IRB, he returned to New York in March 1860 as an IRB envoy. He joined the Forty-second (Tammany) Regiment in June 1861 and for three years he saw active service in various campaigns from the Peninsula to the Wilderness and the siege of Petersburgh, and was twice wounded at the Battle of Antietam (*Cork Historical and Archaeological Journal*, 1969). Downing figures among O'Mahony's lieutenant colonels; above him and below him were many men with similar experience and a burning desire to serve their native land. The problem O'Mahony, Stephens, and company never solved was how effectively to employ such men, to get them, armed and accoutred, across the Atlantic and to time their arrival with a purposeful local insurrection, and, as John Mitchel kept on insisting, with Britain's involvement in a major war.

Recruiting inside and outside the American forces of men with family backgrounds like Downing's was helped enormously by the prevailing popular anti-British sentiment. Britain was believed to have been alarmed at the increasing prosperity of the States, to have deliberately sown the apple of discord among them, by intrigue to have kept the Civil War going, recognizing the Confederate States as a belligerent power and permitting privateers for the South to be built and fitted out in English dockyards. There was another side to this story, of course, but the British government had no success in having it accepted. Their explanations were lost on people who, in the matter of Britain's relations with Ireland, were prepared to give their sympathy, if nothing else, to the Fenian cause.

In November 1863, that is to say some eighteen months before the Civil

War actually ended, the Brotherhood held a first National Convention in Chicago at which resolutions were passed proclaiming the Republic of Ireland virtually to be established, acknowledging James Stephens to be the representative of the Brotherhood in Europe and the Supreme Organizer of the Irish people, and adopting a constitution under which the government of the Brotherhood was entrusted to a Head Center, John O'Mahony, and a Central Council. Thus far the going was easy, but the prospect of impending dissension could be detected when O'Mahony considered it necessary to urge the importance of helping the Irish in Ireland to accomplish the freedom of their country, rather than that with the same intention, Fenian efforts should first be directed against the British dominion of Canada which was being advocated. It was in Ireland, he insisted, that the help of the Fenians was most needed: it was there that English tyranny would receive its death blow. Those who supported the alternative policy aimed to lodge a Fenian army on Canadian soil, to win the local population over, and to use the occupied territory as a base from which to attack Britain. General Thomas William Sweeny had visions of a fleet of Fenian privateers eventually forcing the British to come to terms for the independence of Ireland.

Looking at the two policies, the Irish government—that is, the executive in Dublin Castle—believed that Fenianism would not become a serious threat unless Britain became involved in a war with the United States. In that event there would probably be an open attempt at rebellion in Ireland, the danger from which would depend entirely on the amount of American aid that would be forthcoming; and that, it was thought, would probably not amount to very much. The geographical factor placed the balance of advantage on the British side. It was, therefore, more likely, in their opinion, that the Fenians would make for Canada, where geographically they were not at a disadvantage, and where resources of men and matériel gave them superiority. In the upshot, as we shall see, both alternatives were tried, and both of them failed dismally.

The British, in which I include the Irish government, of course had one enormous advantage in this situation, the possession of an excellent intelligence service. They had all the information they needed regarding the plans and proceedings of the Fenian Brotherhood and IRB, and no move could be made anywhere without their prior knowledge. The IRB was closely watched by the Irish Constabulary and the Dublin Metropolitan Police, while the affairs of the Fenians in the United States were usually conducted in such an open manner that there was little difficulty in discovering what was afoot. The agents of the British Consul General within the Fenian ranks in New York, and the experienced Irish Constabulary officer who had been specially assigned to the eastern cities, supplemented, and acted as a check on, the newspaper reports.

Through 1865, with the U.S. Government ignoring British requests that they should check the Fenian movement, the Irish government became disturbed when groups of Fenians, with arms and money, began to leave American ports with the intention, it was said, of taking part in an insurrection that was to take place toward the end of September. By the middle of that month the government felt they had to do something to contain the threat. They accordingly raided the IRB headquarters which were alongside the castle, arrested the leaders, and, with the exception of Stephens, who managed to escape, put all of them away for long terms of imprisonment. They simultaneously suppressed the influential anticlerical IRB paper, the *Irish People*. In March 1866 the government acted again, this time to even greater purpose. They suspended the writ of habeas corpus and made 700 arrests, and the effect of so doing was described as magical. IRB meetings were abandoned, drilling ceased, public alarm subsided, and, before the end of May, the government believed that, so far as Ireland was concerned, that was the end of Fenianism. But that, however, was far from being the case.

II

In Philadelphia in October 1865 another Fenian Convention abolished the post of Head center and the Central Council and set up in their place a President of the Fenian Brotherhood of the United States and a General Congress consisting of a Senate and House of Delegates: in effect, a government modeled upon that of the United States itself. O'Mahony, by virtue of his new status, proceeded like any American president to appoint a cabinet with a Secretary of War, an Agent of the Irish Republic, an Agent for the issue of republican bonds, and so forth, and he sent John Mitchel, another Young Irelander become Fenian, to Paris to act as a disburser of funds to the order of the peripatetic Stephens when he was available and to his nominees when he was not. All in all this was a colorful piece of stagecraft, and Irish Americans no doubt swelled with pride when they saw the Irish harp and sunburst flying from the Fenian Capitol in New York City. On O'Mahony's government within a government, the suspension of Habeas Corpus and the widespread arrests had the opposite effect to what had happened in Ireland. The American Fenians were spurred to action, but at a time when their leaders were at sixes and sevens, not merely over the fundamental question of where the battle for Irish freedom should be waged, but over an issue of republican bonds, a so-called Senate party, led by William Randall Roberts and Thomas William Sweeny being accused by O'Mahony of corruption and of having accepted British bribes. They retaliated by having O'Mahony deposed by the Fenian Congress, and then proceeded with their plans for an assault across the Canadian frontier. O'Mahony met this revolt by convening a rival Congress from which he secured an endorsement of his policy of fighting England on Irish soil. To keep up the home organization, he told Mitchel, must be our chiefest and greatest care. Without it even an American or French war might fail to free Ireland (*Cork Historical and Archaeological Journal*, 1970). This was in accord with Mitchel's own thinking, and Stephens's, though Mitchel did not think much of Stephens, except insofar as he tried without success to heal the divisions in the American Fenian Congress before coming out in support of O'Mahony against the Roberts-Sweeny faction.

It is not clear where the idea of an invasion of Canada originated. An obvious starting point, of course, was the justifiable assumption that America owed a debt of gratitude to the Fenians for their splendid war service, and it may have been with this at the back of his mind that Doran Killian, an able Fenian lawyer, sounded President Andrew Johnson and Secretary of State William Henry Seward as to how they would react if, simultaneously with a rising in Ireland, the Fenians were to seize some portion of the territory lying north of the frontier of Maine. Nothing in the nature of a specific undertaking was secured, but Roberts and Sweeny and the so-called Senate party went ahead with their plans, confident that they could rely on the support of the American government. The Irish vote in the impending election was, as always, a factor of considerable weight, and this the British fully recognized. They therefore approached Washington with considerable delicacy, hoping that Seward, if reluctant to guarantee to them in advance that there would be no breach of the international obligations of the United States in the matter of neutrality, would see to it at the appropriate time that these obligations were fully respected. Seward was believed to want peace but considered it politically undesirable to appear friendly to the British. But the British left Seward in no doubt as to their unease at observing a Fenian executive with all the paraphernalia of ministers and departments functioning in one of the centers of the American Union. This might not be of much importance practically as regards the peace of Ireland, they noted, but it kept agitation alive and embittered the feelings of the people of the United States against Great Britain, and this could eventually impair the relations of the two governments.

Between 1866 and 1871 the American Fenians made three assaults on British North American territory. The first—in April 1866—was an effort to seize Campobello in the Bay of Fundy on the North Brunswick frontier. The ownership of this island was considered a debatable matter, and an attack on it, it was hoped, might provoke a dispute between the British and the Americans, and perhaps a war from which Ireland would stand to benefit. This was the thinking of O'Mahony and his followers who engineered the attack, hoping thereby to steal a march on the Roberts-Sweeny crowd who were known to be preparing to invade Canada, but had so far made no move. The attempt ended in sheer burlesque at a cost of $40,000, and forced O'Mahony to resign the leadership of the orthodox brethren to James Stephens. The only achievement was the capture of a Union Jack from a customs post. The British were delighted, and derived particular satisfaction from the fact that a naval vessel and a company of artillery put in an appearance to mark the Americans' intention of stopping enterprises of this sort.

The first border crossing into Canada occurred at the end of May 1866 —about a month, that is, after the Campobello affair—when, taking the British somewhat by surprise, despite their superior intelligence, General T. W. Sweeny directed forward movements from Buffalo, New York, and St. Albans, Vermont. These were rather easily dispersed, though not before a contingent of Civil War veterans under Colonel John O'Neill gained a considerable advantage over a party of Canadian volunteers at Ridgeway. The military failure of the attempt as a whole was evident, and a grievous disappointment to the Fenians, but what hurt them most was a proclamation issued by President Johnson in pursuance of which Roberts and Sweeny were both taken into custody, and the movements of persons, arms, and ammunition, destined to violate the laws of the United States, forbidden. Many Fenians were arrested in the frontier areas but were given a discharge and free transport home in exchange for the undertaking not to repeat the offense. The prosecution of Roberts and Sweeny was not proceeded with, captured Fenian arms were handed back, and Roberts went to Washington to agitate for a change in the neutrality laws. He tried to put the blame for the Fenian failure on the administration and called Seward a dirty tool of the English government. He won some sympathy from congressmen but nothing more, while the British reduced the tension by advising the Canadians to treat the prisoners in their hands leniently. Canadian public opinion had understandably been outraged by the deaths of twenty-five of their soldiers and by the expense to which the country had unnecessarily been put.

Roberts, having reflected on the unlikelihood of a second invasion being any more successful than the first, relinquished the presidency of the Senate party at the end of 1867, and was succeeded by the more optimistic hero of Ridgeway, John O'Neill. O'Neill's intentions were, however, hampered both by a shortage of funds reflecting a falling off of popular interest in Canadian adventures, and by further dissensions on issues of policy, and it was May 1870 before a Fenian force again moved toward the frontier, this time to the east and west of Lake Champlain. It was once more a hopeless business from the start. The Canadians and the Americans were well prepared for the raiders. Since their experiences in 1866 the Canadians had created a well-trained and adequately armed militia, and were supported by a force of British regulars. The American reaction also was stiffer and more positive than before. Grant and Hamilton Fish had replaced Johnson and Seward at the head of the administration, and as soon as O'Neill's men began to move, they issued a warning proclamation which was read to the Fenians in their forward positions by a federal marshal. President Grant subsequently announced that Fenians would no longer be permitted the luxury of a government organization within the United States, an *imperium in imperio*. Meanwhile marshals in the troubled areas generally were given orders to deal with all breaches of the neutrality code, and American troops were posted on the border to ensure that the president's decree was enforced. Every move by O'Neill was anticipated. He had elevated the Englishman T. M. Beach, who passed as Major Henri Le Caron, to a position on his staff, and through Le Caron the Canadian and British governments were supplied with all the information they could wish for.

The invasion, or raid, or assault, like its predecessor, ended ignominiously. For a few hours the newspapers gave an impression of tens of thousands of Fenians on the march and of the entire length of the border in a condition of panic, but this was the faintest reflection of the facts. When O'Neill put in an appearance on horseback, there were scarcely twenty men in his company, and though they marched bravely to meet a Canadian outpost, they were quickly driven back in disorder. O'Neill retired to make contact with his scanty reserves, and was arrested by the U.S. marshal of Vermont. For his contribution to the defeat Le Caron was paid a special bonus of $1,000. In addition to supplying in advance the requisite details of O'Neill's intentions, he on the day of battle, deliberately delayed the arrival of the Fenian reserves and rendered unworkable the solitary Fenian gun by removing the breach piece and putting it where it could not be found. O'Neill, of course, knew nothing of this treachery, and, indeed, when he sat down in a Canadian lockup to write his official report, he actually praised Le Caron as being both competent and reliable!

O'Neill made a final incursion into Canada in October 1871. This was not, however, a Fenian business at all, but that made no difference to O'Neill, who was prepared, in Le Caron's view, to do "anything to cripple the enemy." He had just been released from jail, contrary to the wishes of the New York Fenian council, when he accepted an invitation from a Father William B. O'Donohoe, a young priest from Manitoba, who was acting as secretary to Louis Riel, the leader of a Canadian revolt that aimed at annexing the Red River colony to the United States. He duly went into action across the Manitoba border with no more than forty men and the result was exactly as before: He had obligingly in advance let Le Caron see his correspondence with Father O'Donohoe. When arrested, it seemed certain that this time he would go to prison for a long spell, but on being handed over to the U.S. authorities, he was released on the technicality that his offense had not been committed on American soil.

The Fenians have been described by Professor C. P. Stacey as "assiduous but inept practitioners of the art of revolution": And who, looking at the events we have been outlining, would quarrel with that description? They did nothing for their cause except to manifest a self-sacrificing attachment to "the old country," and the unreasoning hatred of England from which we still suffer. Most of them were Catholic, but their cross-border raids worsened the position of their coreligionists in Canada from whom they had asked, but received no collaboration, and they revived the anti-Catholic feeling that had formerly been largely fostered by the Orange Order. The real beneficiaries ultimately from the raids were the Canadian people as a whole and the British government. The raids promoted a sense of Canadian nationalism and caused any lingering pro-American sentiment to evaporate. They expedited the discussion of proposals for a confederation of the Canadian provinces; and they created a lively interest in national defense, making people realize that safety against invasion lay in unity.

This was a policy Britain had long advocated in order to reduce its overseas commitments. And the Washington Treaty of 1871 closed the door on the likelihood of an Anglo-American war by providing for arbitration on outstanding American grievances, the exploitation of which had hitherto helped the Fenian cause.

III

Having dealt with one wing of the American Fenians, we turn to the other, which takes us back to 1865, the first year that Stephens, returning from America, promised would be the year of deliverance. He told everybody he met there that from America would come everything that was required, money, arms, and experienced officers. From Chicago alone "we'll get 3,000 officers," he told John Devoy. A large number of Fenians did, in fact, cross the Atlantic that year, among them Colonel Thomas J. Kelly, who had been a staff officer in the Army of the Cumberland, who had had opportunities of seeing large-scale military movements, and had been wounded in the battle of Missionary Ridge. He came as an observer for O'Mahony, and was impressed by the possibility of a fight in Ireland and the quality of the IRB men. Under him as chief of staff, a military council of American officers was constituted in Dublin, or so it appears, consisting of Colonel Michael Kerwin, who had been with the Army of the Potomac; Colonel William G. Halpin, who had commanded a Kentucky regiment; Colonel Denis P. Burke, a commander of a regiment in Meagher's Irish Brigade; and a Captain Doherty, who had been on the staff of General Owen. Kelly was exceedingly active, and on his initiative was carried out an infiltration of British army units by IRB men.

As a result, however, of the government's action in September 1865, the possibility of a rising taking place in that year, backed by an American invasion, became extremely doubtful; and Stephens secured the agreement of Kelly's military council to a postponement, giving as the reason for doing so, not the government's intervention but the split in American Fenianism which had interrupted the supply of funds on which the IRB depended for the purchase of arms. The government's move in March 1866 was a really shattering blow. Some members of the military council were arrested as well as key IRB men within the British regiments in Ireland. Stephens once more avoided arrest, however, and from America he asserted ever more boldly that 1866, of which there were barely eight months left, would now be the year of action; before it ended he would be back in Ireland leading an invading American army. It is not easy to assess what lay behind this declaration, for he could hardly have believed he was talking anything but nonsense. His principal aim apparently was to raise money for a variety of purposes from a community that was depressed by the divisions in the Fenian ranks and by the Campobello foozle, and he did whip up sufficient enthusiasm for his enterprise to be able to send some men across the Atlantic, to prepare for his coming. This convinced the British that something really serious might be on the way, and not to be caught amiss they took a good hard look again at their defenses. The admiralty diverted ships and marines, intended for foreign service, to the southern and western approaches; the army was reinforced and the latest issue of military rifles was supplied to the Irish constabulary.

That was the situation at the very end of 1866 when the bubble inevitably burst. Seven months of campaigning and speech making had been ineffective. Less than £3,000 had been sent to Ireland, and the war matériel supplied amounted to less than one-fourth of the minimum requirement laid down by Stephens himself, which was 30,000 rifles. Stephens, therefore, sought the agreement of his council of ex-American army officers to have action deferred for a second time, but this, though it was sheer realism on Stephens's part, was more than they were prepared to swallow. At a stormy meeting in his New York lodgings Stephens was accused of incompetence, insincerity, dishonesty, and cowardice, and only the intervention of Colonel Kelly saved his life when Captain John McCafferty drew a gun on him. According to Devoy's *Recollections*, Stephens was then compelled to order the rising to proceed and was then deposed in favor of Kelly. Though the rising was obviously going to suffer from utter lack of preparation, Kelly and company thought that the important thing was to keep the promise that had been made to the Brotherhood as a whole, and particularly to the advance parties who had already crossed or were at that moment crossing the Atlantic. John Mitchel saw all this as yielding to the impatience of the Irish people for immediate results and to their capacity for being deluded (*Cork Historical and Archaeological Journal* 1970, 49).

Kelly was a very different type to Stephens. In the eyes of the Irish police, he was as reckless and determined as Stephens was vacillating and timid. He certainly did not let the grass grow under his feet. He sold a vessel that had been bought for the Campobello expedition and sent the proceeds to Europe for distribution among the officers who had already gone over. By the end of January 1867, he was himself in London, meeting there representatives of a schismatic IRB and forming with them a Provisional Government on which representation was given to two Continental mercenaries—who were to be the Commander in Chief and Chief of Staff respectively in the Army of the Irish Republic—and to Colonel Geoffrey Massey, a Limerick man who had served with the Confederate army in the Civil War. This provisional government fixed a date in March for the rising and prepared a plan of operations which it was anticipated would enable the insurgents to hold out for at least three months, which was considered sufficient to rouse the patriotism of the Irish in America and inspire them to energetic action. An address was drafted as coming "From the Irish People to the World," a production whose style and character indicated to the government that it was the handiwork of Charles Bradlaugh, the English radical.

Kelly and his associates had approached the English republicans for support, and the address to the world contained a special appeal to the English working class. "As for you workers of England," it read, "it is not only your hearts we wish, but your arms. Remember the starvation and degradation brought to your firesides by the oppression of labour. . . . Avenge yourselves by giving liberty to your children in the coming struggle for human freedom." The address was annexed to the proclamation of an Irish Republic, which was to signal the start of the rising, and which emphasized the equality of all men, the determination to replace a cursed monarchical government with a republic based on universal suffrage, the intrinsic value of man's labor, the need to restore the soil of Ireland, held by an oligarchy, to the Irish people, the absolute liberty of conscience, and the complete separation of church and state. This proclamation, Kelly described as "the gauge of our republican principles and our social aspirations," and as "the desire of the Ireland of 1867 regenerated by the story[?] of its exiles in America." There is no evidence that these blood-stirring phrases made any impact on the English working class, and no support that I know of came from the English radicals.

In the early days of the previous November the police reported that Fenians, bent on mischief, were arriving in Britain from the United States at the rate of about fifty a week and were settling down in Birkenhead, Liverpool, Chester, Manchester, Sheffield, and London. What were described as American Irishmen were simultaneously making their appearance in the Cork area. The number who landed at Queenstown in the first fortnight of the month was 800, and most of these had only been away about nine months. They had returned, they said, because they could not find employment in America or because of poor health, but the police doubted their stories. Nine months was just about long enough to be drilled and sent home to lead the disloyal in whatever disturbance was planned. Strangers of military appearance, and evidently Americans, had also started to arrive in the west of Ireland, where a landing was anticipated. The soft felt hat which such people usually wore had been superseded by the square felt hat French style or by caps with French peaks similar to those worn by men aboard ships; and several Irish Americans wearing this gear had succeeded by February 1867 in coming over as engineers or firemen or concealed by the regular ships' firemen among whom they had sympathizers. The Irish newspapers reported some of these items; and the police sought authority to have persons so arriving from America detained and required to give an account of themselves. If this proved unsatisfactory, they should be given the option of returning by the next boat or of being imprisoned under the Habeas Corpus Suspension Act. The prime minister, Lord Derby, warned, however, in December 1866 against indiscriminate arrests. Such a step would involve Britain in the most serious difficulties with the American government, with which they were trying hard to remain on good terms.

We do not know what the provisional government's plan for the March rising was. They were terribly short of arms, and reluctantly therefore they had to accept the idea of raiding Chester Castle in order to secure the large stocks known to be deposited there. The train for Holyhead, and the boats in Holyhead Harbour were to be seized in turn, and railway lines and telegraphic communications destroyed as the Fenians, concentrated in England, moved to assure a landing on the east coast of Ireland in the vicinity of Dublin. This imaginative idea originated with John McCafferty, who had been in the Confederate army as one of Morgan's raiders in the forays through Kentucky, and was recognized by the Irish police as an eccentric self-willed fellow, who usually did what he thought proper without regard to the opinions and feelings of others. (We are talking now of the events of 1867. Fifteen years later McCafferty was still at it. He was then one of the much feared Invincibles and may have been their leader.) His Chester Castle plan, however, was never really put to the test, because once again an informer was at hand to warn the government. The informer, John Joseph Corydon, had also American war experience, and had joined the Fenian Brotherhood at Harrison's Landing, Virginia, when serving as a lieutenant in the Union army.

Through ignorance of the change in the government of the Brotherhood and confusion as regards the date fixed for the rising, another American officer, a Colonel John J. O'Connor, went into action in Kerry in mid-February with a small contingent that included some Americans. They attacked a coastguard station and then, discovering perhaps that a general insurrection had not taken place, they dispersed, leaving it to an *Irish Times* reporter, who had a streak of poetry in him, to describe how they disappeared through the mist, "dropping one by one over a mountain ridge like hares seeking a covert." The government made much of this false start, Lord Derby pouring contempt on a Fenian army reduced to ten men, and on American generals and colonels who came to Ireland only to find there were no soldiers to lead. The incident, trifling and localized though it was, had a prejudicial effect on the prospects of the national outbreak planned for the following month —not that they were ever very great. It revealed to the government the possible weakness of the Kerry constabulary, some of whom on hearing that the Fenians were on the march, put up the shutters on the barracks and hid behind them. On the other hand the army was given an opportunity of which it availed to try out the practice of employing flying columns of commandeered vehicles in disturbed areas, and the experience gained in this way proved particularly valuable when "the real thing" happened.

I do not propose to enter into the details of the rising of March 1867; I have done this already in my book *Fenian Fever*. But as regards the contribution of the Fenian Brotherhood to it I should say that, apart from the individuals I have already mentioned—McCafferty, O'Connor, Corydon, and Massey—a dozen American officers named by John Devoy, probably did as much as could have been expected of them to make the rising a success instead of the shambles it became. They were Patrick Lennan, John Kirwan, W. G. Halpin, William Mackey Lomasney, James Moran, P. J. Condon, John McClure, Larry O'Brien, a Captain Dunn, John G. Healy, a Lieutenant Colonel Leonard, and Richard O'Sullivan Burke.

Late in July or in the early part of August that year what O'Sullivan Burke called a general convention of the IRB was held in Manchester and was attended by about 300 delegates from Ireland, Scotland, Wales, and England. The convention was summoned by Colonel Kelly, who had lain low in Dublin for some months, and it was organized by a couple of American Fenians. We do not pause to consider Kelly's right to convene such a meeting or the authority by which the convention proceeded to elect him as chief executive of the IRB—this ties up I imagine with the replacement of James Stephens. By an overwhelming vote the convention also adopted a plan for the future of the IRB, and Kelly continued, as the organization's chief executive, to live in Manchester and from there to assign officers, most of them Americans, to take general charge of the organization in the home countries, including Northern and Southern Ireland. At this stage Sir Thomas Larcom, the Undersecretary in Dublin Castle, noted a bad spirit abroad which he blamed on a score of newspapers pouring out sedition, and on Americans and other agents who were going about canvassing for recruits to their cause. It was, he wrote sarcastically to Lord Naas on 3 July, truly a most happy Arcadian state of society (NLIMS. 11191 [12])!

That was roughly the situation, with Kelly's caucus resisting the efforts of Roberts and Sweeny to win recruits from the IRB when Kelly, in September, was arrested in Manchester along with Captain Timothy Deasy, another of the Fenian officers who had come over from America for the rising. They were both rescued later in an attack on a police van in which a police sergeant lost his life and for which killing three "Manchester martyrs" were created. Not long after this, Colonel Richard O'Sullivan Burke was also taken prisoner and lodged in Clerkenwell Jail in London. He, too, got away, but, in blasting through to him with dynamite, many unfortunate women and children living in tenements nearby were killed or maimed.

In retrospect Devoy said that the wonder was not that the rising was such a military fiasco, but that it should have been attempted at all. A disaster was what the Supreme Council of the IRB called it when they passed judgment on it in April 1868, a disaster caused partly by the determination of certain American Fenians to sustain their influence and partly by the desire of some very brave men to precipitate the issue. The army that was to have led to victory was grossly unprepared, through lack of military equipment, to attain even the most temporary success, except by fortuitous circumstances and such an expenditure of human blood as no Christian man would sanction. It was, in fact, to prevent a repetition of premature military action and to restrain from violence and outrage men who had sworn allegiance to the Irish Republic and its government, that the Supreme Council itself had been instituted after the rising. This council, without indicating how they had obtained it, claimed authority in the name and on behalf of the Irish people to command that no agents or officers accredited and commissioned from the United States should be received, recognized, or obeyed by the IRB unless and until their authority was ratified by the Supreme Council; further, that no organization in the United States had authority to claim obedience in Ireland. These decisions had become necessary, it was pointed out, to prevent the possibility of the disunion that had occurred in America spreading into the Irish Republican Brotherhood and paralyzing its work. And, in the name of a perishing people, the Supreme Council appealed to Irishmen in America not to get involved in the unhappy party differences over there which had brought about nothing but frustration.

The council, however, went far beyond an *appeal* to the Irish Americans. They announced the *rupture* of formal relations with the Fenian Brotherhood, a rupture that was to last until 1876 when, with much difficulty, a Joint Irish-American Revolutionary Directory was formed. Meanwhile, as if to show that they could dispense with American aid altogether, the Supreme Council began to make outrageous claims about the strength of the IRB, its state of discipline, organization, and spirit. All, they said, was wanted was equipment. When this became available, they in the Supreme Council would choose their time and strike, in Ireland, of course, which was the only place where England could be successfully combated and destroyed.

All of this was egregious exaggeration. And the government knew it.

What worried them was the persistence of the revolutionary spirit. On March 25, 1867, after the rising the able Larcom told his political chief: "We are much as usual—smouldering. We hold Fenianism by the throat as you would a burglar, but the moment you relax, up it springs as strong as ever. The root is in America, in the discontent of a million and a half of people, mourning and brooding over a grievance." And echoing the words of young Grattan, with which this talk began, he explained what the grievance was. It was expatriation, exile from a homeland. This, though it had occurred in the past, lived on as a sentiment that was not to be reasoned about and that fed on itself. He could not see how it was to end, and what means were to be taken to end it. One thing was certain, however. They could not go on throttling forever. They could only go on trying to win away more and more from the malcontents and raise antagonism to them by spreading contentment at home. And that was a long process, he warned Chief Secretary Naas, and a painful prospect (NLIMS. 11191[5]).

IV

The Fenian Brotherhood, in the aftermath of the raids on Canada and the Irish debacle, steadily lost ground to the Clan na Gael (United Brotherhood), another revolutionary body that came into existence in 1867. In 1872—in succession to John Savage, who had been chief executive since 1867—John O'Mahony was elected to a post equivalent to his earlier one, but he resigned in 1874 and died in dire poverty a few years later. In 1875 the Brotherhood was endeavoring to secure the release of Fenians still undergoing sentence but, when some of them were successfully rescued from Australia in 1876, the honors went to the Clan na Gael and the IRB. O'Donovan Rossa appeared to give the Brotherhood a new lease of life a little later when he inaugurated a Skirmishing Fund out of which dynamite operations against English targets were financed in the eighties. But by 1877 the Brotherhood was in a parlous condition and Stephens, then living in France, under a cloud, was invited to come back and assume the leadership. Understandably, he took his time replying to the invitation, and it was January 1879 before he arrived in the States. He failed in the task of reorganizing and reviving the moribund organization and threw in his hand the following year. The Brotherhood finally expired in 1886, leaving the field to the Clan na Gael; and it was with the Clan na Gael that the IRB henceforward did business.

FOR FURTHER READING

The literature of this subject threatens to sink the movement it studies: a movement important and dramatic although not coterminous with Irish and Irish-American public concerns from 1865 onward. Yet Irish independence has been taken as vindicating the colorful revolutionary stream rooted in American Fenianism and partly nurtured from it. William D'Arcy, *The Fenian Movement in the United States* (Washington, D.C., 1947); Michael Funchion, *Chicago's Irish Nationalists* (New York, 1976); Brian Jenkins, *Fenians and Anglo-American Relations During Reconstruction* (Ithaca, N.Y., 1969); and W. S. Niedhardt, *Fenianism in North America* (London, 1975), detail various American phases, while T. N. Brown, *Irish-American Nationalism, 1870–1890* (Philadelphia, 1966), sets them in wider context, and Fergus Mac-Donald, *The Catholic Church and the Secret Societies in the United States* (Washington, D.C., 1946), relates them to church policies. Nonetheless, both the origins of the movement and its long underground aftermath in Clan na Gael and the IRB in the United States await adequate study. Here, memoirs are helpful, together with biographies: John Devoy, *Recollections of an Irish Rebel* (Shannon, 1969), and William O'Brien and Desmond Ryan, eds., *Devoy's Post Bag* (Dublin, 1948–53); John O'Leary, *Recollections of Fenians and Fenianism* (London, 1896); T. V. Powderly, *The Path I Trod* (New York, 1940); J. O'Donovan Rossa, *Rossa's Recollections (New York, 1898)*; Patrick Tynan, *The Irish National Invincibles* (New York, 1894), among the former, and Marcus Bourke, *John O'Leary* (Tralee, 1967); F. G. McManamin, *The American Years of John Boyle O'Reilly* (New York, 1976); Sean O'Luing, *O Donnabhainn Rosa* (Dublin, 1969) (in Irish); Desmond Ryan, *The Fenian Chief* (Dublin, 1967), among the latter. Seamas Pender is editing the "Fenian Papers in the Catholic University of America" continuously in the *Journal of the Cork Historical and Archaeological Society*, which give the often inflated feel from the conspiratorial inside, while M. B. Buckley, *Diary of a Tour in America. . . in 1870 and 1871* (Dublin, 1889), gives the view of an observant and sardonic Cork priest, privileged by nationalist reputation to move in revolutionary circles. Of general studies, the most important are T. W. Moody, ed., *The Fenian Movement* (Cork, 1968); Leon O'Broin *Fenian Fever: An Anglo-American Dilemma* (London, 1971), and *Revolutionary Underground: the Story of the IRB, 1858–1924* (Dublin, 1976); and the essays by E. R. R. Green and K. B. Nowlan in T. D. Williams, ed., *Secret Societies in Ireland* (Dublin, 1973).

THE
POLITICAL IRISH:
POLITICIANS
AND REBELS

THOMAS N. BROWN

The Irish are an old presence in American politics. In the late seventeenth century an Irishman served as colonial governor of New York. A century later other Irishmen were active in the movements leading to the American Revolution and to the adoption of the Constitution of the United States. In the course of a protracted participation in American politics, the Irish have led political lives of almost infinite variety.

Historians have appropriately associated American Irish politicians with the city, but some of the most consequential, such as Senator Tom Walsh of Montana, came from the Mountain West; others like Senator David I. Walsh and Postmaster General James J. Farley were products of small towns in the East. Even among urban Irish politicians, variety abounded. The cities produced orators, such as James Michael Curley of Boston, and men of massive silences, such as Charles F. Murphy of New York; aristocrats like James Duval Phelan of San Francisco and roughnecks like Denis Kearney of the same city. Some Irish were light-fingered in dealing with other people's money. Notable in this regard was Richard Croker, whose impressive capacity to acquire wealth was investigated by New York's Lexow Commission in 1893. But the commission's chief inquisitor was John W. Goff, an Irish nationalist active in the Clann na Gael and a stern protector of the public purse. Most Irish were Democrats, except in Philadelphia, where they were apt to be Republicans.

In this rich diversity it is no easy task to find the constants that can give shape and coherence to the story of American-Irish political development. Some writers have attempted to solve this difficulty by portraying American Irish politics as an expression of the political culture of Ireland. To date, however, no one has done so very satisfactorily, perhaps because we know too little about early nineteenth-century American-Irish politics. Yet the little we do know leaves one with the very strong impression that the politics of Irish-America was very different from the politics of Ireland and suggests that some attention to the differences may provide a useful approach to the study of American-Irish politics.

What gives distinctiveness to the American Irish and what lives most vividly in their consciousness is the sense they have of themselves as a political people. They are aware that they have been seekers of power, adept at politics; in the American language, the term "Irish politician" is a familiar one. As politicians the Irish are an American tradition.

There are in fact two Irish political traditions that animate the contemporary American imagination. To the familiar term "Irish-American politician," we may add another equally familiar, the "Irish rebel." The two images are at odds with one another. The Irish-American politician is an organization man; to him is attributed great skill in the gathering of votes, in the winning of elections. The ability to accommodate differences, to find when in office suitable compromises in moral and other dilemmas, is his particular function.

The rebel is of a different order. He rejects compromise and pursues principles, even unto death. The moral distance between the rebel and the politician is immense: The rebel seeks justice, the politician is content with order. The rebel finds his place in the streets and the hills, the politician in the ancient houses of power. The rebel looks to the future; the politician sits complacently in the present. Irish rebels are heroes; Irish-American politicians are corrupt "hacks." The rebel resides in Ireland; the politician in America. The contemporary currency of these images is manifest in Tennessee Williams' recent play, *The Red Devil Battery Sign*, in which a young man of Irish antecedents becomes the subject of abuse. In Ireland, he is told, you Irish were rebels; in America, you have become politicians.

The stereotype of the Irish-American politician owes much to late Victorian reformers unhappy with the Irish rise in municipal politics. The image they carried about in their heads was in turn shaped by the cartoons of the German-born Thomas Nast in *Harper's Weekly*, in which the Irish active in New York's Tammany Hall in the last decades of the century were portrayed as crude, cigar smoking, corrupt, egregiously Catholic.

The American image of the Irish rebel is old, far older than the image of the politician. In its origins it no doubt goes back to the image of the Wild Irish, a fearsome people whose rebellion in 1641 was understood to be of unparalleled ferocity. With the coming of the American Revolution, however, the Irish rebel was, so to speak, domesticated. The American revolutionaries, as Owen Edwards has shown, were anxious to identify the cause of Ireland with the cause of America. In the century and a half that followed, Americans remained more or less persuaded of that identity. The enduring Irish quarrel with Britain was like the American quarrel of 1776. As William James Mac-Neven wrote in 1807, "What was tyranny against the Americans would necessarily be tyranny against the Irish; and the resistance so glorious in one country, could not be accounted a crime in the other."

American sympathy for the Irish national cause was of course conditioned and limited by regard for American self-interest. Irish nationalists who attempted to involve the United States as a principal in the Anglo-Irish quarrel quickly lost favor. Moreover, Americans during and after the Civil War had to face the contradictions inherent in the effort to put down a rebellion in the South by a nation that traced its origins to the American Revolution. The rebels of 1776 became an embarrassment to American Victorians. But at the same time the Victorians had a very great regard for high-minded idealism, however indifferent they were to its actualization in the rough and tumble of daily life. And the Irish rebels, or many of them, appeared to be the essence of that high-mindedness. So long as the Irish rebels retained their aura of idealism, they were respected. The immense prestige of John Boyle O'Reilly, the former Fenian revolutionary who became one of Boston's poets, rested on the popular view of him as the very embodiment of romantic idealism.

That so many Irish rebels from 1848 onward were writers, poets, and men of letters enhanced the rebel image. Though little read other than by women, writers and poets were highly regarded by Victorians. In the aftermath of the Easter Rising, when the currents of American opinion were running against the participants, Joyce Kilmer shrewdly sought to reverse the current by describing Patrick Pearse and his fellows as poets and idealists, representatives of that high culture of Western civilization for which the war was presumably being fought.

The history of modern Ireland provides ample warrant for the American image of the rebel. The Great Rebellion of 1798, the risings of 1848, 1867, and 1916, the Anglo-Irish War of 1919–21 and the Civil War which followed (1922–23) have made the rebel a conspicuous figure in Irish life. The rebel is active today in Northern Ireland.

The rebel was all but an inevitable figure in a nation whose components were so unbalanced as those of Ireland in the nineteenth century. Ireland entered the century with a small Protestant minority, backed by the power of Britain, exercising a virtual monopoly over social and religious privilege, landed wealth, and political power. Nineteenth-century Irish politics was directed at redressing the imbalance. By 1829 the Irish Catholic middle class had won the right to vote and to hold high political office; by 1870 the Catholic Church had won various privileges and the Protestant Church of Ireland had been disestablished. By the first decade of the twentieth century, after more than twenty years of effort, the Anglo-Irish monopoly of land in an overwhelmingly agricultural society had been broken and the Catholic small farmer was well advanced in the process of becoming possessor of the land he tilled. Three years after the Armistice in 1918, Irish revolutionaries, employing guerrilla tactics, had won from Britain the status for Ireland of a self-governing dominion within the Commonwealth. These accomplishments represented massive political efforts extending over more than three generations. The rebel, born out of the imbalance, was nurtured in these massive efforts.

Ireland in the nineteenth century was in a condition of more or less chronic rebellion. All Irish institutions were in some measure shaped by this condition. The Orange Order, pledged to continued Protestant domination, the secret Whiteboy societies committed to hold the land for the peasantry, the revolutionary and secret nationalist bodies and Dublin Castle, with its network of spies and informers—unique in the British Isles—provided direct institutional expression of the dangerous cleavages in Irish society.

Irish political parties, however much they resembled their analogues in the United States and Britain, were also uniquely shaped by the peculiar condition of Irish society and bore something of the rebel aspect.

The most successful Irish political parties in the nineteenth century were those organized by Daniel O'Connell in the first half of the century and by Charles Stewart Parnell in the decade 1880–90. Like nineteenth-century American political parties, these Irish parties were "grass-roots" organizations. But both O'Connell and Parnell in their leadership were far more authoritarian than their American counterparts. Irish political culture, with its high regard for authority, made such leadership possible and the conditions of Irish life made it necessary. For the causes advanced by these parties ensured that, unlike the major American parties, they could not count upon support from the ruling classes of Irish life. O'Connell's agitation for Catholic Emancipation and particularly for repeal of the Act of Union, which had made Ireland an integral part of the United Kingdom, and Parnell's efforts in behalf of land reform and home rule threatened the people of privilege.

In the absence of support from the affluent, these movements turned not only to the weak Catholic middle class but also to the most volatile elements in Irish society, the small farmers and the landless laborers, the men readiest to join the peasant secret societies. It was not the votes of these classes that mattered, for between 1829 and 1884 the landless laborer was without a vote. What was wanted was control over the threat the volatile offered to the stability of Ireland. Such control represented a political force in its own right.

The Irish parliamentary parties were always on trial. They were in competition with the secret societies, peasant and nationalist, for Irish loyalties. As a consequence, O'Connell was critically dependent upon the parish priest, who alone had an authority comparable to the Whiteboy chieftains. Parnell was far less dependent upon the parish clergy but far more than O'Connell he was hobbled to the overseas Irish in Britain and particularly in America for moral and financial support.

The revolutionary conditions of Irish life demanded skillful politicians. Their reach had to extend from the rebel in the hills and from the Irish overseas to the ministerial benches in the House of Commons. Efforts to maintain control over a volatile following, while retaining credibility in the House, place substantial restraints upon strategy and tactics. Expediency dictated that at times leaders indulge in the rhetoric of rebellion and at other times that they accept a period in jail. All politicians everywhere, of course, are subject to similar if less demanding constraints. But the stakes were higher in Ireland than elsewhere, indeed were of a different order of magnitude. At stake was not only the power of party but also social convulsion. The Easter Rising of 1916 not only destroyed the Irish parliamentary party of John Redmond but was also a prelude to revolution and civil war.

The parliamentarians were politicians, skilled in the arts of conciliation and compromise, but they were something more than politicians. Like the rebels, they were engaged in altering the fundamental social and constitutional arrangements of Ireland. Though they did not share his means, they shared the rebel's goals. They shared his anger, too, and their language of defiance was not always dictated by expediency. They, or some of them, shared in the mythic aura that surrounds the rebel. In Mr. Casey's despairing cry "Parnell, my dead king," uttered at the conclusion of that terrible Christmas dinner scene of Joyce's *Portrait*, we have some measure of the Irish politician as mythic figure.

The unfavorable image of the American-Irish politician is in many respects a particular expression of a more generalized American prejudice against the seekers and holders of public office. In the early days of the Republic men honored with power were supposed to be of severe and disinterested virtue. Inevitably, they proved to be a disappointment. Overweening ambition, greed and venality became associated with the word politician. "I am not a politician," said the mid-nineteenth-century humorist, Artemus Ward, "and my other morals are good." But the very nature of the politician's work was probably more important in promoting his unfavorable reputation than his personal failings. As James Madison foresaw in the "Tenth Federalist Paper," American politics has been concerned with the work of reconciling divergent interests on a rich continent and in an expanding economy. The art practiced has been the art of compromise. The American people have benefited from the work but have not been grateful. Their culture has encouraged in them an incorrigible idealism that sticks at principle and is at odds with compromise. The politician plying his trade appears to be engaged in a conspiracy against conscience.

In the decades following the Civil War this generalized antipathy became focused on the Irish, then assuming dominance in municipal politics, as a particularly reprehensible species of politician. Thomas Nast, the German-born illustrator of *Harper's Weekly*, and others shaped the image of the corrupt, porcine Irish politician that Victorians carried about in their heads. The stereotype was by no means false; it reflected certain unsavory truths and (in a back-handed way) certain vitalities in American-Irish life. But it has lived on too long. Its persistence to the present obscures important developments in the history of American-Irish politics.

American-Irish politics in the nineteenth century appears to have developed in a series of overlapping stages. In the first stage the Irish were engaged in carrying on in the United States the work of O'Connell in Ireland: the fight to open up to Irishmen and Catholics the places of Protestant privilege. We may label this first stage as the politics of causes. As Catholic institutions grew to meet immigrant needs native American opposition increased apace. The religious tolerance characteristic of the first decades of the century declined in the face of increasing Catholic numbers and the revival of evangelical Protestantism. Catholic political action was directed at freeing public institutions from Protestant domination and at protecting from local and state interference the rights of Catholics to build their own institutions. The ties to Ireland and to O'Connell were apparent in the support given by the American Irish to the Catholic and Repeal Associations.

If early American-Irish political activity was influenced by O'Connell's Irish agitations, it should be noted that they moved on a narrower front than he. O'Connell was more than an Irish reformer. His was a humanitarianism of immense scope. O'Connell's voice was joined with American abolitionists, when they were but a small and despised minority, in indignant protest against American slavery. The American Irish did not follow him in this. They could not. The processes of acculturation had brought them to the anti-abolitionist position of the American majority. To have joined their voices to his would have added to their already great burdens.

The second stage of development in American-Irish politics may be characterized as the politics of power and party, what Emerson called the politics of principles and causes. The Irish first learned this kind of politics in the Democratic party. Historians have the habit of referring to the early Irish as natural democrats, inevitable followers of Jefferson. They might more accurately be described as "unnatural democrats." Jefferson's liberalism could hardly have been congenial to the run-of-the-mill Irishman resident in America, however attractive it was to the middle-class revolutionaries who had fled from Ireland in the 1790s as the disasters of the United Irishman movement unfolded. The cast of mind of the Federalists, Jefferson's opponents, was more congenial to the conservative Catholic immigrant. But the Federalists were responsible for the Alien and Sedition laws, which among other things proscribed the activities of refugee revolutionaries such as the United Irishmen. The laws were construed to be anti-Irish, and the Irish became wedded to the party of Jefferson. In this way the Irish peasant was shaped by the American environment into a democrat.

The Irish arrival was timely. The exodus from Ireland, beginning in the 1820s, coincided with American political efforts to expand the base of party participation. What had been in greater or lesser measure a preserve of privilege became by the late 1820s a process in which all (white, adult males) could participate. Property qualifications for voting and holding office were virtually swept away in all but a few states. The Irish peasant, who lost in 1829 the dubious privilege of voting in Ireland, found the polling booths open to him in America. The resulting increase in the size of the American electorate obliged party leaders to develop techniques and strategies that would gather in the votes of the newly arrived and newly enfranchised. As Irish numbers increased in American seaboard cities and in the newer cities of the trans-Appalachian West, their importance to politics and politicians increased. Wherever the electorate was closely divided, as in New Orleans in the 1820s or New York in the 1840s, the Irish vote became critical. In the 1850s when American political parties buckled and splintered under the pressure of the antislavery movement, the immigrant vote everywhere became important to electoral outcomes. The raging anger of the anti-Catholic and anti-immigrant Know-Nothings in the 1850s was testimony to the often decisive influence of the immigrant vote. In this decade in America when issues were paramount and distracted Americans cast off old allegiances to join new parties, the Irish remained solidly entrenched in the Democratic party.

Irish loyalty to the Democratic party endures to the present. The leaders of the Whig party, successor to the Federalists, and of the Republicans, successors to the Whigs, periodically made efforts to win over the Irish by taking up popular Irish or American-Irish issues and by nominating for office candidates of Irish origins. But the Irish, with some notable exceptions, remained loyal Democrats. No doubt this is indicative of the great value that Irish political culture places on the virtue of loyalty. But this virtue was not exercised in a vacuum. The presence of anti-Catholics, Orangemen, and others, in the Whig and later Republican parties confirmed the Irish in their allegiance. The Irish took their stand upon determining where their enemies stood. And with their enemies adopting their own stand by the same process of reasoning, the two tended to fix each other in position.

But factors other than this elaborate minuet were at work. Loyalty was not its own reward. As the Irish rose in the ranks of the Democratic party's municipal organizations, their loyalties were increasingly cemented by more tangible rewards in the form of patronage and office.

The Irish ascent was more a matter of Irish numbers than of Irish issues. Political power was to be had by the accumulation of votes, just as economic power was to be had by the accumulation of dollars. Few Irish immigrants from the south of Ireland possessed the money and the enterpreneurial skills that had made the Irishman John Mullanphy one of the richest traders in the Mississippi Valley. As a consequence, the immigrant poor were barred from the capitalist process of adding the half-pence to the pence. Their numbers and the concentration of those numbers in the cities, however, afforded them opportunities in American politics. The numerous political factions active in these early cities needed votes. Any young Irishman who could command a block of votes and deliver them on election day could make a name for himself. Saloons were the clubs of the poor and saloon-keepers were in an excellent position to command votes. Leaders of street and work gangs were also favored. Not only did votes cling to them, but strong arms and hard fists were often necessary in a politics frequently productive of violence. The ability to command votes could make a some-body out of a nobody. The shrewd trading of votes one held in one's pocket, like the capitalists' shrewd trading of property, could advance one in power. The Irish became skilled in the trading of votes, skilled in the accumulation of bits and pieces of power.

Irish history and tradition and American circumstances favored the process. The Irish had learned English as their native culture degenerated, giving them in the United States great advantages over non-English-speaking immigrants. Although more honored in the breach than in the observance, American ideology esteemed the sanctity of the ballot box and conceived of voting as an act of the individual conscience. There was little in the Irish experience which encouraged this view: The Irish who possessed the franchise voted as they were told by the landlord, by the priest, and by O'Connell. Moreover, Irish respect for authority had the consequence of making the Irish vote cohesive. It facilitated the accumulation of power.

The politics of causes and the politics of power and party did not, of course, lead fully independent lives. One influenced the other. When con-cern about Protestant domination of the public schools led Bishop Hughes (later archbishop) of New York in 1841 to field his own slate of candidates, he so frightened Democratic party leaders that they not only altered the school system but also their own previously hostile attitude toward the presence of the Irish in the councils of the party. And inevitably, the growth of Irish influence within the party and within American politics generally stimulated Know-Nothing activity and so generated a host of issues of importance to Catholics and immigrants. But at some point difficult to determine the process whereby a nobody became a somebody was self-sustaining; it did not need the stimulus of Irish and Catholic issues. Public office, however modest, and political power, however limited, was an attractive force in its own right for the sons of a hitherto powerless and despised people. It is true that down to the present one would be hard-pressed to find an election in which what we call ethnic issues did not somehow emerge. But increasingly in the years following the Civil War, as the second generation of politically active Irish reached maturity, Catholic and Irish issues became the stuff of electioneering but not necessarily of elections. Increasingly, elections in those American cities in which the Irish were organized turned on the realities of jobs, patronage, power.

The Irish were able to pursue the politics of power, confident that they were affirming the promise of American life and of Irish Catholic vitality. Nineteenth-century practitioners of politics, both American and Irish American, assumed with Jefferson that the American government was the world's best hope. Playing the great game of politics was a manifestation of that hope. The opportunity to vote, run for office, win and turn your opponents out was what distinguished the United States from the benighted nations of the Old World. One could serve transcendent purposes by playing the political game. For the Irish this was particularly true. Politics and the wielding of power testified to the resurrection of the once despised Irish.

In the American-Irish alliance with the Jeffersonian party, in their refusal to follow O'Connell on the slavery question, in their increasing attraction to power over issues, we have evidence of the transforming capacities of American society. By the post–Civil War period, the American Irish were engaged in a politics very different from their kinfolk across the Atlantic.

American-Irish politics following the Civil War was urban politics. In city after city, building upon a power base in the dark streets of the city wards, the Irish emerged as leaders in the urban political organizations or machines of the Democratic party. The American Protestant middle classes, whose traditional prerogatives were threatened, reacted adversely. Magazine article after magazine article expressed shock at the "Irish control of our cities." To break this control the middle classes took up urban political reform, organizing for the purpose a multitude of institutions. When Lincoln Steffens set out on his celebrated tour of American municipal corruption, he assumed that everywhere he would find the Irish at the heart of the matter. Steffens's assumptions were based on his experience in New York, home of Tammany Hall, the greatest of the urban political machines, where the Irish first came to power and to national attention.

New York State, as Robert Kelley has pointed out, was the "cockpit of nineteenth century American political life." Of the thirteen men the Democrats nominated for the presidency in the period 1836–1900, seven came from the Empire State. No wonder then that Irish control of New York City was a matter of foreboding to rural and middle-class Americans. In the words of William Jennings Bryan, the Nebraska Democrat, the city was "enemy's country." The enemy was Tammany Hall, for Bryan and others the hated symbol of those urban forces subverting the old rural order of the Republic. Irish association with Tammany Hall more than anything else fixed in American minds the image of the Irish politician. Tammany practices were followed by the Irish in other American cities.

The first Irishman to climb to the top as leader or "Boss" of Tammany was John Kelly. "Honest John," as he was known to his contemporaries, was born in old New York in 1823. It had been his ambition when young to become a priest, but circumstances moved him into business and to the accumulation of a modest fortune. In his career we can observe the transition from the first phase of American-Irish politics, the politics of causes, to the second phase, the politics of power and party. While serving in Congress before the Civil War, the only Catholic in the Thirty-fourth Congress, he won a reputation as a staunch defender of Catholicism. Following the war and the scandals of the Tweed Ring, which almost destroyed Tammany, Kelly took over the leadership and revitalized the battered organization. He recruited distinguished new members from the business community and disciplined operations. He was never able, however, to establish Tammany's control over the Democracy of Manhattan. He was engaged more or less continuously in conflict with rival Democratic factions. A notable antagonist was William R. Grace, the first Irish Catholic mayor of the city; a more notable antagonist was Grover Cleveland, who became president of the United States in 1885, the year of Kelly's death. Cleveland was one of the many presidential aspirants who found political profit in having the Tammany Hall Irish as enemies.

Before dying the pious Honest John chose the high-living Richard Croker as his heir. Croker, an immigrant at an early age from Black Rock, County Cork, had fought his way upward in the hard school of New York's punch-in-the-nose politics. Far more than Kelly, he was successful in bringing rival Democratic factions under control. From Kelly he had learned the importance of unremitting attention to organizational detail, but his successes may more plausibly be traced to the facts of city development and to his skill in adapting Tammany to new circumstances. City growth in size and services provided Tammany with a larger pool of patronage with which to hold the organization together; and improved transportation and communication— the electric railway, the telephone—facilitated control. During his tenure, too, the newer immigrants, the Italians and East European Jews, were absorbed into the Tammany principality.

Under Croker, corruption, particularly police corruption of the most sordid kind, was characteristic. Croker himself accumulated a fortune in dubious ways. "A good cook licks his fingers," he once boasted. Like other Americans of his time, he was fond of conspicuous displays of consumption. When repeated investigations of the sources of his wealth proved embarrassing, he retired to his estate in County Wicklow, Ireland, where he bred racehorses. In 1907, his stable won the English Derby, the Tammany Derby, as it came to be known in racing circles. The burly, taciturn, vulgar Richard Croker, the insouciant Master of Manhattan, was the living image of the corrupt Irish politician.

After a brief interregnum Croker was succeeded in 1903 by Charles F. Murphy, who would preside over the Hall until his death in 1924. Murphy, New York City–born, had followed the traditional path upward; athletics (baseball), saloonkeeper, vote gatherer. It was his task to adapt Tammany once again to changing times. In the years before World War I, American progressive reformers were demanding the reconstruction of American institutions and the elimination of political machines such as Tammany. The working classes were demanding security from the hazards of industrial life. "Silent Charlie," as he was known, reformed Tammany by cutting connections with the police, the single most important source of corruption under Croker. While never forgetting the primary interest of winning elections, he made of Tammany a force for social welfare legislation and for new rights for labor.

Tammany Hall and like organizations elsewhere were called machines. The metaphor suggests the awe Tammany inspired in friends and foe, but the term is not descriptively useful. What Kelly, Croker, and Murphy presided over was a hierarchy, a pyramid of power. The base was composed of the city's Democratic voters, chiefly but not exclusively immigrant. In return for favors, tangible and intangible, this electorate gave their votes to Tammany. The vote-gathering process was managed by thousands of block workers, under the direction of precinct captains, who in turn reported to ward and assembly district leaders, who in their turn reported to the Boss (Kelly, Croker, Murphy) at the top. The votes given and gathered elected officials subservient to Tammany. Businessmen who wanted the city's permission to build this or that paid for the privilege in the form of favors or, as seems clear enough in the case of Croker, in the form of bribes. Their payments made rich men out of some Tammany leaders but also provided the pool of resources out of which came the favors that sustained the loyalties of the voters. Tammany power bound the rich and the poor together in a common enterprise.

The Irish did not invent the machine. Its origins go back to the eighteenth century. Nor were the Irish the sole practitioners of machine politics in the post-Civil War period. In Cincinnati Republicans of impeccable WASP character ran the machine. But most of the large city organizations in the period were Irish dominated. No doubt, as Daniel Patrick Moynihan has suggested, the Irish brought old country ways to the workings and improvement of the machine. Loyalty, for example, was a prime Irish virtue and it was this virtue as much as anything else that held the machine together.

But Tammany politics from Kelly to Murphy was very different from the politics of Ireland in the same period. Tammany politics was the politics of power, the politics of winning elections and of distributing the spoils. The larger issues of public policy were at best of secondary concern. The politics of Ireland were the politics of causes, above all the politics of the nationalist cause, the persistent quest for the Irish nation. Whenever that quest and the turbulence it generated within Irish America threatened to disrupt the voting precincts of New York, Tammany's chief concern was to protect its power. It was as indifferent to Irish nationalism as it was indifferent to other transcendentalisms. There were no ideologues in Tammany. A possible exception was Daniel Cohalan, member of Tammany and the Clan na Gael, son-in-law to Murphy, activist in behalf of Ireland in and after World War I. His zeal led him in 1920 to support the Republican, Hiram Johnson, for the presidency. His father-in-law and other machine politicians, however, did not share his zeal.

Irish nationalist parties, whether the Home Rule or Sinn Fein parties, were more akin to American socialist parties than to the American-Irish machines. Both the nationalist and the socialist had in common a fear that the bread-and-butter reforms of pragmatic politicians would dilute the commitment of the faithful to the cause before the ultimate objective was reached. Tammany, with no long-range objectives in mind, had no such fears. As the careers of Kelly, Croker, and Murphy illustrate, Tammany was highly adaptable to circumstances and was prepared to embrace reforms desired by the electorate.

The career of Alfred ("Al") Emmanuel Smith provides us with perhaps the strongest evidence of Tammany's adaptability to new demands by the electorate. Smith, like Kelly before him, is a major transitional figure. In his career the politics of power become wedded to the politics of causes. And with that consummation the third stage of American-Irish politics begins.

Born in the old Fourth Ward of the Lower East Side of Manhattan, trained in politics by the local saloonkeeper and district leader, Al Smith was one of a number of young and forceful men brought forward in Tammany under the auspices of Murphy. In the course of his career in the New York State Assembly, Smith would develop immense parliamentary skills, a heightened consciousness of the suffering imposed upon the weak by industrial capitalism, and a gift for bringing the earthy language of the Lower East Side to the clarification of complex issues. He tied together the realists of Tammany with idealists in the ranks of reform. The reformers identified the measures to be passed. Smith and Tammany knew how to get them passed. In 1918 he was elected to the first of the four terms he would serve as governor of New York, one of the best the state has ever had. Upon the death of Murphy in 1924, Smith became in effect the head of Tammany and a presidential aspirant. When he ran for the presidency in 1928 as the nominee of the Democratic party, he quickly learned that much of the nation outside New York viewed him as nothing more than an Irish politician. His Catholicism, his gravelly East Side accent, the omnipresent cigar and brown derby, the rumored fondness for alcohol evoked the by now hoary image.

Smith, nevertheless, pointed the way toward the future. In responding to the needs and demands of his East Side constituency, he made himself and the Democratic party into advocates for a new, if moderate, liberalism, rooted in urban industrial America. His appeal ran far beyond the Irish, to the new professional classes and to the immigrant peoples of southern and eastern European stock. The Happy Warrior, as Franklin Roosevelt had called him, laid the basis for much of the New Deal and for much of modern American politics. But when he died in 1944, he was an embittered man. The year 1928 still hurt.

Two years after Smith's death, John F. Kennedy inaugurated his political career by running for the U.S. House of Representatives from the Eleventh Congressional District of Massachusetts. The seat young Kennedy sought had been vacated by the aging James Michael Curley, the Skeffington-like rebel of Boston politics who had just won his fourth term as mayor of that city. The Eleventh District included the North End of Boston, which had once been bossed by the Fitzgerald grandfather of the young man, and East Boston, bossed in the old days by his Kennedy grandfather. The future president began his career surrounded, so to speak, by the past. But he was insistently of a new generation that was determined not to be identified with the old-timers and their old ways. In this and in future campaigns, he kept the past at a distance. Unlike Al Smith, who was a New York provincial, Kennedy was a cosmopolitan figure. In his career he broke through the constraints that the image of the Irish politician had imposed upon ambition. After him the ambitious would not be frustrated as James A. Farley and Edward J. Flynn had been frustrated in New Deal days, when the Irish as mere politicians had been relegated to running the Democratic National Committee.

The fourth and perhaps final stage of American-Irish political development may be said to have come of age with the Kennedys. We now have the complete Irish politician; the politics of causes, which the Irish brought from the land of O'Connell, has been joined to the politics of power in ways acceptable to the American majority. The long Irish residence in the cities prepared them uniquely for a national politics shaped by the new urban America. As the Irish moved outward and upward from city politics to the larger stage of state and nation, Irish political skills—handed down from one generation to the next like carpenter tools—have been employed in advancing the bread-and-butter liberalism of the New Deal. The Irish politician, if one may use the term at all for a largely assimilated people, is now middle class. The old image, so much an expression of class snobbery, has loosened its grip on the American imagination, but it is not, of course, without force, even today. The late Mayor Daley of Chicago, as much a modern bureaucrat as he was a boss, evoked the ancient image and even so benign a figure as Thomas P. ("Tip") O'Neill, the present Speaker of the House of Representatives, has suffered from its enduring vitality. Nevertheless, the tragic career of John F. Kennedy has provided the American people with a more noble image of the American-Irish politician.

It is not without profit to study the history of American-Irish politics against the background of political developments in Ireland. The undertaking reveals that the history and institutional arrangements of Ireland and America produced two very different kinds of politics and of political behavior. The Irish rebel was a product of a poor society in a condition of chronic rebellion; the American-Irish politician was a product of a rich and expansive society of highly diverse character. The historian who studies the contrasting images of the rebel and the politician is directed toward paradox: the Irish in the homeland were outsiders, rebels knocking at the door of power; the Irish in the foreign cities of America were insiders, custodians of power in long-established institutions.

There is irony too in any consideration of the rural American's fear of the American-Irish politician as a subversive. For it is now the considered judgment of many that Irish political machines were engaged in the fundamentally conservative task of maintaining social order in cities undergoing explosive growth. The diffusion of power and fragmentation of authority once characteristic of American cities were brought to an end by the advent of the political machine. The power to get things done was assembled and things got done. Cities grew and prospered. In terms of graft and corruption, the price was high. But continuation of the old ways might have exacted a higher price in terms of political instability and violence. Under Irish leadership, the poor and the newly arrived found places, however lowly in the political process, and a stake in society. In the old city neighborhoods one can glimpse something of a sacral quality. The clubhouse, the neighborhood saloon, the fire and police houses were the material manifestations of a deeper reality. Names, faces, old quarrels, ancient affections were fixed in these places and the whole made up a world. In otherwise brutal cities, Irish political organizations wove a network of friendship and loyalties. Irish political organizations gave reality to the Burkean principle that national political loyalties begin with the "little platoon" of one's neighbors. In this way the American Irish, in contrast to the rebel in Ireland, played a profoundly conservative role.

American prejudice against the American-Irish politician was in considerable measure self-serving. Yankees displaced from old positions of authority and dismayed by the corruption of post–Civil War politics blamed the Irish for their troubles and the ills of political life. Corruption in the

Gilded Age, however, was by no means uniquely Irish and the politics of power was hardly an expression of innate Irish characteristics. Politics in nineteenth-century Ireland, was, after all, by and large the politics of causes. The Irish learned the politics of power in the United States. It is true that the peasant experience had disposed the Irish to accept party politics without the reservations characteristic of Americans for whom party discipline was an affront to conscience. Nevertheless, American party politics, including machine politics and the attendant corruption, antedated the Irish. The Irish arrived early in the process of party development, learned the trade, and were on hand at the conclusion of the Civil War to provide leadership in many of the urban machines. The Irish rise to power coincided with the rise of the cities as new centers of wealth and influence. Those Yankees who deplored the latter fixed on the Irish as special objects of their animus. The old prejudice against politicians was reshaped to become a more intense prejudice against Irish politicians.

The Yankee response to the Irish went beyond indignation to something like awe. Tammany Hall and its counterparts throughout the nation became in the shaping of the American imagination legendary places of evil. This is perhaps understandable when one considers the shocking frankness with which the Irish pursued power in the late Victorian years. American political idealism taught that the exercise of power had to be wrapped in the coverings of transcendental moral purposes. But the Irish seemed to want power for its own sake. They practiced their trade bluntly and without apology.

The pursuit of power had, of course, a significance for the Irish beyond the votes gathered, the offices held. Politics was a way of affirming their strength as a people. Coming from the crabbed fields of home, where the peasant stepped back into the ditch when the gentry rode by, the Irish found in America a place where the politics of deference was dead and where energies could be released. They brought to politics an exuberance not to be found in the grim moral strivings of American reformers or Irish rebels. They ruled for a time over American cities and they built or helped to build the structure of the modern Democratic party. In this work they shaped the future. For a people once trapped by the past, it was no inconsiderable achievement.

FOR FURTHER READING

A comprehensive list for further reading would cover at least a third of the past two decades' publications on the nineteenth-and early twentieth-century politics of two dozen states and a score of major cities. The following are especially important: John M. Allswang, *A House for All Peoples: Ethnic Politics in Chicago* (Lexington, Ky., 1971); Alexander B. Callow, ed., *The City Bosses in America* (New York, 1976);

Alfred Connable and Edward Silberfarb, *Tigers of Tammany* (New York, 1967); Richard Jensen, *The Winning of the Midwest, 1888–1896* (Chicago, 1971); Paul J. Kleppner, *The Cross of Culture, 1850–1900* (New York, 1970); Joel A. Tarr, *A Study in Boss Politics: William Lorimer of Chicago* (Urbana, Ill., 1971); Nancy Joan Weiss, *Charles Francis Murphy, 1858–1924* (Northampton, Mass., 1968); James P. Walsh, ed., *The Irish: America's Political Class* (New York, 1976). That there may have been greater continuity with pre–Famine Irish politics, even with postrevolutionary Ulster Irish politics, than has usually been supposed, is a theme treated in George Potter, *To the Golden Door* (Boston, 1960), pp. 217–41, and is implicit in works such as Joseph I. Shulim, *John Daly Burk: Irish Revolutionist* (Philadelphia, 1964), and in John Coleman's forthcoming study of the second phase of Thomas McKean's career as Jeffersonian governor of Pennsylvania. Connections are also suggested in David N. Doyle, *Ireland, Irishmen and Revolutionary America* (forthcoming), and Earl F. Niehaus, *Irish in New Orleans* (Baton Rouge, La., 1965). The conscious role of American political parties in politicizing the Irish would repay more extended study: See, for example, Alfred D. Young, *The Democratic Republicans of New York, 1763–1797* (Chapel Hill, N.C., 1967), or William Hanchett, *Irish: Charles G. Halpine and the Civil War* (Syracuse, N.Y., 1970) for separate instances.

The place of the Irish background is widely disputed: See Daniel P. Moynihan, *Beyond the Melting Por* (Cambridge, Mass., 1963), pp. 223 ff., and Edward M. Levine, *The Irish and Irish Politicians* (Notre Dame, 1966), *passim*, for estimates, but its influence is probably as pervasive as a general force among a hyperpoliticized people, as it is irrelevant of precise application because of the vastly different character of politics and its opportunities in America, as has been argued here. For recent Irish studies on Irish political culture, see Basil Chubb, *The Government and Politics of Ireland* (London, 1970), pp. 45–57; David E. Schmitt, *The Irony of Irish Democracy* (Lexington, Mass., 1973), pp. 43–80; John M. Whyte's introduction to John Raven et al., *Political Culture in Ireland* (Dublin, 1976), pp. 1–6. Specifically on Daniel O'Connell, see James A. Reynolds, *The Catholic Emancipation Crisis in Ireland, 1823–1829* (New Haven, 1954), pp. 164 ff.; Lawrence J. McCaffrey, *Daniel O'Connell and the Repeal Year* (University of Kentucky Press, 1966), chap. 5; and on Parnell, see Conor Cruise O'Brien, *Parnell and His Party, 1880–1890* (Oxford, 1957), pp. 1–79, 347 ff., and F. S. L. Lyons, *Charles Stewart Parnell* (London, 1977), pp. 608–24.

For a classic portrayal of the machine politician, see William L. Riordon, *Plunkitt of Tammany Hall* (New York, 1905), and for a contemporary account of the machine, M. Ostrogorski, *Democracy and the Party System in the United States* (New York, 1910), pp. 229 ff. But revisions are suggested, especially on the relations of bosses and reformers, in Bruce M. Stave, ed., *Urban Bosses, Machines and Progressive Reformers* (Lexington, Mass., 1972), Warren Stickle, *Bosses and Reformers: Urban Politics in America. 1880–1920* (New York, 1973), and M. H. Ebner and E. M. Tobin, eds., *The Age of Urban Reform* (Port Washington, N.Y., 1977), pp. 68–85, 142–55. Ultimately, as is suggested here, Irish-American politics can scarcely be characterized as such on a liberal-to-conservative spectrum, since their local variants were each distinct. Contrasting studies suggest this as they appear: John D. Buenker, "The Mahatma and Progressive Reform: Martin Lomasney as Lawmaker, 1911–1917," *New England*

Quarterly (1971): 397–419, or Mark Foster, "Frank Hague of Jersey City: The Boss as Reformer," *New Jersey History* 85 (1968): 106–17, as against the antirevisionist treatment of Charles Murphy and Tammany in John M. Allswang, *Bosses, Machines and Urban Voters* (Port Washington, N.Y., 1977), pp. 60–79. That "machine" style politics were not however unknown in Ireland beneath the stratum of "causes" is newly shown in K. T. Hoppen, "National Politics and Local Realities in Mid-Nineteenth Century Ireland," in Art Cosgrove and Donal McCartney, *Studies in Irish History Presented to R. Dudley Edwards* (Dublin, 1979).

MR. DOOLEY
IN CHICAGO:
FINLEY PETER DUNNE
AS HISTORIAN OF THE
IRISH IN AMERICA

CHARLES FANNING

There is something like poetic justice in the fact that the first brilliant American writer born of Irish immigrant parents asserted his genius by asserting his Irishness. This was Finley Peter Dunne, the turn-of-the century journalist whose *alter ego*, Mr. Dooley of "Archey Road," Chicago, forced all America to read with a brogue—and love it. Mr. Dooley has a secure place in the hearts of American historians and newspaper editors as the source of some of the most trenchant short speeches ever delivered on the state of the nation. Ever since his clearheaded critique of the Spanish-American War brought Dunne's fictitious Chicago bartender to the attention of a national audience, analysts of the American scene have been quoting glittering bits of his wisdom. Stretching from 1898 to World War I, Mr. Dooley's tenure as resident American comic sage was remarkable both in its length and in the consistent high quality of the mostly occasional commentary. Anything newsworthy in an offbeat way attracted Dunne's gadfly mind: from Teddy Roosevelt's health fads to Andrew Carnegie's passion for founding libraries; from the invariable silliness of national politics to high-society doings at Newport; from the Boer and Boxer rebellions to the Negro, Indian, and immigration "problems."

For all this, a grateful American nation thanked Finley Peter Dunne by making him the most popular journalist of his time. There is, however, more to his story than the years of center-stage national applause. Before fame overtook him, Mr. Dooley had had a full and productive talking life back in Chicago. Between 1893 and 1898, Dunne had written over 300 Irish dialect sketches, from which he selected roughly one-third for his first two collections, *Mr. Dooley in Peace and in War* (1898) and *Mr. Dooley in the Hearts of His Countrymen* (1899). The other 200 pieces have remained buried in the files of the newspapers where they first appeared. Many of them are concerned with daily life in Bridgeport, Mr. Dooley's South Side

Chicago neighborhood, and Dunne probably considered them to be of minimal interest to his new national audience. It is, however, precisely their parochial setting that makes these forgotten pieces valuable now. Emerging from this accumulation of weekly sketches is the most complete picture we have of an Irish-American working-class community in the 1890s. In addition, even though it is made up of fragments, this picture is broad and deep enough to establish Dunne as a pioneering social historian and an important contributor to the early stages of the realistic movement in American literature.

Peter Dunne had been born on the Near West Side of Chicago, in the middle-class Irish neighborhood where his immigrant father had built a successful carpentry business. The only son to be sent to high school, he graduated last in his class of fifty, then took a job as office boy and police reporter for the Chicago *Telegram.* He was not yet seventeen, and the date in June 1884 marks the real beginning of his education. There was no better vantage point from which to observe American life in the later nineteenth century than the staff of a big city newspaper, and no more exciting place to do it in than Chicago, a sprawling monster of a town that had gained a million inhabitants between its two defining spectacles, the Great Fire of 1871 and the World's Fair of 1893. In eight years Dunne worked on six different daily papers. In 1888, four years into the profession and twenty-one years old, he was named city editor of the Chicago *Times.* Four years later, in November 1892, he arrived as editorial chairman at the *Evening Post,* which soon became Mr. Dooley's first home.

Dunne had been experimenting with Irish dialect in his political reporting; he often enlivened city council news with comical transcriptions of the brogues of Chicago aldermen. Now, at the suggestion of the *Post's* managing editor, he began to write a weekly column featuring Colonel Malachi Mc-Neery, a saloonkeeper in the tenderloin district of the city. McNeery was modeled on a friend of Dunne's, Jim McGarry, whose Dearborn Street saloon was a favorite gathering place of newspapermen and visiting celebrities. The real catalyst for the column, though, was the World's Fair, and the colonel's adventures on the exotic Midway became so popular that his prototype, McGarry, ordered Dunne to stop making fun of him. Dunne acquiesced by shipping McNeery back to Ireland at the end of the Fair.

Two weeks later, the *Evening Post* for Saturday, October 7, 1893, contained the first appearance of Martin Dooley, a saloonkeeper from Archer Avenue in working-class Bridgeport. The shift in location is significant. McGarry's downtown bar was a lively, worldly place, and Dunne had portrayed Colonel McNeery as a sophisticated friend of the great. On the other hand, a bar out in Bridgeport was likely to be a community institution, dispensing entertainment and companionship to a stable clientele of Irish mill-workers and draymen. That Dunne was aware of the special character of a neighborhood saloon is apparent in the very first Dooley piece. Here are the opening paragraphs.

Business was dull in the liquor-shop of Mr. Martin Dooley in Archey road last Wednesday night and Mr. Dooley was sitting back in the rear of the shop holding a newspaper at arm's length before him and reading the sporting news. In came Mr. John McKenna. Mr. McKenna has been exceedingly restless since Colonel Mc-Neery went home to Ireland, and on his way out to Brighton Park for consolation he bethought himself of Martin Dooley. The lights were shining in the little tavern and the window decorations—green festoons, a single-sheet poster of a Parnell meeting in McCormick's Hall and a pyramid of bottles filled with Medford rum and flies—evoked such cheery recollections of earlier years that Mr. McKenna hopped off the car and entered briskly.
"Good evening, Martin," he said.
"Hello, Jawnny," replied Mr. Dooley, as if they had parted only the evening before. "How's thricks? I don't mind, Jawnny, if I do. 'Tis duller here than a ray-publican primary in the fourth ward, th' night. Sure, ye 're like a ray iv sunlight, ye are that. There's been no company in these pa-arts since Dominick Riley's big gossoon was took up be th' polis—no, not the Riley that lived down be th' gas-house; he's moved over in th' fifth wa-ard—may th' divil go with him: 'twas him bruk that there mirror with a brick for an' because I said Carey, th' informer, was a Limerick man. This here's Pat Riley, th' big, strappin' kid iv Dominick Riley, that lived beyant the rollin' mills. He was th' 'ell's own hand f'r sport. What was he tuk up for, says ye? Faith, I'll never tell ye. Th' polis had a gredge again him, like as not. . . . But where 've ye been all these days, man alive? I ain't seen ye, Jawn dear, since ye led th' gr-rand ma-arch in Finucane's Hall, this tin years past."

Immediately, we are in a different world. Mr. Dooley's brogue is thicker than Colonel McNeery's, which signals the social descent from Dearborn Street to Archer Avenue. Also, there is an assumption by the speaker of knowledge common to the Irish-American community, in the reference to "Carey, th' informer," who betrayed the Dublin Phoenix Park murderers in 1883. But most important, we are at once in that community, exposed to the flavor of a particular neighborhood culture, where people are placed by family, geography, and reputation. Here are the seeds of Dunne's accomplishment in the Chicago Dooley pieces—the imaginative evocation of Bridgeport in the 1890s.

Mr. Dooley does belong with Hosea Biglow and Artemus Ward in the tradition of American homespun philosophers, but he is the first city dweller in the group, and the first of these vernacular voices to be rooted solidly in a particular place. Through his painstaking eye for detail, the neighborhood comes alive. All motion is defined in relation to the "red bridge," which joins Bridgeport to the rest of Chicago. "Archey Road" is a vivid main street, extending from Dooley's place, to his rival Schwartzmeister's, "down th' way," to the political capital of Ward Six, Finucane's Hall. Social status is measured by the proximity of one's home to the gas house and the rolling mills. And the waters of Haley's Slough, a swampy Chicago River runoff, provide a meandering backdrop for nearly every scene. These pieces are populated with a large cast of recurrent characters, many of whom were modeled after real people. John McKenna was a genial Republican politician from Chicago's Brighton Park section. His role as chief listener goes back to the Colonel McNeery days, and ceases only after the presidential election of 1896. During the Bryan-McKinley campaign, Dunne had invented Malachi Hennessy, a working-class Bridgeport Democrat, to argue against McKenna, thereby allowing Mr. Dooley to stand comfortably in the middle, exploiting the comic potential of both sides. After the election, Hennessy took over the listening post, presumably because, as a slow-thinking millworker with a large family, he was a more typical Bridgeporter than McKenna, and a better foil for Mr. Dooley's wit. Of the other important characters, Police Sergeant John Shea, political kingmaker William Joyce, Alderman Billy O'Brien, and the local parish priest, Father Kelly, were real-life Chicagoans who lent their names and some of their idiosyncracies to Dunne's cast.

The Chicago Dooley pieces constitute a coherent body of work, essentially different from Mr. Dooley's performance as a national figure after 1900, and worthy of attention on its own. Certainly Dunne was limited by his chosen form, the weekly column of 750 words. These pieces are truly sketches, providing at most telling glimpses into character and motive, particular places and events. Yet there is more of a realized world here than readers of Dunne have suspected until now, and its creation within the restricted Dooley form is a small miracle of American letters. That world can be seen in a thematic arrangement of Dunne's scattered treatments of the various aspects of Chicago Irish life: the experience of immigration, daily life in Bridgeport, assimilation problems, poverty crises, and the preoccupation with politics, both American and Irish.

When he first appeared in the *Evening Post* in 1893, Martin Dooley was already over sixty. In the course of the Chicago pieces, Dunne provided him with a plausible, detailed past, stretching back to a childhood Christmas in Ireland, when "th' lads that 'd been away 'd come thrampin' in fr'm Gawd knows where, big lads far fr'm home in Cork and' Limerick an' th' City iv Dublin—come thrampin' home stick in hand to ate their Christmas dinner with th' ol' folks." In other pieces, Mr. Dooley recalls the Great Hunger, when "thim that was scrapin' th' sod f'r a bare livin' fr'm day to day perished like th' cattle in th' field." He remembers his own emigration ("We watched th' little ol' island fadin' away behind us, with th' sun sthrikin' th' white house-tops iv Queenstown an' lightin' up th' chimbleys iv Martin Hogan's liquor store. . ."), and his youthful illusions about America as the place where "all ye had to do was to hold ye'er hat an' th' goold guineas 'd dhrop into it." Arriving in Chicago, he finds that "there was mud to be shoveled an' dhrays to be druv an' beats to be walked. I chose th' dhray; f'r I was niver cut out f'r a copper, an' I'd had me fill iv excavatin'." Other memories include employment restrictions due to Irish county rivalries between Limerick "butthermilks" and Dublin "jackeens," fights and strikes along the old Bridgeport canal during its heyday as a busy artery, and the effects on Chicago's Irish of the Civil War, an 1867 cholera epidemic, and the notorious fire of '71, that "desthroyed old buildin's so that new wans cud be put up."

Dunne also observed the Bridgeport passing scene in the 1890s with vividness and concision. The Chicago Dooley pieces give us in unprecedented detail the colors of the common life in an Irish-American urban neighborhood at the turn of the century. Mr Dooley reports on the following church-centered activities; the annual parish fair, complete with a shooting gallery, gambling, "Roddy's Hibernyun band playin' on th' cor-rner," and booths selling everything from prayer books to oyster stew; a church production of "The Doomed Markey," starring Denny Hogan; the parochial school graduation of "Hennessy's youngest" that features music by the "St. Ignatius Quintet" and a recitation of "th' speech that Robert Immitt made whin they was goin' to hang him"; and an experimental "temperance saloon" that closes on its opening night, after the patrons have "dhrunk thimsilves into chollery morbus with coold limonade." Mr. Dooley attends secular events as well: a genealogy lecture in the school hall that erupts into a brawl over whose ancestors were kings and whose only dukes (Dooley declares that, "f'r mesilf I'd as lave have a plastherer f'r a grandfather—me own was marrid to th' niece iv th' parish priest"); a benefit raffle for an ailing bartender, at which O'Malley rolls fifty-four, then swallows the dice to ensure victory; a family reunion, during which the emotional climate shifts from nostalgia to name-calling, until "they wasn't two Dooleys in th' hall 'd speak whin th' meetin' broke up"; football games between the "young Parnells" and the "young Sarsfields," and a skating party on a flooded, iced-over vacant lot.

The crooked course of love on Archer Avenue is the theme of several pieces which corroborate Mr. Dooley's opinion that "f'r an impetchoos an' darin' people th' Irish is th' mos' cowardly whin it comes to mathrimony that iver I heard tell iv." One example is "Dacey th' plumber, who'd niver 'v marrid if he hadn't got into th' wrong buildin' whin he wint to take out a license f'r his dog, an' got a marridge license instid." For balance, there is the story of young Felix Pendergast, who courts a girl with singular lack of success by playing "Th' Vale iv Avoca" on the cornet under her window.

In some of the finest pieces, Mr. Dooley illuminates the lives of Bridgeport workingmen, "th' quite people nayether you nor me hears tell iv fr'm wan end iv th' year to another." One such figure is little Tim Clancy, who "wurruks out in th' mills, tin hours a day, runnin' a wheelbarrow loaded with cinders," and supports eight children on "wan-twenty-five a day—whin he wurruks."

Another is old Shaughnessy, who "wurruked f'r Larkin, th' conthractor, f'r near twenty years without skip or break, an' seen th' fam'ly grow up be candle-light." His story reads like an O'Neill tragedy in miniature; driven toward the priesthood, the oldest boy dies bitterly of consumption; the second son, a charming ne'er-do-well, also burns himself out and dies young; further deaths and desertions leave Shaughnessy with a last daughter, who "thought on'y iv th' ol' man, an' he leaned on her as if she was a crutch." When she marries, her father is left alone by the stove, "with his elbow on his knees an' th' empty pipe between his teeth."

Finally, Mr. Dooley acknowledges the civil service route out of the slough of unskilled labor with a series of vignettes about firemen and policemen, heroes and goats, respectively, to Irish Chicagoans in the nineties. Chicago was a wide-open city, full of opportunities for graft, and newspaper campaigns for reform of the police department were yearly events in Dunne's time. Mr. Dooley is often critical too, but mildly so, perhaps because so many of his neighbors were "polismin." He delivers an occasional light jab: to "th' polisman that dhrinks this beat," to backroom card games involving on-duty policemen, to the substitute for the Monroe Doctrine advocated by Officer Jerry Hoolihan: "Niver stop to fight whin ye'er goin' to supper." In other pieces, he mistakes a policeman for a robber, until rough treatment demonstrates that he's been accosted by the former, and he finds it hard to distinguish between police provocation and control of a riot. On the other hand, as Dooley admits, the situation is "altogether diffrent with th' fireman." In an increasingly crowded city, "consthructed f'r poor people out iv nice varnished pine an' cotton waste," the fireman was an undisputed culture hero for Bridgeport and greater Chicago. So it is that Fire Chief Denis Swenie is received as a returning hero when he comes to Bridgeport to fight a fire: " 'Twas 'Good avnin' to ye, Misther Swenie,' an' 'Misther Swenie, will ye have a glass iv beer befure ye go in, f'r th' fire's hot?' " Moreover, Dunne responded to two real Chicago fire-fighting tragedies by creating lasting fictional images of the Irish fireman: Pipeman Shay, a dark, brooding figure whose aloofness, fierce pride, and heroic defense of his calling inspire something akin to awe in the usually ir-reverent Dooley; and Fireman Mike Clancy, of whom "all th' r-road was proud. . . . All th' people looked up to him, an' th' kids followed him down th' sthreet; an' 'twas th' gr-reatest priv'lige f'r anny wan f'r to play dominos with him." In Clancy's story, Dunne has given us a convincing image of the common man as tragic hero. The fireman vows to his wife that he'll retire, "only I want to see wan more good fire, a rale good ol' hot wan."

"An' he did, Jawn [Mr. Dooley continues]. Th' day th' Carpenter Brothers' box factory burnt. 'Twas wan iv thim big, fine-lookin' buildings that pious men built out iv celluloid an' plasther iv Paris. An' Clancy was wan iv th' men undher whin th' wall fell. I seen thim bringin' him home; an' th' little woman met him at th' dure, rumplin' her apron in her hands."

Despite its distinctive coloration, Bridgeport in the 1890s was not a stable community. Many forces for change were operating, most of them related to the complex process known to that time as "melting" into American life. Like other immigrant groups, the Irish found themselves caught between two worlds, and forced to make uncomfortable compromises in order to become "assimilated." By the nineties, the children of the Famine immigrants (those who, as Mr. Dooley remarks, had been "born away from home") were making it into the American middle class in large numbers—but not without cost to their sense of identity as individuals and as an ethnic group. The stairway of upward mobility was strewn with cases of swallowed pride and stifled traditions, and the Chicago Dooley pieces embody the peculiar mixture of fulfillment and frustration that went along with being Irish in America. In the first place, the city itself would not hold still. In keeping with the familiar rhythm of neighborhood invasion by poorer groups while the older residents move up and out, the ethnic make-up of Bridgeport was changing rapidly in the nineties. Mr. Dooley contrasts the "fightin' tinth precint" in the old days, when it was the stronghold of "ancient Hellenic" heroes from Mayo and Tipperary, and the same precinct in 1897, by which time "th' Hannigans an' Leonidases an' Caseys" have moved out, "havin' made their pile," and "Polish Jews an' Swedes an' Germans an' Hollanders" have "swarmed in, settlin' down on th' sacred sites." A particularly disturbing sign of "change an' decay" is the appointment of "a Polacker" as tender of the strategic "red bridge," which takes control of the gate to Bridgeport out of Irish hands.

The American dream of success also drove damaging wedges into the immigrant community, as Mr. Dooley notes in stories about hard-hearted Irish landlords, one of whom "had acres an' acres on Halsted Sthreet, an' tinants be th' scoor that prayed at nights f'r him that he might live long an' taste sorrow." Irish landlords evict Irish tenants in several pieces, which illustrates how land and money hunger are breaking up Bridgeport. (Mr. Dooley explains that a career in real estate "includes near ivrything fr'm vagrancy to manslaughter.") Another force for change is creeping respectability, and the Dooley pieces are full of references to the disappearance of the old rough-and-tumble in favor of the more insidious scramble for status. For example, in Mr. Dooley's youth, only people who were under arrest got their names in the paper; now, "I see hard wurrukin' men thrampin' down to the newspaper offices with little items about a christenin' or a wake an' havin' it read to thim in th' mornin' at breakfuss befure they start to th' mills." Another case in point is the running debate between Mr. and Mrs. Hogan on the subject of naming their children: "Ye'll be namin' no more children iv mine out iv dime novels," says Hogan. "An' ye'll name no more iv mine out iv th' payroll iv th' bridge department," says she. "D'ye think I'm goin to sind th' child out into th' wurruld with a name that'll keep him from anny employment but goin' on th' polis foorce?" At the end of this piece, Mr. Dooley is on hand to watch the tenth Hogan child christened—Augustus.

Signs of dissolving cultural unity naturally appeared early among Bridgeport's young people, and Dunne created a group of characters who reveal the problems of a generation gap compounded by immigration. Most visible here is Molly Donahue, a lively, fad-conscious Bridgeport girl who squares off against her Irish father in a half-dozen Dooley pieces. She first scandalizes the neighborhood by riding a bicycle down Archer Avenue in bloomers, after which she is sent off to church, where she receives "a pinance th' like iv which ain't been knowed in Bridgeport since Cassidy said Char-les Stewart Parnell was a bigger man thin th' pope." In succeeding appearances, Molly campaigns for the vote, for Elizabeth Cady Stanton's revised "Woman's Bible, and for the liberation of "the new woman." Her piano lessons cause a cultural disagreement in the family about the relative merits of "Choochooski" and "The Rambler from Clare." The latter is condemned as a "low chune" by Mrs. Donahue, who tells her husband, "if ye want to hear that kind iv chune, ye can go down to Finucane's Hall an' call in Crowley, th' blind piper."

As for Bridgeport's young men, Mr. Dooley charts two divergent roads toward assimilation, one high and one low, but both causing pain and bewilderment in the older generation. College begins to be possible in the nineties, and Bridgeport boys come trooping home from Notre Dame with bicycles, long hair, and delusions of superiority. (In one piece, an educated son gets his father so scared that "he wore his shoes afther supper an' had to r-roll th' growler f'r a pint in a handbag.") The tragic potential of this generational conflict comes across in Mr. Dooley's capsule biographies of young Bridgeport criminals. Jack Carey was "a thief at tin year, an' th' polis'd run f'r him if he'd showed his head. At twelve they sint him to th' bridewell f'r breakin' into a freight car. He come out, up to anny game." Branded a chronic criminal, Carey is hounded by the police to an early death. The child of exemplary parents, Petey Scanlan "growed up fr'm bein' a curly-haired angel f'r to be th' toughest villyun in th' r-road." His career ends after he has robbed a store, terrorized Bridgeport, and fled to his parents' home. Having berated Lieutenant Cassidy for making a scandal before her neighbors, Mrs. Scanlan leads Petey to the patrol wagon on her arm, and is left "settin' in a big chair with her apron in her hands an' th' picture iv th' lad th' day he made his first c'munion in her lap." Mr. Dooley can only shake his head at these sad examples of dissolving community:

"What was it at all, at all? Sometimes I think they'se poison in th' life iv a big city. Th' flowers won't grow here no more thin they wud in a tannery, an' th' bur-rds have no song; an' th' childher iv dacint men an' women come up hard in th' mouth an' with their hands raised again their kind."

Poverty was probably the greatest force against community in Bridgeport in the nineties. The national depression of 1893–98 was aggravated in Chicago by an exploding immigrant population, labor unrest, and bitter-cold winters. The suffering of Bridgeport's poor is a frequent Dooley topic, and he faces it, not with the detachment of a social scientist, but with the mingled anger, frustration, and compassion of a member of the afflicted culture. The result is a chunk of living social history available nowhere else.

An important theme is the difference between heartless, humiliating organized relief programs and personal charity, dispensed with consideration for the pride of the recipient. Out-of-work laborer Callaghan tells the officious St. Vincent de Pauls to "take ye'er charity, an' shove it down ye'er throats," even though the cost of refusal is his family's health. And Mrs. Hagan, the wife of a blacklisted railroad worker, drives the Ladies' Aid Society from her door, even though "some iv thim was f'r foorcin' their way in an' takin' an invinthry." On the other hand, Dooley, himself, provides examples of the tactful practice of personal charity. He buys Christmas presents for a mother and children who have just been deserted, John McKenna finds him taking care of a baby in the saloon's back room, and when the little Grady girl comes into the shop in a snowstorm to fetch beer for her alcoholic father, Dooley puts five dollars in his pocket, closes up early, and sets off "to lick Grady."

Several pieces underscore the contrast, at its most blatant in American cities in the nineties, between the lives of the rich and the poor. Mrs. Mulligan takes her sick baby to the lake for a change of air, but is refused passage through the Illinois Central Railroad's toll gate, which prompts Hennessy to suggest "a new caddychism. It'll go like this: 'Who made ye?' 'Th' Illinye Cinthral made me. . . .' They's naw use teachin' th' childher what ain't thrue. What's th' good iv tellin' thim that th' Lord made th' wurruld whin they'll grow up an' find it in th' possession iv th' Illinye Cinthral?" In noticing different styles at the funerals of wealthy "Gran'pah Grogan" and a poor "Connock man up back iv th' dumps," Mr. Dooley is led to a meditation on the possible effects of price fixing by the Beef Trust on the Connock man's children: "Spring's come on. Th' grass is growin' good; an', if th' Connock man's children back iv th' dumps can't get meat, they can eat hay." During the famous Pullman strike of 1894, Dooley criticized George Pullman's callousness with a harsh analogy between Chicago during the strike and Ireland in the Famine years: "Musha, but 'tis a sound to dhrive ye'er heart cold whin a woman sobs an' th' young wans cries, an' both because there's no bread in th' house." Meanwhile, Pullman sits up in his mansion, ordering "a bottle iv champagne an' a piece iv crambree pie. . . . He cares no more f'r thim little matthers iv life an' death thin I do f'r O'Connor's tab."

Some of Dunne's strongest poverty pieces were written during the winter of 1896–97, the fourth of hard times in a row, and the worst. Mother Clancy, "a Galway woman fr'm bechune mountain an' sea," holds out proudly against the shame of applying for relief until it is too late, and the man sent to "investigate" her case meets the priest and the undertaker at her door. Banks fail through dishonest deals, sending people whose savings are gone to the icebox for a suicidal "light lunch of paris green." A starving Pole named Sobieski is shot to death by a watchman for picking up bits of coal along the railroad tracks, after which, in Mr. Dooley's bitter words, he passes "to where—him bein' a Pole, an' dyin' in such a horrible sin— they'se no need iv coal iv anny kind." And Clancy, the Infidel, a notorious Bridgeport atheist, is saved from starvation only through an ironic personal sacrifice by Father Kelly. Most of these poverty pieces have not been republished, for Dunne seems to have bridled at their biting social criticism. While preparing the 1899 Dooley collection, he wrote his publisher that "I have piled up my old Dooleys—enough for ten books—none of which could be read by a taxpayer." Still, in spite of Dunne's own misgivings, this group of pieces is a moving testament of concern for the urban poor, and our only firsthand account of a crisis potentially as destructive to the Chicago Irish community as the Famine had been to the peasants of Ireland.

Politics was, of course, the most visible and controversial career opportunity for the Irish in American cities in the late nineteenth century. As an experienced political reporter who had been close to the action in Chicago since the 1880s, Dunne was well qualified to describe the Irish contribution to his city's government, and the Dooley political pieces do not disappoint. They constitute a valuable inside narrative of the Irish-American pursuit of power, and a vivid microcosm of the urban political machine. In addition, because bosses made poor or reluctant historians, Mr. Dooley gives us much new information about the electoral process and the workings of ward politics. Several pieces provide insight into Chicago's yearly tribal rite, the election of aldermen. Dooley recalls with relish his own service as precinct captain in his corner of Ward Six: "I mind th' time whin we r-rolled up twenty-siven hunderd dimocratic votes in this wan precinct an' th' on'y wans that voted was th' judges iv election an' th' captains"; or again, "I mind whin McInerney was a-runnin' f'r county clark. Th' lads at th' ya-ards set up all night tuckin' tickets into th' box f'r him. They voted all iv Calvary Symmitry an' was makin' inroads on th' potther's-field." During one other election, ten votes for the Republican candidate appear mysteriously; to avoid disgrace, Dorsey feeds them to his favorite goat, Monica. Further reminiscences of rioting between rival torchlight parades, brick-throwing incidents, and bone-bruising nomination procedures support Mr. Dooley's judgment that "politics ain't bean-bag. 'Tis a man's game, an' women, childer, cripples an' prohybitionists 'd do well to keep out iv it."

Mr. Dooley also gives us glimpses of the inside operations of the mayor's office and the city council. To dissuade Hogan's son from becoming a priest, Dooley lists the advantages of being an alderman: "Ye have nawthin' to worry ye. Whin ye'er hungry ye go to a bankit. Whin ye'er broke all ye have to do is to give something away that don't belong to ye. . . . Did ye iver hear iv an aldherman bein' arristed? By gar, I believe th' polisman that 'd arrist an aldherman woudn't get off short iv tin years." To illustrate cooperation on legislation between the mayor and the council, Dooley relates an exchange between Mayor Carter Harrison and Bridgeport's Billy O'Brien on the issue of installing a garbage dump on the South Side. The quality of appointments made by the spoils system is questioned in the story of Hannigan, the water inspector who avoided his job to the extent that "he used beer as th' chaser." And the mechanics of dispensing graft become clear in the career of Alderman Dochney, who "was expelled fr'm th' St. Vincent de Pauls, an' ilicted a director iv a bank th' same day."

This group of pieces also contains many political biographies, in which sympathy for the hardships of deprived childhood is tempered by Mr. Dooley's feeling that nothing so qualifies a man for political life as a talent for a rough-house bullying. One young tough with "th' smell iv Castle Garden on him" rises through his reputation as a brawler to become boss of the ward, then commits the unpardonnable sin of betraying his community; he moves up to Michigan Avenue and leads the citizen's committee formed to prosecute his old supporters. In other vignettes, political aspiration ruins the lives of decent men. Convinced by self-serving friends that he can win a seat in the state legislature, little Flanagan throws away his savings, job, and house, then loses the election. A similar fate confronts Slattery, "a dacint, quite little lad," who parlays a successful saloon into an aldermanic seat, then sacrifices his reputation to the lure of easy money. Defeated for reelection and deserted by his customers, "all he had left was his champagne thirst." The "education" of an alderman is the theme of another piece, expressive of Dunne's skepticism about the possibility of political reform in Chicago: "Jawnny Powers . . . didn't meet so manny men that'd steal a ham an' thin shoot a polisman over it. But he met a lot that'd steal th' whole West Side iv Chicago an' thin fix a gr-rand jury to get away with it."

A full survey of Dunne's Chicago accomplishment should include Mr. Dooley's examinations of the American contribution to the Irish Freedom movement. First of all, there is healthy perspective here on the past history of Irish-American nationalism. Mr. Dooley remembers that most bizarre of nationalist events, the 1866 Fenian invasion of Canada, in which his Uncle Mike participated: " 'Uncle Mike,' says I to him, 'what's war like, annyhow?' 'Well,' says he, 'in some rayspicts it is like missin' th' last car,' he says; 'an' in other rayspicts 'tis like gettin' gay in front iv a polis station,' he says." He also recalls the printing and dispensing of Irish Republic Bonds in the old days, and the talk of meetings of the Clan na Gael, the secret revolutionary organization in the 1880s, about sending dynamiters to England to help "the cause." (Dunne often presents Mr. Dooley as a lapsed Clansman, a one-time believer in violent revolution who now espouses a milder view, and he takes satiric advantage of the Clan's alphabetical codes, secret handshakes, and elaborate hierarchy of officers and "camps.")

Nationalist events in his own time also evoked responses from Dunne. The passage of the Second Home Rule Bill in Commons in 1893, Gladstone's retirement in 1894, and the British cabinet crisis of 1895 are all noted by Mr. Dooley, who refuses to be stampeded into believing that Irish freedom is close at hand: "Ye can't grow flowers in a granite block. . . . much less whin th' first shoot 'd be thrampled under foot without pity. 'Tis aisy f'r us over here, with our bellies full, to talk iv th' cowardice iv th' Irish; but what would ye have wan man iv thim do again a rig'mint? . . . No, faith, Jawn, there's no soil in Ireland f'r th' greatness iv th' race." About the contributions of the Chicago Irish to the cause, Mr. Dooley has mixed emotions: sympathy for the rank-and-file nationalists, and suspicion for the motives of their leaders. "Did ye iver," he asks in 1895, "see a man that wanted to free Ireland th' day afther to-morrah that didn't run f'r aldherman soon or late?" He carefully scrutinizes the cluster of nationalist commemorations in his community, including the annual August 15 picnic of Chicago's United Irish Societies and the St. Patrick's Day parade. Invariably, he finds these events to be riddled with hypocrisy and self-delusion, and his reports often include parodies of the excesses and simplifications of nationalist oratory. Dunne made quite a few enemies with these pieces, but, to those who listened, Mr. Dooley offered clear, rational commentary on matters that more often triggered the wildest fanaticism.

Mr. Dooley's Bridgeport chronicle ended on January 22, 1898, with a bitter farewell piece, in which he searches for concrete, positive effects from his talking career in Chicago, and finds none: "What's all th' histhry an' pothry an' philosophy i've give ye an' th' Archey road f'r all these years come to? Nawthin. Th' la-ads I abused ar-re makin' money so fast it threatens to smother thim. Th' wans I stud up f'r is some in jail an' some out iv wurruk." This decision to stop the series is a measure of Dunne's identification with the people of Bridgeport. In the Dooley pieces written during 1897, there is a downhill slide toward the conviction that suffering and poverty cannot be appreciably alleviated. The climax comes at Christmas time, 1897, when Mr. Dooley refuses to be cheered; instead he asks, "What can annywan do? If ye'd cut up al th' money in th' sixth war-rd in akel parts ye cudden't buy a toy dhrum apiece f'r th' fam'lies iv Bridgeport. If isn't this year or last. 'Tis n't wan day or another. 'Tis th' same ivry year an' ivry day. It's been so iver since I come here an' 'twill be so afther I'm put away an' me frinds have stopped at th' r-road house on th' way back to count up what I owed thim." Although some of Dunne's best writing is here, the act of imagining the troubles of Chicago's Irish poor had come to be too painful for him. So, he retreated out of the mounting frustration and pessimism that had become the cost of his observations, and ceased probing the steadily darkening vein.

One month later, in February 1898, the declaration of war against Spain provided a convenient vehicle for the return to conversation of the man who confessed in his January farewell piece that " 'tis har-rd f'r me to lave off talkin'." A safe, generally interesting topic, the war could be handled lightly and with little risk of emotional involvement for Dunne. And so, with the sinking of the battleship *Maine* in Havana harbor, Mr. Dooley returned to the Chicago newspaper scene. In reality, though, it was only his ghost—a disembodied voice, no different, except for the brogue, from its predecessors in the genre of cracker-barrel dialect humor.

The rest of the Dooley story is well known. The American people soon loved him, for that lilting, skeptical voice remained blessedly lucid and rational despite Dunne's embrace of syndication, with its restrictions of topicality and tactfulness. Certainly, America was a better place for the fifteen years of pointed laughter and perspective provided by Mr. Dooley in the second phase of his career. We should, however, appreciate what was lost. Dunne needs to be given his due as an early contributor to the realistic movement in American literature. Throughout the middle 1890s, Mr. Dooley gave Chicagoans a weekly example of the potential for serious fiction of common speech and everyday life. Within his limits, Dunne is as much a trailblazer into the American city as setting for literature as Stephen Crane or Theodore Dreiser. Indeed, he even adds a dimension; unlike Crane's Maggie and Dreiser's Carrie Meeber, Mr. Dooley is relatively comfortable in Bridgeport. He proves that the city can be a home. Had Dunne pursued a career in fiction, "Hennessy's youngest" might well have been the Studs Lonigan of his generation; and we can imagine that his story would have been told, not with James T. Farrell's bitter naturalism, but with subtlety and compassion.

In addition, for students of American urban and immigrant history, these Chicago Dooley pieces take us as close as we are likely to get to the circumstances, customs, and attitudes of an Irish city neighborhood in the late nineteenth century. Understandably, Mr. Dooley measures up very well to his own standard of what history ought to be;

"I know histhry isn't thrue, Hinnissy, because it ain't like what i see ivry day in Halsted Sthreet. If any wan comes along with a histhry iv Greece or Rome that'll show me th' people fightin', gettin' dhrunk, makin' love, gettin' married, owin' th' grocery man an' bein' without hard-coal, I'll believe they was a Greece or Rome, but not befure. Historyans is like doctors. They are always lookin' f'r symptoms. Those iv them that writes about their own times examines th' tongue an' feels th' pulse an' makes a wrong dygnosis. Th' other kind iv histhry is a post-mortem examination. It tells ye what a counthry died iv. But I'd like to know what it lived iv."

FOR FURTHER READING

The material upon which this selection is based is presented in Charles Fanning, ed., *Mr. Dooley and the Chicago Irish: An Anthology* (New York, 1976). See also Elmer Ellis, *Mr. Dooley's America: A Life of Finley Peter Dunne* (New York, 1941), and Michael Funchion, *Chicago's Irish Nationalists, 1881–1890* (New York, 1976). We chose Finley P. Dunne for extended treatment as one of the neglected and yet most revealing of Irish Americans writing about the experience of their community. There are of course many others. Yet remarkably, for so literate and literary a people, the great Irish migration did not produce any novels to equal the work of Ole Rolvaag and Vilhelm Moberg for the Scandinavians, Pietro di Donato for the Italians, Abraham Cahan for the Jews, or Willa Cather for the Nebraska Bohemians, to name only some. On the other hand, the literature of Irish America itself is very considerable. Particularly noteworthy, from the point of reconstructing the sense of Irish Americas now gone are Eugene O'Neill's drama, *Long Day's Journey into Night* (New Haven, Conn., 1955), and the plays and novels of Philip Barry, James T. Farrell, Thomas Fleming, Edward McSorley, Joseph F. Dinneen, Mary Deasy, John Dunphy, Edwin O'Connor, Harry Sylvester, William Alfred, Ramona Stewart, and Finley P. Dunne. The earlier, less realistic, yet often illuminating authors of nineteenth-century Catholic Irish America are treated in Paul Messbarger, *Fiction with a Parochial Purpose* (Boston, 1971). In a class of its own, as the autobiography of an Irish-speaking immigrant laborer, is Michael MacGowan, *The Hard Road to the Klondyke*, trans. Valentine Iremonger (London, 1962). See also the bibliography of Ó hAodha, in this work. It is noteworthy, however, that many Irish-born writers who enjoyed greatest vogue in nineteenth-century America (e.g., Fitz-James O'Brien, John Boyle O'Reilly) wrote little of literary value on their own backgrounds and community.

Since writing this in 1976, Charles Fanning has extended the treatment fully in his *Finley Peter Dunne and Mr. Dooley: The Chicago Years* (Lexington, Ky., 1978).

THE IRISH IN THE NEW AMERICA: 'WAY OUT WEST

JAMES P. WALSH

When the Irish came to California, they arrived not as Famine-driven refugees, disgorged from fever-ridden ships into a stable mature American community in which all places were already taken. California at the start of its Irish time was a rare and desolate land, sparsely settled and loosely controlled by Mexican officials. Few who had the choice wished to abandon life in Mexico City for life on the northern frontier. Those who did found themselves so located, in a warm, soil-rich land, that an easygoing pastoral life-style based on abundant herds seemed preferable to a dynamic Yankee-style acquisitiveness.

Into this environment came Irishmen and their families, not as the out-riders of a mass ethnic migration, but simply in the integrated company of assorted other Americans. These precursors of American acquisition stirred anxiety in the heart of the province's Mexican governor, Pio Pico, who noted, "What this astonishing people will next undertake, I cannot say; but in whatever enterprise they embark they will be sure to be successful." These fears quickly materialized. The Mexican-American War with "these people" followed, and shortly afterward the cession of California and the Southwest to the United States in 1848. The simultaneous discovery of gold created, virtually overnight, an instant state, for California never was organized as a territory. It was dominated by San Francisco, its equally instant metropolis, which served as a base camp and supply center for the interior mining regions. More distant areas of the state advanced by grain production, followed by diversification from hay, wheat, and cotton, to citrus fruit, asparagus, and avocadoes, amongst other specialities.

The first generation of California Irish challenged, at least for the moment, the accepted notion that the American Irish were an urban people. By 1870, one-third of them south of Monterey were successful agriculturists. To the north in Santa Clara, the Irish were also conspicuous, if not numerous, as farmers, as were those Irish who settled the Lucas Valley north of San Francisco's Golden Gate. With other Bay Area Irish, they too came early and prospered. But the attractions and opportunities of the city ultimately proved irresistible to the larger body of Irish and their children. San Francisco became and remained the focus of Irish identity in the West.

For most of those who came to California, the West was at least their second place of settlement after leaving Ireland. Most were processed through cities elsewhere, and thus between Ireland and San Francisco had gained valuable urban experience. Not infrequently their urban understanding exceeded that of transplanted rural Americans with whom they competed for the good things of life in California.

Analysis of the first surviving census figures reveals the patterns and permits cautious inference. In 1852 there were 36,151 residents listed for San Francisco. More were of foreign birth than native and those born in Ireland totaled 4,223 or 12 percent of the total and 22 percent of the foreign-born majority. As the decades advanced to the turn of the century the Irish presence kept pace with the swelling of the city itself. When, in 1900, the total San Francisco population approached 350,000, the Irish and their children constituted 27 percent. It then ranked as the tenth most populous city in America and was home for the sixth largest American concentration of Irish Americans.

A selection of 589 persons of Irish birth in 1852 shows that in this group their initial place of settlement had been Sydney, Australia. Other Irish migrants had come from New York and New Orleans in substantial numbers. Smaller groups were made up of those who came from Boston, Philadelphia, London, and Dublin. These initial Irish immigrants were clearly different from the Americans they met in the new city. It was the habitat of a diverse population which was nonetheless predominantly single, youthful, and male. The Irish were older, already had urban experience, and arrived in family units. The statewide California ratio of workers to dependents in 1852 was 100 to 17. Among the Irish from Sydney, there were 63 dependents to every 100 workers.

Traditional Irish-American occupational patterns were present in San Francisco, but significantly modified. Children of laborers advanced into skilled occupations, and from the start the Irish shared representation among San Francisco's high-status occupations, including ten doctors and twenty merchants among themselves in 1852. By 1870 the Irish work force of Boston was approximately double that of San Francisco, whereas that of Philadelphia was three times that of the new city. In spite of this, San Francisco bettered each city in its numbers of Irishmen in highly paid and prestigious professions and callings. The western city supported twenty-seven Irish-born bankers and brokers to Philadelphia's eighteen and Boston's four.

A statistical examination of the traditional low-status, low-paying Irish-American jobs prompts the same general conclusion. Boston, with twice the work force, had three times San Francisco's number of Irish laborers and domestics. Philadelphia's situation was more favorable to the Irish than Boston's, and was more similar to San Francisco's. In each case the Irish were overrepresented in menial employment, but less so in these cities than in Boston, and least of all for Irish males in San Francisco.

Throughout the 1870s and 1880s wages in San Francisco remained steady and uniformly higher than in New York and Philadelphia at the same time as the net cost of living declined on the west coast. The average work day for San Francisco laborers was nine to eleven hours but the Irish-controlled building trades maintained an eight-hour day. When an early mill owners' association locked out Irish laborers, their union constructed its own mill with union funds and then gate-crashed the offending employers' association! Thereafter, the building trades council under Patrick H. McCarthy simply combined with capitalists to monopolize the industry and pass the costs on to the customer. McCarthy became a pillar of civic respectability, serving as a civil service commissioner and as mayor of the city.

Certainly to judge by a later time, having been Irish in San Francisco seems to have deprived no one of the opportunity for gainful employment. Old-timers who began their working days in San Francisco between the turn of the century and World War I remembered no job discrimination themselves and did not believe that their fathers suffered any either. Such adversity simply was not a part of their family experience. In fact, being Irish and Catholic was on occasion a distinct asset. While a Christian Brother from 1909–20, Edward T. Hannon obtained city employment annually for his father through the chancellor of the archdiocese! The insidious notice "No Irish Need Apply" apparently came no closer to San Francisco than Mendocino County, on a shingle mill owned by transplanted New England Yankees, evoking traditional Irish graffiti in reply.

The economic stimulus of gold from the Mother Lode and silver from the Comstock strikes which followed, called San Francisco into secure existence. As America's first instant city, it achieved overnight a status which took Philadelphia 120 years and Boston over 200 years to attain. The actual effect of such rapid growth was nothing short of astonishing. Before completion of the transcontinental railway in 1869, access to the city was tortuously slow, via the Panama ship and overland route, the long Cape Horn ship route, or the overland trails from Missouri. In such isolation labor enjoyed an enhanced position. Strikebreakers were simply unavailable, particularly during boom periods in the rising business cycle. Moreover, San Francisco's physical setting, though truly beautiful, was an impractical one and therefore required extra labor and services to build and sustain the city initially, and to restore it after its frequent fires and later its earthquake. Far from an economic supply of goods from America's eastern and midwestern industries, it also had to provide its own basic consumer goods. Labor was thus powerful throughout the century, and initially laborers could also depart for the mines whenever they considered it best.

Tied to all this is the paramount fact of the Californian experience, material abundance. Gold first peopled the state and those who came mined $2 billion worth. Possibly an equal amount of Nevada silver passed through San Francisco too. Yet the total value of Californian gold has proved less than that of a single year's agricultural output during the preinflationary 1960s. In 1972 the annual production of income in California ranked the state itself seventh among *nations* of the world after the United States itself, the Soviet Union, Japan, West Germany, Britain, and France. The per capita income of the American West was highest in the world in 1975. Technological innovation, agricultural reorganization, and massive irrigation schemes have made possible this lucrative industrial and farming economy. The trajectory of its gradual development was already well established in the nineteenth century, favoring those Irish who were present at the beginnings.

Possibly, then, the overriding consideration in placing them within this setting ought to be psychological rather than political or historical. Where there is more to go around, maybe adjustment is easier for everyone.

Success and advancement touched every stratum of the local Irish, but did not caricature them as creatures of material fortune, as one-dimensional go-getters and main-chancers. Men as wealthy as John W. Mackay took pains to retain a healthy detachment from their possessions: and the Dubliner who shared the Comstock Lode was reputedly the world's richest man, earning $25 a minute. "Circumstances in the mining business change quickly" he warned a prospective wife, adding "I can always dig a living with my bare hands." Giving the promising quality of local conditions, many Irishmen outran the pack. Apart from the spectacular silver kings, many others established early family fortunes. The Donahue brothers set the city's pace in manufacturing and utilities. From a pool of Irish-American bankers emerged the Tobin family and its Hibernia Bank. In trade, real estate, and finance, James Phelan created an inheritance which enabled his son to devote his considerable energies to the creation of a regional culture, as well as to politics.

Quantification, when applied to admittedly limited materials, sustains the favorable picture of the California Irish. The percentage of the Irish among local elites regularly exceeded their proportion of the total populations, and they contributed 153 members to the state's first club, the Society of California Pioneers. Early county histories confirm this. Unlike eastern cities, San Francisco lacked a *Social Register*, so that money alone determined social status. In the 1870s this put Mackay on top along with the other Irish silver kings, James Fair, James Flood, and William O'Brien. Their Comstock profits were generously augmented by stock market manipulation. Gradually society, or high society, became more formalized on the west coast. Mackay and his family had relocated in Europe by then, but the wealthy Irish remaining helped establish the new social style of the state's elite. James Duval Phelan, after 1900, played host in a discriminating manner. He patronized those who advanced art and learning, science and humanity, patriotism and civic virtue. He opened his country villa, Montalvo, to the rich and the ordinary. His uniformed staff served beef, red wine, and champagne to John McCormack, Al Smith, and Franklin and Eleanor Roosevelt, as well as an appropriate menu to the entire California regiment returned from World War I.

The critical feature in the social formation of San Francisco and the West was the lack of an established elite capable, by virtue of prior arrival and control of resources, of ascribing inferior place to subsequent immigrants. The Irish arrived before any establishment was created and competed on a more equal basis in multiethnic San Francisco than in the East. The timing of the discovery of gold (1848) and then silver (1859) in the West was especially opportune for the Irish. On a frontier easy of rapid occupation advancement, it acted both as the catalyst of several key fortunes and as the lubricant of a dynamic economy which thereby rapidly created a prosperous and proportionately larger Irish middle class. In this it contrasted sharply with the East, where the general rise to middle class status was gradual, so that by 1900 only a fifth of the Irish were middle class and modestly lower middle class, a proportion fairly equal to national norms. In the East they were socially constrained and economically overshadowed by the great wealth of the established elites. In California the affluent Irish were a considerably larger proportion of their community, and overshadowed by nobody.

These differences had decisive effects upon two other aspects of the California Irish experience when contrasted with the eastern: their place in politics, and the position of the Catholic Church. In San Francisco the first Irish Americans availed themselves from the beginning of the general openness of society to engage fully in community life and its making. This was aided in that in most cases the politically active were American-born children of Irish parents, or those for whom the city was at least a second stop, so that they were familiar with American politics elsewhere. Malachi Fallon, for example, a minor officeholder and tavern keeper in New York City, took early control of San Francisco's police department after tiring of the gold diggings which first drew him west. Typically, the areas of the first political emergence of the Irish in the West had been the traditional enclaves of Irish power in the then still natively dominated eastern cities: the police and fire departments, which with their neighborhood connections and access to higher powers, made excellent beginning points. Fallon appointed an all-Irish officership and his force was at least half Irish. Again following eastern patterns, he also surfaced in the local militia. County law enforcement also fell into Irish hands. John Coffee Hays rode into town with his devoted subordinate Billy Mulligan in 1850, and was elected county sheriff on his Mexican War record. The American-born Hays had drifted west with the major stages of U.S. expansion and came to rest and prosperity in California, later donating the land on which the University of California began. Irish-born Mulligan, a tragic figure who satisfied the "wild Irish" stereotype, functioned as his persuader-intimidator, seeing to it that men voted, at least once, for his hero. He craved physical action, stimulation, and excitement, finally dying when picked off by a policeman's rifle during a homicidal rage induced by his own delirium tremens.

The transplanted Irish also used the volunteer fire companies for advancement. The Empire Engine Company No. 1 station—styled by Irish migrants from the Empire State— served as unofficial Democratic party headquarters of San Francisco. The company's cofounder, David Broderick, became California's political impresario, contesting and presiding over the destinies of the Democrats in the state with important national consequence until his assassination in 1859.

Although active in the New York charter convention of 1846, the talented Broderick was restrained by the pre-Irish Tammany establishment. Embittered by this and depressed by the limitations of his defeatist fellow Irishmen, Broderick departed for California. "I was tired of the struggles and jealousies of men of my class, who could not understand why one of their fellows should seek to elevate his condition above the common level." The man's ambition rapidly carried him to a seat in the U.S. Senate, in that chamber where his father had finished the interior stonework. In San Francisco those who coalesced with Broderick were Irish, Catholic, and working class. During those years when nativism was at its peak nationally, Broderick dominated California state politics. He personally shunned graft, "clean" or otherwise, advanced the legal rights of free California blacks, and publicly humiliated the Democratic state leader of the proslavery faction.

His career and its support structure are attributable to the fact that on their arrival the Irish found the city and state both politically unorganized and without a dominant core group. In the very first session of the state legislature, Broderick and his adherents designed the charter of San Francisco, which was modeled on the one he had earlier helped create for New York City. It provided for representation by wards and for annual elections. It was hardly coincidental that this municipal structure favored their own community power sources at the time Broderick and his Irish controlled the local Democratic organization.

Likewise through his control of the state legislature, Broderick determined his own election as U.S. senator in 1857. As such, he opposed the expansion of slavery and spoke for liberalism and reform. Gesturing toward the worthy effects of his father's free labor, Broderick denounced slavery and advocated a rival vision, a truly free society based upon widespread property ownership. His conscious, calculated political advance was exemplary. Unable to advance at a pace commensurate with their abilities, some of the politically precocious, eastern-trained Irish sought the California trail as a shortcut to self-fulfillment. From no other Irish concentration in America could such political potential have been actualized as early as the 1850s.

The synchronous American annexation of California, discovery of gold, and establishment of San Francisco contemporary with the first major Catholic Irish dispersal in the United States made for political and economic success. But timing had relatively little to do with the religious aspect of that congenial adjustment. No Irishman came to California seeking wider boundaries for the exercise of his religious freedom. Nonetheless, it was precisely that which he encountered there.

Catholicism was the area's senior denomination, dating in San Francisco from the Spanish founding of 1776 rather than from American acquisition. Having suffered a period of neglect in the final years of Mexican rule, the Catholic Church revived under new leadership after 1850. Unlike in the East, the church did not have to extract from the Irish major energies for defense in a hostile milieu. And for the laity the contentment and ease which this allowed outweighed the advantages of their economic situation, so that they were better able to concentrate upon success in their secular callings among well-disposed neighbors.

Early and heavy Catholic immigration into California, together with the family and hence reproductive nature of that migration, intensified the state's historical Catholic character. It "reversed the traditional American social etiquette of precedence and subtly affected ethnic and religious relations." The founders of the Catholic *Monitor* stressed that the appearance of their newspaper in no way suggested dissatisfaction. It applauded other local papers as "The Most Liberal in the World." Eleven years later, it advised newly arrived Irish that they need not fear the prejudices of the eastern states: "Irishmen have made themselves a position here fully equal to that of any other nationality in our cosmopolitan population," and newcomers would find no bars of prejudice against their advancement. Retiring in 1884, the first archbishop, Joseph Sadoc Alemaney confessed his preference for the state over the "sunny fields" of his native Spain, stressing the full tolerance the church enjoyed and the civilization based upon diversity and the acceptance of difference which had emerged there. Such minor irritants as the hostility of Frank Pixley's *Argonaut* or George Thistelton's *Illustrated* were best ignored, although one parish priest did not agree, and secured the latter's imprisonment for libel.

Thus too the adversary character which the question of public versus

Catholic schools assumed almost everywhere else in urban America did not arise in San Francisco. Initially, public monies were granted to private schools. Additionally, ward schools were conducted by Catholic nuns who taught religious doctrine from eight to nine, after which non-Catholic children came to class. The laws permitting this were repealed in 1855. With the public school board equally divided between Know-Nothings and Democrats, its members agreed to compromise. A selection of Catholic teachers, excluding nuns, who judiciously withdrew, was retained in the ward schools, and Bible reading was terminated.

Organizational life can hardly be interpreted as part of a process of segmentation of the community into subcultures, as in the East. Perhaps the Catholic institutional life of Boston was created to satisfy otherwise unmet needs of a discriminated against, segregated, and isolated proletariat. But in San Francisco all groups seemed to compete in institutional creation. Protestants, Catholics, Jews, Chinese, French, Irish, Germans, laborers and craftsmen all launched their own benevolent associations, which facilitated the wider welfare in a community in process rather than divided an existent one.

Symptomatic of this broader civic coherence was the fate of nativism in California. The Know-Nothing party of the 1850s and the American Protective Association of the 1890s poisoned the religious and civic atmosphere of much of urban America and complicated its politics. Both focused against the Irish. In each case, San Francisco escaped with only slight discomfort. There the Know-Nothings did not advocate anti-Catholicism, and for good reasons. In a diverse new city the only hope of taking power for any transmuted Know-Nothing party was to frame an appeal not exclusive of Catholics. And without its nativist reason for being, the party had little substance and no future. Indeed, locally it selected Lucien Herman, a Catholic, as its nominee for mayor of the city—a drastic deviation from the national nativist norm. San Francisco Know-Nothingism has to be considered a political rather than a politico-religious movement. Subdued anti-Catholicism existed only as a characteristic of the Protestant merchant class, which while well off was politically impotent in the face of well-organized Democrats.

As the nineteenth century progressed, so too did Catholic security and well-being. Despite the national recrudescence of nativism in the 1890s, the new western variety of antipopery was muted. And well it might be, for in a population approaching 350,000, less than 85,000 were of native parentage. Moreover, as the federal census of religion revealed, in 1906 only 41 percent of the population were sufficiently interested in religion to claim church membership, and church attendance was not recorded. Of the total who did claim it, 116,000 were Roman Catholics whereas only 22,000 were Protestants. Against this, the local wars of the godly were but shadows, reminiscent of the 1850s in California rather than emotions in the East. There was no violence, apparently no actual discriminations, no political movement

—only bigoted talk. The Catholic response, planned and executed by the flamboyant Father Peter C. Yorke from Galway, was a bitter antinativist overkill. He had the local APA infiltrated and published their jejeune proceedings, thereby laughing their bogus patriotism out of San Francisco. It was the same tactic nationally adopted by the APA's chief Catholic opponent, chain editor and Wisconsin progressive Humphrey Desmond, except that he conducted his campaign with some wry sympathy for the small-beer nativists, recognizing that the plural development of America had already doomed their narrow dream of it. In the municipal election of 1896, Yorke actively campaigned for James Duval Phelan against the unsuccessful APA supported candidate. The movement then disappeared locally. In San Francisco, the nativists could represent neither a numerical majority nor an established elite. But it took an encounter or two before the implications of this reality struck home. It was a pity, then, that Yorke knew no restraint. The idol of the Irish crowd and their political adviser, he only embarrassed the hierarchy in its concern for a public show of prudent reticence. By the time the Ku Klux Klan experienced its post–World War I national revival, considerably discomforting the urban Catholic populations of the South and Midwest, San Francisco had formalized its response. Archbishop Edward J. Hannon paraded 10,000 men of the Holy Name Society along Market Street, and thereafter no Klansmen marched in the city.

Protected from nativism by a cosmopolitan ethos and by their economic and social position, the Irish might be expected to have followed the example of Broderick as champions of universal tolerance. This was not to be. They never became the underclass of California, although they did have their less advantaged workers and newcomers for whom Father Yorke and Belfast-born Fenian Frank Roney became spokesmen. Nonetheless the misfortune of being society's underdogs fell to others in California: to the Asian immigrants who arrived roughly the same time as the Irish. While all white California was involved in anti-Chinese and anti-Japanese xenophobia, the Irish have been identified, with good reason, as central to the anti-Oriental thrust. In the earlier years, under Denis Kearney, the movement had been the spontaneous self-protection of job-anxious ordinary Irishmen. Even then, however, few tried to turn the movement from its racist implications: the state's pioneer Jesuit, James Bouchard, was virulently anti-Chinese, although himself part Cherokee. During the years in which Chinese exclusion and Japanese restriction were secured on the national statute books, the California Irish of all classes played a prominent role. Even those such as *Monitor* editor and scholar Bryan Clinch, who despised vulgar prejudice, rationalized that the Chinese would be better off enjoying their own culture at home. Anti-Oriental racism became the cement for labor union organization. Father Yorke used against Asians the very arguments he had refuted when used by nativists against the Irish. James D. Phelan headed the Asiatic Exclusion

League and advanced California's racism as national policy. Throughout the country, even Irish-American editors and leaders hostile to racism as such, as were Patrick Ford and J. J. Roche, espoused the California Irish view of the Chinese immigration "problem."

The presence of so different a minority as the Chinese immediately "conferred instant status on all European immigrants," and for the Irish, the shared bond of race with other white groups provided "a key advantage in law and public opinion." The western Irish were quick to forget the experience of poverty, exclusion, and discrimination as it affected their ancestors or their own early lives when confronted with what they felt was the necessity of curbing the growth of California's own despised minority, the Asians.

By 1900, the gradual uplifting of the Irish throughout the rest of the country was reducing the exceptionality of the California community. As the community matured everywhere, it tended to fragment along the lines of the diverse careers and opportunities of American life, a pattern already presaged in California. Nevertheless, it broadly retained its religious and political coherence in the East well beyond World War I. As Joseph Buenker and others have shown, the old Irish political machines broadened their ethnic base, and provided key groups of legislators to battle for welfare and political reforms in the state legislatures of the Northeast and Midwest during the Progressive era. In California, Irish Americans had never built a consistent political machine, and their variant life-styles and interests precluded a set approach to politics during the Progressive period there. Throughout urban America, there had always been Irish-American opponents of the sleazier machine Irish politicians: reformers such as Dan Bradley and John Goff in New York. In San Francisco, Irish-American politicians acted as individuals for the most part before and after the turn of the century. Several examples will suffice. James Duval Phelan created the board of public health and promoted the secret ballot, independent governmental commissions, financial accountability on all expenditures, and public ownership of power sources and other monopolistic services. He used medical science and advanced technology to combat urban problems. But he surrendered his dream of an expensive and majestic planned city rising from the ruins of the 1906 earthquake to the penny pinchers, taxpayer interests, and corporation politicians who opposed it.

Among these latter were Garrett McEnerney, likewise impossible of easy classification. A millionaire corporation counsel, chief lawyer to the San Francisco archdiocese, co-organizer of the Bank of America, and debt collector extraordinary against the Mexican government, McEnerney opposed those progressive reforms which threatened the free hand of his clients. Nonetheless, he devoted forty-one years to the interests of the University of California as one of its most remarkable regents, committed to the expansion and enrichment of the university's campuses and programs that they might become available to all California's children who might benefit from them. Himself the product of a limited Catholic education, he eventually left half his fortune to the great secular institution. Appropriately, he left the other $3 million to the archdiocese he had also served.

His great antagonist and friend was John Francis Neylan, chief counsel to publisher William Randolph Hearst during the latter's long populistic phase. Neylan pressed progressive reforms and politicians throughout his career, even through the 1920s, when the movement was nationally in abeyance. Strangely, Father Peter Yorke, the popular priest, was to devote his wit and sarcasm to the anti-progressive camp, on issues such as initiative, referendum, and women's suffrage, correctly identifying the elitist element among their protagonists and their antidemocratic possibilities. But when the progressive state administration enacted comprehensive social welfare and industrial protection legislation, the Irish who had previously followed Yorke's voting advice, abandoned him. Also a regent of the University of California, he realized its operations extended far beyond the sphere of his own talents. Having criticized its secularism before his appointment, he thereafter had the good sense to leave it to itself.

The California Irish experience was not that of the rest of Irish America, in the years 1848–1920. It was always closer to what is now the experience of that community generally: affluence, opportunity, individualism, and diversity. In short, California offered both a special variety of Americanization, and a foretaste of the general future. Commentators early noted that the Irish shared the English language and common habits of thought with the other citizens of the state, and hence argued it was simply best to regard them as Californians and Americans. That their heritage was Irish was sufficient. Those fearful of the rapid erosion of explicit Irish identity and organization elsewhere in America should be heartened by these facts. Confidently American, the Californian Irish have long been conscious of their origin in Ireland's culture and tradition, and gratefully, rather than ambivalently, capable of the backward glance.

FOR FURTHER READING

Since this was written, R. A. Burchell has detailed many of these themes in his *The San Francisco Irish, 1848–1880* (Manchester, 1979). Among other studies are Hugh Quigley, *The Irish Race in California* (San Francisco, 1878); Patrick J. Blessing, "West Among Strangers: Irish Migration to California, 1850-1880," Ph.D., UCLA, 1977; see also Gunther Barth, *Instant Cities: San Francisco and Denver* (New York, 1975); Walton Bean, *Boss Ruef's San Francisco* (Berkeley, 1968), and his *California: An Interpretive History* (New York, 1973); and Kevin Starr, *Americans and the California Dream, 1850–1915* (New York, 1973). Biographical studies of Irish Californians include David A. Williams, *David C. Broderick* (San Marino, Calif., 1969); Gabrielle Sullivan, *Martin Murphy, Jr.: California Pioneer, 1844–84* (Stockton,

Calif., 1974); Thomas Prendergast, *Forgotten Pioneers: Irish Leaders in Early California* (San Francisco, 1942); Ira B. Cross, ed., *Frank Roney: Irish Rebel and California Labor Leader: An Autobiography* (Berkeley, Calif., 1931, and New York, 1976); Bernard C. Cronin, *Father Yorke and the Labor Movement* (Washington, D.C., 1943), and James Walsh, *Ethnic Militancy: An Irish Catholic Prototype* (San Francisco, 1972); James P. Gaffey, *Citizen of No Mean City: Archbishop Patrick Riordan of San Francisco* (Wilmington, N.C., 1976) [archbishop from 1885–1914]; On the early period, Roger Lotchkin, *San Francisco, 1846–1856* (New York, 1974); Robert A. Burchell, "British Immigrants in Southern California, 1850–1870," *Southern California Quarterly* 53 (1971): 285–97; and for the material in this work *California Census of 1852*, Daughters of the American Revolution copy (California, 1934), microfilm; and Sherman L. Richards and George M. Blackburn, "Demographic Analysis of the Sydney Ducks," *Pacific Historical Review* 42 (1973): 20–31. Robert A. Burchell, James P. Walsh, Roger Lotchkin, and others are doing current further work on the Irish in California. Some provisional findings are contained in James P. Walsh, ed., *The San Francisco Irish, 1850–1976* (San Francisco, 1978). Alexander Saxton, *The Indispensable Enemy: Labor and the Anti-Chinese Movement in California* (Berkeley, Calif., 1971), is best on that subject.

THE IRISH
AND THE
CHRISTIAN
CHURCHES
IN AMERICA

DAVID NOEL DOYLE

In the 1830s, the sober Alexis de Tocqueville reported that "there is no country in which the Christian religion retains a greater influence over the souls of men than in America." As late as 1957, his words still seemed to hold good, with 96 percent of all Americans reporting themselves as of specific religious identification. From the most shallow social observance to the deeper reaches of dedication and self-sacrifice, the Christian convictions of millions of Americans have helped to shape its culture, social life, and politics. Recent studies have shown that even today a majority of those engaged in voluntary work, in a notedly activist society, are prompted by religious concerns. Religion has thus both leavened America's strenuous secularity, and colored and directed its "virtuous materialism" and its "enterprising individualism."

The Irish role in all this is largely unknown and unstudied, outside the stereotyped story of the Irish "domination" of the Catholic Church in America. In Ireland, the tendency is to take it for granted, as part of a highly distinctive pattern in the establishment of "Ireland's Spiritual Empire" and, relatedly, to speak as though the whole story was essentially a Catholic one. In America, where the historical memory is short, Irish Americans have been seen as tenacious, clannish, and somewhat shallow Catholic Church builders and loyalists. These truisms mask a more complex reality, in which Irish Protestant immigration has played a distinguished part, in which Irish Catholicism in America received new emphases from the established Christianity of the host society, and in which, above all, Irish Christian immigration to America has to be understood as part of a pattern general in European-American relations from the seventeenth century to the present one.

The great majority of immigrants to America from the 1620s to the 1920s came from the peasantry or countryfolk of a score of European societies, and from among the craftsmen and small traders who related closely to them, and shared their culture. This was true whether they came from Somerset or Lincolnshire in the 1630s, Ulster in the 1740s, Munster in the 1840s, Rhineland Westphalia or Baden in the 1850s, Jutland, Silesia, Connacht or Lombardy in the 1870s, Transylvania, Lithuania, Slovenia, or Sicily after 1900. The vast bulk of the immigrants were actively Christian, drawn from strata of society largely unaffected by the secularizing currents affecting the cities in their regions. The central *social* activity of these immigrants when they reached America was the construction of a myriad of congregations, which gave social shape to the religious beliefs and behaviors which were now called upon to act as the "inner supports" of a new life from which the "outward props" had been removed. The 5 or 6 million Irish immigrants of the period 1720–1920 were thus little different from the mass of their fellow–European migrants. The whole process is a warning to us, as to the historians of modern Europe, against assuming the primacy of the political in the European histories of these peoples, whatever the case among the history-making elites of the capital cities. In America, livelihood apart, the Irish—just as the Poles, the Scandinavians, or the Germans—organized first religiously, and only secondly sought the political kingdom. Not that they regarded them for a moment as exclusive! In all this, then, the Irish in America were especially voluble and visible, rather than atypical.

Around 1900, close to half of America's 11 million Catholics were of Irish birth or Irish parentage, many more of Irish descent. Almost three quarters of the American hierarchy from 1790 to 1960 was of Irish birth or descent, their preponderance maintained despite a relative Irish decline in proportion to overall numbers of Catholics. Today, between a fifth and a quarter of America's Catholics are of Irish descent. Probably 4 million Irish Catholic immigrants at least came to the United States from 1820 to 1950, and over 100,000 before that date. Many of these came as secondary migrants from Britain, Canada, and Australia. Obviously, not all newcomers remained actively Catholic—recent studies suggest between 40 percent and 60 percent, and many of their descendants are not Catholic. Yet the flow was sufficient to ensure that for generations American Catholic growth was chiefly Irish based.

From 1720 to 1820, up to half a million Irish Protestants came to the north American colonies and young United States, the majority of them from Ulster; and many of the hundred thousand Catholic Irish immigrants of those years joined their congregations. Presbyterians constituted the main flow, but were not alone, and in fact only a minority of the immigrants' descendants were to remain Presbyterian, the majority becoming Baptist or Methodist. Although never studied, a continuing Protestant migration brought at least another half-million immigrants from Ireland over the next hundred years, and probably many more. The earlier period, however, is more noteworthy, since the movement was collective, and therefore more influential. It also gave part of the leadership of the colonial churches, particularly in formative frontier zones. Francis Makemie of the Laggan Presbytery in County Donegal became the founder of America's first Presbytery (1706) and first synod (1717) and early called out John Henry from Dublin to assist and follow him. The Tennents from Ulster became leaders of an evangelical revival, and founders of the first Presbyterian college in America, at Neshaminy (1726). Francis Alison of Donegal launched a series of academies in Delaware and Philadelphia, became the most respected "Old Side" Presbyterian leader of the 1750s, helped reunite the church in 1758, and won the respect even of Benjamin Franklin for his learning, for he was a prime conduit of the Scottish Enlightenment into the colonies. He and other Ulster-educated clergy helped ensure the prorevolutionary stance of much of their denomination in 1775. Philip Embury and Barbara Heck, of Limerick Palatine stock, founded American Methodism in 1766, not as its organizers so much as its pioneers. James Logan, secretary to William Penn, was one of several Irish Quakers playing a critical role for their faith in Pennsylvania, one, like Alison among Presbyterians, who helped ensure that rising enlightenment and prosperity were reconciled with past tradition. Thomas Barton helped organize Episcopalianism from 1756 throughout central Pennsylvania among Ulster migrants, as did other Irish pastors among their fellow countrymen in Maryland and the Carolinas at an earlier time. Thomas Campbell, shortly after his arrival in 1807 from Ulster, disturbed by the sectarian disunity of the frontier, founded the Disciples of Christ with his son Alexander: it is now a major denomination. After this early period, Irish newcomers continued active and constructive. Robert McBurney, a shrewd and sensitive schoolteacher from County Monaghan, a Young Ireland sympathizer despite the sectarianism of his father in Castleblayney, built the YMCA in America into a vigorous force to combat the impersonality of American cities and lay a foundation of basic decency and Christianity among hundreds of thousands of young men in the tawdry era of the Gilded Age. His early experiences caused him to save it from the impress of a too obvious Protestantism, such as Dwight Moody desired: he had a good understanding of just how much godliness the average young man could take. At the same time, Jerry MacAuley, a converted river thief, an immigrant, worked as an outstandingly successful "apostle to the lost" among the semicriminal elements of New York's underside, while a third Ulster-born arrival, of a very different sort, E. L. Godkin, brought his moral earnestness to the attempted reform of public life through the columns of the *Nation*.

Involvement by Irishmen in so many areas of America's religious life would need more than a volume for its full summation: I have stressed Protestant presence at this point, because it is less known. Moreover, like the Catholic, it was an element active in its American-born generations, as the names James O'Kelly (founder of Republican Methodism), James Mc-Gready (early southwest frontier evangelist), or John W. Nevin (the great theologian of "evangelical catholicism"), and others attest. Obviously, one must pick certain themes for short treatment. Here I shall contrast the two mainstream Irish immigrant denominations, at comparable points in their development: the Irish Presbyterians, from 1740 to 1800, and the Irish Catholics, from 1820 to 1900. Some unexpected analogies, as well as differences, emerge as a result, many of them simply because Irishmen had had their faiths tested in a similar environment, and therefore shaped their responses to a common Gospel more closely than they admitted. In America, this was thrown into relief: the rich pietism, conscious learning, political caution, and musical heritage of the German Lutherans and German Catholics, now sharply set off the thin culture, hyperorthodoxy, stripped-down piety, and usually anxious moralism of both Irish Catholics and Irish Presbyterian—characteristics which had the advantage of already reducing to serviceable essentials those convictions which Tocqueville and others believed flourished best when basic in America. In Germany or Ireland, the difference of creed, so strongly pressed, obscured all similarities. Again, the poverty and disestablishment of Irish Presbyterianism and Catholicism drove their clergies close to their people, caused them to share, or sympathize with, their laities' politics of discontent, and prepared them for the early poverty, initial disfavor, and permanent nonestablishment of the years in America. Both these mainstreams faced many of the same problems in America.

Firstly there was the problem of building up the church organization itself, locally and generally. This apparently practical matter involved a deep question of policy. Did one proceed by a backward-looking conservatism, harvesting the immigrants by touching their nostalgia, expressing cautious pastoral solicitude by seeing in strongly Irish congregations and styles the guarantee of churchly strength? Or did one confidently try new methods, assume that the immigrants and their children would not be content with old ways in a new land, and instead respond to an evangelical imperative, in which new methods were tried, immigrants included in interethnic "American" congregations, and the church's vitality vindicated in its wider reach and purpose? To say there was a simple struggle over whether the Presbyterian Church or later the Catholic Church should be either Irish or American, as so many scholars have, would be gravely to oversimplify this. Both parties, the solicitous and the confident, were strong, active, and realistic; often the same man was himself divided; both parties agreed that their goal was a viable church in America, not the pickled preservation of an expatriate sect. One's sympathy constantly shifts between them. Secondly, and more briefly, some sort of characterization of Irish Christianity in America would seem necessary to complete the analogies.

For both Presbyterians and later Catholics, the adjustments to America were limited or contained by the character of the body of their adherents on the one hand, and by the authoritative and European foundations of their organization on the other. Both churches presided in Ireland over a strange contrast between the theological and organizational richness of their traditions elsewhere, and the suppressed, unschooled, and impoverished congregations which confronted them in Ireland for the most part, and reduced their operations to the pastoral essentials. The danger was that they would carry these weaknesses to America in the nature of the immigrations, while removing themselves even further from the sustenance of Europe: of Edinburgh and Rome, of the middle classes who produced a polished clergy, and gave body to those traditions, a middle class slowly emergent too in Belfast and Dublin.

Most Ulster farmers were close to their Scottish origins, by kinship, dialect, outlook, custom, and livelihood: Presbyterianism was but the most obvious link. Indeed, in Dublin, incoming northerners remained distinct from the Anglo-Irish Presbyterians of the city with their roots in English Puritanism. Most Ulstermen, wearied by plough and byre, harassed by rent, prices, shortages, taxes, and magistrates, had only a fragmentary, if tenacious grasp of the Presbyterian essentials, much of these in turn the common currency of the Gospels. The body of them held to the Westminster Confession, or at least its thought patterns if they belonged to the non-subscribing congregations. It was a reasonable Calvinism in which God covenanted with man through Christ, so that His predestined elect, by fidelity to the way of Holy Scripture and obedience to church and civil order, might have some reassurance as to their final state, while in no way earning it. The arbitrary God of Calvin was thus domesticated to a sensible bargain. Others argued that Christ's atonement was universal, that the "Covenant of Grace" was no closed shop: a point taken up by the Marrowmen reformers in Scotland under Ebenezer Erskine, imprecisely influential in America until the Baptists would make a wide sweep through emigrant congregations preaching the same essential idea in a democratic evangelical style. Generally, Ulster's ministers adhered to the strict Westminster Standards, even the Secessionists of 1746 who claimed to follow Erskine but were in fact challenging the "moderatism" of their fellows, which they construed as laxity and worldliness, and which today would be interpreted as liberalism. But it is probable such quarrels did not deeply affect their people, except insofar as probably all Ulstermen did not incline to presume too much on the Deity, and allowed the severities of long sermons, church discipline as enforced by elders, and unornamented psalmody, to reinforce the toughness that was partly native, partly rooted in the proximity to so many native Ulster "papists." Nonetheless, taken seriously, complacently, or easily, Presbyterianism did not eliminate the Ulsterman's wit and balladry, his delight in hare coursing and whiskey drinking, his literate but unlearned spiritedness. Indeed the snobbery of certain elders, the scholasticism and social conformism of many ministers to Anglican standards, insulated him against any chilling effects of doctrines like election and damnation, and underlay his sympathy with nonsubscribing, secessionist, and antiburgher movements within the church, or gravitation toward other groups like the Covenanters.

Symptomatically, Baptism and later Methodism were to grow rapidly at the expense of mainline Presbyterianism on the American frontier. They may be seen not merely as harvesting the effects of "Americanization" but as drawing upon these earlier polarities in the Ulster character. In the absence of sufficient clergy, and of sufficient social order, the peasant characteristics of the Ulster countryman flourished. Studies have revealed that the hymnody created by emigrant stock in the vast Appalachian zone abandoned strict psalmody, and returned to the musical patterns of the folk music of the Scottish Lowlands and of Ulster: pentatonic, melodic, with Jesus the Saviour and His Grace replacing earthly love as the central simple image, sin and the world's weariness replacing hardship and betrayal as the context. Tunes and stanza structure are often identical to their secular Ulster predecessors. Thus, in America, Baptism and its music may have reconciled the Calvinist convictions of the Ulsterman with the inner spring of his emotional life and culture.

America, in short, intensified many of the problems of creating a unified and coherent Presbyterianism. Simply by scattering people from Ulster over such an enormous belt, from Orange county in New York south to the Georgia frontier, it made ministerial service and control very difficult, a point Francis Makemie early recognized in his *Plain and Friendly Persuasive to the Inhabitants of Virginia and Maryland for Promoting Towns and Cohabitations*. The same theme was to be pressed 150 years later by Archbishop John Hughes of New York against the sponsors of Irish Catholic colonization in the West! Moreover, the isolation of the frontier bred moral decay, callousness, and cynical unsociality, as a score of commentators from Charles Woodmason to J. F. D. Smyth observed. The inhabitants themselves often took steps to remedy this, as did those of Paxtang, Pennsylvania, when they invited Reverend John Elder among them in 1754, "Being deeply Sensible of the great loss & disadvantage we & ours may sustain . . . by our living in such a condition in this Wilderness." Ministers, however, were very scarce; and few came from Ulster after the 1740s. Moreover, even fewer were inclined to go to the huge swathe of backcountry, where the majority of immigrants settled, nor were the American-trained clergy. As Jacob Green wrote in 1775: "The method we have been in has been first to make men gentlemen and then to make them preachers and our candidates have no idea of being gospel ministers without living politely.

This . . . will always leave the great part of the Churches destitute of ministers." Instead, the ministry concentrated where there was a settled and prosperous Presbyterian community in its second and third American generation after the 1740s: the merchant and cash farmer regions of north Delaware, southeast and south central Pennsylvania, and New Jersey. This was but the northeastern corner of the great 1,700 mile crescent of Ulster settlement, and here, by the year 1789, the bulk of the organized 220 congregations and 15,000 full church members were found. Elsewhere, except in the Valley of Virginia, Presbyterianism tended to be skeletal, disappearing among the majority by default.

This outcome had been foreseen by a strenuous minority within the church who sought measures to prevent it. The "New Side" or reform party, headed by Ulstermen Gilbert and William Tennent and Samuel Blair, sought to revitalize Presbyterian piety, infuse the clergy with a flexible, evangelical spirit, and take educational and organizational measures to meet the challenges of the frontier. They saw in the tendency of the orthodox "Old Side" to remain in established centers, and to absorb the enlightened, easygoing spirit of the times, a danger to the church. They thus anticipated by a few years the Secessionists in Ulster who saw middle-class "moderatism" as undermining the church and therefore vilified it as mere laxity. Certainly, in such men as Francis Alison (himself the introducer to America of the ideas of his teacher, Ulster-born Francis Hutcheson of Glasgow), the "Old Side" had men closer to the secular ideas of the century, and thus to the "new light" element in Ulster Presbyterianism's mainstream. But these developments seem to have been quite separate in actuality, even if there are obvious parallels between them, and between the "New Side" in America and the Secessionists in Ulster. In America, the reformers espoused the revival, carefully prepared and followed up, to spread the church, although opposing that collective emotionalism which James McGready and others would later borrow from Baptism as the answer on a further frontier. They established new churches and schools, and carried the church southwest into Virginia's inner valley. They cooperated interethnically, outside the Ulster Presbyterian connection, with George Whitefield, Theodore Frelinghuysen, and other non-Presbyterian revivalists, notably Jonathan Edwards, as well as with native American leaders such as Samuel Davies and Jonathan Dickinson. They feared the complacent predestinarianism of the Ulster establishment in America, as the Secessionists did in Ulster. Expelled from the church in 1741, they returned in 1758, winning a formal victory in that many of their positions were adopted as the basis for reunion, but losing insofar as incoming young American-born recruits to the ministry failed to follow their example. Thus the most promising possibility of containing the majority of Ulster emigrants and their offspring in a dynamic, reformed, and expanding American Presbyterianism was lost. The thrust to respectability among the majority remaining found expression in the ever-closer links with New England's Congregational establishment, culminating in the Plan of Union of 1801, and in the ease with which the incoming handful of later Presbyterian ministers found immediate status (the Reverend John Grendy, a United Irishman, becoming chaplain to the House and Senate, and a friend of Madison and Monroe). The undemocratic tone, assured theological superiority, often Federalist politics and middle-class style of the church alienated the backcountryman, accustomed to find in himself (as contemporaries noted) the measure of things, in his isolation and ingenuity. Baptism, as preached by farmers and tradesmen, took up where the "New Side" had left off, and multiplied.

Nonetheless, the achievements of Presbyterianism should not be underestimated either. It was the strongest organized force and the largest denomination in the middle colonies by the 1760s (predominant in pivotal Pennsylvania), and provided a link with Calvinist New England which helped forge a common culture and politics as the Revolution approached. Likewise, it set the educational and theological standards to which the more backward and popular denominations of the region eventually aspired. Thus its formative hold on Ulster American Christianity survived in several respects despite its failure to contain it within its own congregations. It provided the elementary beliefs on which Baptism, the Disciples of Christ, and other denominations would build, and it continued to influence those groups by direct example, and indirectly by shaping the culture about them to some degree.

The Irish Catholic experience in the United States is more widely known and better understood. On the eve of the migrations, it had an even more vagarious religious tradition in Ireland than did Presbyterianism, although attempted streamlining and improvement had been under way for some time. This process was assisted by the energetic activities of bishops like Archbishops James Butler of Cashel, John Carpenter of Dublin, and above all John Thomas Troy of Dublin in the later eighteenth century, and many more in the nineteenth; by the foundation of Maynooth for the training of clergy in 1795, as of smaller institutions such as that at Carlow; and by the gradual shift of the mass of the population from Irish speaking to English speaking, a process facilitated and furthered (but by no means started) by the establishment of state primary schools after 1831. A basic catechetical knowledge could now be impressed upon most Catholics as children, and reinforced by religious services through life. This but supplemented Christian traditions and practices deeply rooted in the rural Irish-speaking past, many of which carried over in weakened form into English. On the other hand, among townsmen, it assisted the beginning of a deeper practice rooted often in English Catholic sources. The majority of Irish Catholics, however, just as of Ulster Presbyterians, were countryfolk of religious traditions and emphases varying within families or neighborhoods; their lives were too harsh to permit a religious existence which was more than customary, fragmentary, and inconsistent. There were the inherent conflicts of the Maynooth Catechism versus the superstitions of the folk festivals of Bealtaine, Lughnasa, and Samhain; of the sermons of their clergy, earnest rather than sophisticated, versus the immediacies of surviving Irish folk hymns; of the popular prayer gatherings or patterns observed even close to Dublin versus the new readings of the spiritual guides of Richard Challoner. Such antitheses and others crosslight Irish Catholicism on the eve of the migrations. Emigrants from different areas and different classes had different backgrounds in Catholicism, no less—at a later time—than those from Italy, although the tendency was toward increased practice and standardization of response, especially from the 1850s. Nonetheless, just as one could falsely antithesize the dour orthodoxy of Ulster's Shorter Catechism with the surviving spirit of Tam O'Shanter among Presbyterians, so one could make too much of these elements. Plain folk, weather-beaten and hardworked, the country immigrants from 1820s Cork or 1850s Cavan were but fitfully mindful of God, longing for distraction while craving final salvation, and hardly changed their inner habits overnight on taking a loading job in a goods yard in Philadelphia, or a laboring job on canal or railroad.

Welding these people into one church was easier for their leaders in America than had been the case for Presbyterians the century before. This has not been evident only because the Catholic story is usually related separately from those of other denominations. In 1899 Cardinal Domenico Ferratta attributed the great growth of the church in America and elsewhere to the Divine Providence which had unified the world with the fruits of human ingenuity. For the Irish Catholics were spread across America after 1840—in the era of the railroad, the telegram, ready money, and easy bank loans—in a broad swathe corresponding exactly with the greatest concentration of urban and transportation facilities: from Boston down to Baltimore across to Minneapolis down to St. Louis. Here, in America's industrial heartland, 85 percent of them settled, and this helps to explain their singularly rapid emergence as an integrated national mass denomination. It took a Presbyterian pastor of 1790 eight weeks to travel from Lexington, Kentucky, to a synodal meeting in New York in 1790. Catholic bishops could travel to the Third Plenary Council of Baltimore in 1884 by rail in at most a matter of days, even from California. Telegraphed news services and railroading missioners, priests aided by cheap postal services and mail-order church furnishers, a vast turnover of population between parishes and dioceses and a far-flung press cribbing assiduously from the Boston *Pilot* and New York *Freeman's Journal*, all ensured a cohesive national consciousness among Irish American Catholics, especially when allied to the strategic diocese and parish building of church authorities.

Since John Carroll's time as first American bishop, the importance of concentration and communication as keys to retaining the allegiance of Irish Catholics has been understood; their absence accounted for the loss of the great mass of the 100,000 indentured Irish servants and their offspring in the previous century. Parishes, established in the port cities in the 1790s, thereafter kept pace with the spread of the national economy. This connection also ensured that priests could everywhere be supported. Even when the community was at its poorest, before the 1860s, bank loans, Irish construction companies, and the regular wages of thousands of communicants, made their maintenance, and the construction of churches, possible. Only one Irish bishop out of several hundred, John Purcell of Cincinnati, managed to bankrupt his archdiocese, in a century of business, bank, and even governmental, insolvencies. Presbyterianism in the previous century faced a huge, ill-connected, and dispersed swathe of Ulster settlement everywhere on the brink of pure subsistence. Only the promise by twenty or thirty families to come up with five pounds a year could guarantee them a minister, or even the prospect of one. In short, Catholics were fortunate that their chief influx coincided with the broader era of the nationalizing of American life, from 1840 to 1900, and that the Irish newcomers never migrated *en masse* beyond the reach of their clergy.

All this also meant that localism, the mother of difference, was a dwindling force among them after the 1820s. More dynamic forces of unity existed also than the mechanical and geographical, however. The doctrine of the Catholicity of the Church was never really forgotten. In the 1890s, crusty lay editors such as William Hughes, Humphrey Desmond, Patrick Ford, and William Dillon took to task Irish American priests or people who antagonized each other, either locally, as in East St. Louis or Chicago, or nationally, in the disputes over schooling, Americanism, and other matters. They also criticized strongly those who made German or Polish Catholics uncomfortable in the Irish-dominated parishes. In both cases they appealed explicitly to the doctrine of Catholicity, and to the fact of the progressive Americanization of all Catholic nationalities in America, so evident in their second generations. The bulk of the hierarchy likewise thought and acted interethnically or catholically (however high-mindedly and insensitively they behaved on occasion). In the 1840s and 1850s they succeeded in diplomatically reconciling the strains between the assertively Irish poor, and the assimilating middle classes, and in the 1880s and after, in maintaining the principle of a common church organization while conceding the practical utility of short-term national parishes. Thus the trusteeism of the 1820s was overcome by the 1840s, and the German and Polish separatism implicit in the Cahensly program and explicit in the Polish National Church in the 1890s was largely contained and dissolved.

Indeed Irish-American Catholicism in the nineteenth century, dutifully if unimaginatively Roman, was so little given to insistence upon its own identities and peculiarities as such, much less to finding expression for them, that the principal failure of accommodation, that of reaching the Italians comprehensively, was a matter of style, personnel, and attitude, rather than of policy differences. The rapid erosion of Gaelic cultural residual elements in Irish Catholicism in Ireland had made easier the ordering of a basic orthodoxy suited in advance to the generalized and workable Catholicism favored by American bishops, one which might assimilate other nationalities, and withstand the Americanization of its adherents. If Irish Catholicism in America was thus Irish by numbers rather than by essential characteristics, and therefore less interesting than it might have been, it is probable that its intrinsic vitality and viability were thereby enhanced in these regards. Certainly it avoided the tendency to fragmentation which Presbyterianism brought from Ulster, as also a clannish refusal of close relations with other nationalities, including native Americans, which eighteenth-century American Presbyterians had noted of the Ulster majority before 1760.

Likewise, whereas the problems of response to America had split the Ulster Presbyterians between Old and New Siders, similar issues led only to differences of opinion among Irish-American prelates, and in fact never affected more than a minority of them. There were those, from John England to John Ireland, who argued that the church in America should resolutely Americanize. There were also those who argued that it should seek first to retain the immigrants by cultivating a mode and flavor congenial to them. The first assimilationist and cosmopolitan tradition, liberal in its estimate of secular and Protestant culture, derived its strength from the period before 1840, when the Irish were but an element in the Church, and their own most sensitive spirits were attracted by the eclecticism of America and realized they could not build an exclusive Irish church even had they so desired. In this they were analagous to the Tennents and Makemie of a century before, with their pastoral concern also for Americans generally, and for the immigrants' children. Among Catholics, this phase waned after 1840 due to vast German and Irish immigration, and the rise of nativist bigotry. Yet it remained an influential substream, and defined the final goals to which most bishops gave their final allegiance, in that they foresaw a pan-Catholic future, an American Catholic Church, and worked for it *programatically* in the statutes of the Councils of Baltimore.

Nonetheless, if scholars such as JoAnn Manfra and Ralph Nary have demonstrated this for the 1850s and 1890s, yet it is equally true that from the 1840s through the 1880s the *tactical* task of most churchmen was the construction of the conservative, immigrant-responsive church, as Jay Dolan has emphasized, and the assimilationists as such were a minority. Few bishops were as conservatively Irish in their exploitation of the ethnic-religious possibilities of American liberty as Archbishop John Hughes of New York in the mid-nineteenth century, or William Cardinal O'Connell of Boston in the early twentieth. Most, like the various incumbents of Chicago, San Francisco, and Philadelphia, neither advocated defensive withdrawal from American life, nor rapid dismantling of Irish group identity, but were content to act as cautious yet dynamic pastors to a changing situation which was allowed to define itself. All parties agreed on the urgency of Catholic schooling. Yet, as Howard Weisz demonstrated, Catholic parents were allowed, in return, to dictate the largely secular and American content of the new Catholic schools. Again, even the most conservative bishops relied on the beneficence of capitalists who were more American than Irish: men like Thomas Fortune Ryan, James Rend of Ohio, William Connors of Buffalo, or the Creightons and Cudahys of the Midwest. Probably the laity shaped the level of immigrant emphasis, and of Americanization, to a much greater degree than is usually allowed in studies concentrating on church policies, even if their formal voice was weak. Were the sources available for a full study of eighteenth-century Ulster Presbyterianism, it is possible that the same theme might emerge.

This in turn leads to a brief characterization of these two chief Irish Christian denominations in America. Both were very much shaped by the type of human material available to them. Almost everything else said upon Irish immigrants elsewhere in this volume has its bearing upon their character as Christians, and their group Christian cultures. Two salient constraints are everywhere apparent: poverty and politics. They were interrelated by the stringency which poverty lent to Irish politics, and both were closely related to Irish Christianity because the lines of political cleavage in Ireland coincided with those of religion, and because the manifold effects of poverty both weakened and strengthened aspects of religious commitment. These are commonplaces in the study of Irish society, but only lately have their repercussions in America been broadly portrayed. If life in America was materially and politically a considerable improvement over life in eighteenth-century County Antrim, or nineteenth-century County Cork, in that it ensured a basic subsistence and essential civic rights denied Presbyterians and Catholics by the agrarian system and by Anglican hegemony in Ireland, yet there were analogies of condition which caused both religious groups in turn to rebuild in America a politico-religious landscape of the mind, and to act accordingly. Relatively deprived Presbyterian backcountrymen saw themselves as victims of a coastal establishment of Anglicans in the Carolinas, and Quakers in Pennsylvania. Certainly they were short-changed in political representation, the provision of public services, and general influence; where this was not the case, in Virginia, politics did not develop along such polarized lines. The resultant organization of Presbyterians as a political grouping allied with other Calvinists against Anglicans and Quakers had fateful results when they turned tables to become the cutting edge of the American Revolution in the pivotal mid-colonial region, and later the base of Jeffersonianism in the same area: Pennsylvania, New Jersey, and Delaware. From the first, the Catholic Irish faced a middle-class native Protestant hegemony in the cities in which they settled; this they gradually overthrew in the quest for congenial law enforcement patterns, patronage, employment, and a favorable social climate generally. By the 1880s, the confrontation had moved into the state legislatures, and the Irish sought antiprohibitionist and propluralist allies among German Lutherans, Polish Catholics, and others, later broadening their appeal to workingmen's interests generally, just as urban Ulstermen in the Society of St. Tammany had turned to radicalism in the 1790s. Neither Ulster Americans nor later Irish Americans instigated or created ethnoreligious politics in America. But their presence intensified it, and they in turn welcomed it as a natural and traditional way of seeing and doing things, if not the only one.

Not surprisingly neither group produced deep Christian scholars nor notably holy individuals from the midst of so political a religious understanding. In the period of the maturation of Ulster America, after 1760, thoughtful Calvinists were not Irish: John Witherspoon, Jonathan Dickinson, Samuel Davies, David Rittenhouse, Benjamin Rush. Francis Alison was atypical, transformed, like the Tennents earlier, by his own cosmopolitan eclecticism. Likewise, in the period of Irish-American Catholic maturation, 1880–1910, despite the emergence of a score of their universities, the Catholic scholars in America confronting Darwinism were not Irish: John L. Spalding, Timothy Dwight, John Thein, John Gmeiner, Auguste Thébaud. The absence of heroic piety among eighteenth-century Ulster immigrants was a byword of the time. Less well known, yet equally apparent despite a mass of group-congratulatory rhetoric in the past, is the scarcity of real sanctity among the later Irish. However we understand their final import, Catholic criteria for the official establishment of a reputation for such goodness are scrupulous, systematized, and hypercritical. Those who have faced such testing among nineteenth-century American Catholics have included almost every nationality but the Irish: Frances X. Cabrini, Teresa Demjanovich, John Neuman, Frederic Baraga, Katherine Drexel, Joseph Rosati, Philippine Duchesne, Elizabeth Seton.

Political religiosity and religious tribalism, the products of poverty and confrontation, lessened but did not disappear in America. Much in the new country reevoked their defensive and ego-assertive functions. The tribe of immigrants, Presbyterian or Catholic was despised by men as tolerant as Benjamin Franklin in the first instance, Ralph Waldo Emerson in the second. They could not destroy by individual variation the sacred rites which dignified their often tawdry group interests. Such a climate was not congenial to reflection or moral heroism. Yet this does not divest their Christianity of its basic importance or sincerity. The contemporary scientific study of religion has reestablished, if in irritating terminology, the empirical reality of many of Christianity's own insights into its operations among men. Damaged and stunted men cling to their faith to order their impulses, steady their sense of self, strengthen their social obligations, organize their communities, and find some hope in a world of coercion, repression, necessity, or drudgery. Few of them scrutinize that which heals their fragmentation. Still fewer sustain the self-forgetfulness of rising to the prophetic, activist, or devotional heights suggested by their own tradition. Presbyterians and Catholics from Ireland, between 1717 and 1914, seeded the country with myriads of families devoted to the essentials of virtue, self-respect, and public order, and stimulated a minority to service, reform, and piety. They produced thousands of mechanics and teachers, businessmen and clerks, who although often as self-interested as the American Dream seems to encourage, yet spurned the rewards of being predators upon the public good, and often contributed directly to it. The political founders of the republic, Washington, John Adams, and the rest, believed virtue the central foundation of liberty, political passion and activity its expression. Irish Christianity, despite its narrowness, provided both.

FOR FURTHER READING

Systematic study of the Irish element in both religious groups is lacking, yet material is as rich in the literature as it is unorganized. Sidney Ahlstrom, *A Religious History of the American People* (New Haven, Conn., 1972), Thomas McAvoy, *The History of the Catholic Church in the United States* (Notre Dame, Ind., 1969), and L. J. Trinterud, *The Forming of an American Tradition: Colonial Presbyterianism* (Philadelpia, 1949), provide context. Thomas Witherow, *Historical and Literary Memorials of Presbyterianism in Ireland*, 2 vols. (London, 1879–80), and Patrick J. Corish, ed., *A History of Irish Catholicism*, vols. 4 and 5 (Dublin, 1967–71), detail the backgrounds. Marvin Buxbaum, *Benjamin Franklin and the Zealous Presbyterians* (London, 1975), and Owen Ireland, "The Ethnic-Religious Dimension of Pennsylvania Politics, 1778–1779," *William and Mary Quarterly*, 3rd ser., 30 (1973): 424–25 on the earlier politics, and Paul Kleppner, *The Cross of Culture* (New York, 1970), and James Walsh, ed., *The Irish: America's Political Class* (New York, 1976), on the later, offer indications and further reading. Jay Dolan, *The Immigrant Church* (Baltimore, 1975), and Howard Weisz, "Irish-American Attitudes and the Americanization of the English-Language Parochial School," *New York History* 53 (1972): 157–76, are not easy to reconcile. JoAnn Manfra, "The Catholic Episcopacy in America, 1789–1852," Ph.D. (University of Iowa, 1975), and Ralph Nary, "Church, State and Religious Liberty: The Views of the American Catholic Bishops of the 1890s," Ph.D. (Georgetown University, 1967), demonstrate these matters were far from exhausted. Of most recent studies, James W. Sanders, *The Education of an Urban Minority: Catholics in Chicago, 1833–1965* (New York, 1977), and Jay Dolan, *Catholic Revivalism: The*

American Experience, 1830–1900 (Notre Dame, Ind., 1977), are most noteworthy, and Irish related. Guides to the considerable literature will be found in the works of Ahlstrom and McAvoy, and more fully in Nelson R. Burr, *A Critical Bibliography of Religion in America* (Princeton, N.J., 1961). Local studies, as yet unsynthesized, are listed in David N. Doyle, "Irish America: A Regional Bibliography, 1830–1930," *Irish Historical Studies*, 21(1979), and of these the most recent are Emmet Curran, *Michael A. Corrigan and the Shaping of a Conservative Catholicism in America, 1878–1895* (New York, 1978); Martin J. Becker, *History of Catholic Life in the Diocese of Albany, 1609–1864* (New York, 1977); James F. Connolly, *The History of the Archdiocese of Philadelphia* (Philadelphia, 1976); and William Faherty, *Dream by the River* (Saint Louis, 1973).

THE IRISH
IN AMERICAN
BUSINESS AND
PROFESSIONS

E. R. R. GREEN

I remember as a child in Northern Ireland a small corner shop we always passed on our way to town and once being told that the people who owned it were related to an American millionaire who had died and left them all his money. The reason this incident has stayed in my mind, I am sure, is because it was my first awareness of America as a real place. What is significant is the identification with money and success, and in some such way the idea of America as a land of opportunity must have been planted in the minds of countless Irish boys and girls and so conditioned them to the possibility or certainty of emigration.

Historians on the whole have not emphasized the promise of America as a factor in Irish emigration, nor have they been all that interested in the careers of those for whom it became a reality. For them there is no pot of gold at the end of the rainbow. Skepticism is no doubt a worthy attribute, but the study of Irish history seems sometimes to induce a sense of helplessness as disaster follows upon disaster like the rain clouds hurrying in on the westerly gales. Moreover, such a view of history was paralleled by a now slightly outdated sociology which regarded migration and especially urbanization as essentially traumatic and the source of a plethora of social ills.

Yet the hopelessness at home which made emigration an unwilling necessity, the wretched conditions of travel, the growing misery in the slums of great cities, the ethnic and religious prejudices of those already settled in America, do not tell the whole story. Many thought of emigrating and never went, some went who should have stayed, but most of those who left did better in life or saw their children do better than they could have at home, and there were always a few who did exceptionally well.

The source of information for this minority of emigrants is the old filiopietistic history with its lists of those who had brought credit to themselves and the land that gave them birth or to the Irish race if the connection was a generation or two removed. Such lists, and they can be supplemented from the various biographical dictionaries, are meaningless in themselves. As they stand, they tell us nothing more than that individual Irishmen or their descendants achieved prominence, became powerful, and made money. If success was due to things such as inherited advantages, an appropriate education, or even to the coincidence of ability and opportunity, Irish identity is virtually irrelevant. By definition we are concerned only with the success of individuals within an immigrant group in achieving material gain or professional status. What is important then is to see whether Irish immigrants brought any special skills, showed any particular aptitudes, or could look forward to any advantages which might give them a head start in America. Basically, this must be done by the old method of stringing together biographies, but in the hope that patterns of some sort may emerge. A final word of caution: the method involves the selection of only a very few names from a very large number who are themselves a tiny fraction of the Irish-born in America.

Ireland and America intertwine in the story of English overseas expansion. In the seventeenth century, the flow of emigrants from England went in three directions, to Ireland, America, and the West Indies. In the last forty years or so of the century, large numbers of Scots came to Northern Ireland in addition to the English there and in the rest of the country. Eighteenth-century emigration from Ireland was in the main a remigration of these immigrants. Although Presbyterians from the North predominated, other Protestants from all over the country and Catholics also went. The last are a particularly elusive element, as they found it difficult to maintain their identity in a new country almost without priests or churches.

The eighteenth-century picture has been dominated by the presence of the Scots-Irish pioneer, a discovery of historians writing toward the end of the past century. There is no need to start that hare which amateur historians and propagandists have so loved to pursue. Our concern is with a commercial group which has no place in the pioneer concept and has consequently suffered from neglect. There were plenty of Irishmen among the merchants of the principal American ports, especially in Philadelphia and New York. In those days, the slowness and uncertainty of communications meant that business carried on between distant places required a high degree of confidence in the individuals concerned. Accordingly, it was often felt necessary that a member of the family or the firm should reside in the chief center with which trade was carried on. For such men, there was no element of risk in emigration nor any need for it to be permanent, while it also gave opportunities of achieving wealth and prominence which were not so easy to find at a later time in America's history.

Fortunately for us, these merchants are more easily identified by their custom of forming societies named for their patron saint. There was nothing peculiarly Irish about this; the other nationalities of the old Kingdom of Great Britain and Ireland also associated under the names of their own saints. Their purpose was charitable as well as social, and they did valuable work among the immigrant poor. The oldest of them was the Charitable Irish Society of Boston, founded in 1737. The Friendly Sons of St. Patrick of Philadelphia and the St. Patrick's Society of Charleston, South Carolina, were both established in 1771. The Friendly Sons of St. Patrick of New York did not come into existence until 1784.

John Maxwell Nesbitt of Philadelphia is a good example of these merchants. He was born in County Down and came to Philadelphia in 1747 at about the age of seventeen. He had a recommendation to Redmond Conyngham, a shipping merchant and importer, who had originally come from Letterkenny in County Donegal. Nesbitt was first employed as a clerk and then eventually became a partner. Conyngham returned to live on his Irish property in 1765, and the firm eventually became J. M. Nesbitt & Co. During the American Revolution, they were deeply involved and subscribed to the bank which was organized to supply the Continental army. Nesbitt's partner, David Conyngham, acted as a secret agent for the Americans both in France and the West Indies. On the organization of the Bank of North America in 1781, Nesbitt became a director. He was the first president of the Insurance Company of North America, founded in 1791. The Irish Club, which was the predecessor of the Friendly Sons in Philadelphia, was actually made up of members of the firm of Conyngham and Nesbitt. When the latter was founded, Nesbitt became vice-president and subsequently served as president in 1773 and again from 1782 to 1796. The first president was Stephen Moylan, brother of the Roman Catholic bishop of Cork, and a merchant who became a distinguished cavalry commander under General Washington.

Oliver Pollock, who emigrated at the age of twenty-three, had a wider-ranging career. Soon after his arrival, he began trading to the West Indies and soon made his headquarters at Havana. He had the good luck to arrive at New Orleans with flour from Baltimore when the town was facing famine. He let Count O'Reilly, who was in command, have the flour on easy terms and received in turn the far more valuable privilege of freedom to trade to Louisiana. Pollock grew rich by the sale of English cloth, African slaves, and American flour, and as a banker, contractor to the Spanish army and planter. Come the Revolution, he was in a position to give important service to the American cause. His three nephews later became prominent merchants, associated in business in New York and New Orleans.

The material advantages of independence first came to the United States with the outbreak of a major European war in 1793. For more than twenty years, the Americans reaped a rich harvest as neutral traders despite British efforts to hinder trade with the enemy. Although all the American ports flourished, it was Baltimore which had the most spectacular rise from a small Chesapeake port to a position of rivalry with Philadelphia. There were accordingly great opportunities for energetic men during these years of rapid growth.

William Patterson was born in County Donegal in 1752 and was sent to Philadelphia at the age of fourteen to be trained in the office of an Irish shipping merchant. As events moved to the point where armed conflict between Great Britain and the American colonies became inevitable, Patterson invested his total assets in two vessels and their cargoes and set sail for France. The proceeds were reinvested in military supplies. Profits and risks were equally high in this trade, and Patterson gave it up in the summer in 1778 when he brought $100,000 in cash and merchandise into Baltimore in fast-sailing vessels. With this capital, he was able to achieve a leading place in the commerce of the city. It was Patterson's daughter Elizabeth who unwisely married Napoleon's brother Jerome when he came to Baltimore as a French naval officer in 1803.

Robert Oliver apparently went out as a commission agent for one or more Belfast merchants at the end of the war in 1783. From 1785 to 1796 he was in partnership with Hugh Thompson, who came out from Northern Ireland in 1784. He then formed a new firm of Robert Oliver and Brothers to include his brothers who had come to Baltimore in 1790 and 1791. His great fortune was largely made in the West Indian carrying trade in which the connections of his brother-in-law, John Craig of Philadelphia, were most important. Through Spanish officials and Baring Brothers in London, Oliver eventually secured a near monopoly of trade from Veracruz in Mexico to the United States by which he netted about three quarters of a million dollars in just three years.

The greatest of the Baltimore merchants was Alexander Brown, a Ballymena linen merchant and bleacher who emigrated in 1800. To start with, he imported linens and exported flaxseed to which he added cotton and then tobacco. Brown was fortunate to have four sons, all of them men of conspicuous ability. As each son came of age, he was taken into partnership and sent to establish a new branch of the business. William, the eldest, was sent to Liverpool in 1808 and became probably the greatest merchant of his generation there. By 1840, it was reckoned that a sixth of Anglo-American trade, primarily in cotton, passed through his hands. The Brown family had an important part in the introduction of railways into the United States. George Brown called a meeting at his house in 1827 to discuss possibilities even before the completion of the Liverpool and Manchester railway. The result was the Baltimore and Ohio line, of which the first sleeper was laid on Independence Day, 1828, by Charles Carroll, the last surviving signatory of the Declaration. Alexander Brown died in 1834, leaving the then vast fortune of nearly $2 million. Under George Brown, the business concentrated more and more on banking, which eventually became the sole concern of Alexander Brown and Sons.

The young man, without family connections or money, could get ahead by venturing into remote places and taking up hazardous occupations. The immensely lucrative trade with the Indians for furs and skins, with the attendant advantages of land speculation, was such a possibility. Sir William Johnson does not fit all that easily into this category as he originally came to America to look after his uncle's 13,000-acre land grant on the Mohawk River in the colony of New York. The uncle, Sir Peter Warren, had been in the Royal Navy and gained great acclaim by his part in the capture of the French fortress of Louisbourg. He had also married into the great New York de Lancey family. At home, the Warrens and the Johnsons were landed gentry in County Meath. Johnson became a key figure in relations with the Indians and in countering French expansion. His Indian diplomacy and his military success brought him a baronetcy in 1755, and in the following year he was given sole responsibility as superintendent of Indian affairs. His deputies in this post were his nephew, Guy Johnson, and George Croghan, who had emigrated from Dublin in 1741, and was also a highly successful trader and land speculator.

There were also many Irishmen to be found in the southern Indian trade, based in South Carolina and Georgia. James Adair, the author of a *History of the American Indians* (1755), was undoubtedly the most remarkable of them. He must have been a very able linguist as he knew Greek, Latin, Hebrew, Spanish, French, and Irish in addition to the Indian languages needed in his everyday work. Not much is known of his life other than what is mentioned incidentally in his book, but he apparently came to South Carolina about 1730 and died soon after the outbreak of the American Revolution. John Rea, from near Ballynahinch in County Down, was one of the earliest settlers in Georgia. He became an Indian trader and eventually a partner of Patrick Brown, another Irishman. Another partner in this firm was George Galphin, who had emigrated from County Armagh. In 1765, Rea and his partners, Galphin and McGillivray, obtained a grant of 50,000 acres on which to settle Irish immigrants. The settlement, which was called Queensborough, was near the present Louisville, Georgia, and in its day represented an important stage in westward expansion. The episode is also interesting as showing the close connection between Indian trade, land speculation, and settlement.

In the eighteenth century, printers and booksellers were the equivalent of the journalists and broadcasters who inform opinion today. It is not altogether fanciful to regard the appearance of Irishmen in printing and publishing as an indicator of the aptitude for politics which later generations developed in America. John Dunlap was born in Strabane in 1747 and sent to his uncle William in Philadelphia at an early age to be apprenticed. William Dunlap had originally worked with Bradford, the pioneer printer of the middle colonies, and later acquired Benjamin Franklin's former appointment of postmaster in Philadelphia. However, in 1766 Dunlap decided to enter the church and made over his printing business to his nephew. John Dunlap's first venture was to publish a newspaper, the *Pennsylvania Packet*, which appeared in 1771. Beginning as a weekly, and then being published three days a week, the *Packet* became the first American daily in 1784. Dunlap, as is well known, is famous as the printer of the Declaration of Independence. He also printed the U.S. Constitution, and its first publication was in the pages of his newspaper. As printer to Congress, Dunlap was paid for some of his work with Philadelphia building land, the only asset available, which eventually became extremely valuable. Indeed, soon after the Revolution, Dunlap gave up his printing business and turned his attention to real estate, in which he was most successful, and died a wealthy man in 1812.

Hugh Gaine learned the printing trade in his native Belfast, came to New York at about the age of twenty, and worked for James Parker, who had been set up in business by Benjamin Franklin. Seven years after his arrival, he was able to start on his own as printer, publisher, and bookseller. In the same year, 1752, he began to publish the *New York Mercury*. He became printer to the colony in 1768 and continued to do all the government printing for many years. Gaine also diversified into the import of drugs, soaps, and what would be now called cosmetics, the success of which depended on advertising, which he could do at little or no cost. As a newspaperman, Gaine steered a successful neutrality; he was even able to continue the publication of his paper all through the British occupation of New York and still remain acceptable to patriots on the day of victory. He had traded at the sign of the Bible and Crown and continued to do so with the removal of the last two words.

Matthew Carey was born into a prosperous Dublin Catholic family in 1760, and despite his father's disapproval persevered in his intention of becoming a printer. In 1779 he published a pamphlet defense of the Catholics which caused a great outcry and was even condemned by conservatives of his own religion for its vehemence. As a matter of prudence, young Carey fled to France, where he secured an introduction to Franklin and worked for a time on his press at Passy. After a year or so, it was felt safe for him to return to Dublin, and his father advanced the capital to start a newspaper. It was not long before Carey was again in serious trouble, and this time he decided to go to America. In Philadelphia, with financial help from Lafayette, he again became a newspaper publisher. Through the magazines which he edited, his publishing and bookselling business, his own writings, and his active participation in public life, Carey became a prominent man in his adopted country. Historically, he has considerable importance in the development of economic thought in America, for although it was Alexander Hamilton who laid the foundations of a protective system, the theory was worked out by Carey.

In another way, Carey is significant as the precursor of a new kind of Irish emigrant. The failure of the revolutionary policies of the United Irishmen brought professional men to America as refugees who ordinarily would never have dreamed of emigrating. Thomas Addis Emmet, disillusioned with Bonaparte, came to New York in 1804. A special act of the state legislature was required to admit him to the bar because of Federalist opposition. He soon built up a lucrative practice and appeared in many famous cases. Emmet combined in an extraordinary way both the respect of New Yorkers and the affection of the Irish immigrant community. On the day of his funeral in 1827 the whole city came to a standstill for several hours.

William James McNeven belonged to the Catholic gentry and was sent to Vienna to be educated, where he had an uncle who was personal physician to the Empress Maria Theresa. On receiving his degree in medicine there, he returned to Dublin to practice. As one of the leaders of the United Irishmen, he was first imprisoned and then banished. McNeven, too, lost confidence in Napoleon and followed Emmet to New York in 1805. Within a very short time he had been appointed a professor at the College of Physicians and Surgeons and was recognized as a leading member of his profession.

The United Irish triumvirate in New York is completed by William Sampson. While in Belfast, he acted for the defense in most political cases which came before the courts and busied himself in publicizing acts of violence committed by members of the armed forces. Arrested in 1798, he agreed to emigrate, but the Americans would not have him. Eventually, after several years abroad, the Jefferson administration allowed him to enter the United States in 1806. He was admitted to the bar almost at once and soon achieved prominence. It is interesting to note that Wolfe Tone's son entered his law office and later became his son-in-law. Sampson appeared in 1813 in one of the earliest cases in America involving organized labor.

As we get toward the middle of the nineteenth century, the method of selection which has served reasonably well so far and which does provide a framework within which the success of Irish emigrants can be studied as a group rather than simply as unique individuals is less satisfactory. Now we are faced with a situation in which much larger numbers are emigrating, where the growth of the American people and economy has outstripped anything dreamed of in colonial days, and when the commanding social and economic heights are becoming rather less accessible to newcomers. The sample secured by picking individuals here and there is becoming increasingly less representative and even creating apprehensions about whether it is meaningful at all.

There are a number of lines of opportunity which can be tentatively followed. One is the linen industry which characterized the regional economy of the northeast of Ireland and which by the later nineteenth century held a dominant position in world markets. There is without doubt a connection between this background and the success of A. T. Stewart in New York as a pioneer of the modern department store. Brought up by his grandfather, Stewart joined his mother in New York in 1820 and taught school for a time. When he went back to claim a legacy, he invested about two-thirds in Irish embroidery, which he used to stock a small shop on Lower Broadway. By 1846 his trade had expanded so much that he was able to buy a run-down hotel near the city hall and build his famous Marble Store on the site. He moved once again in 1862 when he opened the largest store in the world at that time. Although the foundation of his fortune was probably the stocks of failed merchants which he bought at auctions during the 1837 financial crisis, he showed real genius as an organizer and innovator. At his death, Stewart was probably worth about $40 million.

The great Chicago store of Carson, Pirie & Scott originated with two young men from Newry in County Down. John T. Pirie came from Scotland to serve his time in his uncle's drapery shop. He later went to Belfast and persuaded Carson, whom he had known in Newry, to go into partnership with him. On second thoughts, they decided to emigrate and worked for a time in a shop belonging to friends of theirs in illinois. They finally started up in business on their own in 1854 and expanded rapidly after they persuaded George and Robert Scott to come out from Newry to join them. The firm did not move to the Louis Sullivan building on "the busiest corner in the world" in Chicago until 1904.

In the nineteenth century, mining was probably the equivalent of the Indian trade at an earlier time in the risks and rewards which it held out. Again, emigrants who had severed ties with familiar places and people in crossing the Atlantic and were prepared to go anywhere in search of fortune are to be found among the handful who really struck it rich. The two most famous are James G. Fair and John W. Mackay. Fair was born in County Tyrone and went to America with his parents at the age of twelve. Mackay was born into a poor family in Dublin and emigrated with them as a small boy in 1840. Both Fair and Mackay went to California in the gold rush, gained experience, and became successful. In 1864 Mackay went into partnership with James C. Flood and William T. O'Brien of the Auction Lunch Saloon in San Francisco to promote mining operations. Fair joined them in 1868, and a year later they gained control of the Hale and Norcross mine at Virginia City, Nevada. Then, in 1873 they struck the fantastically rich Big Bonanza in the Virginia Consolidated mine from which $100 million in gold and silver was taken in the next six years. Marcus Daly was born in Ireland in 1841, came to America at the age of fifteen, and in due course became a miner in California. He worked with Fair and Mackay for a time, and then went to Montana in 1876, where he became a partner in the Alice Silver Mine at Butte. He next persuaded George Hearst and others to buy the Anaconda Mine, where the silver soon ran out but vast deposits of copper were found just as great new markets were opening up with the development of the electrical industries. Philip Argall differs somewhat from the others by having learned mining in County Wicklow and then gained wide experience all over the world before becoming manager of a smelter at Leadville,

Colorado. It was Argall who designed and built the first plant to treat Cripple Creek gold ores by the new cyanidation process.

There were also internal lines of advance along which immigrants could move. Minority groups have their own service sector. Religion and education, food and entertainment, law and savings, and credit and insurance all provide opportunities to give leadership or to become better off. The Irish, for instance, had an aptitude for politics, providing them with a power base among their own people which made them influential first at municipal and state and then at national levels. Again, special skills may enable immigrants to acquire a monopoly position in a particular industry or in certain kinds of work. The Irish, though, as a rural people undergoing urbanization were forced initially in large numbers to accept unskilled employment. Consequently, the construction industry was about the only one in which the immigrant could conceivably gain any advantage from his national identity.

To pursue this line of inquiry very far involves accepting a different meaning of Irish. So far, we have considered only those actually born in Ireland. Possibly those who were brought to America at an early age should also have been excluded on the grounds that emigration strictly speaking results from a personal decision. Besides, an American environment and education will in many situations enable the young immigrant to compete on equal terms with the native-born. Any wider definition of Irish at once involves us in two things, a concern with those who are merely Irish by descent and with urban groups which retain a separate identity, believed by them to be Irish. The former cannot possibly be regarded as other than individuals whose Irish origin is the proper concern only of the biographer or family historian. The latter are certainly not immigrants; they would react vociferously and very properly to any suggestion that they are foreigners. What it all adds up to, in fact, is that so far as America is concerned being Irish has two meanings. The first applies to those who emigrated, and the second to their descendants, only a proportion possessing an identity based on that fact.

Eugene Kelly fits uneasily enough into even the flexible framework which we have been trying to create. He was born in County Tyrone in 1808, served his time in the drapery business, emigrated to New York as a young man, and secured similar employment. He first moved to Kentucky on behalf of his employers, then built up his own business in St. Louis. In 1850, Kelly went to California and prospered in the hectic conditions of the gold rush. There, he extended his interests to banking and was a founder of Donahoe, Kelly, and Company. He then moved to New York, where his main concern was with banking and insurance. Kelly was a founder of the Catholic University of America in Washington, D.C., and treasurer until his death in 1894. Although not very active in politics, he was a friend of John Dillon and treasurer of the Irish parliamentary fund. Hugh McCloskey in New Orleans is similarly detached from and at the same time involved with the Irish community. He emigrated at the age of twenty-three in 1837, when an economic blizzard was about to sweep the United States. Consequently, it was a long haul before he became a prosperous soft-drinks manufacturer in New Orleans, where he had started as a laborer laying water pipes. Among the more important of his interests were the Hibernian Bank, which he promoted, and the Hibernia Insurance Company, of which he was the first president. His concern in a streetcar company also led him inevitably into municipal politics. Because none of his children lived beyond an early age, McCloskey brought out no fewer than five nephews who succeeded him in business. A far more characteristic line of advance within the immigrant community was that of President Kennedy's family. Patrick Kennedy, who emigrated from County Wexford to Boston in 1848 and died of cholera ten years later, worked as a cooper. His son became a saloonkeeper, was active in politics, ran a coal business, and organized a trust company and savings bank. From this base, the grandson Joseph Kennedy advanced to a prominent place in American business and public life.

The special position of the Irish in building and contracting was connected not only with the concentration of their labor in the construction industry but also with the rapidity by which they gained power in politics. John B. McDonald was born in County Cork in 1844 and brought to New York at the age of three. The father prospered in his own way, starting as a day laborer and becoming a contractor, alderman, and Tammany stalwart. After his death, John McDonald rapidly expanded the business and became one of the leading railway contractors in the country. His final achievement was the building of the New York subway. The Rapid Transit Subway Construction Company was organized by August Belmont, the banker, and McDonald. There was a grim political struggle before obtaining a charter from the state legislature, but work began in 1900 and trains were running four years later. John D. Crimmins was born in New York and was the son of a contractor. His business was on a very large scale, often employing as many as 12,000 men at a time. Crimmins as a rule did not seek city or county contracts as he did not like the kind of politics associated with them. He did, though, build most of the elevated railway mileage decided on by the New York Rapid Transit Commission in 1875. The work of placing electric wiring underground, required by the city after 1884, was largely carried out by his firm. Crimmins was also much interested in Irish-American history and published work on the subject.

Thomas Addis Emmet had set a splendid example by his distinction at the New York bar, but this could not be all that easily followed by the young emigrant, even of reasonable education, who had to support himself while studying law. Again, it is the second or third generation before a family became substantial enough to put sons into the professions. The great jurist, Morgan J. O'Brien, was the son of a County Limerick emigrant and born on the Lower East Side, but he was able to get to Fordham and Columbia.

From there, his ability carried him to the office of state supreme court justice. He was also a prominent layman and gave help to the Land League and later headed the American Committee for Relief to Ireland in 1920. Pierce Butler, who became a justice of the U.S. Supreme Court in 1922, was the son of a County Wicklow emigrant and pioneer farmer in Minnesota. Again, he was able to attend Carleton College and develop the talents which gained him admission to a prestigious law firm.

In concluding, it can hardly be claimed that anything has been added to entrepreneurial theory. The little work that has been done on American business leadership confirms the preponderance of the older stocks. William Miller, in articles published in 1949 and 1950, looked at a sample of some 200 businessmen about the beginning of this century and found that "poor immigrant and poor farm boys" accounted for only 3 percent of the total. As regards national origin, some 80 percent could be traced to the United Kingdom, Canada, and other parts of the then British Empire. It is interesting that 11 percent were of Northern Ireland origin and only 3 percent came from Southern Ireland. The obvious explanation lies in the earlier date at which Ulster emigration began and ties in with Miller's conclusion that the longer a family had been in the United States, the greater the advantage to its members. A survey such as this, dealing with a small number of men of obvious ability, simply tells us, as we might have expected, that they were likely to seize whatever opportunity offered. Still, certain trends have been isolated, such as the importance of transatlantic commerce in providing business opportunity and the significance of hazardous undertakings like Indian trading and mining where risks and rewards could be very great.

FOR FURTHER READING

The literature is fragmentary, but more substantial than is usually thought. On the early Irish Indian traders, see James Flexner, *Mohawk Baronet: Sir William Johnson* (New York, 1959); Leroy R. Hafen and William J. Ghent, *Broken Hand: Thomas Fitzpatrick* (Denver, Colo., 1931); and N. B. Wainwright, *George Croghan, Wilderness Diplomat* (Chapel Hill, N.C. 1959). On the early mercahtile figures, see Edwin J. Perkins, *Financing Anglo-American Trade: The House of Brown, 1800–1880* (Cambridge, Mass., 1975); James A. James, *Oliver Pollock* (New York, 1937); Stuart Bruchey, *Robert Oliver* (Baltimore, 1956); Julian Gwyn, *Enterprising Admiral: The Personal Fortune of Admiral Sir Peter Warren* (Toronto, 1974); John C. Campbell, *History of the Friendly Sons of St. Patrick* (Philadelphia, 1892); and Richard C. Murphy and Lawrence J. Mannion, *The Society of Friendly Sons of St. Patrick in the City of New York* (New York, 1962), pp. 1–234. On the United Irish and other radical immigrant penetration of business and the professions, see R. R. Madden, *The United Irishmen: Their Lives and Times*, 4 vols. (Dublin, 1857–60). For later developments, there is much information in the regional studies of Irish America on Irish business in cities such as New York, Boston, Philadelphia, and New Orleans, in the studies by Moynihan, Shannon, Handlin, Clark, and Niehaus cited previously.

Stephen Birmingham, *Real Lace: America's Irish Rich* (New York, 1973), is impressionistic yet suggestive. On several great chain store founders, from North and South respectively, see Harry E. Resseguie, "A. T. Stewart and the Development of the Department Store, 1823–1876," *Business History Review* 39 (1965): 301 ff., and on Pirie and James Butler, Godfrey A. Lebhar, *Chain Stores in America, 1859–1959* (New York, 1959). On the mining kings, see particularly Richard H. Peterson, *The Bonanza Kings: Social Origins and Business Behavior* (Lincoln, Neb., 1977), and J. W. Caughey, *Gold is Cornerstone* (Berkeley, Cal., 1948). The career of Harry O'Reilly, the Monaghan-born rival of Samuel Morse, may be followed in R. L. Thompson, *Wiring a Continent, 1832–1866* (Princeton, N. J., 1947), and that of J. D. Crimmins in his *Diary* (New York, 1925), and in W. F. Reeves, "Elevated Lines in New York," *New York Historical Society Quarterly Bulletin* 18 (1935): 59 ff. Earlier and continuing penetration of commercial and manufacturing life, followed by large-scale enterprise and financing on the part of post Famine immigrants, can be deduced from the contemporary accounts and biographical sketches in John F. Maguire, *The Irish in America* (New York, 1868); Jeremiah O'Donovan, *A Brief Account of the Author's Interview with his Countrymen* (Pittsburgh, 1864); John O'Hanlon, *Irish Emigrant's Guide for the United States* (Boston, 1851), whereas of later compilations, J. B. Cullen, *Story of the Irish in Boston* (Boston, 1889); Charles Ffrench, *Biographical History of the American Irish in Chicago* (Chicago, 1897); and C. E. McGuire, *Catholic Builders of the Nation*, 5 vols. (Boston, 1923), the last being noncontemporary for the most part, are more reliable. Apart from businessmen, there are several sources on Irish-American lawyers, notably James McGurrin, *Bourke Cockran* (New York, 1948); K. E. Conway and M. Ward, *Charles Francis Donnelly: A Memoir* (Boston, 1909); John Riordan, "Garret McEnerney and the Pursuit of Success," in Walsh, ed., *The Irish in San Francisco* (San Francisco, 1978), pp. 73–84; Anon., "Pierce Butler," *Georgetown Law Journal* 28 (1939): 163 ff. What is now most needed are social and contextual studies of Irish business and professional life for all periods in America, along the lines of the pioneering W. E. Rowley, "The Irish Aristocracy of Albany, 1798–1878," *New York History* 52 (1971): 275–304, or of the Perkins study of the Browns of Baltimore. In the meantime, the careful accumulation of further biographical data should itself reveal which patterns, other than those suggested here, might be also further pursued. The Irish mercantile community of Philadelphia, 1750–1820, and the professional and entrepreneurial community of New York, 1840–1900, would repay detailed study. Alice C. Cochran, *The Descendants of John Mullanphy* (New York, 1976), attempted this unsuccessfully for the "Irish Aristocracy" of St. Louis.

THE IRISH AND THE AMERICAN LABOR MOVEMENT

DAVID MONTGOMERY

Workers of Irish birth or lineage have been so prominent in the struggles of American labor that any attempt to sort out what is peculiarly Irish in their contribution to the labor movement must proceed with caution. German immigrants obviously dominated the woodworking, baking, and brewing industries of the nineteenth century, and the mark which they left upon the unions in those occupations is as distinctive as that which Jewish immigrants stamped upon the unions of the needle trades. There were no industries in which the Irish formed a numerical majority, after the decline of handloom weaving in the 1850s. On the contrary, workers of Irish descent were scattered throughout the length and breadth of American industry. They were everywhere and into everything.

A *Biographical Dictionary of American Labor Leaders*, published five years ago, offered brief summaries of the careers of some 503 men and women of eminence in the labor movement of the United States between the 1830s and the 1970s. Twenty of them were born in Ireland, another 93 can be clearly identified as being of Irish Catholic descent, and at least a dozen others probably were. In other words, between one-fifth and one-fourth of the notables in this list were Irish Americans. Only two other countries surpassed Ireland's contribution to the *Dictionary*'s list of immigrant leaders, the Russian Empire (with 42 entries, all of them Jews) and the United Kingdom (with 37). Neither of them, however, equaled the mark left on American unions by the children, grandchildren, and great-grandchildren of immigrants from Ireland.

On the other hand, the importance of Irish Americans in labor organizations rose as their share of the total working-class and immigrant populations declined. From 1820 to 1855 between 43 percent and 47 percent of the immigrants who disembarked in American ports each year were from Ireland. During those years, however, Irish activists in workingmen's movements were rare indeed, and those who could be identified were either handloom weavers, veterans of the movement in England, or Protestants (and some-times all three). The prominence of Catholic Irish Americans in the labor movement was achieved in the 1880s; yet by that time new Irish immigrants represented less than 16 percent of the annual influx of newcomers, and they had been clearly replaced by Germans as the most numerous foreign-born group. During the first decade of the twentieth century, when Irish Americans occupied the presidencies of more than 50 of the 110 unions in the American Federation of Labor, the Irish proportion of the foreign-born population had fallen to 10 percent and their annual share of the new arrivals was only 3 percent.

These considerations suggest two lines of inquiry for this paper. It is evident that the typical Irish-American activist in the labor movement was not an evicted cotter, but rather an immigrant's child or grandchild, who had been reared in an American industrial town. In what ways, then, did this activist's mentality differ from that of his or her parents? Conversely, did such activists impart any peculiarly Irish qualities to the national labor movement?

Because Irish-American communities themselves changed fundamentally over the course of time, one cannot answer these questions without first attempting to demark three successive periods of time in which the experiences and roles of Irish-American workers differed significantly from those of the preceding and subsequent epochs. First, the "making of the American working class," to borrow a familiar expression, is best identified with the period of rapid economic development between the 1820s and the 1860s. By the end of this epoch the population of the United States matched those of France and the Austro-Hungarian Empire, and the value added by manufacture in the United States was second only to that of Great Britain.

Immigration from Ireland had swelled steadily during those years. As early as the 1830s, the employers and workmen alike in the burgeoning communities of handloom weavers, which appeared around Philadelphia, Fall River, Pawtucket, and other textile centers, were practically all Irishmen. The canal network, which occupied the center stage in the nation's party controversies, was dug largely by Irish hands. But in the grim wake of the potato famine and subsequent enclosures, 1,187,000 Irish men, women, and children came to America in only eight years (1847–54). A third of all the Irish to migrate to the United States during the nineteenth century came during those years, and it was then that the Irish established themselves as the most highly urbanized ethnic group in the country, and as the backbone of the unskilled labor force in industrializing America.

The second period is that in which the modern labor movement took shape, and Irish Americans became so prominent in its leadership. That epoch extended from the 1870s to the great depression of the 1890s. During those years, 1.3 million Irish crossed the Atlantic. The bulk of them were young and unmarried. They came with prepaid tickets and headed directly for the established Irish communities of the cities. One consequence of this pattern was identified by Sam Bass Warner, who found that the Irish immigrants of Philadelphia resided in more tightly segregated neighborhoods in 1930 than their predecessors had in 1860. Almost half of the Irish immigrants of this phase were women, and in some decades more than half. Large-scale migration by young, unmarrried women, traveling on their own, took place with no other nationality. It served to maintain the ranks of the largest occupational group in the society—domestic servants—and to root Irish immigrants quickly in American life. Moreover, the Irish had a lower rate of returning to the old country than any other immigrant groups of the time, except the Russian Jews. When they came, they came to stay.

The third period is that in which American life has been dominated by giant corporations, giant depressions, and giant wars—the era extending from the depression of the 1890s to the present. During this time, immigration from Ireland has slowed down to a trickle (except for a significant burst in the last half of the 1920s), and Irish Americans have been found in every walk of life from Skid Row to the White House. David Doyle is quite right when he says of the early years of this century: "Numerically, Irish Americans *dominated* few trades (except plumbers and steam fitters), politically they dominated a majority of the unions of organized trades."

That political hegemony was apparent in the new industrial unions formed during the 1930s, just as it had been in the older craft unions. In the industrial unions above all, however, Irish Americans have led members who were largely of other nationalities and races. The social policies promoted by these unions were significantly different from those advocated by the older organizations. Moreover, the Irish-American leaders of this century have brought to their union offices political views as disparate as those of Frank Fitzsimmons and Peter Brennan, two Nixon Republicans, James Carey and Philip Murray, liberal Democrats of a Catholic Trade Unionist bent, William Z. Foster and Eugene Dennis, Communists, and the Trotskyist Dunne brothers, Grant and Ray. For all these reasons a distinctively Irish imprint on the labor movement has become increasingly difficult to identify.

I propose to discuss a few highlights of the first and second eras, that is to say, the developments of the nineteenth century. I hope to be able to indicate how Irish Americans rose to prominence in the labor movement, what changes in their own attitudes and behavior were involved in that process, and what distinctive qualities they imparted to the movement as a whole.

THE FORMATIVE YEARS, 1820–70

Early immigrants knew the meaning of solidarity well, but the cohesiveness which they exhibited followed the lines of family, clan, county of origin, and religion—seldom those of trade. Few of them had any trade.

The earliest detailed national survey of immigrants' occupations is provided by the census of 1870, too late to portray the initial impact of the Famine immigration, but early enough to reveal what patterns had taken shape since that time. The 947,243 Irish immigrants who were gainfully employed at that time constituted 8 percent of the country's total labor force. Less than 15 percent of the Irish worked in agriculture, in contrast to 47 percent of Americans generally. On the other hand, the Irish immigrants provided somewhat more than their share of wage earners in mining and manufacturing. Almost 28 percent of the Irish were found there, as compared to 21 percent of the total labor force. They were spread so widely over American industries that only among a few groups, such as linen mill operatives, morocco dressers, and gas works employees, did they provide as much as 30 percent to 40 percent of the total force. But four Irish immigrants out of every ten toiled as unskilled laborers or as domestic servants. Although only 16 percent of the total labor force engaged in these two occupations, 39.6 percent of those who had been born in Ireland were found there.

It is at this point that the local studies of Dennis Clark, Estelle Feinstein, Laurence Glasco, Paul Faler, Stephen Thernstrom, Carl Degler, Vera Shlakman, Herbert Gutman, and other reveal far more than national statistics. They suggest that in mill towns where textiles and shoes were fabricated, young Irishwomen tended machines in the factories, while their brothers and fathers labored for railroad and building contractors. In larger cities almost every teenage girl of Irish parentage left home to work as a servant between the ages of eleven and fifteen, then married sometime in her early twenties. Her brother left home between eighteen and twenty-two, and he was probably married before he was twenty-five (in startling contrast to the late marriage customs of the home country). He most likely headed for the docks, building sites, or road-building gangs in search of work. Here was a world of fierce competition for irregular employment, a picaresque world of bribes and battles for jobs, pilfering, and convivial but hard drinking, in which one could survive only by ties of unswerving loyalty with one's friends.

Those friends were fellow Irish Americans, but more, they were from the same city block and probably had come from the same region of Ireland. In fact, Dennis Clark found by surveying Philadelphia's tax records that "those from the same area in Ireland concentrated in the same city neighborhood. Bradys, O'Donnells, and Gallaghers, for example, would cluster together; owing to the legacy of the clan system, many families unrelated by blood carried the same surname."

Around the firehouse, parish, and teenage gang each neighborhood asserted its mastery of its own turf. Immigrants also used threats and violence against outsiders in an effort to corner the market on various local laborers' jobs, much as the Whiteboys had tried to do in the Irish countryside. Murderous clashes took place on the New York and Baltimore waterfronts between the newcomers and the many blacks, who had previously unloaded ships there. By June 1863 links among work gangs on the New York docks had been developed sufficiently to enable the workers to conduct a successful port-wide wage strike and to create a loosely structured society to which all dockers had to belong. A month later the dockers' union, firehouse, and neighborhood gangs were all involved in an outbreak of enraged demonstrations against conscription and against emancipation of the slaves, which began with four days of massive assaults on draft offices, dwellings of the rich, arsenals, Protestant missions, and blacks, and which ended in armed combat between the barricaded poor of New York and regiments of veteran troops, fresh from the recent battle at Gettysburg, who advanced through the city's streets under cover of artillery fusillades.

Never again would America experience an insurrection so fiercely fought or so ruthlessly suppressed as this one, not even in the Great Strikes of 1877 or the Detroit insurrection of 1967. New York's Police Commissioner Acton estimated that 1,200 lives had been lost. By no means were all the rioters Irish Americans, despite the lurid claims of the contemporary press, but a vast proportion certainly were. What this bloody rising did reveal, however, is the intensity of the neighborhood loyalties, which were characteristic of the immigrant poor, and the degree to which a common sense of outrage could spur half a city into violent action against its familiar enemies.

On the other hand, the trade unionists of the time were horrified by the New York insurrection. Although their papers denounced the draft and lauded the dockers' strike, and thousands of artisans and shipyard and factory workers had left their jobs to join the crowds which swarmed up New York's West Side to protest the draft on the first day of the rising, trade union spokesmen quickly dissociated themselves from the fighting. Large contingents of their members joined volunteer units to assist the police by the third day, and skilled workers formed armed bands to reopen their workplaces.

The distance which separated native craftsmen from Irish immigrants in that crisis was nothing new. Throughout the 1840s and 1850s native-born artisans and trade union activists had contributed heavily to the ranks of anti-Catholic movements such as the American Republican party and the Know-Nothings. Thousands of them had poured into the streets to do battle with the Irish, or with troops defending Catholic churches, in the bloody riots of 1844 in Philadelphia's suburbs of Kensington and Southwark, as well as in lesser engagements throughout the land. In the mid-forties Philadelphia's unions of shoemakers, tailors, printers, and other artisans had openly barred Irish Catholics from membership, and their officers were active in the nativist Order of American Mechanics.

During the mass rallies and petition campaigns for the ten-hour day late in the 1840s, and especially during the great strike wave of 1850–51, many workers' organizations did try hesitatingly and awkwardly to enlist the immigrants, whom they had so recently spurned. Owenite radicals, like John Ferral and William English, who had constantly preached to deaf ears against the sectarian hostilities of the forties, now found their oratory much in demand. But old habits were hard to overcome. At a rally for the ten-hour day in the textile town of Manayunk, for example, the organizers made special efforts to attract Irish mill hands, only to see their rally disintegrate into a brawl, when the Methodist temperance band, which they had invited, struck up its favorite tunes.

In fact, in spite of the draft riots, it was during the Civil War decade that the great wall of hatred between the basically Protestant trade union movement and the Irish Americans was first breached. A few thousand Irish immigrants and many more of their sons found jobs in plumbing, carpentry, bricklaying, and iron foundries and rolling mills, where trade unions had a significant presence. By 1870 almost 17,000 Irish immigrants worked in shoe factories and 23,000 in coal mines, where the two largest unions in the country flourished (the Knights of St. Crispin and the Workingmen's Benevolent Association). Two central labor councils appeared in New York City, the Arbeiter-Union embracing most of the German organizations and the Workingmen's Union with 22 of the 86 unions which conducted their affairs in English. Although the predominantly Irish groups, like the 8,000 strong Longshoremen's and Laborers' United Benevolent Society, held aloof from the Workingmen's Union, two recent immigrants were among the leading lights of that council: Thomas Masterson, a Fenian shoemaker, and Robert Blissert, a tailor and organizer for the International Workingmen's Association. The Fenian Brotherhood was warmly welcomed as an ally by the American labor movement, because of its ardently republican and anti-British stance, and the Lincoln administration itself had encouraged the Brotherhood to proselytize within the ranks of the Union army.

These developments made possible the first significant participation of Irish Americans in unions which were not based on neighborhood or nationality. Sons of immigrants, like William McLaughlin the shoe worker, Terence Powderly the machinist, and Patrick Collins the upholsterer, and veterans of British industrial life, like John Siney and John Welsh of the miners and Hugh McLaughlin of the iron puddlers, played major roles in this transition. They deliberately juxtaposed Irish and American poetry and songs in the pages of labor newspapers, made sure that there were Catholic as well as Methodist bands, and stressed their common devotion to "the Union of the States and the union of the workers." The great parades in Massachusetts's shoe towns, which celebrated the first anniversary of the Knights of St. Crispin in 1869, all were led off, in the words of one press report, by "American and Irish flags, typical of the unity of race and feeling on the occasion."

Years later Terence Powderly summed up his perception of the task he and his colleagues had faced in these days:

When I began my work I found men arrayed against each other in hostile camps, on religious lines, on political lines and on race lines. My constant plea was to think for themselves. If a man made bottles, stoves, shoes, locomotives or shoveled the refuse off the streets as a scavenger, he, of all men, should know what his labor was worth and should not be obliged to go to a clergyman, a politician or some big man of his own race to tell him how much he weighed in the industrial scale.

THE LABOR MOVEMENT, 1870–1900

The Irish-American community and the American labor movement came of age together in the last quarter of the nineteenth century. The rapid development of urban life had given rise to clear social differentiation among Irish Americans, including some rich and powerful families, and to middle-class hegemony over many of the community's political and social organizations. As E. P. Hutchinson has pointed out, 5 to 6 percent of the Irish Americans were manufacturers, professionals, bankers, and other members of the upper middle class of 1900, and 16 to 17 percent occupied lower middle-class stations, a stratification which was quite similar to that of urbanized native Protestants.

Although some Irish Americans had risen to the top in almost every line of economic endeavor, they were especially prominent as contractors in the construction of buildings. No less than 17 percent of all the contractors identified by the 1870 census had been born in Ireland. They were three times as numerous as either the Germans or the Englishmen in this business, and doubtless many American-born contractors were of Irish parentage. Construction is of special interest to us for three reasons. First, the complex network of subcontracting and low capital requirements which characterized this steadily expanding sector of the economy created an ideal setting for the ambitious poor man, who was determined to get ahead in the world. Second, the decisive role of building permits, government inspection, and public contracts in this industry forced contractors to be involved deeply in local politics, preferably those of the dominant party. The rise of James P. "Sunny Jim" McNichol to the top of Philadelphia's construction industry and Republican party machine simultaneously personifies this link. Third, Irish-American contractors preferred Irish-American employees. A disproportionate number of brick masons, stone cutters, plumbers, steam fitters and boiler-makers were of Irish ancestry, and in newer trades like electricians, elevator riggers, and structural ironworkers their preponderance was even more marked.

The building trades of the larger cities provided the most highly unionized body of workers in late nineteenth century America. They also produced more strikes than any other industry (9,564 between 1880 and 1905, almost three times the number in their closest rival, coal mining), though their average strike involved fewer than 100 workers. The fact that they also held the record for lockouts and sympathetic strikes suggests something of the intensity of organized industrial conflict in this industry. Union practices in construction were determined by two basic facts of life; several employers

were involved in the erection of any one building, and few workers remained longer than a couple of weeks on any one job. Because of the fluid
character of the industry, union wage scales and work rules could be enforced only by the persistent solidarity of the workers themselves—only by
ostracism of the scab.

Thus the building trades provided a case study of two interrelated phenom-
ena. One is the much celebrated rise of some immigrants from rags to riches.
The other is the much ignored forging of a working-class ethical code,
which exalted mutuality over acquisitive individualism and promoted the
group welfare in preference to individual success. The work rules of building
trades unions illustrate this code clearly. Every union had some rule designed
to prevent the subcontracting and sweating practices which everyone knew
provided the first rung on the success ladder and which also made of life a
Darwinian jungle, where they prevailed. The carpenters banned piecework.
The bricklayers prohibited any member from taking employment from a
contractor who did not buy his own bricks. All of them prohibited an
employer from working with tools alongside of his men. Such rules drew a
clear line between worker and boss. Surely if the emergence of a bourgeois
mentality among "upwardly mobile" Irish Americans deserves the attention
which it has received from recent historians, some consideration might be
spared for the corresponding appearance of a working-class consciousness,
which was devoted not to success, but to sober and deliberate group self-help.

Did that word "sober" appear by some prank of my subconscious mind,
or does it also suggest an important aspect of the transformation of consciousness with which we are concerned? At labor congresses of the late
nineteenth century T.A.B. buttons were very much in evidence. Irish Catholic
labor activists who had taken the pledge were as numerous as their Protestant
counterparts. The two accusations which union officials used most often to
discredit their rivals for office were those of pilfering the funds and being
drunk. Many unions had bylaws like that of the Sons of Vulcan, which
specified: if any "member . . . shall be habitually drunk, or neglect his family,
or injure the reputation of the Association . . . there shall be a charge preferred against the offending member."

Terence Powderly devoted the longest chapter of his autobiography
Thirty Years of Labor to the evils of drink, and the revolutionary tailor
Robert Blissert, who conceded that the social atmosphere of the tavern was
better than that of the tenement flat, contended that "liquor was the invention
of hell, and that all its distributors were the devil's imps." What is evident
here is that the cultural values which developed around the labor movement
were different from *both* those of the peasant immigrant and those of the
successful middle class. It is unlikely that Robert Blissert pleased middle-
class ears when he testified that workers who had won shorter hours of toil,
"instead of furnishing their wives with black eyes as they used to, after

spending the evening in the beer-houses, were now found wending their way home reading *Progress and Poverty.*"

Before probing more deeply into the ideology of the labor movement, however, it would be useful to identify two more centers of trade union activity in which Irish Americans were prominent: the metal trades and dock work. The history of Irish Americans in metalworking was a peculiarly fortunate one. Precisely because so many of the Irish immigrants had no manufacturing skills, they became laborers and helpers in iron and steel furnaces, foundries, rolling mills, and fabricating works during the 1850s and 1860s. Over the next twenty years these heavily capitalized industries expanded very rapidly. Their wage levels far exceeded those of the declining handicrafts, such as tailoring and woodworking, into which the more skilled German immigrants had been locked, and the opportunities they afforded for advancement into a skilled craft were great. Iron rollers, heaters, puddlers, and molders had little or no tradition of apprenticeship. They learned the art by doing it. They also had a gruesomely high death rate. Moreover, during the seventies and eighties puddling and molding expanded more by the addition of new furnaces than by technological innovation. Consequently, these crafts, which had been clearly dominated by English and Welsh immigrants in the 1860s, were largely Irish-American domains by the 1880s. The Iron Molders' Union and the Amalgamated Association of Iron and Steel Workers were two of the century's strongest labor organizations.

Longshore work had quickly come under Irish sway, as we have already seen. In southern ports the docks were shared by Irish Americans and blacks, often under elaborate arrangements dividing the piers or, as in the case of the New Orleans screwmen, establishing racial quotas, designed by the organized longshoremen themselves. Dock unionism was resilient, rather than continuous. Unions in all the major ports were incessantly formed, broken, and reformed. In the Deep South, where black dockers were too numerous to be driven out, some of the most impressive manifestations of biracial unionism in the country's history developed. Two general strikes, one in 1892 and the other in 1907, saw black and Irish-American dockers battling shoulder to shoulder against the combined might of the city's astounded and irate establishment.

Old Irish traditions of popular struggle blended with the new lessons of trade unionism and with boycott practices recently made famous by the Land League in the activities of dock workers. New York's once-proud longshoremen's society was broken in a strike of 1874, and the endless flood of immigrants to that city frustrated all efforts to revive unionism for the rest of the century. But the predominantly Irish-American freight handlers, who ferried railroad cargoes across the Hudson River, waged massive strikes in 1882 and 1887. The three most prominent leaders of the 1882 strike

(Jeremiah Murphy, John R. McNamara, and P. J. O'Sullivan) were all from Cork and were all ardent nationalists. They sustained the strike by large street demonstrations and solicited funds from Land League branches, other unions, and municipal governments. Their boycotting committee distributed lists of scabs at the Catholic churches on Sundays, advising that the offenders be "left severely alone." In these strikes, as in those of transit workers during this decade and the next three, neighborhood solidarity proved the key to the strikers' effectiveness in keeping replacements away from the workplace. This may help explain why the few unions of unskilled workers which were able to survive as long as a year or two were made up largely of Irish Americans.

Let us now look more closely at the question of the old and the new in Irish-American attitudes and practices during the late nineteenth century. It may be possible to specify more precisely both how the labor movement affected the Irish-American community and how the Irish-American presence influenced the labor movement. As Terence Powderly had implied in his statement about workers' learning their own worth, the formation of a trade union consciousness involved an important step away from purely ethnic loyalties and traditions. The Irish American bricklayer who walked out on strike together with his mates of English, Welsh, and German stock, against an Irish-American boss, was a common figure in the 1880s. The work rules, standard wage, and closed-shop principle did not come from the Old Sod, nor did the working-class conception of mutuality, which they embodied. Irish immigrants learned them in America (just as migrants from the countryside the world over were learning them in the cities), and more often than not their first teachers were workers of other nationalities. Along with the art and mysteries of a skilled trade one learned the craftsman's moral code. Irish Americans within a single generation became both eager learners of this code and effective teachers of the next wave of immigrants.

Two anecdotes may serve to illustrate the process whereby immigrants learned then transmitted working-class values. The first scene took place at a party thrown by the Allegheny Lodge of the Amalgamated Association of Iron and Steel Workers for an Irish-born puddler, John Morran, who was retiring from the trade to open a grocery store. When Morran had enrolled in the lodge, fourteen years earlier, its members had been mostly Welsh, and it was the veterans of that group who saluted Morran upon his farewell. John J. Morgan orated at length on the subject of how Morran had entered their fellowship:

As I have been very closely associated with Bro. Morran ever since he came into this district, I feel as though I must say a few words in his behalf. When he came here he came from a place where the iron heel of oppression was most sorely felt. So severely had this iron heel pressed upon the necks of those with whom he had been associated that all the manhood had been crushed from them. His nature revolted at such a condition of his fellow men. And finding his attempts to better their condition treated with scorn and contempt, he came to Pittsburgh, and he came freighted with the knowledge of what tyranny would do if not opposed by the strong will of united minds. . . . Brothers, need I tell you what we have gained by the brother's association with us? No! The condition of this lodge testifies to the fact that he has been loyal to the cause he espoused.

It is understandable that Brother Morran's voice was choked with tears, and that even the pounding gavel of the chairman could not stop Brother Abel Jones from leaping to his feet with a Welsh cheer and shouting: "Mr. President and fellow workers, Johnny Morran is a bully good fellow and don't·you forget it." But can one not detect a patronizing tone oozing through this celebration of fraternity? Despite his unpromising origins, Brother Morran proved himself worthy to be one of us.

Yet at almost the same time another ceremony was taking place in New York City. There Abraham Rosenberg was one of hundreds of Jewish cloak makers, recently arrived from Russia, who had gone on strike, then enrolled in the Knights of Labor. Years later Rosenberg wrote:

I still retain in my memory a vivid picture of the scene which took place when the District Master Workman and his deputies, all Irish, came to perform the ceremony of installing us. We were all new in America and we did not understand a word of what was said. We could only see how one of them took a piece of chalk and drew a large circle on the floor and told us to stand around the circle. Then another deputy placed a small sword on the table, and a globe was hung on the side of the door of the meeting-hall.

Many of us seeing the sword were not sure whether we were all going to be slaughtered or drafted into the army. Many of us had already made their peace with themselves. . . . Only later did some of those who understood a little of the ceremony explain to the rest the meaning of it all, namely, that if anyone of us broke his oath and became untrue to the interests of labor, he would be pursued by the sword, and be unable to escape because the Knights were strong the world over. . . .

Pupils and professors of labor's cause in the same years: but note also how different ethnic flavor was imparted to the same working-class institutions. In fact, it was precisely in the ideology and the cultural tone of labor activities, not in the nature of trade union practice, that the Irish Americans left their distinctive mark. As Rosenberg's story suggests, it was in those labor organizations which were largely created and led by Irish Americans, like New York's famous District Assembly 49 of the Knights of Labor, that secrecy, oaths and elaborate rituals survived most strongly, and survived despite the strictures of the Catholic Church against secret societies. By way of contrast, the German tradition of organizing rings within rings, with each successive circle representing greater secrecy and greater commitment to the cause (as was exemplified by Wilhelm Weitling's League of the Just) passed into oblivion after the Civil War.

Similarly the great attraction of the cause of land reform for the American labor movement, though it was rooted in George Henry Evans's influential National Reform movement of the 1840s, was clearly kept alive and potent by the Irish. Terence Powderly wrote in 1883 that the "key note which will reach the American heart" was the attack on "the alien land lord who first drives his victims from Irish soil and [then] heads them off in this land by buying (stealing) up the land and compels his slave to go up in an eight story tenement in a large city and live on a crust or pay an exorbitant price for land which God made for all honest men instead of for thieves."

The popularity of this idea is illustrated by the tactic employed by Samuel Gompers and Peter McGuire to defeat a socialist motion for collective ownership of the means of production at the 1894 convention of the American Federation of Labor. They put a successful countermotion for nationalization of the land.

This fixation on the landlord as the worker's mortal foe both helped keep labor organizations of late nineteenth-century America alive with political agitation and provided a major stumbling block in the path of socialists' efforts within the movement. Henry George, who was put forward by New York's Central Labor Union in a dramatic campaign for mayor in 1886, had become known to the city's workers through his frequent columns in the *Irish World*. The Central Labor Union itself had come into existence as a result of a series of trade union rallies of 1881 and 1882 in support of the No Rent campaign in Ireland. At one of those rallies 500 of the freight handlers, who would undertake their famous strike eight months later, marched behind banners and a band to St. Michael's Institute in Jersey City, where they heard Parnell's mother speak.

The closer one looks the more strands appear connecting the labor movement, land reform, and Irish nationalism. Terence Powderly was General Master Workman of the country's largest labor organization, the Knights of Labor, in 1883. At that time he was also mayor of Scranton, Pennsylvania, and a vice-president of the Irish National Land and Industrial League of the United States. After the Philadelphia convention, at which that organization had given way to the new Irish National League of America, Powderly presided over a rally in Scranton, at which Thomas Brennan from Ireland was welcomed to the city. Many Knights of Labor local assemblies and nationalist clubs marched in the grand parade, but it was headed by the Parnell Rifle Club and the Father Mathew Guards, after whom trooped the local branches of the Father Mathew total abstinence union.

Although historians continue to this day the debate initiated by the (London) *Times*'s lawyers against Parnell in 1888–89 over the role of the Clan na Gael in that Philadelphia convention, one thing is certain: Powderly was also a national leader of the Clan na Gael. That connection is very fortunate for historians, because the well-preserved correspondence of the general master workman is filled with Clan na Gael letters. From them we learn that in city after city, leading activists of the trade unions and the Knights were also members of that secret, militant nationalist group. In the little rolling mill town of Woods Run, adjacent to Pittsburgh, for example, forty workers and the priest of St. Andrew's Catholic Church belonged to the Land League, forty-five people had contributed to the Fenian "skirmishing fund," and twenty-one members belonged to the Clan.

Almost every resident of this town was a millworker, and it was a union stronghold. Consequently, we are not surprised to learn that Joseph Good, a puddler from County Cork, who was Master Workman of the local assembly of the Knights and district deputy of the Amalgamated Association of Iron and Steel Workers (as well as being prominent in the Total Abstinence and Beneficial Society) was also Junior Guardian of D.221, Clan na Gael. James Cain, a staunch supporter of the Greenback Labor party and President of Bishop Lodge of the iron and steel workers, was Senior Guardian of the D., and he used union stationery freely in connection with its affairs. Thomas Purcell, a common laborer and uncommonly prominent socialist, Michael Woods, a union leader and Democratic politician, Christopher Burns, a pioneer of the puddlers' union, and Andrew Stewart, his local's delegate to the founding convention of the Federation of Organized Trades and Labor Unions—all were active in the Clan na Gael.

These personal links embedded the causes of Irish nationalism and land reform deeply within the American labor movement. They also reinforce the conclusion that one simply cannot rest content with Dennis Clark's conception of the late nineteenth-century Irish-American community as divided into an upwardly mobile middle class and a disreputable "underclass" of drunkards, thieves, and Fenians, however popular that style of thinking may be in America today. The success ethic inspired but one segment of Irish-American society, and however powerful that segment may have become, it is misleading to interpret everyone's history in its terms.

The iron puddlers and rollers of Woods Run produced their own leaders, men of broad political vision, most of them devoted to temperance and all of them staunch trade unionists. They organized themselves into an elaborate network of societies, both public and secret. In some, they advanced their national cause. In others, they joined with fellow workers of other nationalities and religions to promote the welfare of the trade or the political interests of their class. The cultural legacy which they had brought from Ireland blended with the new moral code, which they learned in the factory and the factory town, to produce the complex and resilient ideology, which was their gift to all of American labor.

FOR FURTHER READING

Little specific attention has been given the Irish in this field, which, once again, is so inextricably enmeshed with the Irish presence in the nineteenth century that as with urban politics and the Catholic Church, it is difficult to judge whether it is legitimate even to attempt to extract "Irish" elements: Gary M. Fink, ed., *Biographical Dictionary of American Labor Leaders* (Westport, Conn., 1974); Michael Gordon, "Labor Boycott in New York City, 1880–1886," *Labor History*, 16(1975), 207–11; David Doyle, "The Irish and American Labour, 1880–1920," *Saothar: Journal of the Irish Labour History Society* 1 (1975): 42–53. A great deal can be gleaned from Francis Broderick, *Right Reverend New Dealers: John A. Ryan* (New York, 1963); Henry J. Browne, *The Catholic Church and the Knights of Labor* (Washington, D.C., 1949); John R. Commons, *History of Labor in the United States*, 4 vols. (New York, 1918–35); Marc Karson, *American Labor Unions and Politics, 1900–1918* (Boston, 1965); David Montgomery, *Beyond Equality, 1862–1872* (New York, 1967); from autobiographies and biographies of Mary Ann Harris Jones, "Mother Jones" (1925), Frank Roney (1931, 1976), Father Yorke (1943), Terence V. Powderly (1940) among the Irish-born; from the histories of unions which were heavily Irish, such as those of the plumbers, steam fitters, building trades, teamsters and skilled textile and iron and steel trades, listed in standard bibliographies; and from the official state and national censuses of occupations. Early social reform, and its weakness, is touched on in the works of Cross and Brown, cited previously, and in James E. Rochan, *American Catholics and the Social Question, 1865–1900* (New York, 1976), Aaron I. Abell, *American catholicism and Social Action* (New York, 1960), and in Henry J. Browne and Francis Broderick, here cited. Its culmination, and transformation from a labor and religious movement to a political one, is treated in the works of Huthmacher, Buenker, David O'Brien, and George Q. Flynn, cited elsewhere. Incredibly, the only full work to deal specifically with Irish-American workers, and with a very special case, is Wayne Broehl, *The Molly Maguires* (Cambridge, Mass., 1964), although almost all the local studies, such as those of Handlin, Thernstrom, Clark, Feinstein, Walkowitz, Faler, Shumsky, Degler, Laurie, listed p. 124-25, p. 444, n3 or in Doyle, "Irish America: A Regional Bibliography, 1830–1930," have much material on working lives and culture. Montgomery annotates his own sources fully in his "Na Gaeil agus Gluaiseacht an Lucht Oibre," in S. Ó hAnn-racháin, *Go Meiriceá Siar* (Dublin, 1979), 138–53, in Irish.

THE IRISH
AND THE
AMERICAN
MILITARY
TRADITION

MICHAEL J. COSTELLO

When the American War of Independence began, there were about 4 million white people in 13 states that declared independence. Of these about 60 percent (2.4 million) are estimated to have been of British origin. The highest estimate of the number of Irish birth or descent is 400,000, or 10 percent.

The Irish seem to have been made up of about equal numbers of Presbyterians from Ulster and of Catholics from all parts of Ireland, with a sprinkling of descendants of other planter stock including prominently some of those who came to Ireland with or in the wake of Cromwell or William and became assimilated even to the extent of becoming Irish speakers.

Of the Catholics some were the offspring of indentured servants and of people shipped out by Cromwell as slaves. But the great majority were, like the Ulster Presbyterians, fleeing from oppression in Ireland.

In the words of Ramsay, who wrote the best contemporary history of the period, "they fled from oppression in their native country and could not brook the idea that it should follow them here." The quality, the spirit and the sentiments of the Presbyterians of Ulster at this time can best be understood from the writings of Dr. Dickson, a distinguished founder-member of of the Irish Military History Society.

To the Catholic and Presbyterian emigrants alike the words of the Devon Commission about a later generation may be applied: ". . . the young, the strong, the enterprising and industrious . . . leave us, whilst the old, the idle and the indolent stay with us."

It required great courage and even greater powers of endurance to face and survive the Atlantic crossing and, as most of the Presbyterian immigrants did, to penetrate the wilderness which began in those days in western New York, Pennsylvania, Virginia, Georgia, and the Carolinas. They were the first frontiersmen of whose advance Alistair Cooke has said "the timid never started; the weak died on the way."

Then and for two generations after, they manned the frontiers, kept off the hostile Indians, and thus permitted the Puritans of New England, the planters of the South, and the cosmopolitan traders of New York and Philadelphia to prosper in the peaceful pursuit of trade allied in the case of the more self-righteous Puritans to a dedicated pursuit of religious intolerance.

Among the Catholic immigrants it is important to note the large number of schoolteachers who communicated their spirit of independence and hostility to England to the large proportion of the leaders of the Revolution who were their pupils. Historians who believe that the Irish were at this time almost totally illiterate except for the aristocracy and the urban populations appear to be unaware of the hedge schools and of the fact that literacy in government statistics meant only literacy in English.

Of the 60 percent of the population of the colonies who were of English origin, only a minority supported the Revolution and most of these served in local militia forces scathingly criticized by Washington for their lack of zeal, discipline, and dedication. John Adams said, "One third took up arms, one third were openly or secretly loyalists [Tories] and one third didn't give a damn." New York furnished more soldiers to George III than it did to Washington.

It is therefore not surprising that the Irish 10 percent of the population, according to one well-documented estimate, supplied 38 percent of Washington's soldiers. The British and Loyalists exaggerated the proportion at 50 percent. Most of them served in the Regular Forces (the Continental line), who were almost half the total and the only reliable and mobile part of Washington's forces. The most famous unit was the Pennsylvania Line, which, said General Henry Lee, "might with more propriety have been called the Line of Ireland."

Even more significant than their numerical strength was the quality of the Irish troops. They exhibited the military qualities so often demonstrated in the service of England, France, Spain, and Austria. There are many tributes to their fighting spirit, their joy in battle, and the continuing attitude noted by Spencer of being "great scorners of death." All this was powerfully reinforced by their hostility to or hatred of England and the English. Sir Henry Clinton reported to London that "the emigrants from Ireland are our most serious opponents." A contemporary said: "On more than one occasion Congress owed its existence and America possibly its preservation to the fidelity and firmness of the Irish."

But they had other Irish characteristics besides courage. "Bold and daring, but impatient and refractory"—again the judgment is that of General Lee. They were also fond of whiskey.

The leadership that would get the best out of them had therefore to be good and to be capable of understanding and controlling such highly emotional material. And it was so provided mainly by officers of Irish birth or ancestry. At the outset the leaders came mainly from officers with experience as such in the colonial militia and, to a lesser extent, from men who had been officers in the British army. Later there was an influx of soldiers of fortune from continental Europe, but as the war progressed those who remained or rose to command were mainly Irish. By the end of the war the foreign-born officers who were brigadiers general or higher numbered twenty-six, of whom sixteen were Irish (that is, 61 percent); three were Germans; two each were French and Scottish, and there was one Dane, one Englishman, and one Dutchman. If militia generals and administrators be counted, there were twenty-six Irish generals. Some of these like Montgomery, from Enniskillen, who led the unsuccessful invasion of Canada and was killed at Quebec, Hand from Clyduff, Offaly, and Irvine, also from Enniskillen, had served in the forces of the Crown but adopted the cause of independence. Others, like Knox and Wayne, were from British families that had settled in Ireland, but several, like Sullivan, Moylan, Shee, and Butler, were Irish Catholics whose rise to positions of importance was due to natural ability and to proven successes which caused even the bigots to overlook their race and religion until the war was won. That Washington himself did not share these prejudices is evidenced by his choice of aides-de-camp (ADCs). These were in succession: Joseph Reed, Joseph Carey, Stephen Moylan, John Fitzgerald, and James McHenry, all of Irish birth or extraction.

General John Sullivan was probably the best and was certainly, with Antony Wayne, the most successful general of the Revolution. He was the son of a Kerry schoolmaster and a Cork-born mother who settled in New Hampshire, where their children were born. Four sons fought for America, and Owen, the father, lived to see them hold office as one of Washington's most highly valued generals, as a governor of New Hampshire, as a governor of Massachussetts, as an attorney general of New Hampshire, and federal judge for New Hampshire. From Owen Sullivan's school also came men who became leaders in almost every walk of New England life.

John Sullivan was a prosperous lawyer in Durham when, in 1772, he attended the first Continental Congress in Philadelphia, where he was a strong and able advocate of independence. On 13 November of that year he struck the first blow of the war when he attacked and captured Fort William and Mary at Portsmouth. Included in his booty were fifteen cannon which formed the foundation of the American artillery and played an important part at Bunker Hill. Within six months he was a brigadier general and, fourteen months later, a major general. He had been a keen student of military literature, and this strengthened his natural powers of command. He commanded a brigade at the Siege of Boston and in the Battle of Long Island, where he was taken prisoner. He was exchanged and succeeded General Charles Lee in command of the right wing of the American army. He led the two most successful night attacks of the war at Trenton and

Staten Island, took command of the expeditionary force in Canada when it was disorganized and demoralized after the death of Montgomery, and brought it back successfully to American territory. He fought also at Brandywine, Germantown, and Quaker Hill. In 1779, with 4,000 men, he attacked the combined forces of the New York Loyalists and their Indian allies, the Iroquois, and decisively defeated them at what is now Elmira, New York. He burned their villages and destroyed their orchards and crops. For this he was severely criticized by the Loyalist elements and those Americans who were half-hearted in the struggle. But he was voted the thanks of Congress for his conduct of the campaign. Washington wrote of him that "he had a little tincture of vanity but along with it military genius."

General Anthony Wayne was born in Pennsylvania. The family came originally from Yorkshire, but both his father and grandfather were born in County Wicklow. I would rate him and Sullivan as the best fighting generals of the American Revolutionary army. He recruited, organized, and trained the Fourth Battalion of the Pennsylvania Line and led it in the invasion of Canada. Later, and for most of the war, he commanded the whole Pennsylvania Line. He and his men were well matched and, in the words of General Henry Lee, "singularly fitted for close and stubborn action hand-to-hand." He was known to his men as "Mad Anthony" and he has gone down in history with this nickname.

He distinguished himself for gallantry and good leadership at Three Rivers, Brandywine, Germantown, and Monmouth, where his coolness and courage saved the day after the retreat of General Charles Lee. Wayne's most spectacular effort was the surprise and capture of Stoney Point and not the least valuable of his services was that of overcoming a mutiny of the Pennsylvania Line when, being without pay, without rations, and practically without clothing, they decided to march to lay their grievances before Congress.

In 1792 he was made commander in chief of the American army and led it successfully in a campaign against the Indians, which opened up Ohio and and Indiana to white settlers.

General Henry Knox was born in Boston of Irish parents of Ulster Presbyterian stock. He took part, under Ethan Allen, in the brilliant surprise and capture of Fort Ticonderoga, when 100 cannon were captured. He became chief of artillery to Washington and brought this arm to a high level of efficiency. He was one of Washington's closest friends and became the first secretary of war when Washington became president. He was succeeded by another Irishman, James McHenry of Ballymena, who filled the same office under President Adams as well.

General Stephen Moylan was, like Sullivan, one of a remarkable family of brothers. Born in Cork, where their father was a prosperous merchant, one became Catholic bishop of Kerry and later of Cork. Three went into the shipping business on the Continent, Stephen at Lisbon, John at Cadiz, and

James at l'Orient. James became the agent of the American Congress at that port and rendered important service in fitting out privateers and other vessels turned over by the French to the new American navy. These included John Paul Jones's famous ships *Ranger* and *Bonhomme Richard.*

Stephen, John, and another brother, Jasper, went to America and all gave distinguished service in the Revolution—Joseph became a captain in the Pennsylvania militia, John became clothier general of the army but never got sufficient funds to provide for its needs; Stephen became famous in many capacities. After organizing and leading a Pennsylvania regiment of dragoons in the Continental army, he served for a while as ADC to Washington. Next he was given the almost impossible task of quartermaster general, then the command of a light cavalry group and eventually became chief of cavalry for the whole American army. A close and trusted friend of Washington, he won much admiration for his services and, like Washington himself, made not a few enemies.

He is described as a man of high spirit, of fierce independence, and one not averse to ruffling feathers! Here is the material for a great military tradition, one of which Ireland as well as America could have been justly proud, but it quickly faded and for several reasons.

The regular regiments and especially the Regimental Depots, which are the custodians of the powerful traditions in the British army, did not exist in America. The Continental line, the regulars without whom the war could not have been won even with the powerful aid of France, was disbanded. A regular army, minute in relation to the vast area of the United States and very small even in relation to the population, was widely dispersed over a coastline and frontier of thousands of miles and its traditions became more related to those of the frontiersmen and Indian skirmishes and wars than to the War of Independence. The Irish origin of these frontiersmen was forgotten. They came to think of themselves only as Americans. No element of the population then or since was so quickly assimilated. Theirs was a new tradition having no reference to Ireland and the Irish race. It was a half-century later when religious bigotry again became a powerful force and when it was directed especially at the new wave of Catholic Irish immigrants who came penniless, disease ridden, and broken in spirit to huddle in horrible slums that the descendants of the Ulster Presbyterians began to describe themselves as Scotch Irish.

The depth and the extent of the anti-Catholic and anti-Irish sentiment are some of the most persistent themes in American history. Although founded on the narrow-minded bigotry of the New England Puritans, it was enhanced by several other factors:

1. The assimilation of the Tories and the dominance of English culture made England the main source of opinion and ideas for a most influential

section of the population in the East. English writing and English cartoons of Paddy and his pig had a wide circulation. People of this section became the chief historians and the most influential educators in the nation.

2. The hostility that forced the Irish in on themselves in the city ghettos made them also a homogeneous and powerful force in city politics. This, in turn, intensified the fear and hostility of the classes and groups that now began to call themselves "native" Americans. These factors have been further explored by Lawrence McCaffrey in his essay.

The Regular Army, which might have been expected to carry on the traditions of the Irish soldiers who were dominant in the War of Independence, was for a time extinguished altogether by the following astounding legislation of 2 June 1784.

Whereas standing armies in time of peace are inconsistent with the principles of republican governments, dangerous to the liberties of a free people, and generally converted into destructive engines for establishing despotism;

It is therefore resolved,

That recommendations in lieu of requisitions shall be sent to the several States for raising the troops which may be immediately necessary for garrisoning the Western posts and guarding the magazines of the United States. . . .

Resolved, That the commanding officer be and he is hereby directed to discharge the troops now in the service of the United States, except 25 privates to guard the stores at Fort Pitt and 55 to guard the stores at West Point and other magazines, with a proportionate number of officers, no officer to remain in the service above the rank of captain.

In fact it was of course found necessary to have more than eighty regular soldiers to defend the United States, and there were repeated panic measures to authorize more, followed, when the panic passed, by drastic reductions. The velocity of such expansion and contraction inevitably made the growth of any military tradition impossible in the first quarter of a century of that nation's existence.

It slowly dawned on the legislators that it took more than resolutions of Congress and laws of authorization to make an army. Congress decreed their recruitment but the recruits did not come in. During the most violent of these concertina-like changes, the strength of the Regular Army remained steady at the following pitifully low figures:

1805	2,732 all ranks
1807	2,500 all ranks
1809	2,965 all ranks

If the New Englanders did not win the War of Independence, they wrote its history as well as assuming for a long time the government of the nation, together with the Virginians. Boston's writers emphasized the fact that their region furnished the largest number of the militia mobilized in the war, but ignored or minimized the distinguishing features of these militia units, their continuing history of wholesale desertions, their want of discipline, their repeated panics in battle, and their more or less general refusal to fight or even serve outside New England. They totally excluded from their histories the story of the Irish presence, so much so that Woodrow Wilson could write, in his capacity as a historian, this travesty of history: "The Irish were for the most part heartily loyal to England" and "the Revolutionary war was a conflict between men of the same race and blood."

But in every subsequent war the Irish again became important to the U.S. armed forces. Their military virtues were almost universally recognized in time of need and if the stereotype of the Irishman in peace was the hard-drinking, rough and reckless navvy or the wily politician, the stereotype in time of war was the fighting Irishman. Common expressions such as "getting his Irish up" shows this. So also do cartoons such as one pirated from *Punch* during World War I, and widely republished in America. It shows a respectable character remarking to Paddy, "This is a terrible war Pat." Paddy, on this occasion, is shown without his pig, but otherwise complete with his caubeen, his tattered knee britches, the short clay pipe, and his vacuous face resembling that of the absent pig. His reply is to agree: "Indade a terrible war, your honour, but sure isn't it the only war we've got."

And America had plenty of war (25 years of it in its first 100 years, counting the Indian Wars). Its original 4 million people were submerged in the flood of 45 million immigrants from Europe plus those absorbed with the acquisition from France, Spain, Mexico, and Canada of about 2.5 million square miles of new territory, with their variety of races. Its military tradition up to the great Civil War was the tradition of the frontier, of the tough, brutal, but formidable fighter in the wilderness and a small and neglected Regular Army. Until the Civil War involved the whole nation, the frontier wars and even that in Mexico touched only a small proportion of the population on the ever-moving western frontier.

The advance of the frontier and the opening of the West to settlement played a fundamental role in the development of the American character and in making Americans what they are today. It was a long and variegated conflict with the Indians, the real history of which has been largely obscured in a fog of myth and sentimentality generated in Hollywood and by eastern writers of modern stories. The Indians were superb fighters, because fighting was a condition of their lives and they developed military skills admirably suited to the terrain over which they fought. From early childhood they were trained as warriors and in the calm endurance of pain, hunger, cold, and heat with an almost incredible patience.

Against these the pioneers, mostly the descendants of the Irish who were the core of Washington's army, and the new Regular Army had to equal or better the Indians in military skills and in powers of endurance. The non-commissioned officers (NCOs) and men of the new army included a large proportion of Irish immigrants recruited in New York and New Orleans, with Boston and Philadelphia as less important recruiting grounds. Hollywood is right in portraying the typical NCO as a tough, aggressive Irishman, with many of the characteristics of the frontiersman. Indeed, their life-style as soldiers was very similar to that of the Daniel Boones and Davy Crocketts.

Here we find the main body of the American military tradition, supported by and intertwined in the other constant tradition—that of West Point Military Academy.

Andrew Jackson, the seventh president of the United States, exemplifies and personifies the traditions of the frontier fighter. His parents came from Carrickfergus, and he inherited the stubbornness of his tough Presbyterian ancestors. As a youth he fought in the War of Independence in a minor capacity, and in Indian wars. He had a lifelong hatred of the English and the Indians, mingled with some contempt for them. He was an irreconcilable opponent of the eastern aristocracy and the commercial and banking interests of the larger eastern cities. From his time dates the long-lived tradition of the western log cabin as the best source of presidential material. He first became famous for his leadership of frontier militia and regulars in successes against the Creek Indians in Georgia and Alabama. In the War of 1812 he became a major general, captured Pensacola, and inflicted a crushing defeat on Packenham's British army at New Orleans. This was America's only victory on land in this war, which was otherwise a series of debacles almost comic opera in character.

He was a tough combative person who fought several duels. He was vigorous, brusque in manner, uncouth, and relentless, but absolutely straightforward and open. He not only represented "the spirit and the temper of the American of his day" but also represents the tradition which has been dominant in the U.S. Regular Army and in the militia and National Guard of the states other than those on the north and center of the eastern seaboard.

THE CIVIL WAR

Like the contribution of the Irish in the War of Independence, their role in the Civil War has been minimized by American historians, but it has been generously acknowledged by the best historians of the period, especially by the British General Henderson in his classic *Stonewall Jackson and the American Civil War*, and is more widely recognized than their earlier contributions to independence and frontier defense.

The immense importance of the Irish contribution has been obscured in Ireland by the focusing of attention on T. F. Meagher and the Irish Brigade in the Army of the Potomac. This, in part, accounts for the fact that Irish historians have largely ignored the far more significant contributions of other Irish regiments—Confederate as well as Union. It also accounts for our neglect of possibly the greatest of all the generals who have served America—the Cavan-born Philip Sheridan. He was and is appraised at his true worth in Germany and France and albeit grudgingly in England. Significantly, he was the first Irish-born West Pointer, and to gain his admission his nominator thought it necessary to pretend that he was American-born.

As modern American historians, notably Bruce Catton and D. S. Freeman, give a balanced and professional picture of the Civil War, the decisive importance of Sheridan has become better appreciated in America but not yet in the land of his birth. In the persons of James Shields and Pat Clebourne Irishmen can salute with pride two other fellow countrymen whose contribution to the American military tradition has never been surpassed. Established during the Revolutionary War, it was a tradition of ready participation in the nation's wars by Irish immigrants and their offspring, and of risk taking and courageous efforts on the part of their officers. They in turn helped to establish the respectability of successive generations of Irishmen in the mind of America, a mind which, despite its inconstancy to the value of military tradition, has always admired the integrity of soldierly courage.

FOR FURTHER READING

Russell Weigley, *History of the United States Army* (New York, 1967), outlines the tradition and reviews the literature; Fritz Kredel and F. P. Todd, *Soldiers of the American Army, 1775–1954* (New York, 1954), study its manpower. Don Higginbotham, *The War of American Independence* (New York, 1971), is best upon its military aspects. Early organization, in which Knox, McHenry, Barry, and others were prominent, is covered in Harry M. Ward, *The Department of War, 1781–95* (Pittsburgh, Pa., 1962), and Marshall Smelser, *Congress Founds the Navy, 1787–1798* (Notre Dame, Ind., 1959). The Irish element in the revolutionary war is best followed in Arthur Alexander, "Pennsylvania's Militia," *Penn. Mag. Hist. Biog.* 69 (1945): 15 ff.; Robert C. Pugh, "The Revolutionary Militia in the Southern Campaigns," *William and Mary Quarterly*, 3rd ser., 14 (1957): 154 ff.; William B. Clark, *Benjamin Franklin's Privateers* (Baton Rouge, La., 1956); Jack and Marian Kaminkow, *Mariners of the American Revolution* (Baltimore, 1967); Burke Davis, *Cowpens-Guilford Courthouse Campaign* (Philadelphia, 1962); Freeman Hart, *The Valley of Virginia in the American Revolution* (Chapel Hill, N.C., 1942); Lyman C. Draper, *King's Mountain and Its Heroes* (New York, 1929), and in the works of Dunaway, Metzger, and Doyle noted previously. Specific figures have been studied in Richard D. Knopf, ed., *Anthony Wayne* (Pittsburgh, Pa., 1960); Charles P. Whittemore, *General of the Revolution, John Sullivan* (New York, 1961); B. C. Steiner, *Life and Correspondence of James McHenry* (Cleveland, 1907); North Callahan, *Henry Knox* (New York, 1958), and W. S. Murphy, "Four Soldiers of the American Revolution," *Irish Sword: Journal of the Military History Society of Ireland* 5 (1962): 164–74.

W. S. Murphy, "Four American Officers of the War of 1812," *Irish Sword* 6 (1963–64): 1–12, and Blanche M. McEniry, *American Catholics in the War with Mexico* (Washington, D.C., 1937), can be supplemented by Potter, *To the Golden*

Door, pp. 473–98. The emergence of an Irish-American, as against immigrant, tradition, is also implicit in these, as in Thomas Kearny, *General Philip Kearny* (New York, 1937); Dwight L. Clarke, *Stephen W. Kearny* (Norman, Okla., Richard O'Connor, *Sheridan* (Indianapolis, Ind., 1953); and Philip H. Sheridan, *Personal Memoirs* (New York, 1888). Papal nuncio Gaetano Bedini believed with his visit in 1853 that the U.S. navy was the one area of national life fully free of anti-Catholic prejudice, a fact perhaps owing to its founding Irish elements: see, for example, William B. Clark, *Gallant John Barry, 1745–1803* (New York, 1938), and Joseph Gurn, *Commodore John Barry* (New York, 1933); Carroll S. Alden, *Lawrence Kearny* (Princeton, N.J., 1936); and Homer L. Calkin, "James Leander Cathcart and the U.S. Navy," *Irish Sword* 3 (1957–58): 145–58.

For the Irish in the Civil War, apart from considerable material in the regional histories of the Irish, and the general studies of the Civil War and its campaigns, see James F. Maguire, *The Irish in America* (London, 1868), pp. 545–89; Robert F. Athearn, *Thomas Francis Meagher* (Boulder, Colo., 1949), pp. 89–142; Paul Jones, *The Irish Brigade* (New York, 1969), journalistic and undocumented, but loosely based upon obvious standard sources; Ella Lonn, *Foreigners in the Confederacy* (Chapel Hill, N.C., 1940) and *Foreigners in the Union Army and Navy* (Baton Rouge, La., 1951); Joseph M. Hernon, *Celts, Catholics and Copperheads: Ireland Views the American Civil War* (Columbus, Ohio, 1968); William Hanchett, *"Irish": Charles G. Halpine in the Civil War* (Syracuse, N.Y., 1970); J. L. Garland, "Irish Soldiers of the American Confederacy, " *Irish Sword* 1(1949–53): 174–80; William Corby, *Memoirs of Chaplain Life* (Chicago, 1893); Alf McLochlain, "Three Ballads of the American Civil War," *Irish Sword* 6 (1963–64): 29–33.

On the Spanish-American War, see Doyle, *Irish Americans, Native Rights and National Empires* (New York, 1976), pp. 165–223, and on Irishmen in the subsequent Filipino war, Edmund Mc Devitt, *The First California's Chaplain* (Fresno, Calif., 1956). Awards to the Irish-born are documented in William D. O'Ryan and Robert M. Gaynor, "Irish Recipients of Awards for Bravery in the U.S. Armed Forces," *Irish Sword* 8 (1967–68): 274–76, and listed in *Irish Sword* 12 (1975): 149–51. The support of the Catholic Church for the tradition is found in Dorothy Dohen, *Nationalism and American Catholicism* (New York, 1967), and standard biographies of the bishops. As yet, the *Congressional Record* is the source for that of politicians such as Congressman John F. Fitzgerald and Denis Hurley in the 1890s, and their successors, who took a prominent role in funding a modernized army and navy.

PART THREE
INTERPRETING
THE TRADITION

THE AMERICAN ACHIEVEMENT: A REPORT FROM GREAT IRELAND

ANDREW M. GREELEY

Somewhere in the Icelandic saga of Eric the Red, that marvelous character (and himself doubtless seven-eighths Irish) sails beyond Iceland and beyond Greenland to a place which he refers to as "Great Ireland," a great land across the sea already inhabited by Irish monks. If we are to take Eric the Red at his word—and, of course, we must—then substantially after the Holy Navigator Brendan and substantially before Christopher Columbus there was an Irish settlement somewhere on the North American mainland. Serious scholars will tell you that Great Ireland, if it existed at all, was probably in Newfoundland or Nova Scotia; but those of us who really understand such things know better. Great Ireland was either Queens in New York or Cook County in Illinois.

Let me make it clear before I begin that if I refer to the Irish in North America as "Great Ireland," I intend no qualitative comparisons, only quantitative. There are in Great Ireland 22 million people who claim to be Irish—presumably most of them have some justification for the claim. This is five times as many, give or take a few million, perhaps, as there are on the ancestral isle. As to qualitative matters, ah well, those of us from Great Ireland will be very modest indeed. We have a long way to go to catch up with "Little Ireland."

Before I set about my principal task of describing the economic and social achievement of the American Irish and the costs of that achievement, let me make some preliminary observations.

First, Bernard Shaw once said that England and the United States were two nations separated by a common language. If I may modify his paradox, Great Ireland and Old Ireland are two nations separated by a common heritage; and if the two Irelands are to understand one another (to say nothing of the other Irelands that have sprung up in England, Canada, New Zealand, Australia, and all the other places of the world to which the Irish made pilgrimage), we must be conscious of those things about which we differ.

I am always struck when I get off the plane at Shannon or Dublin that everybody in Ireland looks Irish. It is like I am back home on the South Side of Chicago except that the Slavic, Latin, Teuton, and Anglo-Saxon faces are all gone. But each time I must make the mental adjustment to the fact that the people at the airport may look like the crowd that used to come pouring out of Christ the King Church in my neighborhood in Chicago in the 1950s and 1960s, and in many critical respects they are the same kind of people; but they have had different experiences for the past hundred years. If I wish to understand them and they wish to understand me, we must be clear about these different experiences.

The first thing to note is that although there has been a stream of Irish immigration to the United States up to the present, most of the immigration was finished by 1900. Eighty percent of the Irish Catholic population in the United States are third or fourth generation, which is to say that their grandparents or their great-grandparents were the immigrants. That means that many of our predecessors left Ireland quite unaffected by what I take to be two of the most critical cultural influences that shaped contemporary Ireland, the Celtic revival and the political conflicts that led to the emergence of the Republic of Ireland. My own grandparents, as far as I can calculate, left about the time of the Land League; they were certainly gone before the fall of Parnell, and knew, for the most part, only what they read in American newspapers about the political history of Ireland after the turn of the century. What's more, they had their own political and cultural problems in the United States, and although some of my parents' and grandparents' generation may have bothered to be interested in what was going on in the home country, it was an interest from a distance for the most part. More recent Irish immigrants to the United States often complain to me about the low levels of interest among the American Irish in either the Irish literary heritage or (depending on the immigrant's particular cause) the political struggles in the North. My answer to such complaints is that most of us were gone before Easter Rising, indeed long before the Irish language revival. For us, these events took place in another country; we were more than sufficiently preoccupied in the country that was now our own.

I do not mean, as I hope to demonstrate in this paper, that we have ceased to be Irish, but our experience of the past 80 to 100 years has not been the same as that of those who remained in Ireland. On both sides of Brendan's ocean, we ought to be clear about that.

Secondly, I shall confine myself to that slightly less than half of the Irish-American population that is Catholic. I do so neither to slight the contributions of the so-called Scots-Irish to American life (more presidents, according to some counts, than other ethnic groups, for example); not do I intend to slight the contributions made by Protestant citizens in the Republic of Ireland. I make my decision for two reasons: first of all, it would appear that much of the Irish Protestant immigration came before 1800, and that this so-called

Scottish-Irish group had a very different cultural and historical background from the later migrations of "mere Irish," most of whom were Irish Catholic (as still are most of their descendants). Also there is very little literature available about Irish Protestants in the twentieth century. Paradoxically enough, they are a relatively unknown segment of the American population, perhaps in part because they tend to live in southern rural and mountainous districts. To try to discuss these two groups with different cultural backgrounds and different experiences in American life in the same essay would confuse and obscure the issue, I think. So I shall limit myself to the perhaps 10 million Irish Catholics in the United States, virtually all of whose ancestors migrated from what is now the Republic of Ireland (and the Catholic districts of the Six Counties) and who came from the late 1840s to the late 1890s for the most part.

Thirdly, there are many different ways to judge the achievements of a people. My concern as a sociologist is not with the individual but with the general population. I do not intend for a minute to deny the achievements of the artist, the poet, the tycoon, the general, the entertainer, the athlete, the novelist; my concern as a professional sociologist is with the ordinary people and their efforts to climb out of poverty and misery, to overcome the obstacles of oppression, bigotry, and fear, and find a new and better life for themselves and their children. To anticipate one of my major theses, the economic and social achievement of the American Irish is one of the most remarkable accomplishments in social history.

My final preliminary remark has to do with terminology. I intend to make use of four "tool words" in stating my theses. "A tool word" can have many different meanings, and a writer is free to attach any one of the various available meanings that suit him so long as he is precise about which meaning he is using. A writer has the right to ask his readers to accept the fact that he is using his tool word only in the narrow sense in which he defines it, and presumably the reader will extend to writers the privilege of defining their own terms. My four terms are:

1. *Population.* By "population" I mean the collectivity of people of whom a given attribute can be predicated without any implication that the members of this collectivity relate to one another in any institutionalized or self-conscious way. When I speak of the Irish-American population, I mean that group of Americans who when asked their nationality background will say "Irish" and when asked their religion will say "Catholic."
2. *Community.* By "community" I mean a population insofar as it is institutionally organized or psychologically self-conscious.
3. *Culture.* By "culture" I mean, here at any rate, those characteristics of a population on which its members have higher or lower mean scores than do members of other populations on measures such as family structure, the nature of interpersonal styles, political propensities, attitudes and

values (particularly those concerning the ultimate nature of reality), eating and drinking patterns, attitudes towards child rearing, and so on.

4. *Heritage*. By "heritage" I mean self-conscious culture; that is, a person is aware of his heritage when he realizes that in some respects his culture is different from that of other populations and when he understands and appreciates the most important, most significant, and most excellent creations of his cultural history.

Now, after this all too lengthy preliminary, I am in a position to state my thesis: the Irish population has flourished economically and socially in the United States, but the Irish community is loosely organized, if at all, and only intermittently strong in its self-consciousness. The Irish culture has persisted, indeed sometimes with remarkable tenacity; but self-consciousness about the Irish heritage is almost nonexistent. However, because of the survival of an unselfconscious Irish culture, there is always room for a revival of the heritage and some signs that it is in fact reviving.

I shall say little in my remarks about the institutional organization of the Irish-American community except that it ought to be self-evident that there are no national organizations or journals which speak either for or to more than small segments of the Irish-American population.

First of all, then, the facts of the social and economic achievement of the American Irish. They can be stated rather briefly. The Irish Catholics in the United States are the most successful economically, occupationally, and educationally of any of the Gentile groups in American society. The national average in educational attainment is 11.5 years; for the Irish Catholics it is 12.5 years (one-tenth of a year higher than that of the British Protestants, though less than the Jewish attainment of 14.0 years). On a scale running from 0 to 100, the national occupational prestige score is 40; the Irish Catholic score is 44, again higher than any other Gentile ethnic group in American society (British Protestants score 43), though less than the Jewish score of 48. In income, the Irish Catholic annual family income is $2,473 above the national average—less than the $3,387 above the national average for Jewish families but substantially more than the $401 above the average for British Protestants.

Let me fill in with some technical comment for the social scientists who may be lurking in the wings. We are working with a national probability sample of 18,000 respondents, the largest ever used in religio-ethnic research in the United States. The comparisons being made are limited to whites (so the Protestant average is not pulled down by the lower income and educational levels of black Protestants), and we have taken into account the possibility that the concentration of the Irish in cities in the northeastern and midwestern sections of the country might have given them some disproportionate geographic advantage. Finally, the superior achievement of the Irish in income does not result from the fact that there are more wage earners among the Irish families than in other families.

These data run counter to much of the conventional wisdom about Irish Catholics in the United States; indeed, the data are at variance with the conventional wisdom among many of the Irish themselves. Distinguished American-Irish commentators such as Senator Daniel P. Moynihan and Ambassador William Shannon once lamented the failure of the American Irish to be economically, socially, and educationally successful. Many of the Irish and non-Irish writers on the subject have evolved all kinds of complex explanations for the economic "failure" of the American Irish, including rigid church control, lower middle-class respectability, and, of course, "the creetur." Many such writers (though scarcely Senator Moynihan) have not tried to find an explanation for the Irish success that these data suggest. Indeed, not a few of them reject them out of hand. One crypto-Irishman on the Harvard faculty told me that he once attended a Harvard faculty dinner party in which the report containing these findings was ridiculed as being patently absurd.

(Let me simply note here that our findings are unassailable and that no competent specialist in demography would ever expect them to be reversed.)

What is more, it would appear that the Irish success in the United States goes back a long time. Our data enabled us to estimate that college attendance rates for Irish Americans was high as far back as World War I. At that time the national average for college attendance of young people of college age was 17 percent, but one quarter of the Irish Catholics who came of age in that era went to college; and the national college attendance rate for Irish Catholics has been substantially above the national average ever since. At present a little more than two-fifths of American young people in their twenties have attended college, but three-fifths of the Irish Catholics have, which is an attendance rate approximately that of American Episcopalians.

It is perhaps the misfortune of the American Irish that the group to which they have always been compared is the Jews, whose success in American society has been even more spectacular. But the Jews, while victims of persecution and discrimination in eastern Europe, were a literate, urban or at least townspeople; many of them had several generations of background in small commercial activities. The overwhelming majority of the Irish, however, were land-hungry rural proletarians. In the first decades of the immigration, at any rate, the Irish were often illiterate and even non-English speaking or speaking English only as a second language. Comparisons are odious—especially when they are between two groups that have fought, cooperated, competed, and joined hands in a complex relationship in the cities and in the Democratic party of the United States. One can simply say that the Irish have not been as successful as the Jews, but neither has anyone else; and the Irish are more successful than any other Gentile group in the United States. Who would have thought it?

In fact, who believes it?

My second point is that a very heavy price has been paid for this achievement. To detail the nature of this price, let me sketch out very quickly what I take to be four critical components of the Irish heritage—hoping that readers will excuse me for drastically oversimplifiying.

First, I take it that most of the things that shaped modern Europe did not happen in Ireland. Therefore the line between Irish culture—stories, poetry, language, music, dreams—and the remote past is cleaner, purer, and more direct than it is in most European countries. Ireland was never invaded by the Romans, the Teutons, or the Goths. It was far distant from the religious controversies of the early councils of the church; it was relatively uninfluenced by the Reformation, the Renaissance, the French Revolution, and, until very recently, the Industrial Revolution. The ancient ways survived much longer in Ireland than in any other place in western Europe. For example, it seems that our ancient ancestors had far more extensive vocabularies than we moderns do. They may not have been able to read and write, but they had much richer and more flexible ways of expressing their thoughts to one another. In the modern world this has been lost. The typical human vocabulary for ordinary usage is about 4,000 words; but among the Irish speaking in the west of Ireland, it is 6,000 words, and the closer one gets to the Gaeltacht, the more words one has in one's vocabulary. The love affair with words that is part of being Irish, and to a very considerable extent part of being Irish American, represents a direct line to the very ancient and very rich past. That this old Irish culture was worth anything began to be appreciated only with the Celtic revival that began around 1900. I would note again that by that time most of our ancestors had left the country.

My second comment is that Irish politics has rarely been the politics of ideology and issue but of loyalty, friendship, coalition, compromise, consensus (this despite Ireland's history of revolts, which were exceptions). My friend and colleague Professor Emmet Larkin has pointed out that the modern Irish political style grew up in the nineteenth century when men like Daniel O'Connell and, later, Parnell combined the skills of the British parliamentarians with west-of-Ireland clan loyalty. Larkin points out, appropriately, I think, that this was precisely the kind of political style that would prove indispensable in American urban politics. Contrary to popular belief, many of the Famine immigrants came not knowing the language necessarily but knowing politics, which was, in fact, more important.

My third comment is that the Irish Catholic tradition is very ancient, perhaps the oldest in Europe. It is thoroughly Catholic, of course, but also very, very Irish, which makes it also unique and special. (Incidentally, I do not mean by "Irish Catholic tradition" the set of rigid pieties that some people equate with it. As Larkin has pointed out, this is mostly a middle nineteenth-century addition to a much older religious tradition.) In truth we do not know how Ireland was converted; King Leary of Tara was not, after all, converted by Patrick, and 150 years later, his descendant, King Dermot, was still not a Christian. By the time the great missionary saints like Brendan and Columkille set forth to other countries, Ireland was still probably only half-Christian. Yet it is the only country in Europe to become Christian without conflict, without martyrs, without compulsion. Slowly, gently, it would seem almost without knowing it, the land became Catholic. As the result of this gradual and gentle change, much that was good and rich and wonderful in pre-Christian Irish paganism was preserved. For example, the Celtic cross was originally a fertility symbol. The monks did not throw it out—they merely used it to represent Jesus and Mary and the reflection of the unity of masculine and feminine in God. We also know that the Brigid cross, which I like to wear on my lapel, is an ancient, Indo-European, sun symbol that represents the wheel of the sun moving back and forth across sky. The pre-Christian goddess, Brigid, was the goddess of the sun, and that cross was her symbol. Her feast was February 1 and her sacred fire burned in Kildare. Conveniently enough there was also a Christian Brigid, who wears on her religious habit (and on the ancient Celtic brow, be it noted) the sun symbol. The Christian Brigid's feast is February 1 and her monastery just happened to be in Kildare. To make the tie-in with the femininity of God just about perfect, at least some of the early Irish Christians, not completely cured of their pre-Christian past, thought Brigid might just possibly be the Virgin Mary reincarnate—a nice touch if theologically untenable.

There was a very strong rule of penitential discipline in the Irish monasteries. (Many writers today think that its rigors were exaggerated in order to impress the Romans in the controversy over the dating of Easter in the seventh century A.D.—and, after all, exaggeration is an Irish trait with which we are not unfamiliar. Incidentally, the Irish lost the fight with Rome over the dating of Easter. On historical grounds it is now clear that the Irish were right—we usually are, though it is only official when a Roman admits it.) There was also a great love for nature, for color, for human friendship, for argument, and for warm sensuousness (in the good sense of the word). The old pagan stories and tales of people like Deirdre, Maeve, and Finn McCool were not suppressed but lovingly written down, in beautifully illustrated and illuminated texts in the same way the Bible was written down. Warmth, beauty, softness, sensitivity to the God that lurked everywhere in nature were and are very much a part of the essence of Irish Catholicism. St. Brigid (or more likely the monkish bard who put the words in her mouth) pictures God as an Irish King come to a great feast that has been prepared for him. She says she would like to have a great pool of ale for the King of Kings, and she would like the heavenly host to be drinking it for all eternity—a religious sentiment that I think would hardly be held inappropriate here at the Cumann Merriman.

Now this poem is very Catholic, and I would suggest that only in the Irish Catholic tradition would anyone be so brave and so daring as to picture God coming to a party and actually enjoying it (much the way Jesus must have enjoyed the marriage feast at Cana). So when I occasionally refer to God as "the Old Fella," I am doing so right out of the old Irish Catholic tradition.

Another part of the Irish tradition is learning. The druids may not have had an elaborate written language, but they were passionately interested in understanding how things worked. Their successors, the monks, were committed scholars as well as holy men. They wrote down all the ancient pagan folktales and sagas of Ireland and at the same time preserved European culture during the terrible invasions of the fifth, sixth, and seventh centuries. It is no exaggeration to say that had it not been for the Irish monasteries, much of the Greek and Roman learning would have been lost. The modern world might never have come to be.

(Incidentally, no one can read the tales of ancient Ireland that the monks set down and think that the Irish were rigid, narrow puritans. Such characters as Finn McCool, Dermot, Grania, Deirdre, and Maeve were no better than they had to be —and it turns out they did not have to be very good.)

Let it be noted in winding up this point that now the modern world has suddenly rediscovered the importance of these things I have suggested Ireland has had all along. We are now convinced that in folk song, dance, and story there are rich resources from the past that should not be lost. We are also becoming increasingly convinced once again that neighborhood, freedom of choice, pluralism, and the politics of coalition and consensus are the way free humans ought to govern themselves; that loyalty is saying that after all we do encounter God not merely in abstract philosophy books, dry catechisms, or tiresome sermons but in the experiences of the warmth and beauty of daily life. Characteristic of all things Irish, we are finally praised when it is almost too late for us to enjoy it.

As I have said, the performance of the American Irish in the social and economic world has been remarkable—and not easy. They said we were too poor, too ignorant, too contentious, too church-ridden, and too often drunk to make it. They pictured us as no better than an ape in a stovepipe hat, clutching a mug of beer in one fist and a shillelagh in the other. They laughed at us, and now we can laugh all the way to the bank and the country club.

One of the reasons for our success was our immense store of political skills. We knew how to put together coalitions, to arrange compromises with which everybody could live even though they made no one completely happy. We did so, I think, usually unselfconsciously, not realizing that we were engaging in particularly Irish behavior but just taking it for granted that that was how people acted in the politics of neighborhood, precinct, ward, city, and nation. Similarly, in the ecclesiastical area, despite many disasters past and present, the Irish leadership of the American church, including that great man of Chicago in the first decade of this century, Archbishop James Quigley, held together a coalition of incredibly variegated immigrant groups. And in his case it was done with a style and a pluralistic delight that I am sure will awe historians for centuries to come.

But even though the Irish political style (with the neighborhood manifestations of which Professor McCready deals in this volume) has been immensely successful in holding together urban coalitions, we were never able to articulate a rationale for it; we left the political philosophy and the political science to the "goo-goos" or the "goody-goodies," the reformers, the "better" people, those who thought that government could be run like a corporation, the "rational," scientific bureaucratic types who think that politics is about universal principles, abstract issues, and bureaucratic regulations. Now we have permitted ourselves to be ashamed of machine politics, and if we are sufficiently well educated and successful, we rejoice when periodically it is announced that the last of the great urban political machines is dead. (Chicago has a machine, the city is not bankrupt; New York has no machine and is bankrupt.) Our young people at colleges and universities are put through the deracinating experience that university life is supposed to be and frequently end up with hatred and contempt for a political style and approach (called by my colleague Terry Clark "non-ideological particularism") that is the only way to build effective urban coalition governments in America's polyglot, polychrome society. So just now, precisely when neighborhood communities, coalition, decentralization, and affective politics are becoming fashionable among the most advanced and radical, or, alternatively, the most thoughtful and perceptive, of American thinkers, we are abandoning a political style that had all these characteristics from the beginning. It is an example of what I call Greeley's Law: when Catholics give something up, other people are just beginning to discover it.

We still have our love affair with language and many of us still speak poetry without realizing it, but we have pretty much left behind, at least in any self-conscious and explicit way, an appreciation for the Irish cultural heritage. Oh, we may sing songs on St. Patrick's day (though they are usually Irish-American songs—we have not heard of the Chieftains, for which God forgive us), but we do not read much poetry and (God forgive us again) we write less of it, and as the greatest storytellers the world has ever known, we do not tell very many any more. Now I am not making this as a critical comment; I do not see how it could have been any different for us. Perceive what happened: we came to America desperately poor and clearly unwanted; we were told we could never become respectable Americans. All our efforts

were bent at proving them wrong, that we could become Americans, successful Americans, and still remain Catholic. It meant we had to give up some of
our Irish ways, but, after all, they did not seem to be all that important.

Let me speak of my own family for a moment. Given the time and place
my grandparents were born, they were certainly Irish speakers; they spoke
English too, but Irish was their first language. Yet there is only one word in
our family memory from that fantastically rich and culturally valuable
language, and that is *amadan* ("male fool"). Obviously, my grandparents
made the decision that to become Americans they had to suppress their
own language. I remember very clearly riding downtown on a Lake Street
"El" with my mother and noticing that the people across the aisle were
speaking Italian. She shook her head in dismay. "You really can't be an
American," she told me, "unless you speak English." My mother must have
heard that from her parents. I think that losing the old language was a
heavy price to pay; even if we had no choice, it was still costly. Oddly
enough there are now thousands of young people all around the country
(including two of my nieces) who are taking courses in the Irish language.
There are 400 students enrolled in such courses at the University of Pittsburgh
alone. History has a funny way of doing things.

Or take the matter of names. In my family there are two female names
that keep recurring, "Grace" and "Julia." Well, those are certainly not Celtic
names. We never could figure out where they came from until I went back to
the old country and discovered all kinds of relatives who were "Granias"
and "Sheilas." The grandparents must have decided that they even had to
Anglicize their names. And then, of course, the common culture played a
trick on us and Sheila became perfectly legitimate as a name for Americans
—as did Brian, Kevin, Eileen, Sean, Kathleen, Maureen, and even Deirdre.
(One of my associates at NORC is named Deirdre, and she's black. You see
what I mean about history justifying the Irish in the long run? It reminds me
of Mr. Dooley's famous comment that history always vindicates the Democrats but only after they are dead, "f'r nothin' is iver officially true 'til a
Repooblic'n admits it, and by th' time a Repooblic'n admits anthin' is true,
all th' Dimocrats are long since dead.") I've even known people who changed
their names from Brigid to Beatrice when they came to this country because
they felt that Brigid was too Irish to be "respectable" (to say nothing of
those marvelous nicknames, Bridey and Biddy). The name of the great
goddess of light and of the great Irish saint not respectable enough? No. But
that is what many of our ancestors thought. You cannot blame them for
thinking that way. In the circumstances in which they found themselves
they had no choice.

Nor is there in Irish-American culture much of the softness, the warmth,
the love of nature, the sensuousness, the earthiness that is characteristic of
the Irish Catholic tradition at its best. It may be that that part of the tradition is not strong in Ireland just now either, or so it seems to me; but I can

tell you that Catholicism in Ireland is less uptight, more relaxed, and more playful than it is, or at least has been until very recently, in the United States.

Sometimes, just for the sake of making trouble, I tell people (particularly young radicals who are convinced that their generation has developed something new in the way of sexual freedom) that trial marriage, wife swapping, swinging, and equal rights for women is something the Irish invented. I go on to describe the customs of the Brehon laws and some of the practices of the Irish nobility up to at least the time of the Synod of Kilkenny. Well, they are shocked. That is not the way the Irish are or ought to be. Fair enough, but "The Midnight Court" was a popular poem, and we could do with a lot more of Brian Merriman's attitudes toward sexuality in the church (both in Ireland and the United States) and in the non-Catholic world too. Sex without laughter, Merriman seems to be saying, is also sex without love.

I guess the best way to sum it all up is to say that I do not suppose 99 out of 100 American Irishmen have ever heard of Brian Merriman. I had not myself until about five years ago. Such a lack of awareness of something authentic, unique, and remarkable out of one's past is just plain tragic.

On the other hand, and I think this is critically important to my argument, as well as to the future of the American Irish, we have not stopped being Irish. Perhaps the best way to demonstrate this is to point out that my colleague Professor McCready thought to investigate some time ago the extent to which one could be accurate in predicting the scores of various American ethnic groups on a wide variety of attitudes, values, and behaviors merely on the basis of what one could derive as hypotheses from the European literature about the cultures from which these groups came. McCready's hypotheses were overwhelmingly sustained. Interestingly enough, even though they were relatively early immigrants to American society, the Irish were more distinctive from the British-American mainstream than many of the ethnic groups that came after them. You do not have to realize you are Irish, in other words, to act Irish.

For example, the Irish are the most politically activist group in American society; they are also the most likely to drink and the most likely to have a serious drinking problem; they overchoose journalism and law as professions; their family structure is strong on authority and low on explicit affection and is sharply distinct from that of other American ethnic groups. Their basic world view is the highest of all ethnic collectivities on both fatalism and hope—which is for others a contradiction but for us merely a paradox that makes sense. The Irish are also the American urban ethnic group most likely to visit siblings each week. (Jews and Italians are most likely to visit parents.) They are, despite the adverse publicity given to them in international media, the most socially and politically liberal of Gentile groups in America; and they are also that group which is best able to cope with the problem of growing old. In other words, in politics, in profession, in basic belief, in drinking, in family life, and in growing old, the American Irish are still distinctively and recognizably Irish. (There are some data that show the Irish are more likely than other American ethnic groups to have frequent sexual intercourse. I do not know whether to believe this or not, and I shall refrain from all judgments about how much they might enjoy it!)

How can culture persist if heritage does not? The answer to that question gets us into one of the most fascinating and fundamental research topics in the study of cultural diversity in the United States. Our tentative answer, however, is that certain basic attitudes, traits, values, and behaviors are transmitted across generational lines in the very early years of life, not so much from explicit instruction from parents as from clues provided by the subtle interpersonal environment created by the interactions and atmosphere of family life, particularly that atmosphere of intimacy between father and mother. If ethnic characteristics are passed on at an early stage of life in such a subtle fashion (and all available evidence indicates that they are), then such characteristics will have remarkable durability and can persist largely undiminished for many generations even without self-conscious intention to transmit such characteristics. Thus, for example, to take two of the most characteristic of American-Irish traits, their political activism and their weakness for "the creature," we could find no diminution of this effect either by education, occupation, or length of time a family has been in the country; also there was no relationship between Irish self-consciousness and these two effects.

It is precisely the fact that some ethnic traits can be transmitted across generational lines without any self-conscious intent that makes it possible for a heritage to revive. Young Irish Americans are still writing poetry and short stories without any realization for the most part, of the link between singing and storytelling on the one hand and their past on the other. In fact, the present generation seems more likely to sing and to tell tales than its predecessors perhaps because it feels more free to indulge its literary propensities. Amazingly enough, some of these young people write poems and tales—or so it seems to me—that are quintessentially Irish. One young Irish-American poet to whom I gave a collection of Frank O'Connor's translations of the old poems said to me after devouring the book, "Hey, those people think just like I do!"

As these young people become more and more conscious of the origins of their heritage—and the current ethnic revival in the United States makes this heightened self-consciousness likely—I would suspect that their Irishness will be strengthened and reinforced.

Hence I am more optimistic than people like my friend Professor McCaffrey about the revival of ethnic self-consciousness. I do not say that such a revival will occur; I simply say that the raw material is present for such a revival. If you ask me for my prediction, I will respond with an appropriate mixture of Irish fatalism and hope. For as you know, in any serious Irish conversation two things must be said. First of all, "Ah, they were great times and great places and marvelous people, but, sure, it's all over, it's done with; they'll not see our like again!"

Then, as the evening wears on and more of the creature is consumed, "Well, sure, there's still some of us around."

So by way of brief summary, we became successful, we kept our political style (though unselfconsciously and unexplicitly), but we forgot about or pushed down into our subconscious or unconscious minds the rich memories of our cultural and religious traditions. Yet these traditions still lurk in our personalities because of our early socialization experiences, and they can be recalled and revitalized—with surprising ease, perhaps.

What about the future of the Irish Americans? First of all, I think we should not kid ourselves about the persistence of a residue of anti-Irish feeling in American society. In the environments where most of us live and work, it does not exist, but it is powerful indeed in the great universities, the elite national media, the large foundations, and in many of the more intellectual government bureaucracies. Few Irish Catholics are to be found there, and they are not wanted—not unless they have apostasized and have turned vigorously against their own heritage and their own people. Neither Mayor Richard Daley of Chicago nor Ambassador Daniel Moynihan would be subject to as much hatred and vituperation as they are if they did not have the "misfortune" to be Irish. Recently, for example, I read two insanely vicious attacks on Pat Moynihan, both quite explicitly explaining that he hates little starving children because he is Irish. In the world of lots of people who do the thinking, writing, interpreting, and funding for American society, the old anti-Irish prejudices are fairly strong—and usually unconscious. When you ask, "Don't you think it's bigotry to suggest that most Irish politicians are dishonest or that Pat Moynihan is a stage Irish comedian?", the response is likely to be, "But isn't it true that most Irish politicians are corrupt, and isn't it true that Moynihan says most of the things he does for effect? And isn't that the Irish way of doing things?" These people may not affect our lives directly, but let me assure you, my friends, they affect the world in which we live and in which our children grow up.

Incidentally, on the subject of Richard J. Daley, I have been asked repeatedly by Irish journalists and intellectuals how the Irish Americans ever managed to be captured by such a reactionary fascist. My standard response is that I did not know Irish journalists and intellectuals judged a political leader by what they read about him in a half-column article in *Time* magazine. Like all political leaders Daley made his mistakes; even at his death, he was considered to have been, by almost universal agreement, the best municipal administrator in America. Every time he ran for office, he was reelected not by the Irish but by the blacks and the Poles, capturing 80 percent of the vote from those two very different ethnic groups. In the last election, Daley polled 65 percent of the Jewish vote against a Jewish opponent. No man who was either a reactionary or a fascist could possibly do that. Daley was a very astute, skillful, and sensitive Irish politician—perhaps the best in the twentieth century. It is a measure of the pervasive influence of anti-Irish feelings in the elite sectors of American life that Daley's image in the world press is what it is.

But the anti-Irish feelings ought to be no effective barrier to us. In the final analysis, what comes of the American Irish is something that is up to them. Let me tell you what I think.

The future challenge for Irish Americans will be to recover the spirit of scholarship and learning that is part of our heritage. We are well educated—indeed, the best-educated Gentile group in American society—but we are thin on scholarship and learning. Although we have produced writers like O'Neill and Farrell, O'Connor and Power, they have been alienated from, one might say even pushed out of, the Irish-American community. Let me illustrate what I mean by pointing to the unbelievably brilliant and beautiful book *World of Our Fathers*, by Irving Howe, a book about the New York Jews. No one could write such a book about the Irish-American experience. And it is not that we do not have writers as skilled as Howe, though he is indeed a superlative writer, but because an Irish Catholic Irving Howe would not have available the scholarly and literary resources with which to work. Our Jewish brothers have produced a fantastic amount of scholarly research and literary publications describing their experience in this country. There are Jewish research centers, Jewish studies programs, Jewish-endowed chairs at universities, Jewish scholarly conferences, Jewish literary prizes, Jewish artistic and literary commissions. Even though we are only slightly behind them in income, we have little if any comparable resources for culture study. We cannot talk about our politics, we cannot recapture our experience in either Ireland or America; we cannot rediscover the roots of our own immense cultural heritage without such resources. I am not suggesting that we are inferior to the Jews because they have done it and we have not; I am simply pointing out that we have had different histories in the United States and that now we are beginning to enter an era, I think, when the institutes, the research centers, the funded chairs in Irish or Irish-American studies, the literary prizes, the historical competitions could be as useful a part of Irish-American life as their like are to Jewish-American life. It would be an effective way to refute the bigots and an even more effective way to equip our young people to realize how rich a resource their own tradition is as they begin to enter the worlds of the foundation, the national media, and the university.

There is one very strong response that might be made to this plea of mine for a rediscovery of Irish scholarship and learning, as well as the encouragement of literary and poetic activities. And that is, who needs it? Who cares what they think about us? Who cares what others say? Let the Jews have their novels, their poetry, their magazines, and their chairs of Jewish studies —why should we be bothered?

It is an arguable position. However, it seems to me that there are two weaknesses to it. First, we cheat our fellow Americans that way. There is much in the Irish tradition of politics, culture, and religion that responds to the needs and desires contemporary humans are feeling again—for a warm religion of emotion, the politics of neighborhood, coalition, and loyalty, and for a culture that reaches far into the past and deep into the roots of the human personality. We have that from our tradition—however much we have forgotten it; it would be a shame not to share it with others.

But there is a more important reason, I think, why we should recapture our tradition of scholarship and learning. It is the Irish thing to do. Granted that we first had to establish ourselves in America, granted that much of our education was practical and pragmatic; but now we have made it, and not to be interested in scholarship and learning, not to try do rediscover and share with others the riches of our past would be a horrendously un-Irish way to act. How dare we say that ideas, history, and learning are unimportant, we whose ancestors kept alive the light of civilization for Europe through the Dark Ages? How dare we not respect poetry and storytelling among our own kind, we whose predecessors were the finest poets and the greatest storytellers in the history of the human condition? That we had not the time or the resources to do it until now is understandable, but, God forgive us— and I fear Brigid, Patrick, Columkille, Brendan and all the rest will not—if we turn aside now from the scholarly dimensions of our own tradition.

Let me be blunt about it. For a people whose past is filled with writers, storytellers, poets, and scholars, we have produced in America very few if any of these and have encouraged even fewer. In truth, and again, heaven forgive us for it, we have often discouraged those who wished to pursue learning and culture. And too often it was not merely what one wrote —since what one wrote was rarely read— but the mere fact of writing was sufficient to make people suspicious of one of their own who dared to pursue the literary arts. (And if this sounds like a comment on personal experience, let me assure you that it is.) We did not even have to read our own writers to know we did not like them.

Well, the past is the past, and it had its own reasons, which we must try hard to understand sympathetically. We are still Irish. We are not Irish like our relatives in Ireland are, because for several generations now we have had different experiences. But we are in love with language, we dream great dreams, we are masters of politics, we are paradoxically hopeful fatalists, and we tend to drink too much. We are still Irish. We are the heirs to one of the richest religious, cultural, scholarly, and political traditions of human history. It is time we learned more about it, time for us to understand it better, time for us to give more self-conscious thoughts to who we are and where we came from. It is time we shared our rich resources with our fellow Americans.

FOR FURTHER READING

The interpretation of Irish America herein also draws on the general works cited for L. J. McCaffrey's article, but aspects have been more specifically developed in Andrew Greeley, *The Catholic Experience* (New York, 1967); *Most Distressful Nation: The Taming of the American Irish* (Chicago, 1973); *Why Can't They Be Like Us* (New York, 1975); *Ethnicity in the United States* (New York, 1974); and in various papers in the journals *Ethnicity* and *Journal of Ethnic Studies*. Since this paper was completed, he has amplified many of the points in his *Ethnicity, Denomination and Inequality* (Beverly Hills, Calif., 1976); *An Ugly Little Secret: Anti-Catholicism in North America* (New York, 1977); and in *The American Catholic: A Social Portrait* (New York, 1977).

THE IRISH NEIGHBORHOOD: A CONTRIBUTION TO AMERICAN URBAN LIFE

WILLIAM C. McCREADY

I should like to begin this presentation with a caveat taken from the dedication of Flann O'Brien's *The Dalkey Archive*.

> I dedicate these pages
> to my Guardian Angel
> impressing upon him
> that I'm only fooling
> and warning him
> to see to it that
> there is no misunderstanding
> when I go home.

Today I am a long way from my home on the South Side of Chicago, but I would like to use it as an illustration of one of the most significant contributions of Irish immigrants to American culture, the neighborhood.

It is by now no surprise to even the most casual observer that the United States has become an urban society. This happened in a very short period of time—basically this century. In 1920, 60 percent of the population lived on farms or in small-town rural areas, whereas in 1970, 73 percent of the population lived in large metropolitan areas. The shift has been observed by demographers and social observers for many years, but many of its consequences have gone unnoticed. I would like to discuss the quality of life in an urban environment, and, more specifically, to comment on the unique Irish contribution to the creation of neighborhoods. Other ethnic groups have created neighborhoods in our society, that is true, but it seems to me that none of them has done it in quite the same way as the Irish.

First of all, the Irish neighborhood has persisted long beyond the point of immigration. Even now you can still find some of them in the large cities in the United States. A neighborhood is one of the most creative ways to cope with an urban environment that has yet been devised by man. But before I launch into a detailed discussion of why this is so and what it might mean for the future, I would like to begin with three images of my own neighborhood, which I believe show the essential qualities I am going to be talking about.

FIRST IMAGE

It's Sunday morning, and the sun is out, and it is nearly time for the 11:00 Mass at St. Barnabas. Many of the families on our block are getting ready to go to church; the children are out all dressed up; and the dogs are barking at the strangers who have parked their cars on our street. Sebastian, the Labrador retriever, and Shamoo, the bloodhound, are tracking a little old lady down the street, hoping that perhaps she will turn around and throw them something good to eat. All of a sudden, around the corner, comes a large green and brightly painted bus filled with smiling faces, most of whom are well over the age of sixty. This is known in the neighborhood as "the green bus" or "the fantasy bus." Actually it is chartered by the parish for Sunday mornings to go around the streets of the neighborhood to pick up those parishioners who are too old or to infirm to drive or walk to church. The peasant village had its church bell, we have our "fantasy bus." These buses have become a dramatic and highly visible symbol of the church's presence in the neighborhood. They do more, perhaps, than any other organization or set of sermons or community involvement to tell people that there is a church in the neighborhood and that it is concerned about them.

SECOND IMAGE

It is late summer, just after Labor Day. The schools have opened and we have some new neighbors next door. Three young men bought the old Horton mansion, a large, white Victorian house, with plans to restore it to its original splendor. They are busily cleaning out the basement, the driveway, and the backyard area when one of them gets the bright idea that he will hook up a firehose to a hydrant to wash away the debris that had accumulated on the driveway and the street. Now these are three very nice young men, they make good neighbors and have done a beautiful job with their house; but they did not know very much about fire hydrants. They got the hydrant on, flooded the street, and then tried to shut it off. They could not do it. The fire department was called; they could not do it. The water department came out; they did it, but in the process they turned the valve too fast and the back pressure blew a hole in the street about forty feet down the hill and also blew out the water main underneath my house. (I noticed this because water started bubbling up through my basement floor as I was watching television.) Naturally I complained to the water department people that they ought to fix the hole in the pipe in my basement. They said that it was a city law that they could fix only the water main in the street; they could not go into private property. This was beginning to assume the proportions of a disaster.

To dig through the basement floor, repair the main, and to put a new section in was going to cost me $500 to $1,000. I called my precinct captain, who gave me a number to call, who gave me another number to call and ask for so-and-so, who then led me down the corridor to talk to Mr. What's-his-name. The end result of all these machinations was that a city crew appeared at my door the next morning, dug up my basement, replaced the water main, patched the basement floor; and today you cannot see any ill effects from the broken water main except the signs of new cement.

I am not a politician, but there were politicians in my neighborhood who could ease me through the bureaucracy. In effect, they had made the city work for me in a way I could not have done for myself. I could have spent hundreds of dollars hiring lawyers to argue what I felt was a just case; I could have written to the newspapers and gotten "Action News" on my side to go out and harass city officials; or I could make a couple of phone calls to people who could be trusted to keep their word and to do their best to make the city responsive. I chose the last, and it proved to be the most efficient, the most economical, and the most humane way to get the problem solved.

THIRD IMAGE

It is a nice, warm summer day in the middle of this current year. My friend and colleague Father Andrew Greeley comes into my office and says, "How would you like to go to the Merriman Summer School in Ireland to give a paper on neighborhoods?" I say, "Yeah, sure, fine, Andy," figuring it's another one of his leprechaunish jokes. However, a phone call comes from Con Howard of the Irish Department of Foreign Affairs, and I find it is no joke but a genuine invitation. Not only do I have to finish all the work I had planned to do in the latter part of August by the 15th, but there are arrangments to be made, things to buy, and, last but not least, the children have to be cared for while we are gone.

Now Liam and Nora are very active and energetic six- and three-year-olds. Nancy's mother is seventy-six years old with a very poor memory, and my parents are both working full time at my father's medical practice. So there's a dilemma. There is no time to call a professional babysitter (they usually have to be booked months in advance), and the question is what to do with the children so that we can spend this marvelous time in Ireland.

Well, Liam is staying with Lou and Collette Briody and their six kids, even though we have known them only two years; and Nora is staying with Brian and Catherine Burns, even though we have known them for less than three years. To the outside observer it might seem questionable that we would leave our children with people whom we have known for relatively short periods of time. However, both these families are neighborhood families and people we feel we can trust, people we feel will treat the children as we would. Because of this we were able to go to Ireland unencumbered with worries about our children's well-being. We know they will be treated like the Briody and Burns children would be if they stayed with us—which on many occasions they have.

These three images reflect the genius of the Irish neighborhood in American urban life. It is a blend of religion, politics, and social structure that creates a humane environment in which city people can live. The neighborhood has a way of combating the dehumanizing and alienating forces of the city, and instills in its inhabitants feelings of security in a place that is their very own. The parish, the precinct, and the neighborhood: when they are combined with flair and style, they can provide a unique alternative to many of the deadening and dehumanizing forces that exist in our large cities.

THE PARISH

For most urban American Catholics there is very little distinction between the parish and the neighborhood. The parish is the neighborhood and the neighborhood is the parish, and in Chicago, when you want to find out where someone was born or where they are now living, you do not usually use neighborhood names or street coordinates but rather parish names. "I'm from St. Stanislaus," or "I used to live in St. Killian's, but now I live in St. Barnabas." When I was growing up even Protestants used the Catholic parish name as a means of neighborhood identification.

Many of the immigrant groups attempted to re-create in their new surroundings the culture from which they had recently come. For example, the Polish community in Chicago, which was led by the Resurrectionist Fathers, was built along detailed and rational plans. The large cathedrals that dot Milwaukee Avenue were put there to remind the immigrants of their hometowns in Poland. To the Resurrectionists the creation of this kind of community was a way of preserving the faith of the Polish immigrants. It was also a way of ensuring the continued support of and pressure for a free and independent Poland.

The Italian immigrants, however, led by the Scalabrini Fathers, had a much more relaxed conception of parish community. There was no need to stress weekly mass attendance as a prerequisite of being loyal to the church. Given the fact that Italy was a one-church country, there was no question of people's loyalty to the church, and given the strong ties of Italian family life, a community could be constructed without emphasizing the central function of the church.

The Irish immigrants and clergy, apparently without much in the way of conscious planning, continued to do what they had always done in rural peasant Ireland. As soon as the community was established and the church constructed, it became the social, religious, and political center of the entire community. It is not unusual at my parish church, for example, to see on the same evening a collection of teenagers playing basketball in the parking lot or just "hanging around" waiting for something to happen; an Alcoholics Anonymous meeting going on in the basement of the rectory; and a political strategy meeting of community leaders involved in dealing with one of the local savings and loan institutions gathering on the rectory's second floor. Not all of the people who attend these meetings and gatherings are members of the church; some of them are probably not Catholic, some of them may be of different races. Yet they all identify the church as a powerful and central institution in the community.

The parish is a visible symbol of stability in the community not because it represents the investment of a large impersonal bureaucracy such as the Roman Church but because it represents the investment of many people who consider themselves to be members of a parish and who therefore form a core around which a community can be organized. For Catholics the parish is more than just a focus of social organization; it is also the focus of their faith. Most people do not think of the church as the Pope or the cardinals; they think of it as their local parish. This is where their faith rests in its daily dimensions; this is where they pray, this is where they send their children to be educated.

In a church that is changing as rapidly as the Catholic Church is, the local parish provides a point of stability and a point of contact with the past that enables change to occur with less disruption, fear, and alienation. Many commentators within the church see parochial life as being a narrow, particularistic and confining force within the church. Thet maintain that people cannot be concerned about the global problems of the church, nor can they be concerned about the less fortunate in other lands, nor can they be concerned about the struggles for liberation from oppression in other lands if they are so closely focused upon their own narrow community interests. This point of view reveals a romantic and unrealistic definition of human nature. Humans are social animals; as a result, they tend to live in closely bonded groups when they can. This gives them the strength to go beyond their own survival concerns and begin to think about larger questions. Without the close personal bonds forged in social communities, human beings tend to become atomistic and, as a sociologist would term them, anomic. They lose the sense of belonging that their social nature requires.

In human community particularism and universalism are clearly joined. It is only when we are comfortable and secure in our particularistic communities, such as urban parishes, that we can look with objectivity and compassion upon the situations of other people. An excellent example of this on the current American scene is the conflict over the parochial school system.

The parochial school system is perhaps the greatest achievement of the American Catholic Church. The immigrants built the schools to preserve their culture and their faith. Parochial schools provided an alternative to the discrimination the immigrants felt in the public school systems. Gradually, the clientele of the parochial schools changed so that today it is no longer the immigrants who populate them but the children of immigrants or the children of the children of immigrants. The goal of the schools has changed, too. No longer is it the narrow focus of preserving the immigrants' faith, but rather a true concern for developing Christian perspectives in the modern world.

However, the enemies of particularism see the Catholic schools as evil. We are accused of providing schools for white parents to use to avoid sending their children to school with blacks. This stereotype exists even though the data show the contrary. Most Catholics live in areas that are at least partially integrated. Most Catholics send their children to schools that have at least some black children in them. Catholic schools are probably less lily-white than most other private schools in the country.

The distinguishing characteristic of Catholic schools is that they are responsive to local control. There is no large Catholic school board in the Archdiocese of Chicago that makes policy for all the neighborhood schools and that insists that all the schools abide by the same set of rules. Rather, policy is set down by local boards of education residing in each parish. This method has the advantage of utilizing local talent and local resources rather than alienating them. And all this goes against the conventional wisdom that bigger is better. Bigger may be better in terms of lowering the cost of producing automobiles or lowering the cost of delivering food to people, but it is not necessarily better in all things.

The great asset of the parochial school system is the sense of ownership and possession that the people who attend the schools share. "The parochial school is *our* school, not someone else's." Just as Nancy and I feel comfortable in leaving our children with two neighbors, we also feel comfortable sending our children to the parochial school, because we know that the religious, moral, and social values that we hold are also values held by those who teach in the school.

The parish as a center of worship and liturgy, the parish as a center of community organization and involvement, the parish as a center of locally controlled education—all of these characteristics produce a strong sense of social cohesion within the community. It is no wonder that for most people who live in them, parishes are neighborhoods and neighborhoods are parishes.

THE PRECINCT

The precinct is the smallest political unit in the city. It is the creature of large urban political machines, and it is intended to be a reporting station for keeping track of the vote. In a city that is organized into wards and precincts, the responsibilities are very clear. The ward committeeman is responsible for delivering the vote of his ward, just as the precinct captains are responsible for delivering the vote of their precincts. The voter gets services in return for his vote; it is a straight bargaining situation. The central figure in the urban political machine is the precinct captain. He is an individual from the community who acts as a go-between for the interests of the community and those of the larger political machine. He translates the needs of the community into political issues and translates policies back to the people in terms of their self-interest. Most precinct captains would probably not recognize such an intellectualized description of their work; they would more likely think of themselves as simply listening to people's gripes and then trying to get something done about them. The streetlights do not work, the roads are full of potholes, nobody has taken down the dead trees for the past two years—these are the common complaints of city dwellers. The factor that makes the process work is that the precinct captains are in touch with the identities, the heritage, and the culture of the people they serve. A well-run precinct organization is very hard to beat, as many of the independent candidates in Chicago know all too well.

In addition to being an efficient political organization, the precinct is also an efficient delivery system for social services. Just as central issues in the parish revolve around local control of the schools and the high visibility of the parish as a serving institution, so the central focus of the precinct is around the local control of community services. People in effect trade their votes for services. I do not mean to romanticize political organizations or precincts in this discussion. However, it should be pointed out that they are a relatively efficient system through which leaders and the people they serve can communicate with one another.

The political organization can be mobilized by an individual to remedy specific problems. And that is how I got my water main fixed. But the political organization can also be used by the community at large to make its feelings known about important political and social issues to the larger political entity, that of the municipal government. As cities become larger, more and more urban bureaucracies are spawned. City planners are forever coming up with new ways to modernize the urban environment, but all too often such modernization is done at the expense of the neighborhoods and the communities that exist within them. I do not believe that planners are consciously opposed to neighborhoods; they firmly believe that the modernized bureaucratized and tightly organized planned communities are better places for human beings to live in than the often ugly, seemingly inefficient and disorganized neighborhoods. But they are wrong. It has been proved time and time again that if you take a community of people and put them into brand new high rises or carefully plannned new towns, they will eventually form their own social structures and social organizations. It is the nature of the beast to do so. Why, then, is it necessary to destroy existing social structures and traditional neighborhoods when with a little foresight they could be revitalized and make important contributions to the well-being of the entire society?

The style of political organization represented by precinct captains, ward committeemen, and strong party affiliation is a style that was born out of the urban ethnic experience, and particularly out of the Irish Catholic urban experience.

It comes as no surprise to anyone who has had contact with the Irish in America that they have become consummate politicians. Even though the present Democratic machine in Chicago was started by Anton Cermak in the 1920s, it did not reach its full strength and power until the Irish mayors, Kelly, Kennelly, and Daley, made it work at its optimum.

The hard school of British domination formed the Irish political sense, and the ancient Celtic traditions of language, the telling of stories, and the creation of myths helped them develop their political style. What is politics, after all, but the convincing of those with divergent self-interests that they have more in common than not, while managing to move the amalgamated group forward just a bit farther than it wants to go? And if that is not an engagement in storytelling and mythmaking, I do not know what is.

The Irish language was never really meant to be written down, although Ireland has produced many great writers. It is essentially an oral tradition, meant to be spoken, a tradition of the great story and the tall tale. An Irishman will never tell you a story in the most direct fashion, it seems. He will always approach it with a roundabout way that leaves you wondering if he will ever get to the point. A good example of this is from the beginning of "John Duffy's Brother," by Flann O'Brien.

Strictly speaking, this story should not be written or told at all. To write it or to tell it is to spoil it. This is because the man who had the strange experience we are going to talk about never mentioned it to anybody, and the fact that he kept his secret and sealed it up completely in his memory is the whole point of the story. Thus we must admit that handicap at the beginning—that it is absurd for us to tell the story, absurd for anybody to listen to it and unthinkable that anybody should believe it.

It is clear that the Irish like to "fool around" or to play with language; they like to tease it, cajole it. This is a pastime that can be traced back into the dim prehistory of the Celtic race. The cynical might say that politicians need to play with words in order to avoid being pinned down to a given position or in order to avoid getting caught in a lie. However, there is a much more serious side to it. A politician needs to play with words in order to avoid splitting delicate coalitions that support him.

The Irish political style is something unique in the world. Research in the area indicates that both Irish Catholics and Irish Protestants in the United States have similar political styles; that is, they engage in a wide range of political activities in a particular kind of way. Their political participation levels, for example, differ, with the Irish Protestants being very low-level participators and the Irish Catholics being high-level participators; but when they do what they do, they do it very much alike. The Irish political style tends to be one of personal confrontation that involves all forms of political activity at a very personal level. In other words, they are not limited to petition signing, campaigning, or personal contact with politicians or constituents; they do all of these things and more.

One of the most salient characteristics of the Irish political organizing style is that it works. To many people in America the very mention of the words "Irish politician" conjures up images of smoke-filled rooms, big black cigars, shiny cars, parades, and thousands of vague promises. However, the pertinent question might well be, what else works any better? The quality of life in Chicago is probably no worse and maybe a little better than most other large cities. Our tax base is relatively secure, and the relationships among various ethnic, bureaucratic, and structural components of the city are at least not destructive if not always smooth running.

It is difficult to say why the Irish have taken to politics in such a dramatic fashion. Perhaps it was their history of living under the Penal Laws, perhaps their history of dealing with a repressive British government that has made the Irish so adept at politics. Whatever the reason, the Irish politician in America can be characterized by one word: flair. It may be that they engage in politics for the same reason they tell stories and play around with language; they simply enjoy it; it is fun.

As in all things Irish, there seems to be a paradox here. Although the Irish enjoy word games and like to tell tall stories, the one thing Irish politicians are noted for in the United States is that they keep their word. It is not uncommon, for example, in the bureaucracies of the city of Chicago to hear Poles, Italians, or blacks say that they would much rather deal with an Irish supervisor than anyone else because they know he will keep his word. This also may be traced back to the early times of oppression when the Irish had very little else to go on except the word of another Irishman.

The great advantage of the precinct, therefore, is that it is a political institution human beings can deal with. They can make it responsive to their needs, they can complain to it, they can deal with it as they would another human being. It is not a vast impersonal bureaucracy filled with forms and blinking telephone and computer lights. If you remain loyal to the precinct and continue to vote for its candidates, it will remain loyal to you. A man is only as good as his word.

THE NEIGHBORHOOD

When many of my academic colleagues go away for a portion of the summer either on vacation, to a seminar, to teach summer school or a summer institute, or the kinds of things that academics do, they tend to worry about whether their house will be broken into, whether their possessions will be cared for, whether they should hire some college students to stay in the house, whether those students would have wild parties, and so on. I am over here in beautiful Ennis, several thousand miles away from my home, and my situation is quite different. Two neighbors are staying in my house; they are not charging me anything (nor am I charging them anything). There are twenty or thirty watchdogs on the street led by Sebic and Shamoo, lazily sunning themselves during the day and baying at the moon at night (or at any stray burglar who should happen along); my grass is being cut by neighborhood boys, and my children are being cared for by two neighbors I know will care for them as I would. That is why neighborhoods are good places in which to live.

Neighborhoods are places where people can trust one another, and that is an attribute that is becoming all too hard to find in modern society. I do not mean to romanticize my neighbors; they are pretty much like any other people in the United States, and probably the world. What does make them different is that they are neighbors. The trust they have for one another forms a social bond that makes urban living more than just tolerable.

The concept of neighborhood offers two humanizing characteristics to modern urban society. First is the principle of subsidiarity—that is, that nothing be done by larger organizations if it can be done by a smaller one. Second is the principle of an organic community. Both of these are traditionally Catholic social concepts, and both exist to a high degree in the Irish Catholic neighborhoods of large American cities. The parish school and the political precinct are both classic examples of the principle of subsidiarity; they are both institutions responsive to human initiative rather than determinants of human behavior. Subsidiarity is critically important at this time in our social history because it ensures the maximum individual freedom and the minimum social disruption. The principle of subsidiarity puts the emphasis on individual freedom and the dignity of the individual person rather than on the maximum social efficiency. In the same fashion, an organic community is a natural community, one whose members trust each other, are vulnerable to each other, and have close social relationships. People are allowed to feel that a community is theirs and that what is most important in life happens at the local level. Care must be taken, however, that this security does not turn into exclusion, and that the neighborhood boundaries are kept permeable.

THE FUTURE

The kind of neighborhood we have been describing is a blend of religion, politics, and social structure pulled together with the flair and natural wit that the Irish brought with them when they came to the United States. It is questionable whether such neighborhoods will continue into the future, and any rational person would say that the cards are stacked against them. Neighborhoods are not a national priority; many of the cultural and intellectual elites in the society have the feeling that neighborhoods are a negative influence, that racists live there, and that no social progress is possible as long as urban government is dominated by people from the neighborhood.

Poor leadership decisions on the part of many of the Catholic hierarchy have also begun to sap the traditional wells of support for the church that characterized the neighborhoods. In our recent survey we found that the probability of Irish Catholics wanting their sons to become priests had declined by half, and Mass attendance was down in many areas. It is questionable whether the cohesive combination of religion, politics, and social support can withstand such blows and still survive.

Recently things have begun to change, however. There are signs on the horizon that the future of neighborhoods is not all that bleak. There are people now in neighborhoods who are actively fighting the large banking institutions that exploit the neighborhoods for their own purposes. There are young professionals who are returning to the neighborhoods as places to live and raise families. My own children are living three blocks away from where their great grandparents lived sixty years ago. Neighborhoods are benefiting from the nostalgia boom in that now they are seen by some segments of the population as quaint and charming places to live. (It remains to be seen whether quaintness can be converted into economic stability.) Parochial schools are being viewed as sources of strength for the future of the church as well as educational bargains.

The outcome largely hinges on the extent to which neighborhoods can be made visible in American society as opposed to allowing them simply to fade away. This, it seems to me, is where the Irish contribution is most important. At a time when neighborhoods are seeking eloquent spokesmen, men and women who can speak to the issues with flair and wit and persuasiveness, the Irish, who are uniquely capable of doing that, are busy seeking respectability. This trend needs to be reversed.

One of the things the Irish Americans do not do much of any more is to write. For centuries the Irish were noted as storytellers and mystics and people who could cast a spell with words and music. Now if Irish Americans are seen as distinct at all, we are known by the population at large as politicians and drinkers, perhaps successful in a materialistic sort of way. Ireland produced writers as its rivers produced salmon. There were so many of them they fell all over each other in the pubs. It was not a professional writing class such as can be found in the "artistic" sections of most cities; rather they lived scattered throughout the land. Writers and storytellers were everywhere—driving milk lorries, directing traffic in uniform, pouring drinks behind a bar, or tending babies in a park. The Irish were in love wtih language; they played with it as a kitten plays with a ribbon. They spun dreams and created visions of what their life would be like in some far-off better day. They inspired one another to strive, to endure suffering, and to throw off the shackles of the oppressors. They came to America and successfully entered the mainstream of American life. One might think the dreams had come true except that there are very few songs and stories now, and by and large the Irish in America have let their traditional love affair with language cool to very dull, gray ashes. Why?

It may well be that silencing the storytellers was the price of acculturation for the Irish. It was almost as if the natives said, "Listen, you Irish, you will be allowed to struggle up from your impoverished condition and enter our respectable ranks, but you've got to get rid of that troublesome teller of tales and singer of songs. He is embarrassing; he just won't fit." And much to our shame we agreed to keep our mouths shut and work diligently at becoming good little Americans. Recent events prove that such pressure is still around. The former ambassador of the United States to the United Nations, Mr. Moynihan, is clearly in touch with his Irish heritage. His flair with words is one of his more appealing characteristics, yet it is also a talent that gets him into a lot of trouble. Pointing up foibles and exposing social and political inconsistencies are acceptable enough if done with proper seriousness and bowing and scraping; if they are done with humor and just a slight edge or irony or tongue-in-cheek, however, all the demons of the establishment come falling on your head at once. Ask Mr. Moynihan.

The pushy, mouthy Irishman lost out to the sedate, rational professional, and hardly a whimper was heard. Jimmy Cagney's brawling, smart-alec, charming "Rocky Sullivan" was co-opted in both the movies and real life by the tame side of the Irish personality played by Pat O'Brien's "Father Jerry." You have to worry about how you look if you are going to get ahead, and being in love with words does not allow much time for looking in the mirror and checking up on yourself every day.

There is little doubt that the Irish in America have been very successful, perhaps the most successful of the major immigrant groups with the exception of the Jews. However, success has come at a high price. The Irish in America are generally quite removed from their rich heritage and culture. One suspects, however, that the fires have just been banked, not extinguished. When we consider the young people taking courses in Gaelic or in Irish music, and when we hear the poems of some of our current minstrels, we wonder if there might not one day be a resurgence of storytelling and spellbinding among the American Irish.

The Irish-American culture is filled with latent songs and tears mixed together with bravado and the trappings of success. Underneath the social science jargon, there is something of the Celtic past which remains in the Irish no matter where they land. It may lie dormant for a long time, but every so often it raises its head just to let you know it is still there. A poet emerges here or there, a politician rises who teaches the rest of them what politics is really all about, a statesman conducts the affairs of a great nation with unusual wit and flair. These are not "odd occurrences" but signs of what lies beneath. It may well be that as time progresses and as materialism takes its toll of the Irish spirit, we shall see less and less of these signs until until they are no more. It may well be, but do not count on it.

FOR FURTHER READING

These ideas are further developed and evidenced in William C. McCready, "The Persistence of Ethnic Variation in American Families," in Andrew Greeley, ed., *Ethnicity in the United States* (1974), 156–76; McCready and Andrew Greeley, "The Transmission of Cultural Heritages," in *Ethnicity: Theory and Experiences*, ed. Nathan Glazer and D. P. Moynihan (1975), pp. 209–35. General studies of the metropolis in relation to both ethnic groups and neighborhoods begin with N. Glazer and D. P. Moynihan, *Beyond the Melting Pot* (New York, 1963), through to recent works such as Allen F. Davis and Mark H. Haller, *The Peoples of Philadelphia, 1790–1940* (Philadelphia, 1973), and Jay Dolan, *Immigrant Church: New York's Irish and German Catholics* (Baltimore, 1975), on the ethnic dimension; and from Jane Jacobs, *The Death and Life of Great American Cities* (New York, 1961), to Sam Bass Warner, *Private City* (Philadelphia, 1968) and his *Streetcar Suburbs* (New York, 1969) on the neighborhood dimension, from the nostalgic and critical viewpoints respectively. The interpretation here is explicitly Chicagoan, on which there is a large literature, dating back to the Chicago School of sociology and urban ecology under Robert Park in the 1920s, and influenced by the specifics of the Chicago situation. On these see Robert E. Park and others, *The City* (Chicago, 1925); Harvey Zorbaugh, *Gold Coast and Slum* (Chicago, 1929); Allan H. Spear, *Black Chicago* (Chicago, 1967); James Sanders, *The Education of an Urban Minority, Chicago's Catholics, 1833–1965* (New York, 1977); and most notably Bessie Louis Pierce, *A History of Chicago*, 4 vols. (1937–) and H. M. Mayer and Richard Wade, *Chicago: The Growth of a Metropolis* (Chicago, 1969), ably summarized in Sam Bass Warner, *The Urban Wilderness* (New York, 1972), pp. 85–112, which complements this treatment.

THE IRISH-AMERICAN LITERARY CONNECTION

PEGGY O'BRIEN

During the spring of 1975 when I was living for a year at home in the United States, I went to hear James Wright give a reading of his poems. I hoped to compensate for the years spent in Ireland at a distance from the most recent developments in American literature. The opening of Wright's reading presented me with an irony in light of my expectation: the American poet began with an enthusiastic recitation of at least a dozen translations of early Irish poetry. He said simply that these poems were close to him, objects of his love. He did not explain more, as it is not his wont to explain overmuch. Perhaps it is a finally recalcitrant mystery in the poems from the Irish past which appeals to him, since an appreciation for the resistance to rational imposition is expressed through one of his own poems which concerns a collection of Swift's poetry sent on to a friend:

> I promised once if I got hold of
> This book, I'd send it on to you.
> These are the songs that Roethke told of,
> The curious music loved by few.

Notice, underscoring the subliminal enthrallment in Swift's poems, that Wright calls them "songs." He then recalls an earlier Irish poem about Swift that unlike some recent efforts at explaining the Dean begins by acknowledging his mystery:

> I think of lanes in Laracor
> Where Brinsley Mac Namara wrote
> His lovely elegy, before
> The Yahoos got the Dean by rote.

MacNamara's "On Seeing Swift in Laracor" actually speaks of the compulsion the unexplained creates:

> Now when they mention of the Dean
> Some silence holds them as they talk;
> Some things there are unsaid, unseen,
> That drive me to this lonely walk.

This walking up and down the "Lanes in Laracor" imitates Swift's movements with his friends, male and female, and with his own mind out of which, MacNamara speculates, Gulliver sprang, perhaps induced by the back and forth of the peripatetic rhythm. Mac Namara, driven by mystery to the "lonely walk," hopes to simulate Swift's movement and by that his life, then through empathy to unlock his secrets. In the end MacNamara confesses. "And yet no comfort comes to me, / Although sometimes I see him plain, / That silence holds the Hill of Bree." As for Wright, he seems to savor both the need to probe the mystery and the failure to elucidate it, to keep pacing back and forth over the inscrutable, maybe coming at insight through a kind of hypnosis, certainly through indirection. Indirectness, even secretness, is firmly built into the structure of his poem starting with the title: "Written in a copy of Swift's poems for Wayne Burns." It is to be regarded as a poem by one man written in a book of poems by another man addressed to still another man and bearing internal reference to two further men, Brinsley MacNamara and Theodore Roethke, who seems to have introduced Wright to Swift in the first instance. Everything is hearsay, back and forth like MacNamara's "Lanes in Laracor," from one sympathetic ear to the next. "The curious music [is] loved by few" because it fails to satisfy curiosity. Similarly,

> Only when Swift men are all gone
> Back to their chosen fields by train
> And the drunk chairman snores alone
> Swift is alive in secret Wayne.

Swift is alive when all the "Swift men," the fast men who travel speedily because directly and not on foot in lanes but by trains on straight tracks, depart. In a less direct way, "Swift is alive in secret" because Swift found his life and we find his life, the imaginative quick of it that is, in secrecy, latency, not dead explanation.

Although Wright's poem is not specifically about Irish literature but about some poems by Swift which he admires, I think in the poem he is touching the nerve that connects him to Ireland: its appreciation for mystery. Roethke actually lived in Ireland for a while, and Richard Murphy has written a poem, "The Poet on the Island," about the American's unfulfilled need to be accepted by a culture which embodies the transcendence of logic found in his poems. Roethke displayed a particular interest in Yeats, probably because of the Irish poet's tireless pondering of the final mystery, death. In Roethke's poem "The Dying Man: W. B. Yeats," he recalls many of the insights explored by Yeats particularly in *The Tower*. Roethke too considers the role imagination plays in relation to death, Yeats's great question, and ends somewhat at variance with the close of "Sailing to Byzantium"; indeed Roethke's stance has more in common with Yeats's later poem "Lapis Lazuli," which explores the positive faith man must have to remain poised in an absurd position, maintaining life for its own sake in the face of inevitable destruction. Roethke writes, with more emphasis then Yeats would put, however, on the inadequacy of imagination:

> Nor can imagination do it all
> In this last place of light: he dares to live
> Who stops being a bird, yet beats his wings
> Against the immense immeasurable emptiness of things.

The paradoxical "immeasurable emptiness," a nothingness which exceeds measure, not only typifies absurdity but combines man's simultaneous and contradictory intuition of eternity and annihilation. Earlier in the poem Roethke dwells on the way finality lends itself to infinity, that death creates a sense of the eternal present: "I know as the dying know, / Eternity is now." What Roethke shares on the deepest level with Yeats is a rootedness in contradiction, the bifurcated product of the mind dwelling on mystery.

I was not surprised to read in the collection of Sylvia Plath's letters to her mother that when Plath first encountered Roethke she exclaimed, "I've found my influence." Both shared a love of nature with its evidence of regenerative life in contrast to death, another mutual obsession. Both also shared a love of Ireland; perhaps for all we know Roethke helped foster that love in Plath. All we do know through the letters is that Jack Sweeney and his wife brought Plath to Ireland when her marriage was beginning to break up and that Ireland provided both a sympathetic reflection of the poet's troubled mind and a soothing mist in which to drape her angular thoughts. When she felt herself near the edge of a breakdown, she expressed a desperate compulsion to return, but what prevented her from coming was an event deeply related on a psychic level to Ireland. While house hunting in London she found, quite accidentally, the perfect flat, the one Yeats had lived in. In order to muster the courage to persuade the estate agent to rent the flat to a separated woman with the unreliable job of poet, she consulted occult sources, feeling a deep kinship with Yeats on the level many find off-putting, the supernatural. She put her finger at random on a line from Yeats's plays which read, prophetically, "Get wine and food to give you strength and courage, and I will get the house ready." She got the flat, the one in which she died.

This habit of reference to Ireland is not exclusive to Sylvia Plath, Roethke, and Wright. Marianne Moore writes with her characteristic, wry tone in the poem "Spenser's Ireland":

> a match not a marriage was made
>   when my great great grandmother'd said
> with native genius for
> disunion, "although your suitor be
>   perfection, one objection
> is enough; he is not
> Irish."

Moore is one of those modern American poets with a highly developed respect for the physical world, yet she combines an almost scientific stance with an equally religious one, which in this poem she allies with Ireland.

> Outwitting the fairies, befriending the furies,
>   whoever again
> and again says, "I'll never give in," never sees
>   that you're not free
>   until you've been made captive by
>   supreme belief—credulity
>   you say?

One could hardly ally "credulity" with Marianne Moore, a woman whose adherence to the physical world is so strong that she will never refer vaguely, to her mind sacrilegiously, to an animal or a plant but will speak of a pangolin or a *Camellia sabina*. With her, as with the Irish poet Patrick Kavanagh, naming is an act of love, a participation through the logos in the act of creation. It is also a form of accuracy which to Moore is also morality. She says in her poem "Poetry," "we do not admire what we cannot understand." Here is a plea for clarity. On the other hand, she is not ruling out the possibility for belief in things beyond our understanding; but she is condemning without equivocation minds that, not understanding, rationalize and produce an obscurity which is heresy beside the luminous mystery. Out of this darkness of mind which is unconnected to the world come the furies, while the fairies are born of light and are the offspring of simplicity, of fidelity to what man can see when he is not twisting his vision with pretension. Patrick Kavanagh would heartily agree with Moore but would probably put her discreet statement into stronger language, dismissing the "phonies" along with the "furies." As with Roethke and ultimately Yeats, the heart of Moore's poem "Spenser's Ireland" is a paradox: "that you're not free until you've been made captive by supreme belief . . ."

Man's relationship with what is unknowable, call it the "fairies" or "God" or "immeasurable emptiness," is what I take to be the dominant concern of both American and Irish literature. "Man in this world and why" is how Kavanagh put it. Because the attempt to understand the unknowable is uppermost, conflict, man's failure counterbalanced by his effort, also predominates. As I have been hinting, a great part of the conflict is between man as a seeker of metaphysical truth and man as a sensuous appreciater of physical fact. Both postures are strongly evident in both literatures and are the complementary poles of a full, rounded religious attitude which ranges from a devout appreciation of this world to intimations of another.

These common spiritual stances, however, may be contingent on some broadly similar historical conditions. First, Ireland and America share the difficult but stimulating problem of inheriting a tongue without its tradition. People in Ireland and American speak English but they are not Englishmen. They write books in English which are not British books. Here I shall not be considering literature in Irish, since I do not want to complicate my problem hopelessly nor, what is crucial, court more incompetence than is already necessary wielding such generalities. I believe that the English language is the bridge over which literary exchange between Ireland and America began. This does not mean that the Irish writer in Irish and the American writer in English cannot have enjoyed mutual matters of sensibility and therefore found an affinity; this is entirely possible, since the writer who uses Irish still shares the same history as his countryman who writes in English, and that history bears an important resemblance to America's, especially in relation to language and literary tradition.

"Severance" is the key word. However much Ireland had suffered invasion of foreign cultures from medieval times on, it was the English who managed, albeit not completely but enough to matter, to sever the Irish from their own past. What one can forget, in the face of American patriotism, is that the first settlers in America did not consider themselves founders of another country but Englishmen in self-imposed exile. The goal behind their Puritan idealism was to erect, in Augustine's phrase, which they borrowed, "A City on a Hill," and that this city, Boston, elevated by virtue, would by throwing its rays across the Atlantic eventually attract the notice of the mother country which, chastened and instructed, would reform and welcome back its righteous children. While they were in America, these early settlers were cut off from their culture, since their extreme Protestantism made cultural assimilation with their more moderate home impossible. When the inhabitants of that continent actually asserted their independence from England, a problem greater than division loomed. They were people severed from a cultural past. Later immigration only aggravated this problem, since several diverse pasts could not be woven together without either intolerable clash or futile dilution. I would suggest that Ireland has provided on many occasions the symbolic past America requires; it can perform this role because it, like America, uses the English language, while not being English and, further, rejects any cultural domination by England.

I am not talking here of the often sentimental attachment to Ireland which many Irish-Americans flaunt; for this tack in no way leads an American who is conscious of being *sui generis* to a symbolic past; it is merely an evasion of the recent past in America in exchange for a distant past in Ireland, yet another form of disconnection. No, there exists a much more subtle and useful mode perhaps exemplified by Wallace Stevens's interest in Ireland formed through a long friendship and correspondence with Thomas Mac-Greevey, the Irish poet. Stevens has written two well-known poems with a specifically Irish frame of reference: "The Irish Cliffs of Moher" and "Our Stars Come from Ireland," which is based on the MacGreevey poem "Homage to Hieronymous Bosch." In the first poem Stevens centers on the theme which makes the more oblique, second poem comprehensible. In "The Irish Cliffs of Moher" he allies the famous landmark with his search for a spiritual father:

> Who is my father in this world, in this house,
> At the spirit's base?

He seeks a source, as permanent and awesome as the grey, towering cliffs, looming like the Patriarch over the infinite sea:

> the cliffs of Moher rising out of the mist,
> Above the rest
> Rising out of the present time and place, above
> The wet, green grass.

Notice that this paternal source is "above the real," transcending natural life, "above / The wet, green grass" and therefore not landscape but something more. Because it is totally metaphysical, it is beyond language and even poetry which must relate to the physical. It is what lies behind poetry, a sense of elemental belonging:

> This is my father or, maybe,
> It is as he was,
> A likeness, one of the race of fathers: earth
> And sea and air.

The elements are as close to the source as one can get, and yet even they are multiple, and the cliffs themselves are not raw and essential but products of nature's artifice, contained in the forming process from which in a hierarchy, landscape leads to man, actual fathers, and on to words and poems, and in a circular pattern the need to return to a source. Because it is impossible to arrive at a pure, single source, because there will always be several elements, at the end of the poem Stevens must speak of the cliffs not as the spiritual father "at the spirit's base" but as "a likeness" of that source: "This is my father or, maybe, / It is as he was, / A likeness. . . ." There is no escape from the present —It is as he was. . . ." The inevitable duality contained in *as* dooms everything thereafter to likeness, not absolute source, but transcends that doom when likeness becomes metaphor and metaphor blooms into poetry. Everything is a matter of likeness to partial-sighted man, of one half searching for completion in another half. Much as Protestantism and Catholicism in healthy situations have often served this imaginative function for each other, so Ireland has often served American writers.

In the second poem I mentioned, "Our Stars Come from Ireland," the poet, if I may crudely simplify the poem, sees Ireland and America as being both west of England, which is important, since he also sees westwardness as the inevitable drift, another crucial word, of all growing things. All life in death must complete the circle of Life, however, and return east, thus mystically to unify east and west. Since in relative terms Ireland is more east than America but is still west of England, there is a balance between likeness and opposition, and a merging, a unifying, is possible. Stevens sees in Ireland the image of young boy and old man, an ancient fetus, his own birth and ancestral father. This is all accomplished by using the persona of MacGreevey, who as a man is looking back on his life as a child in Ireland; but the voice of the poem is double, that of MacGreevey merging with that of the poet Stevens. In other words, doubleness abounds, and the poem attempts to create a unity, with the wholeness of Ireland and America combined as its overarching metaphor.

One of the reasons why Stevens found his friendship with MacGreevey so fulfilling, I suspect, is because the Irish poet not only evoked his nation, but as a traveled man who lived for a long time in France and knew what was happening in important European circles, particularly those around Beckett, he satisfied Stevens's need for horizons wider than America or even that tight mystical circle binding Ireland and America. One gets from Stevens's letters to MacGreevey a sense of pleasure and freedom in talking to a man who in a corresponding position is not self-consciously nationalistic, as Stevens was not. For example, in one letter the American shares a carp with his Irish friend over certain English reviewers who disparaged Stevens's use of a French phrase in a poem. Stevens knows he is talking to a Francophile as well as an Irishman. On the other hand, in the same letter Stevens is quick to assert a personal necessity for confinement in his native land. He had never seen the cliffs of Moher and I am sure he never wanted to, for he says, "a man that is always himself seems to do very much better than, say, the cosmopolitan. Whatever I have comes from Pennsylvania and Connecticut and from nowhere else. That too, no doubt, is why Ireland, green as it is, seems to me so much greener than it is. . . ." One thinks of the green light at the end of Daisy's dock which disappeared as an ideal for Gatsby when his relationship with the real person, not the symbol, was accomplished. There is, in the end, in both countries a similar tension between internationalism and nationalism and an interdependence between the two poles as demonstrated by Stevens. There is a need to reach out into the world to complete oneself; but at the same time the pressure of idealism necessitates an enclosure in one's own world.

I think idealism is born out of an urge for unity, for completion, and, as I have suggested, in both countries history provided an impetus for this search for wholeness. Ireland and America at relatively the same time (the latter half of the nineteenth century) were engaged in the process of creating or, as in Ireland, resurrecting, mythologies which, because they were of heroic proportions, would lend confidence to races that for separate but similar reasons had suffered an amputation from the past and with that a diminution which required Cuchullain-like stature and strength as compensation. If we turn to Melville's prose, a famous passage urging the American people to have pride in their own writers rather than certain English counterparts, one can hear the echoes of analogous pleas uttered by Irishmen:

Believe me my friends, that men not very much inferior to Shakespeare are this day being born on the banks of the Ohio. And the day will come when you shall say: who reads a book by an Englishman that is modern?

It is no wonder that Patrick Kavanagh, great champion of parochialism over provincialism, of the belief that the essence of life can be contained in the microcosm of the parish or even the corner of a field, if accurately observed, was also a great champion of Melville. He knew another great parochial when he saw one.

But Ireland and America, both, provided writers who grew to see the above philosophy as stifling, as cutting them off from a great inheritance, wider even and more promising than the English tradition on its own. Writers like Eliot saw value precisely in being a provincial, since this position meant relating to and benefiting from a great metropolis, like Rome. James's biography of Hawthorne stands as a typical criticism of one type of mind of the other. James faults Hawthorne for never venturing in his imagination beyond the confines of grey New England into the rich hues of Europe with its art and its past. A writer like Joyce seems to embrace both stances. He expanded in both space and time beyond Ireland, escaping to the Continent and choosing as the structure of *Ulysses* a myth from a tradition beyond Ireland's, yet fleshing out that ancient myth with the present, actual life of Dublin, where the author started his own Homeric journey. There is a circular completion here which is echoed by the cyclical structure of *Finnegans*

Wake. I should like to examine briefly these other Janus faces, nationalism and internationalism. Advocates of both points of view, or a complex double perspective, found allies in the other country. Irish and American writers have shared the need to create a mythology whether by contraction into idealized countries inhabited by heroes or by expansion into the rest of the world, exchanging a less impressive stature for a secure base in a recognized and diverse tradition.

To provide neat examples of alliances on the basis of, first, nationalism and, then, internationalism is impossible because the two impulses are more complementary poles than unconnected opposites in the psyche of nations searching for a tradition. Still, to speak broadly of writers who found a common meeting ground primarily as passionate nationalists, let me examine for a moment the correspondence between T. W. Rolleston and Walt Whitman. Rolleston, who was deeply concerned about the future of Irishmen, found a model in Whitman's vision of the free, strong, independent man, a virtual superman; and, significantly, in his letters to Whitman, Rolleston speaks on many occasions of his admiration for Standish James O'Grady as a man and a thinker. One needs only to turn to O'Grady's *History of Ireland* briefly to understand the affinity Rolleston would feel between the vision O'Grady possessed of Ireland's heroic legacy and Whitman's prophecy of America's heroic potential. O'Grady proclaims:

The forefront of Irish History we find filled with great heroic personages of a dignity and power more than human. . . . Century after century the mind of the country was inflamed by the contemplation of those mighty beings whom, too, men believed to be their ancestors. All the imaginative literature of the country revolved around this period, was devoted to the glorification of the gigantic creatures with whom it was filled.

O'Grady will go on to insist that heroic energy is still latent in the Irish. He must explain Christianity in terms of the Irish past, therefore, he argues that the superhuman characteristics of the heroes provided the fervor for the Christian movement which followed, that it was truly a matter of conversion, conversion of energy from one form into another, rather than the creation of faith out of nothing: "It was the Irish bards and that heroic age of theirs which nourished the imagination, intellect and idealism of the country to such an issue [Christianity and its propagation through Europe]. Patrick did not create these qualities. He found them, and directed them into a new channel."

How compatible that holy trinity—"imagination, intellect and idealism" —is with not just religion but society in general, became a problem for both Irish and American writers who espoused the national myth. Think of Yeats's disillusionment with the aftermath of the Revolution, modern Ireland.

Whitman too in his late essay "Democratic Vistas" had to doubt his early sanguinity. Although O'Grady tried to rationalize Christianity in Ireland as an extension of the heroic period, Rolleston in a letter to Whitman sees it in another light, as a skin to be shed before the naked child of nature can stand straight. He identifies organized religion as the future's greatest block to imaginative energy and philosophical freedom—to "imagination, intellect and idealism":

What a country this is. Or would be but for savage misgovernment, and Protestant bigotry. The orangemen in the North are a source of much evil and will be of more, unless some miracle should turn them into sympathetic Irishmen. There was a time when I thought that Ireland could never be set free from English rule because the Catholic church would instantly become dominant and inaugurate a system of religious tyranny which would crush liberties more important than national liberties. Now I begin to see that this would not be for long. The Irish are much less Catholic than they were—dogmatic religion is loosening its hold upon them in a very remarkable way, and hatred for Protestant England as Ireland's ruler is a most potent cause at present in supporting the Catholic religion here. This is felt even by the more cultivated and far-seeing of the clergy, who consequently oppose the national movement as far as they dare. I have no doubt that in a free Ireland the Church would persecute as naturally as a wasp stings, but I am equally certain that a revulsion of feeling would come which (though attended perhaps with terrible struggles) would mark a real moral and intellectual advance such as seems out of our reach at present.

After a bland but good-natured description of the harmless local people, Rolleston sketches a picture of his father, a Whitmanesque giant of a man, a Gulliver towering over the local Lilliputians: "He is a man you would like to see. He is over seventy now, more than average height even for our family, where the men grow very tall (about six-foot-four inches) and still sturdy." Since several six-footers in a family do not make a race of giants and since infinite ideals cannot be measured in feet and inches, all great national idealists must suffer disillusionment. Whitman experienced the cycle from promise to disappointment in his own body. He begins "Song of Myself" with an image of himself as a specimen of the unfallen man: "I, now thirty-seven years old and in perfect health begin." Whitman's letters to Rolleston in later years focus not on the poems so much as on his failing health. Whitman was suffering from advancing paralysis, a terrible irony.

Perhaps because the national myth does contain this trap, that people do not live up consistently to poetry, another opposite but complementary urge, to connect with a strictly literary tradition beyond one's national boundaries, geographical and temperamental, emerged in both countries. I mentioned that the Whitman-Rolleston alliance was not an unmitigated exercise in respective nationalisms. The pretext of their friendship was Rolleston's effort to get Whitman published in Germany and Whitman welcomed a broad audience, since universality through the particular was part of his creed. O'Grady hailed Whitman as "the noblest literary product of modern times" and the word "modern" is significant, for Whitman and O'Grady share the same understanding of time. Recalling the passage where O'Grady tries to show that it is the same imaginative, racial energy working through Irish Christianity that prevailed in heroic, pre-Christian Ireland, one sees the urge to concertina time, to speak not of revolution or linear history, but of a constancy of homogeneous, imaginative energy. A similar vision prevails in Whitman's poem "Crossing Brooklyn Ferry," with a different emphasis appropriate to the author's nationality. Whitman's focus is more on the future, since hope and a sense of potential guide him, than it is on the distant past, where the Irishman found the promise of continuity. Whitman writes:

> It avails not, time nor place—distance avails not,
> I am with you, you men and women of generation, of ever so
>   many generations hence,
> Just as you feel when you look on the river and sky,
>   so I felt,
> Just as any one of you is one of the living crowd, I was one
>   of the crowd.

All history is felt in the experience of the single individual in the single instant of time in the single place. There is no need to move into another skin, another age, or another country. It is no wonder that in the poem there is an image of the author's head reflected in the water with a halo of light around it—"the fine centrifugal spokes of light round the shape of my head in the sunlit water"—since he feels a celestial centrality in himself, in all men paradoxically.

In counterbalance to Whitman's vision, there is in both traditions another perspective on man's position, that he is not central and complete but partial and contained in a collective whole. To speak of literature from this premise, one writer may be regarded, however accomplished, not as encapsulating all of experience through the agency of revelation but as being an accretion to an ongoing, historical tradition which has provided models from which we can learn, if not by revelation, through example. A self-consciousness about style, about where one fits into a larger than national tradition, became the common concern of several important writers from Ireland and America. In England and continental Europe at the beginning of the twentieth century four writers crossed paths, and the configurations of their encounters are the only map anyone would ever need as evidence of the fertility in Irish-American literary relations. Yeats, Joyce, Pound, and Eliot did a great deal to create the norms of what we call "modern" in literature. The paradox is that they accomplished this by acknowledging the past in a disciplined and far-reaching way. They also acknowledged a literary tradition which extends not only beyond their respective nations but beyond Europe. It was an extension in time and space. Perhaps the same vision behind Stevens's "Our Stars Come from Ireland," of east mystically uniting with west, led Pound and Yeats at an earlier time to discover and use Fenobsa's exhumations of the ancient Japanese Nō dramas. If Whitman saw his own living gestures repeated in the future, these writers saw certain of their literary gestures repeated in the past. Both were attempts at unity.

Given this urge for unity, it is curious that most Americans and Irish writers eschew authorial objectivity. The novel, which in its early stages enjoys a narrator with some objective distance and comprehensive authority over the truth of his incidents, undergoes a great change as a form in the hands of modern writers particularly from these countries. Circumstances, social and spiritual, in Ireland and America make it impossible for their writers automatically to join the line of writers proceeding out of the main English tradition. Through the narration of Joyce's *Dubliners* there is a weaving of different voices which reflect and merge with the characters, an effect which militates against any overall, objective voice and makes the situation seem more a collection of subjective presences. Henry James presents us with similar narrative patterns in his novels. A book like *The Wings of the Dove* can explore the most intricate problems of interpretation that arise out of a situation created by several people precisely because, as it is narrated with characters presented as isolate sensibilities and with a subtle collusion reminiscent of Joyce between author and character, no single objective vision is possible.

This adherence to the individual consciousness, to the point of preserving human isolation even in novels, seems to me at least partly the result again of history in both countries. We need only underscore certain words in the first piece of formal prose written in America, *Of Plymouth Plantation*, to feel palpably that isolation at its source. The author, William Bradford, is describing what it was like to be among those pilgrims who landed in Plymouth:

Being thus passed the vast ocean, and a sea of troubles before in their preparation, they had now no friends to welcome them nor inns to entertain or refresh their weather-beaten bodies; no houses or much less towns to repair to, to seek for succour. It is recorded in scripture, as mercy to the apostle and his shipwrecked company, that the barbarians showed them no small kindness in refreshing them, but these savages were readier to fill their sides full of arrows than otherwise. And for the season it was winter, and they that know the winters of that country know them to be sharp and violent, and subject to cruel and fierce storms, dangerous to travel to known places, much more to search an unknown coast. Besides, what could they see but a hideous and desolate wilderness, full of wild beasts and wild men—and what multitudes there might be of them they knew not. Neither could they, as it were, go up to the top of Pisgah to view from this wilderness a more goodly country to feed their hopes; for whichsoever way they turned their eyes (save upwards to the heavens) they could have little solace or content in respect of any outward objects. For summer being done, all things stand upon them with a weather-beaten face and the whole country, full of woods and thickets represented a wild and savage hue. If they looked behind them, there was the mighty ocean which they had passed and was now as a main bar and gulf to separate them from all the civil parts of the world.

Although Bradford is speaking for the whole band of Pilgrims, his writing by its immediacy and intimacy with the reader speaks as though for one of the band, an archetypal member who like the central person in "Crossing Brooklyn Ferry" sees and feels for everyone else. Bradford, having cataloged all the places one cannot bear to look, never mentions looking into another person's eyes. A sense of community has vanished: "They had now no friends to welcome them nor inns to entertain or refresh their weather-beaten bodies; no houses or much less towns to seek for succour." Without the structure of civilization—inns, houses, towns—each man is self-encased, missing the artificial but comforting links between man and man. The physical surroundings are those which demand mental withdrawal, what with the barbarians and the cold and the monotony of noncolor, the grey of the winter sea and the dirty white of the winter landscape. In this sensuously nongratifying environment, mark the recourse of the Pilgrim: "for whichsoever way they turned their eyes (save upward to the heavens) they could have little solace or content in respect of any outward objects." They must, there-fore, focus on inward objects and this focus is clearly indicated by the phrase, in parenthesis ironically since it conveys the kernel of truth, "save upwards to the heavens." The only possible activity is religious meditation, something done on one's own.

The Irish, though not physically exiles from a civilization, suffered its loss. Patrick Kavanagh reflects on this fact and the contrast it creates between Irish literature and the English literary tradition in his essay "Nationalism and Literature," where he also suggests that self-conscious nationalism fails for the writer basically interested in personal truth:

I know a few writers in Ireland who have not cottoned on to the fact that Ireland as a myth is no use. Johnson said that patriotism was the last refuge of the scoundrel. He was once again right on the mark. There have been many fine patriots but there must be some inherent defect in the whole business, seeing that men of little or no principle can readily weigh in with it and be accounted fine men.

Regarding the mighty corpus of English literature, this seems to me largely divorced from England the nation, the often scoundrely nation . . . it seems at first blush that English poetry grew to its plenitude in a myth void, that it was entirely individual. But there was a myth and a true one.

This curious myth has to do with faith in one's own judgement and the courage to pronounce it. Wherever there are a number of men with that faith and courage you have a myth-making society . . . for some reason or other this source of strength has never been lost in England. It goes on quietly unconcerned, undeceived by the latest reports on anything. As one goes on in the country, knowing exactly who is down in the valley sowing turnips or levelling the potato drill and who is not, and what they are all thinking about.

It is this kind of parish myth regarding literature that has been totally lacking in Ireland. Instead we have this national thing which is no use to anyone. . . .

It is no mere coincidence that the writers from these two countries are inordinately bound up with the question of tradition. Kavanagh's major point about the English is that their tradition is unselfconscious, and can contain naturally what under self-conscious conditions would seem illogical and contradictory. It rests on a myth that each man has "faith in one's own judgement and courage to pronounce it." On the other hand, there is a collective response, an intuitive knowing of other people's failings, a family feeling, that of a healthy family where the balance is struck between individual will and community good. Gertrude Stein said English literature is about "island daily living," a different thing from "man in this world and why." What Ireland lost, though it may have it now in certain parts of the country, is this community strength. The parish was as an official unit destroyed and with it the delicate interdependence of the individual and society. What was left was human isolation at one pole and at the other the abstract vision of the nation, Ireland.

The word Kavanagh associates with the connective tissue which guarantees health and balance is the "parish." The word is auspicious for this discussion, since it can be argued that an increased sense of human isolation came to America via the destruction of the parish. The brand of Puritanism, covenant theology, which the settlers brought to the New World was based on the conviction that only regenerate Christians should be members of the church, not all people who lived in a circumscribed place, the parish. Faith not geography should decide the church. Such idealism created a split between the individual experience and the collective idea. There was, on the one hand, a tortured, occasionally ecstatic soul and on the other, again, the growing abstraction of a nation.

In America the widening of literary response to embrace experience beyond the range of that very special Protestantism imported to the new continent is associated with a growing respect for sensuous nontranscendental truth. William Carlos Williams's poem "Catholic Bells" praises this kind of experience, one that does not point with inevitable duality to a higher meaning. The bells ring for the joy of ringing, which is refreshing. It is logical that this feeling should be associated with a religion which pays attention to works on earth, as opposed to early New England Puritanism, which as a strict brand of Calvinism considered only faith as evidence. Joyce's anti-Protestantism, anti-Platonism, with his strong adherence to the physical world, finds a counterpart in the American tradition, particularly with Pound, who begins his "A Retrospect" with the principle, "Direct treatment of the 'thing' whether subjective or objective." It also makes sense that Pound met and helped Yeats when the latter was emerging from a self-consciously nationalistic and, as Kavanagh's logic would have it, relatively abstract phase into a more physical poetry, a transition recognized and applauded by Eliot. Eliot's own need to delineate a tradition that goes back to Rome makes sense given the kind of Protestant culture which dominated his early life. Indeed, one might see the whole compulsion to trace a tradition beyond America defined by New England as a need to assuage the loneliness and isolation the Calvinist sensibility imposes; it is a desire to be surrounded, even subsumed by otherness.

The balance between transcendentalism and nationalism, revelation and reason, is proverbial and the two poles, whatever names you attach, usually coexist in all these writers. Kavanagh with his bias said *Ulysses* "is not so much about Dublin but is the journey of a soul." It is also a faithful compendium of the body's processes, in loving, in eating, in excreting. These writers, whatever pole or poles they tend toward, reveal what I would call religious tendencies. Eliot's attachment to religion in the orthodox sense is obvious; but what I am calling religious is his assertion in the essay "Religion and Literature" that man reads as a whole person, that certain parts of a man's sensibility, say, the religious, cannot be divided off from others, like the literary. This is part of a general urge toward unity of being, Yeats's constant obsession. Yeats's belief in an *anima mundi* indicates the need to see all visible manifestations as part of a larger reservoir of meaning which unifies partial, sensory experience. Joyce's literary concept of the "epiphany" borrows its name from liturgical language because it is related to the experience of revelation.

I regard it as significant that both countries also have enjoyed a high proportion of what may be called mystical visionaries. I would regard Kavanagh as such a writer, and it is significant that his favorite book was *Moby Dick*. He says referring to it, "When we are unconscious we are close to the Eternal. We have to shut our eyes to see our way to Heaven. *Moby Dick* is an evocation of that unconsciousness to which I am referring. It was written out of the blind life." The imaginative value of "the blind life" has been recognized and celebrated by many other writers, Synge in *The Well of the Saints*, who through Martin Doul and Mary Doul, the blind beggars, asserts the value of inner, nonphysical vision, and Yeats in *The Tower* with his appreciation of Raftery, the author of the song in praise of Mary Hynes: "Strange, but the man who made the song was blind / Yet now I have considered it, I find / That nothing strange; the tragedy began / With

Homer that was a blind man, / And Helen has all living hearts betrayed."
The American tradition includes writers with a similar appreciation for the
"blind life," notably Emily Dickinson. Kavanagh says, "We have to shut
our eyes to see our way to Heaven." Dickinson writes:

> Before I got my eye put out
> I liked as well to see
> As other creatures that have eyes
> And know no other way.

Although many of the continuing parallels between Kavanagh and Dickinson
are those that adhere to the morphology of mysticism in every instance,
nonetheless one of the postures, common to the mystical tradition but
especially evident in many Irish and American writers, is that of finding a
truth which eludes language. Describing the genesis of a mystical insight,
Kavanagh tells us: "I am conscious of something within me that plays
before my soul and is as a light dancing in front of me. Were this light
brought to steadiness and perfection in me it would surely be eternal light."
Dickinson in a similar mood conveys a similar sensation, only with her the
fickering of Kavanagh's light becomes the fluttering of a bird and eternity is
called "Hope":

> Hope is the thing with feathers
> That perches in the soul
> And sings the tune without the words
> And never stops at all.

"And sings the tune without the words / And never stops at all." The absence
of language, which however sublime is always limiting, guarantees eternity.
This was the insight at the root of Stevens's "Our Stars Come from Ireland."
Although all these writers seem to be asserting the value of language and
literature as vehicle not as end in itself, they are the same writers who
struggle to make the literary artifact equal to and like in kind to their vision.
Perhaps Beckett, along with MacGreevey and other artists, in the document
Poetry Is Verticle can add to my argument. He says: "Aesthetic will is not
the first law. It is the immediacy of the ecstatic revelation, in the a-logical
movement of the psyche, in the organic rhythm of the vision, that the
creative act occurs." Stevens could have said: "The creative act *occurs*."
Art is active not passive, not describing an experience but enacting it. This
is one reason why traditional forms have undergone such radical changes in
the hands of such writers.

Another reason, I think, relates back to my point about the human isolation prevalent in both traditions. Literary forms have been expected to
embody and communicate, which is extremely important, the human

personality behind the content. Since what writers from these countries have possessed is themselves and what they have not possessed is an unbroken written tradition, this development was inevitable. Charles Olsen and Robert Creeley have tried to transform prosody and make it correspond not to arbitrary measure but to the flexible length of the human breath. In the same vein Joyce said of *Finnegans Wake* in response to criticisms about the book's obscurity: "It is all so simple. If anyone doesn't understand a passage all he need do is read it aloud." In other words, the text relates to man as he is living rather than to some preconceived notions of literature.

I said at the outset that writers in both countries shared the "difficult but stimulating problem of inheriting a tongue without a tradition." The difficulty has been transcended, and the challenge met. Other peoples may not have this specific conflict between national reality and an imported language, but they have others and, above all, the profound sense of individual separateness. Maybe this is why Ireland and America have done so much to create a modern literature which has influenced even English writers. Melville's prediction—"And the day will come when you shall say: who reads a book by an Englishman that is modern?"—exaggerates; but there is an indication of truth in making the last word "modern" when one considers the literatures in English which emerged outside England, chiefly in Ireland and America.

FOR FURTHER READING

Since the subject of my essay is still of a speculative nature, I cannot provide a bibliography of standard texts. I have relied for the most part on my reading of the basic literature of both countries, along with certain letters, essays, and a few works by contemporary authors. I have made direct reference to or use of the following: James Joyce's *Ulysses* (London, 1960), *Dubliners* (New York, 1961), and *Finnegans Wake* (New York, 1971): W. B. Yeats's *Collected Poems* (New York, 1956); *The Complete Plays* of J. M. Synge (New York, 1960); Herman Melville's letter to Hawthorne from *Herman Melville*, ed. R. W. B. Lewis (New York, 1962); and *Moby Dick* (New York, 1967); and Henry James's biography of *Hawthorne* (London, 1967), and *Wings of the Dove* (New York, 1902); T. S. Eliot's essays from *Selected Prose* London, 1958); the *Literary Essays of Ezra Pound*, ed. T. S. Eliot (London, 1950); *Pound/Joyce: The Letters of Ezra Pound to James Joyce*, ed. Forrest Read (New York, 1970); *The Classic Noh Theater of Japan*, by Ezra Pound and Ernest Fenollosa (New York, 1959); Patrick Kavanagh's *Collected Poems* (London, 1964), *Collected Prose* (London, 1967), and *November Haggard* (New York, 1967); *The Complete Poems of Emily Dickinson*, ed. Thomas H. Johnson (Boston, 1960); Whitman's *Leaves of Grass* (Cambridge, Mass., 1959); *Whitman-Rolleston: A Correspondence*, ed. Horst Frenz (Dublin, 1952); *Wallace Stevens: Poems*, with an introduction by the editor, Samuel French Morse, which includes the letter Stevens sent to Thomas McGreevy (New York, 1959); Samuel Beckett's introduction, the essay "Poetry Is Verticle," to the book by Thomas McGreevy, *Collected Poems*, ed. T. D. Redshaw (Dublin, 1971); James Wright's *Collected Poems* (Middletown, Conn., 1971). *The Oxford Book of Irish Verse* (London, 1958) contains the poem by Brinsley Mac-

Namara cited; see also Theodore Roethke's *Collected Verse: Worlds for the Wind* (London, 1968); Richard Murphy's *Sailing to an Island* (London, 1963); William Carlos Williams's *Selected Poems* (New York, 1969) and *In the American Grain* (London, 1971); Marianne Moore's *Collected Poems* (New York, 1961); Sylvia Plath's *Letters Home*, ed. Aurelia Schober Plath (London, 1975).

Many books giving an insight into the cultural background of both countries provided the general foundation of the essay. I actually cite only two works: from Perry Miller's *The American Puritans: Their Prose and Poetry* (New York, 1956) William Bradford's "Of Plymouth Plantation"; and Standish James O'Grady's *History of Ireland* (London, 1878).

IRISH TRADITIONAL MUSIC IN THE UNITED STATES

W. H. A. WILLIAMS

The history of Irish traditional music in the United States is a vast and intricate subject on which very little has been written. Here we are concerned with two major questions: the contribution of Irish music to American folk music, and the survival of the music within the Irish-American community. We shall first consider the Irish folk song tradition (section I) and then the instrumental tradition (section II).

I

Generally, American folk music is a variety of hybrid musical forms developed out of the union of two powerful traditions. The first is European and primarily Anglo-Celtic—the folk music of Britain, Scotland, and Ireland. The other major influence is African, consisting of the complex traditions of harmony, rhythm, vocal coloration, and song structuring which the slaves brought with them from their old homelands. These two great traditions have continually intermingled, and over the years have produced music which is distinctly American. Therefore, to look for Irish influences in American folk music is to search for strands in a tightly woven cloth.

Most of what has been written about American folk music has been produced by American scholars. And, with some notable exceptions, it has been sufficient, from the American point of view, to identify a ballad or fiddle tune as "British" in origin. Moreover, there is a general American tendency, from which not all American folklorists are exempt, to use the words "British" and "English" interchangeably. Therefore, there has been no careful, consistent attempt over the years to differentiate between the English, Welsh, Scottish, and Irish elements in American folk music. Even so fine a scholar as Malcolm Laws, Jr., in his *Native American Balladry*, notes the prevalence of "Scotch-Irish" settlers in the South, goes on to describe the music of the region as "English" and "Scottish" in origin, and ends by covering everything with the blanket term "British" (pp. 102–3).

One must have a certain sympathy for American scholars, however. After all, how does one distinguish *Irish* songs and tunes from those of England or Scotland? A. L. Lloyd in his *Folk Song in England* has noted that many tunes are common on both sides of the Irish Sea. "Such tunes incline to sound English in England, Irish in Ireland and Scots in the mouth of a Lothian harvester or a Buckie trawlerman." If the same tunes happen to be collected in Kentucky, they will certainly sound American. It is little wonder that an attempt to pin down song and tune origins beyond a general British background has not appealed to very many American folk song scholars in the past.

In spite of these difficulties, it is evident that Irish traditional music has had a considerable influence in America. Bruno Nettl, in his *An Introduction to Folk Music in the United States*, suggests that there are some 200 "British broadside" ballads in circulation in the country, and that "A considerable number, perhaps as many as a third . . . are of Irish origin." Lloyd has noted that English folk song itself became "saturated" with Irish melody during the eighteenth century, creating new styles and types of songs which became indigenous to many parts of England.

The essential clues to the role which Irish tradition has played in the formation of American folk music lies in patterns of immigration and settlement in the United States. These suggest that Ireland's initial impact upon American music came predominantly from Ulster. Some 250,000 emigrants from Ulster came to the thirteen colonies prior to 1776, another 100,000 between the end of the Revolutionary War and 1815. Most of these Ulster immigrants were Presbyterians descended from the Lowland Scots who moved to Northern Ireland during the seventeenth century. After the English, these Ulster settlers constituted the largest group of eighteenth-century immigrants to America.

Although they were at first simply referred to as "the Irish," by the middle of the nineteenth century it became customary to call them the "Scots-Irish" or "Scotch-Irish," in order to differentiate them from the vast numbers of Catholic Irish who were then flooding into the country. Although the term "Scotch-Irish" is not often used outside of America, James G. Leyburn, one of the settlers' principal historians, defends the term, saying, "The people who began to come to America in 1717 were not Scots, and certainly they were not Irish: already they were Scotch-Irish." E. Estyn Evans apparently agrees that these Ulster Presbyterians had a distinct culture of their own, and he maintains that "their major lasting contribution to the American scene was their broad imprint on the American landscape and way of life" (*Essays in Scotch-Irish History*). Whatever their influence in terms of cabin and barn styles, field layout, town planning, and so on, it seems likely that the greatest and most lasting contribution of the Scots-Irish was music. And however one may define their particular religious and ethnic identity, musically they should be considered Ulstermen, for they brought with them the mixture of Scottish and Irish tunes which is still characteristic of large parts of Northern Ireland.

Most of these Ulster immigrants settled on the long frontier line, first in New England and Pennsylvania, then, moving southward through the valleys of the great chain of the Appalachian Mountains, into Virginia and the Carolinas. This westward and southward migration was important, for the Scots Irish helped to settle the upland parts of the South, which Malcolm Laws, Jr., has identified as the region most successful in maintaining and developing a folk music tradition. There is a certain amount of irony as William H. Talmadge has pointed out in the fact that when the great English folklorist Cecil Sharp went into the Appalachians to rediscover "English" folk song, he was in fact often dealing with people of Ulster descent. Wherever they settled in large numbers and remained in relative isolation, balladry has been found "live and in a healthy condition."

In spite of this, the Scots-Irish elements in the folk song tradition of America are no easier to spot than any others. There are relatively few songs which are of obvious Irish origin or of Irish character. Among the exceptions are "The Irish Girl" (sometimes this is "The Blackwater Side," sometimes Joyce's "I'm a Poor Stranger and Far from My Own," often it is a collection of floating verses some of which form the American folk lyric "Handsome Molly"), "Erin's Green Shore" (used by the Confederates for "Dixie's Green Shore during the Civil War), "Brennan on the Moor," "Early, Early in the Spring," and "The Boston Burglar."

Norman Cazden, in his collection of New York State ballads claims that the air to a version of "Captain Wedderburn's Courtship" which he collected was "obviously" Irish. A few years ago, the American folklorist D. K. Wilgus gave a paper before the Irish Folk Music Society which suggested that the American ballad "Rose Connally," which is still often sung, was of Irish origin.

Certainly the question of tune origins (as distinct from text origins) is always difficult, even for trained musicologists. Moreover, relatively few American scholars in the past have made any effort to consult collections of Irish music. One exception was George Pullen Jackson, who devoted his life to the study of southern folk and quasi-folk hymns. In his *Spiritual Folk-Songs of Early America*, of the multitude of tunes for which Jackson cited transatlantic origins he attributed Irish connections to about one quarter of them. This in itself is impressive. However, I feel that the figure is too low. Skillful as he was, Jackson seems to have missed a few things. He goes to great pains to attribute the hymn tune "Greenfields" (allegedly Abraham Lincoln's favorite hymn) to a remote German source when "Rosin the Beau," which has had strong Irish connections, seems a more likely source. Also he failed to note the striking similarity between "The Lonesome Valley" and a lullaby tune Petrie printed in the second volume of his *Ancient Music of Ireland*, a correlation which, to the best of my knowledge, no one has yet commented upon. This tune is best known in Ireland today as one of the settings for the Gaelic hymn "*Dia do Bheatha.*" If Jackson had had access to more Irish material, his estimate of the Irish content in his hymn tunes might have been higher. Out of a bibliography of 127 books, Jackson cites only two Irish collections: Joyce's *Irish Music and Song* (1901) and Sandford's edition of Petrie's tunes.

Noting that most of the people who took up the "fa-so-la" or "shape note" hymn-singing tradition were either of Scots-Irish or German descent, with only a small minority of English background, Jackson suggests in his *White Spirituals in the Southern Uplands*, that the German contribution to this form should have rivaled the Irish. However, the German language apparently proved a sufficient barrier to prevent any large body of German tunes from passing into folk and hymn traditions. As he states, it was the "secular song flavor [of] . . . [the] Scotch-Irish" which gave to much of the area's music its "Celtic melodic idiom." Interestingly enough, the Irish element is smallest in that category which Jackson calls "revival spirituals." These Baptist and Methodist camp-meeting songs seem to reflect a largely American idiom, possibly because of their close connections with Negro tradition. At any rate when the Catholic Irish found their way to America, they generally regarded them as strange and off-putting. An amusing satire in *The Cross and Shamrock or How to Defend the Faith* (by "a missionary priest") illustrates the point. Two of the boys of an Irish family newly arrived in America are enticed into a Methodist meeting. The mother later asks them what they heard there. One of the boys tells how first the women in congregation sang, "O for a man—O for a man—O for a mansion in the skies." Then the men answered, "Send down sal—send down sal— / Send down salvation to our souls." The Irish listeners burst out laughting, and then urge the boys to sing something the Christian Brothers taught them. The boys dutifully join hands and sing the "Ave Maria."

This book was published in Dublin in 1853, obviously for those emigrating to America. By that time the emigration of Catholic Irish had long been in flood tide. As a result, the old eighteenth-century habit of referring to "the Irish" as a single group had disappeared. Religious antagonism between Catholic and Protestant ran as high in some parts of the United States as it did in Ireland itself. It is this new wave of Catholic Irish emigration to America, commencing around the 1820s and reaching mammoth proportions after the Famine, that brings us to a new phase in the history of Irish music in America.

The Irish immigrants of this second, mainly Catholic, phase tended to become urban dwellers. As we shall see, they established a strong musical subculture of their own in American cities. And to an extent their impact upon American folk music was limited because of this. American folk music was thriving and evolving in rural areas and mountain regions which, especially in the South, received relatively few of the new Catholic Irish. Nevertheless, Catholic emigration from Ireland, which continued at a high level even after the American Civil War, did have a definite impact upon several notable rural occupations.

In their search for work, Irishmen in the nineteenth century took to navvying on canals and railroads, lumbering in the northern woods, mining, fishing, sailing, and punching cattle. Wherever they went, these Irish workers left their musical imprint. Since most of the occupations which attracted them were outside of the South, the contribution of the nineteenth-century Irish immigrant lies mainly in the musical traditions of the North, Midwest, and Far West.

Many of these immigrants were Gaelic speakers who brought with them songs in Irish. As noted in the case of the Germans, however, foreign language impeded the transmission of songs into the American oral tradition. I have found no Gaelic songs printed in American collections, although editors sometimes refer to having heard that some were once sung. A few macaronic ballads, or at least songs with English verses and Irish choruses have survived, though, as often as not, they antedate the nineteenth century and cannot be associated with nineteenth-century immigration. Of these "Shule Aroon" is the most common. The song was easily adapted to the circumstances of the American Revolution, when it was generally know as "Johnny Was Gone for a Soldier." According to Alan Lomax the tune has also served Americans for a sea chanty, a play-party song, a lumberman's ditty, and even—allegedly —a Cherokee Indian chant. In whatever form, however, even in the "Johnny" versions, the Gaelic chorus had degenerated into nonsense syllables. Typical is this example collected in Missouri.

> Shule, shule shule-a-mac-a-me
> Shule-mac-a-rac-stack, Sally Bobby Lee
> Shule-a-mac-a-rac-stack, Sally Bobby Lee
> Come Bubble-ue-a-boose—said Lora.

Not all of the Gaelic choruses disintegrated, however. It is reported in Eckstrom and Smyth's *Minstrelsy of Maine* that there was a version of "The Gay Wedding" that had "a chorus in Irish which it wouldn't be safe to sing in some parts of Bangor." Parts of the song are reprinted, but not the chorus.

Judging from the songs which have been collected from the oral tradition in the United States, it seems clear that Ireland's major contribution to American folk music sprang from broadside or street ballads. With their compelling rhyming patterns and relatively simple tune structures, they were not only apparently easy to remember, but served as convenient models for anyone who might set out to compose his own song. A. L. Lloyd suggests that these "come-all-ye" street ballads were "probably of urban origin (from Dublin)," and seem to have crystallized during the eighteenth century, being by the end of it well established in Irish song. Emigrants spread the Irish broadside style to many parts of England and the Lowlands of Scotland, to Australia and of course to America (p. 334).

It was the Irish laborers who spread their broadside tradition among the quasi-folk occupational groups of navvies, miners, and most especially among the lumberjacks. They seem to have virtually dominated the singing in the northern lumber camps, from Maine to Wisconsin. Malcom Laws, Jr., quotes one folklorist to the effect that "in the logging camp, the hegemony in song belonged to the Irish. . . . The Irish street song was the pattern upon which a liberal portion of the shanty [logging] songs were made" (p. 107). Phillips Barry, one of the few American folk song specialists of the past who was sensitive to Irish music, once commented that the song tradition of eastern Maine showed that the "Irish element . . . is much greater and much earlier than it is generally supposed to be. . . . It has done more than its share in preserving the old songs." "It is from singers with some Irish blood that we have obtained the most songs" (Talmadge, p. 273).

Thus, as opposed to the earlier Ulster Irish tradition of the southern mountains, a large number of post-1750 urban Irish songs have been collected in the northern and midwestern states. Most of these are of the streeet ballad type. Many of them can be found in Colm O Lochlainn's collections made in Ireland. Even a partial listing is fairly impressive; "The Croppy Boy," "Rinodine," "Willy Tailor," "The Battle of the Boyne," "Morrissy and the Russian Sailor," "The Green Mossy Banks of the Lee," "My Bonny Irish Boy," "Wild Rover," "Banks of the Claudy," "Dick Darby the Cobbler," "The Old Oak Tree," "The Green Linit," "The Grand Conversation of Napoleon," "The Wild Colonial Boy," "Finnigan's Wake," "Exile of Erin," "Lannigan's Ball," "Sweet Gramachree," "The Kerry Recruit," "The Bonney Labouring Boy," "The Girl I left Behind Me," "Pretty Susie, the Pride of Kildare," "The Dawning of the Day," "Skewball," "Rose of Ardee," "Patrick Sheehan" (the words of which were written by Charles J. Kickham, author of *Knock-na-gow*), and even so late a song as "Kevin Barry."

Occasionally, a song which is rare even in Ireland may turn up in an American collection. In Missouri in 1911 a collector found a single version of "Jimmy Murphy" or "Joe Jimmy Murphy" (who was hanged not for sheep stealing, but for courting Kate Wheelin). Except for a few minor details and a fourth verse, it is essentially the same version occasionally heard in Ireland today. Unfortunately, no tune is given. However, the chorus of the Missouri version is even more extraordinary than the one found in Ireland.

Then rall-a-bony lass now
From the east to Dan Pathrow's
To entice poor Jimmy Murphy
From the green mossy banks of the
Jam-spooder-fadler-ram-jam-fa-de-fa-da-riddle-die-do-too-yi-ya.

There are many other songs, some of which may have originated in Ireland but most of which have an Irish-American smack. The titles, of course, suggest little of their contents: "Dublin Bay," "Son of a Gambolier," "Steve O'Donnell's Wake" (at which they all, naturally, got drunk), "I Left Mother and Ireland Because We Were Poor," "Barney Mavourneen" (I won't let you in), "When Pat Malone Forgot That He Was Dead" (when he smelt the whiskey at the wake), "Clarence McFadden Learning to Waltz," "Paddy O'Rourke," "Jack Haggerty" (a widely spread lumberjack song which probably originated in the Far West), "Barney McCoi," "Patrick's Baby," "Pat O'Brien" (a murder ballad), "James MacDonald" (another), "I'm a Tight Little Irishman," "Larry O'Gaff" (We fought like the Devil, like Irishmen always do).

Many of these Irish-American ballads were sentimental, hopelessly so by our attitudes today. Take for example the "Three Leaves of the Shamrock." In the song the girl gives the leaves to someone saying, "Take them to my brother, for sure I have no other, and they are the shamrocks from his dear old mother's grave." Such sentimentality was soon commercialized in popular songs aimed at Irish Americans. It is too easy to forget, however, the effects of the uprooting experience of emigration and resettlement in a new land. The broadside ballads, no matter how crude or sentimental they may have been, were always addressed to emotions which were genuine.

Others of the Irish-American ballads, some of which certainly originated on the minstrel or vaudeville stage, were in the comic tradition of the stage Irishman. When not celebrating the Irishman's alleged capacity for drink and combat, they often gloried in simple Irishness by supplying long lists of Irish names. An excellent example of this type of ballad is "Naming the Boy," submitted by Patrick McKenna to the *United Mine Worker's Journal* in 1910, and reprinted in George Korson's *Coal Dust on the Fiddle*. In the song Mr. McShane asks his neighbors over to his house to assist in picking a name for the new boy child.

> "I've invited the Brady's, the O'Grady's
> And O'Brien, Gilhooly and Dennis McCoy
> Pat McConnell and Fagin, Dan Hagin and Flynn—
> Will be there when I'm naming the boy."

A list of rather ordinary names is produced, but McShane protests:

"These names have a good Irish ring, sir,
But they're just a bit common for me
What I want is a good up-to-date Irish name
For the front of McShane's boy, you see."

Twas a notable gathering that evening,
And names that were hard to excel
Were sprung from the days of Old Brian Boru,
Up to those of Charles Stewart Parnell.

But they wrangled between drinks till midnight
Argued strong over this name and that
And finally agreed that the Broth of a Boy
Should have the best of all Irish names—Pat.

Not all the songs were mere funny pieces, however. The lot of the average Irishman and his Irish-American neighbors was a hard one in the nineteenth century and early decades of the twentieth. Miners, lumberjacks, mill hands, steelworkers, they all worked long hours for low wages in often dangerous conditions, when they could find work at all. Therefore, although songs like "Pat Works on the Railroad" (or "on the Canal") or "No Irish Need Apply" are comic, the humor has the tough, bitter bite of irony. In the soft-coal regions of Pennsylvania they sang of "Mickey McGinn" (Everyone said he was ugly as sin), who saved the lives of fifty miners. The tragic Maine lumberjack ballad, "The Jam on Gerry's Rock," was probably composed by an Irishman and certainly bears in both tune and words the Irish stamp. Irishmen and Irish Americans were often in the forefront of trade union activities. And not just men were involved. "Mother" Jones, born Mary Harris in County Cork, was a tough active organizer in the coal fields and steel mills from the 1870s until the age of eighty-nine, when she participated in the great steel strike of 1919. The radical Industrial Workers of the World was full of Irishmen. As a result, there are scores of protest and union songs which clearly reveal the Irish imprint.

II

The fiddler bein' willin',
His elbow bein' strong,
We danced The *Wrongs of Ireland*
For four hours long

(from *Body, Boots & Britches*
by Harold W. Thompson)

Unfortunately, very little of real substance can be said about the Irish contribution to the instrumental tradition in American folk music. There does not seem to be very much published on the origins of American fiddle tunes which goes beyond the usual "British" denomination. Nor is there very much available which attempts to compare American fiddling styles with those of England, Scotland, or Ireland. In one of the few articles on the subject, Linda C. Burnam-Hall notes that American fiddle tunes in the South exhibit fewer complexities of melodic figuration, less difficulties in bowing and fingering, "and correspond more closely to the relatively straight forward English style of playing than the ornate Gaelic tradition."

To this several objections must be made. Compared with his Irish and Scottish counterparts, the American fiddler has played in a very different cultural environment. The Irish fiddler, performing for his dancers, plays more slowly, has time for ornamentation, and seeks a fluidity which nicely supports the dancers' jigs, reels, and hornpipes. The American fiddler provides music for the "hoedown" or "square dance," which is generally faster, less graceful, and demands sharper and heavier rhythmic accents. Alan Lomax neatly summed up the situation of the American fiddler when he wrote in his *Folk Songs of North America*, "The hoedown fiddler plays with less polish and tunefulness than his Scotch-Irish brothers, but his stronger beat, his more rhythmic attack, his syncopations, and his rapid, heavy bowing make the old reels fairly sizzle. His motive is to play 'music as hot as a hen in a basket of wool trying to lay a goose egg.' " Playing a "markedly wilder and more aggressive" style, the American fiddler has inevitably responded to that "hot" element in the American musical character—the need for rhythm and speed, that has long characterized the country's popular music.

It is this "Americanization" of the old tunes and dances, rather than any powerful influence of the "straight forward English style" which has caused American fiddling techniques in the South to drift away from the Ulster tradition which was originally one of the most powerful musical forces in that region. Burnam-Hall, like so many other American commentators on their folk music, has failed to keep in mind the ethnic origins of southern mountain music. In the North and Midwest, which experienced a later and more continuous arrival of Irish fiddlers in the nineteenth century, one is more likely to find fiddle tunes and modes of playing closer to present-day Irish styles.

As for the tunes themselves, we find ourselves faced with the same problems which we discussed in the section on the song tradition. In the South, where the fiddling tradition, like folk singing, has remained stronger than in most other parts of America, there are only a relatively small number of the common tunes which are easily recognized as Irish in origin. "Miss Macleod's

Reel," common to both Irish and Scottish fiddlers, has been transferred to America with a few changes, although it has picked up a set of words. The Irish tune "The Beggar Man" or "Johnny Dhu" is easily recognized (in the American "The Red-Haired Boy," a favorite among blue-grass fiddlers), as are "The Fairy Dance" (usually called "Old Molly Hare" in America), "Speed the Plow," "Haste to the Wedding," "Pig Town Fling," "Fisher's Hornpipe," and of course "The Irish Washerwomen" and "Garryowen."

More often Irish tunes have undergone powerful changes in America. An Irish fiddler would have to listen carefully to hear the remnants of "The Coockoo" and "The Mason's Apron" among the vast tune families which these two pieces have spawned in the United States. Often one hears bits and pieces in American jigs and reels that seem lifted directly from Irish tunes. "The Rakes of Mallow," for example, is not commonly played in the American South today. However, its two sections have been appropriated for parts of other tunes, "Mississippi Sawyer" and "Soldier's Joy."

There is a whole group of tunes—those which contain sudden shifts from major to minor modes and then back to the major—which commentators often describe as having an "Irish" sound. Two good examples are the oft-played "Billy in the Low Ground," and "Paddy on the Turnpike." Clearly, while some Irish fiddle tunes have remained intact, many more have been absorbed and become the raw materials for American folk music.

What about Irish music as such, pure and unadulterated, as played by Irish fiddlers and pipers? Was everything destined to end up in the American musical melting pot? Not at all. In 1940 the M. M. Cole Company of Chicago published a book entitled *One Thousand Fiddle Tunes*. What is interesting about this particular book is that, out of its vast number of tunes, there are only fifteen or twenty which one might expect a southern mountain fiddler to recognize by their titles. Now nothing can be more misleading than tune titles in folk music, but in this case they suggest something important. Instead of the titles common to the southern Appalachian fiddling tradition, we have titles which are for the most part Irish and Scottish, many of them still well known in Ireland and Scotland today. The homegrown American efforts in the book reek of the minstrel show—"Nigger in the Wood Pile," "Camp Meeting Jig"—or of the early vaudeville circuits of the northern cities —"Belles of Omaha Reel," "The Flowers of Michigan Reel," "The Cincinnati Hornpipe." The presence of these pieces and the large number of Irish tunes suggests that the book represents a distinctly twentieth-century, northern, urban, and largely Irish-American fiddling tradition.

For those familiar with the works of Captain Francis O'Neill, the existence of such a tradition comes as no great surprise. Captain O'Neill was the superintendent of police in Chicago around the turn of the century. He put together several volumes of Irish music, all of it collected in the United States. Perhaps the most famous of these is *O'Neill's Music of Ireland*, published in

1903, which contains 1,850 tunes. O'Neill was dedicated to the cause of Irish traditional music. After his retirement from the force he devoted himself to the propagation and revival of this music. In addition to his tune collections, O'Neill published two other books, *Irish Folk Music: A Fascinating Hobby* (1910) and *Irish Minstrels and Musicians* (1913). It is from these two books that most of what we know of traditional music in the Irish-American communities of the nineteenth and early twentieth centuries may be found.

Naturally, a number of traditional musicians, amateur and professional, were part of the great Irish migration to the United States. In America they found not only a ready audience for their talents but, what is more, an audience which was ready and able to pay for its music. In the United States the traditional musician could support himself professionally in a style not often possible at home. O'Neill himself noted, in his *Irish Folk Music*, after a visit to Ireland in the early twentieth century, that "More and better music can be found in dozens of American cities than in Cork or even Dublin. Why? Because it is encouraged, appreciated and *paid for*, and because the musician's calling is no way suggestive of mendicancy." Irish saloonkeepers in the States were prepared to feature pipers as a part of their entertainment. Some pipers even managed to establish their own saloons, with themselves as the feature attraction. William Connolly, a restless piper originally from Milltown, County Galway, ran several such establishments. Thomas F. Kerrigan, who died in 1901 at the age of sixty, was a fine piper who established "Kerrigan's Pleasant Hour" at West Forty-second Street in New York City. He was relieved during his nightly performances by his waiters, all of whom were musical. Patrick Fitzpatrick, a businessman and piper from Leitrim, was only twenty-one when he built Celtic Hall in New York City in 1892. It was long a center for Irish traditional music in that city.

There were various Irish plays and variety shows which toured America and featured Irish pipers and fiddlers. Power's *The Ivy Leaf* is one such show mentioned by O'Neill. Fitzpatrick, of Celtic Hall, toured the country with *The Top of the Morning* company. Other pipers and fiddlers, some of them developing comedy routines, appeared on vaudeville programs all over the country.

O'Neill was quite distressed at the decayed state of Irish traditional music in Ireland. He blamed the clergy (for stopping the "patterns" and curtailing house dances), the arrival of the "German accordion," and the lack of patronage by the wealthier classes. Certainly, there were few Irish families in America who were prepared to follow the ancient tradition of retaining a household piper. America, however, had its own brand of patronage for worthy musicians. O'Neill mentions John McFadden, a fiddler, who managed to find friends who kept him on the Chicago city payroll, regardless of which party, the Republicans or the Democrats, were in power. Chief O'Neill himself once used his position on the police force to lure Bernard Delaney, a great piper, back to Chicago, when Delaney went off touring with the *Ivy Leaf* company. Contacting the New York City police, no doubt, O'Neill had Delaney intercepted and offered him a position with the Chicago police if he would only return to the Windy City. Delaney accepted.

Indeed, one gets the impression that the Chicago police force provided a kind of subsidy for Irish music in that city. Captain O'Neill relied very heavily on Sergeant James O'Neill (no relation) to note down the pieces played by pipers and fiddlers who turned up in Chicago. In cases where they had only a fragment of a tune, the sergeant would "reconstruct" it. The results were then submitted before an "Inquest Committee" made up of the "Chief" and other musicians who passed on the authentic "Irishness" of the piece. This might account for certain oddities sometimes found in O'Neill's collections.

So strong was traditional music within the Irish community in America that many of the musicians, both Irish-and American-born, learned their fiddling and piping in the United States. Selena O'Neill (no relation), who received some formal music training in Chicago, was apparently a first-rate Irish-American fiddler. "She goes at it so wicked—so vicious that she'd lift you off the floor." O'Neill claims she was the first person to play "The Fox Chase" in public in Chicago.

When the great Columbian exposition was opened in Chicago in 1893, a "Donegal Castle" was one of the attractions. It boasted no less than two pipers. Outside the gates there was the legendary Turlough McSweeney (Toirdhealach Mac Suibhne), who claimed that his great talent came from the fairies. McSweeney had been "imported" especially for the exposition and apparently smuggled some of the "good people" along with him. Even in Chicago, he was known, at certain times late in the evening, to throw open the door, place the jug of whiskey in the doorway, turn his back upon his human listeners, and play exclusively for "them."

Inside "Donegal Castle" was the great Irish-American piper "Patsy" J. Touhey, who left County Galway at the age of four. O'Neill was obviously proud of the accomplishments of the new generation of American musicians, for he commented:

While Turlough McSweeny, the "Donegal Piper," may have fittingly represented an antiquated and oppressed Ireland, playing his ancient instrument outside the entrance of the Castle, the hopes and aspirations of a regenerated nation were pleasingly typified in Patsy Touhey, the spruce young man in corduroy breeches and ribbed stockings, whose expert manipulations of a great set of Taylor pipes made him the center of attraction within.

Touhey's Taylor pipes were themselves an important product in the development of Irish traditional music in America. "Willy" Taylor, O'Neill's candidate for the best pipe maker in America, was born in Drogheda in 1830, where his father made organs and bagpipes. Taylor, with his brother Charles, came to America in 1872. Discovering that the "puny" sound of the traditional Uileann pipes was inadequate for American saloons and large music halls, the Taylors settled in Philadelphia and set about developing a new kind of pipes. Brought up to concert pitch, with a bigger and brighter sound, the Taylor pipes soon became the favorites among American pipers and doubtless had some influence upon pipe making back in Ireland.

Taylor died in 1901, and O'Neill fretted that there was no one of his caliber to take his place. However, in 1975 Lawrence McCullough from Chicago published an article in *Eire-Ireland* about one Patrick Hennelly. Hennelly, although in his seventies, was still making and repairing pipes in Captain O'Neill's city.

In an earlier article in *Folklore Forum*, McCullough has suggested that Irish music in America had reached the peak of its "Golden Age" about the time O'Neill began publishing his great collections. O'Neill himself was afraid that a decline was already setting in by 1910. But as McCullough claims the arrival of the commercial sound recordings gave Irish traditional music a brief new lease of life. In the early days of the gramophone industry, there was almost no such thing as a mass audience. Record companies had to scramble for buyers within a highly diversified market. Every ethnic group, from blacks and Italians to white "hillbillies" in the mountains had records produced exclusively for them, recorded by musicians drawn from their own ranks. The Irish-Americans were no exception.

"Patsy" Touhey, prior to his death in 1923, cut four records for the Victor company. In fact Touhey had earlier hit upon a clever idea. He circulated a list of 150 pieces which he was willing to cut on Edison cylinders at $10 per dozen.

McCullough points out that commercial recordings of Irish music, most of which were made between the 1920s and the 1940s, captured a wide variety of styles in both fiddling and piping. There were the older Irish styles dating from the post-Famine years in Ireland, and the newer Irish-American modes of playing. Some of these recorded renditions came to be regarded as "classics" on both sides of the Atlantic, and have served as "test pieces" for aspiring musicians. However, the Depression of the 1930s, which slashed record company budgets and consumer spending alike, hit the "ethnic" record business heavily. McCullough, who has examined the catalogs of recording companies, states that numbers of Irish traditional musicians recorded and numbers of Irish records kept in stock steadily declined during the 1940s, so that by the end of World War II, the "Irish" market had almost evaporated. A few small American companies continued to record traditional Irish musicians until around 1950, but eventually they too faded away.

Irish America was fast losing touch with its musical roots. Moreover, emigration from Ireland had so dwindled after 1920 that, until recent years, there was no longer enough new blood to keep up the old interests. Remnants of the once powerful tradition, however, still remain. Brendan Breathnach in his *Folkmusic and Dance of Ireland* states that a school of Uileann piping is still maintained in Philadelphia. McCullough suggests that New York City, with its 315,000 Irish Americans, is perhaps the real center for Irish traditional music in America today. This was the city that received many of the post–World War II immigrants from Ireland. Currently, it supports between forty and fifty schools of Irish dancing and about a half-dozen schools of Irish music. There are, according to McCullough, numerous opportunities there for musical performances. Elsewhere, the musical interest among Irish Americans is markedly lower. I can testify, however, that even in the desert fastnesses of Phoenix, Arizona, there is a group called the "Donegal Dancers." The name of their fiddler is Saul Rudnick.

Decline, yes. Obliteration, no. McCullough, himself a champion tin whistle player, says that at the 1973 Fleadh Ceoil na hEireann more than 100 Americans entered the competitions.

The United States is not, of course, about to mushroom out with hordes of pipers and Irish fiddlers and tin whistle players. Americans are eclectic, and I expect that many will pick up Irish tunes and even instruments, but they will use them in a variety of new ways. Already a group of hammered-dulcimer players who call themselves *Trapezoid* has put out a record with three or four of O'Carolan's pieces on it. The tin whistle is sometimes used, but the main instruments, the hammered dulcimers, are German in origin. This is a far cry from O'Neill's golden age of Irish-American pipers and fiddlers. Nevertheless, thanks to modern recordings, and the appearance in America by professional groups such as the *Chieftains*, Irish traditional music has now reached beyond the Irish-American community and has begun to charm and influence a new generation of Americans. The great days may be past, but the end is not yet within sight.

FOR FURTHER READING

Malcom Laws, Jr., *Native American Balladry: A Descriptive Study and a Bibliographical Syllabus* (Folcraft, Pa., 1959, 1969); R. L. Wright, *Irish Emigrant Ballads and Songs* (Bowling Green, Ohio, 1975); A. L. Lloyd, *Folksong in England* (St. Albans, Herts, 1975) (1967); Bruno Nettl, *An Introduction to Folk Music in the United States* (Detroit, Mich., 1967); James G. Leyburn, "The Scotch-Irish," *American Heritage*, (December 1970); E. Estyn Evans, "The Scotch-Irish: Their Cultural Adaptation and Heritage in the American Old West," *Essays in Scotch-Irish History*, ed. E. R. R. Green (London, 1969); Norman Cazden, *The Abelard Folk Song Book* (New York, 1958);

George Pullen Jackson, *Spiritual Folk Songs of Early America* (New York, 1964) (1937); George Pullen Jackson, *White Spirituals in the Southern Uplands* (New York, 1965) (1933); George Petrie, *The Petrie Collection of Ancient Music of Ireland*, vols. 1 and 2 (Farnborough, Hants., England, 1967) (1855); F. H. Eckstrom and M. W. Smyth, *Minstrelsy of Maine: Folk-Songs and Ballads of the Woods and the Coast* (Ann Arbor. Mich., 1971) (1927); Huddie Ledbetter, *Leadbelly: The Library of Congress Recordings*, Elektra, EKL-301-2; William H. Talmadge, "The Scotch-Irish and the British Traditional Ballad in America," *New York Folklore Quarterly* 24 (December 1968); Colm O Lochlainn, *Irish Street Ballads* (Dublin, 1960) and *More Irish Street Ballads* (Dublin, 1965); George Korson, *Coal Dust on the Fiddle: Songs and Stories of the Bituminous Industry*, (Hatboro, Pa., 1965); John Greenway, *American Folksongs of Protest* (New York, 1960); Deac (T. C.) Martin, *Deac Martin's Book of Musical Americana*, (Englewood Cliffs, N.J., 1970); Harold W. Thompson, *Body, Boots & Britches: Folk Tales, Ballads and Speech of Country New York* (New York, 1962) (1939); Linda C. Burnam-Hall, "Southern American Folk Fiddle Styles," *Ethnomusicology* 19 (January 1975); Allen Lomax, *Folk Songs of North America in the English Language* (Garden City, N.Y., 1960); *One Thousand Fiddle Tunes* (Chicago, 1940); Francis J. O'Neill, ed., *O'Neill's Music of Ireland* (New York, 1963) (1903); Francis J. O'Neill, *Irish Folk Music: A Fascinating Hobby* (Darby, Pa., 1973) (1910); Francis J. O'Neill, *Irish Minstrels and Musicians* (Darby, Pa., 1973) (1913); Lawrence McCullough, "An American Maker of Uileann Pipes: Patrick Hennelly," *Eire Ireland* (Winter 1975); Lawrence McCullough, "An Historical Sketch of Traditional Irish Music in the U.S.," *Folklore Forum* 8 (July 1974); Breandan Breathnach, *Folkmusic and Dance of Ireland* (Dublin, 1971).

SOME IRISH AMERICAN THEATRE LINKS

MICHÉAL Ó hAODHA

For over three centuries, Ireland has been a hotbed for actors, most of whom, for the greater part of their lives adorned many countries' capitals but their own. During the eighteenth and nineteenth centuries, the best actors had, of necessity, to leave Ireland for London and later for the United States. Despite the contribution of playwrights of Irish birth from Farquhar to Shaw to English drama, the theatre in Dublin up to the beginning of this century was mainly a colonial creation and as a consequence had little influence or impact on the people as a whole.

The beginnings of American theatre were equally tentative not only because of the slow growth of an indigenous drama but since New York and Philadelphia, like Dublin, were to a large degree dependent on guest stars from the London theatres. In those early days, Irish actors like Tyrone Power and John Brougham had established reputations in London before they visited the States. Power, the first of an illustrious theatre family, was also a playwright and author whose death by drowning in the S.S. *President* in 1841 was a loss to London and Dublin theatres, where he was much admired for his performances in comedy. The film actor Tyrone Power and the stage director Sir Tyrone Guthrie, founder of theatres in Stratford, Ontario, and Minneapolis, were among his descendants.

A more influential figure on the American scene was John Brougham, who was born in Dublin in 1810. After abandoning his studies as a medical student in Trinity College, he made his first appearance on the London stage in Pierce Egan's *Tom and Jerry*. After a short period as manager of the Lyceum Theatre, London, he left for New York in 1842, where he had considerable success as an actor-playwright with adaptations of Dickens and Bulwer-Lytton, before he opened his own theatre, the Lyceum on Broadway in 1850. This theatre passed into the control of James William Wallack in 1852, and it was later to become a base for the greatest Irish purveyor of melodrama, Dion Boucicault.

Tyrone Power, Barney Williams, and James Florence, whose real name was Bernard Conlin, had cultivated a taste for Irish melodrama with plays like *O'Flannigan and the Fairies* and *Rory O'Moore*, but whenever nineteenth-century melodrama is discussed, one inevitably thinks of Dionysius Lardner Boucicault.

An air of mystery shrouds the playwright's birth and ancestry—a mystery which he himself encouraged. To add to the confusion he changed his name rather frequently in his early years; it appears, at different stages, as Dionysius Lardner Boursiquot, Dion Boursiquot, Lee Moreton, even Viscount Boucicault, after a short stay in Paris, until finally he settled for Dion Boucicault as "a suitable patronymic to suggest the subtle magical qualities of a necromancer." He was always ready to invest his own life with a share of the sensation and melodrama so characteristic of his plays. Once in reply to the question "Are you an Irishman?" he replied—a shade cryptically—"Sir, nature did me that honour." And right enough, nature, colloquially speaking, seems to have done its share.

It is now generally accepted that he was the natural son of Dr. Dionysius Lardner, a lecturer and editor of Lardner's Cabinet Cyclopedia, at whose residence, 47 Lower Gardiner Street, Dublin, he was born on St. Stephen's Day, 1820. His mother, Anne Darley Boursiquot, had separated from her husband, a Dublin wine merchant of Huguenot descent in 1819. She was a sister of the poet George Darley, whose upstaged verse-play on Thomas à Becket may have given the lead to Aubrey de Vere, Tennyson, T. S. Eliot, and Jean Anouilh, who have treated the subject since.

After his early success as a playwright with *London Assurance* Boucicault became one of the best-known actor-playwrights of the century in Ireland, England, and the United States. His output was enormous; he is credited with 150 plays, most of which were adaptations of novels or French farce.

With his first wife, Agnes Robertson, he arrived in New York in 1853 and toured the eastern and midwestern states. One of his earliest successes in New York was *The Octoroon* or *Life in Louisiana*, staged at the Winter Garden in 1859. This was one of the first plays to treat the slavery question in the southern states fairly seriously but without giving offense to either side. He always had an eye for the topical, and a year earlier the Indian Mutiny had paved the way for another success, *Jessie Brown* or *The Relief of Lucknow*. He always tried to exploit local appeal in his adaptations. A French melodrama, *Les Pauvres de Paris*, was "boucicaulted" as *The Poor of New York*, *The Poor of London*, and so on. "I localise it for each town" he explained once "and hit the public between the eyes—I can spin-out these rough and tumble dramas as a hen lays eggs."

Boucicault's dictum—"plays are not written, they are rewritten"—gives a clue to his methods. He adapted and rewrote between rehearsals of his plays and between revivals of his plays while all the time in search of another novel, French farce, or historical incident on which he could exercise his undoubted talents as a theatre craftsman and dramatic retoucher. When he hit on the idea for his famous dramatization of the *Colleen Bawn*, he wrote to the New York theatre manager Laura Keene enclosing six engravings of scenes around Killarney, with an order for the scene painter to get to work on them at once, and a book of Irish melodies marking those which he wanted scored for orchestra. He added that he would have the first act finished soon and hoped to have the play upon the stage within a fortnight. He was as good as his word. The play opened at the Laura Keene Theatre, on 29 March, 1860, to become one of the best-known Irish plays of the century.

Boucicault has been accused of plagiarism and of making a romantic hotchpotch of his source, Gerald Griffin's novel *The Collegians*, by those who forget that the Colleen Bawn story has a factual background. Of course, Boucicault never bothered with first sources, but he made due acknowledgment to Griffin in a program dedication "to the undying memory of his illustrious countryman Gerald Griffin whose beautiful romance *The Collegians* furnished the subject of the play." It in turn, provided the libretto for Benedict's opera *The Lily of Killarney* .

Boucicault's greatest success in New York was with *The Shaughraun*, first produced at Wallack's Theatre in 1874. As "Con the Shaughraun, the soul of every fair, the life of every funeral, the first fiddle at all weddings and patterns," Boucicault presented an endearing picture of the harum-scarum happy-go-lucky Irishman of romantic melodrama. Even as stern a critic as Henry James could not resist the charm:

Our drama seems fated when it repairs to foreign parts for its types, to seek them first of all in the land of brogue and "bulls." A cynic might say that it is our privilege to see Irish types enough in the sacred glow of our domestic hearts, and that it is therefore rather cruel to condemn us to find them so inveterately in the consoling glamour of the footlights. But it is true that an Irish drama is always agreeably exciting; whether on account of an inherent property in the material or because it is generally written by Mr. Boucicault we are unable to say. *The Shaughraun* will, we suppose, have been the theatrical event of the season; and if a play was to run for four or five months there might have been a much worse one for the purpose than this. There is no particular writing in it, but there is an infinite amount of acting, of scene shifting, and of liveliness generally; and all this goes on to the tune of the finest feelings possible, love, devotion self-sacrifice, humble but heroic bravery, and brimming Irish bonhomie and irony are the chords that are touched. . . .

These were the qualities which endeared the stage Irishman of the past century to this compatriots in Dublin, New York, and Chicago. He had made himself part of the American dream for the thousands of Irish emigrants who flocked to Boston and New York after the Famine. It was a sentimental and romantic picture of mother machrees and wild colonial boys in their little grey homes in the west. The word "melodrama" has now outlived its usefulness as a term of critical abuse. It can now be seen as a phenomenon of the Industrial Revolution when thousands of the scarcely literate flocked to the popular theatres in the same way as millions of their descendants sit nightly before television screens to view "Kojak" or "Hawaii Five-O."

As one reads of his success as a purveyor of sensation dramas, Boucicault takes on the appearance of a Houdini or a Maskelyne; bodies roped to railway lines, heroines trapped in caves with rising water, the parading of Derby winners on the stage, earthquakes, volcanoes, and the throwing of dubious Christians to real lions—all these were child's play to Boucicault. Like the good showman he was, Boucicault gave his public just what they wanted. He wrote a dozen or more Irish plays, but his interest was in Irish subjects, not in Irish theatre. He professed to be opposed to the stage Irishman of the blood-and-thunder school. Replying to some critics who did not admire the new stage Irishman à la Boucicault he wrote:

The fire and energy that consist in dancing about the stage in an expletive manner, and in indulging in ridiculous capers and extravagancies of language and gesture form the materials of a clowning character, known as "the stage Irishman" which it has been my invocation as an artist and a dramatist to abolish.

He certainly did not abolish the stage Irishman but he refined him in his delineations of Shaun the Post, Myles na Coppaleen, and Con the Shaughraun. In a way, Boucicault may be said to have perpetuated a type who survives in a still recognizable but attenuated form in plays by Shaw, Synge, O'Casey, and Brendan Behan, and other Irish playwrights.

His influence on his fellow dramatists in the United States was widespread but in general harmful. Taking their cue from Boucicault other writers attempted plays in Irish historical themes. The most popular subject was Robert Emmet, the ill-fated young hero of an abortive rebellion in 1803. His speech from the dock delivered in Green Street Courthouse after he had been sentenced for high treason has echoed around the world wherever the Irish gathered.

The earliest record of a public performance of the oration was in a New York theatre in May 1806 when it was recited by a Mrs. Hamilton described in contemporary journals as "formerly Miss Peters of Dublin." Indeed it is on the stage rather than in history books that one can best explore the mystique of the Emmet cult.

At least a score of writers have attempted plays on the subject. The trouble is that he attracted too many authors with no discernible talent as dramatists. For example, there may have been worse playwrights than the American James Pilgrim, but there cannot have been many. This actor-playwright staged *Robert Emmet: The Martyr of Irish Liberty* in New York, in 1853, appearing himself in the part of Darby O'Gaff, whom he describes as "a sprig of the Enerald Isle." According to the published text, Emmet was married, not to Sarah Curran as one might expect but to one Maria so that he can sing to her "I'm sitting on the stile, Mary" before he leaves her a widow.

An American play on Emmet by Dr. P. T. Cunningham, produced at the Olympic, St. Louis, included Napoleon and Talleyrand among the characters. Another attempt, by B. M. Boylan of Ohio, entitled *The Rebels: The Insurgent Chiefs of 1803*, has the familiar disclaimer: "The drama was written with the view to putting a true and clean picture of Irish life on the stage. I have always held in abhorrence the thing known as the stage Irishman, and I feel confident that this play will be received with applause, by those who offer no excuse for, but rejoice in being sprung from the Irish race."

Another Emmet play staged at the Fourteenth Street Theatre, New York, in 1902 deserves a niche to itself in theatrical history, if only for the fact that it had a cast of 150. Despite this enormous cast, only outnumbered by the anachronisms, it earned a lot of money for its author, Brandon Tynan. Born in Dublin, he was a son of Patrick J. Tynan, author of *The Irish Invincibles and Their Times* and who was once believed to have been Invincible No. 1 in the secret revolutionary organization responsible for the assassination of Burke and Cavendish in the Phoenix Park in 1882. Brandon Tynan was a successful actor who ran his own theatre in New York for a period. One of his last appearances was in the film *Parnell*, which starred a beardless Clarke Gable in the title role.

An Irish journalist, Joseph Ignatius Constantine Clarke, who worked for the *New York Sun* as Japanese correspondent, published a play on Emmet in 1888 in which he acknowledges his indebtedness to Dr. Thomas Addis Emmet, the grandnephew of Robert Emmet, for making available to him "the rare collection of family documents, illustrations, which he had gathered, and which he treasures with such loving care." Despite its historical accuracy, there is no record of a production and Clarke is best remembered as the author of the ballad "The Fighting Race" with its well-known refrain "Said Kelly and Burke and Shea."

For a final example of the mythologizing of history, one must return to Boucicault and his treatment of the Emmet legend. In 1881, Sir Henry Irving commissioned a play on Emmet from Frank Marshall with a view to production at the Lyceum Theatre, London. The Lord Chamberlain, however, notified Irving that it would be wholly inadvisable, because of Land League troubles in Ireland, to stage any play about Emmet at that particular time. Although he had paid Marshall an advance royalty of £500, Irving had no option but to comply. He later handed over the script to Boucicault, who rewrote it with his customary theatrical skill.

Although he must have known the Emmet story since his Dublin childhood —he was the compiler of a short history of Ireland—Boucicault took considerable liberties with the facts in order to heighten the melodrama. Knowing that an audience at McVicker's Theatre, Chicago, would not be greatly concerned with historical fact, he presented Emmet in romantic fashion as a sea-green incorruptible betrayed by spies and informers who rejoice that they have "a country to sell." In the final allegorical tableau, the scaffold in Thomas Street where Emmet was hanged and beheaded and where the dogs of the road lapped his blood did not appeal to Boucicault as a suitable ending for a romantic melodrama. Instead he has Emmet shot by a firing squad of English redcoats. When he falls to the ground, the half-drop curtain is raised so that the allegorical figure of Mother Erin "in palest green with a coronet of shamrocks in her hair" can be seen embracing her dead son in the manner of the *Pietà* of Michelangelo. Here was the apotheosis of Emmet as the hero who fought and fell. The symbolism is obvious and effective.

In the next generation Abbey playwrights like Conal O'Riordan, Lennox Robinson, and Denis Johnston tried to refine the melodramatic elements of the dramatic prototype, which was far more an Irish-American creation than they realized at the time. The poetic realism of the Irish theatre movement founded by Yeats and Lady Gregory and which reached its zenith in the plays of Synge was put to the test when the Abbey Theatre Company first visited the States in 1911. The Abbey's first date was at the Plymouth Theatre, Boston, a city with a large Irish community, where the company expected to be hailed as old friends. But the new realism clashed with the romantic dream, and the players were booed and hissed. Some weeks later, the whole cast of *The Playboy of the Western World* was arrested in Philadelphia and charged with presenting immoral and indecent plays. In court, an American witness for the prosecution was asked if anything immoral had happened on the stage. Back came the rely—"Not while the curtain was up."

The real life tragicomedy of that first American tour has been fully chronicled in Lady Gregory's *Our Irish Theatre* and other books about the Abbey. But the last word on the American protests can best be left to George Bernard Shaw:

The arrest of the Irish players is too ordinary to excite comment. All decent people are arrested in the United States—that's why I won't go. Who am I to question Philadelphia's right to make itself ridiculous. I warned the Irish players that America, being governed by a mysterious race, descended probably from one of the lost tribes of Israel calling themselves American Gaels, is a dangerous country for a genuine Irishman. The American Gaels are the real Playboys of the Western World.

But the riots and disturbances on that first American tour made it clear to intelligent theatregoers that for the first time in its history, Ireland had a theatre of its own and a school of playwrights of its own who had set out to mirror "the deeper thoughts and emotions of their people." That some people at home and abroad called it a distorting mirror did not matter greatly because gradually it became clear to audiences that what the Abbey set out to do was to correct a falsely sentimental and romantic view of the country and its people—cottages with roses around the door, mother machrees and purty colleens in old plaid shawls, swaggering boyos with caubeens and clay pipes—all this sunburstry, shamroguery, and stage Irishry was part of what the National Theatre had set out to destroy.

Despite the organized opposition of many Irish-American societies, including the Ancient Order of Hibernians and Clan na Gael, to the production of *The Playboy of the Western World*, the Abbey style of acting won the attention of discerning critics like John Quinn, the New York lawyer and patron of the arts:

These plays are given in a lower (and I think a finer) key than the people here are accustomed to, even if they are not great plays. An appreciation of the art of these players is a little like an understanding of Chinese painting or old tapestries; a matter that does not "grab" hold of one at the first jump.

Quinn was well aware that most Irish Americans rarely went to serious plays of any kind and was incensed to find that the works of Synge should be denounced by political leaders who were totally ignorant of the content of the plays. He was enraged, as he always was, by amateur criticism of any work of art by largely irrelevant moral and political criteria. Earlier he had written a scathing denunciation of his compatriots in a letter to W. B. Yeats:

An Irishman can't ever be a sane critic. He cannot criticize anything without thinking it fair to make it a basis of a personal attack. The true critic dissects a thing lovingly and carefully. The Irish critic goes at the subject of dissection like a drunken sailor, and with a shillelagh and a sledge-hammer batters the poor corpse all round the room, and when he has mashed the poor thing into an unrecognizable pulp, or thinks he has, he points to the poor mess and says it is only jelly or calls it poison and he thinks he has done something great.

Such sweeping generalizations did not win new friends for the Abbey. They were fortunate that they had a more conciliatory supporter in the Sligo-born politician and orator Bourke Cockran, who not only hailed the Abbey Company as "missionaries of Irish culture who have already given to the world a new conception of dramatic art" but introduce Lady Gregory to Theodore Roosevelt, who attended the New York production at the Maxine Elliott Theatre. He made a valuable contribution to the "Playboy" debate when he invited American writers to profit from the Abbey experience:

The Irish plays are of such importance because they spring from the soil and deal with Irish things which the writers really knew. They are not English or French; they are Irish. In exactly the same way any work of the kind done here, which is really worth doing, will be done by Americans who deal with the American life with which they are familiar; and the American who works abroad as a make-believe Englishman or Frenchman or German—or Irishman—will never add to the sum of first class achievement. This will not lessen the broad human element in the work; it will increase it. These Irish plays appeal now to all mankind as they would never appeal if they had been tempted to be flaccidly "cosmopolitan": they are vital and human and therfore appeal to all humanity; just because they wrote from the heart about their own people and their own feelings, their own good and bad traits, their own vital national interests and traditions and history.

Tolstoy wrote for mankind but he wrote as a Russian, about Russians, and if he had not done so he would have accomplished nothing. Our American writers, artists, dramatists, must all learn the same lesson until it comes instinctive with them and with the American public.

Such heartfelt and uncomplicated pleas for a national literature may now appear somewhat simplistic, but they gave valuable publicity to the Abbey Company's achievements and extended the range of their influence. The 1911/12 and 1914 tours gave a marked impetus to the growth of the Little Theatre movement in the United States. The movement grew in America, like the Abbey Theatre in Ireland, in opposition to the commercialism of the professional stage. The Abbey rejected the star system, substituting for it ensemble playing and teamwork in order to achieve a deeper interpretation of the playwright's text. One of the first of these Little Theatres whose principal aim was artistic merit, not long runs and profit, was the Washington Square Players, who made their debut in Greenwich Village with a production of an Abbey play by Lord Dunsany, *The Glittering Gate*, in the backroom of a little bookstore. They later rented a small theatre, where they flourished to such an extent that they made theatre history as the New York Theatre Guild, which became the cradle of many famous actors including one of the original Abbey Company, Dudley Digges. In Chicago, Maurice Browne founded a Little Theatre on the lines of the Abbey, and the lead was followed in nearly every state and in Canada. The Abbey was no longer, as Max Beerbohm had described it "the only oasis amidst the sandy desert of the theatrical world generally."

But the spirit of Boucicault, who died in comparative poverty in New York in 1890, lived on in the works of his protégé, David Belasco, who decried what he described as "the toy playhouse," the little repertory theatres of enthusiastic amateurs. Another great exponent of romantic melodrama was the Irish actor James O'Neill, who claimed to have made his debut in *The Colleen Bawn* in Cincinnati but who scored his greatest success in *The Count of Monte Cristo*. He has won a posthumous immortality as the prototype of James Tyrone, the skinflint, whiskey swilling Shakespearean actor manqué of his son's great play, *Long Day's Journey into Night*. But the fictional James Tyrone should not be too clearly identified with the

James O'Neill who emigrated from County Kilkenny in 1856, at the age of ten, and who became one of America's most successful actors. When faced with the predicament of how to care for a wife who became a drug addict and who needed constant medical care and protection, he did everything possible to help her. He was not aided in his efforts by his two sons Eugene and Jamie, who seldom drew a sober breath in his presence or lost opportunity to scoff and sheer at a peasant father who could not "wipe the bog off his face."

For although the playwright, Eugene, was proud of his Irish blood in a romantic way, he despised his Irish father, who had a fear of poverty but who was not mean by normal standards. In *Long Day's Journey* there is little attractive in the father's character except a somewhat maudlin capacity for forgiveness, but he emerges as a strong dramatic creation even if the real life James was viewed through a distorting lens.

The nearest that Eugene O'Neill ever got to Ireland was when the S.S. *New York* on which he had signed as an able seaman (A.B.) called at Cobh (then Queenstown) in 1911, but the crew was not allowed shore leave. His father, James, visited Ireland in 1906 and when the Abbey Players toured the States in 1911, he made friends with some of the company. His friend and manager, George Tyler, who was associated with Liebler and Company, was largely responsible for the Abbey's visit. Although on a prolonged binge at the time, Eugene using the entrée provided by his father's connections, attended all the Abbey performances at the Maxine Eliott Theatre, New York, in November 1911. It was then he first felt the urge to write.

"It was on seeing the Irish Players that first gave me a glimpse of my opportunity," he told an interviewer years later. "I went to everything they did. I thought then and I still think that they demonstrate the possibilities of naturalistic acting better than any other company." With a touch of the blarney, he even went so far as to boast that in his opinion "the Moscow Art Players could not hold a candle to the Abbey Theatre Company." Of the *Playboy* rumpus his only recorded comment was "The Irish can't laugh at themselves."

O'Neill was particularly impressed and influenced by Synge's *Riders to the Sea*. A few years later he began to write short sea plays for the Provincetown Players, another of the Little Theatres which sprang up after the Abbey visits. This group later moved from Cape Cod to MacDougal Street, New York, where they staged the first plays of Susan Glaspell. The subject matter of T. C. Murray's *Birthright*, the clash between two brothers for the inheritance of a farm, had a marked influence on O'Neills handling of his first full-length play, *Beyond the Horizon*.

In 1924 both O'Neill and Murray published two plays with a similar theme— an old farmer marries a young wife who is coveted by his son of a former marriage. O'Neill's *Desire Under the Elms* is the more powerful play even if it depicts sex repression and sex satisfaction in the primary colors of melo-drama. Murray's *Autumn Fire* shows a classical restraint which is nowadays out of fashion. The West Cork dialect is pared of every excrescence so that the dialogue is fresh, clean-cut, and poetic. O'Neill's dialogue, as Joseph Wood Krutch commented, is often clumsy and repetitious. Some of his Irish characters speak a spurious "Synge Song," but he compensates for this deficiency by demonic energy and a splendid sense of theatre.

But if O'Neill remained conscious of his Irishness, it is mainly the darker and less attractive traits which are reflected in his semiautobiographical plays. There we find the Joycean rejection of family, country, and religion. His mother, Ella Lundigan Quinlan, alias Mary Tyrone, was the child of Irish parents who emigrated after the Famine, but who prospered in the retail trade and in real estate dealings. Her upbringing was that of a pampered daughter of a highly conventional middle-class Catholic home. She was "Lace-Curtain Irish" who were often slightly ashamed of their Irish origins now that their brothers and sons were distinguishing themselves at Harvard and at Yale. The O'Neills remained "shanty Irish," suspicious of their more ambitious and successful compatriots who in their opinion were aping their betters.

These conflicts were reflected in O'Neill's life and work. The yokels in *A Touch of the Poet* and the dossers in Johnny the Priest's saloon in *The Iceman Cometh* reveal the obverse of the stage-Irish coin minted by Boucicault. It is an image etched in acid, but the outlines are clear-cut to those who recognize the darker side of O'Neill's Irishry.

Drink, whores, the sea, suicide, and death were his subjects. The death wish was strong in him. In twenty-five of his forty-four published plays, a total of forty characters suffer violent and unnatural deaths. The playwright's own life story is an equally tragic record of violence and attempts at suicide by himself and his associates. This will for self-destruction goes hand in hand with a search for redemption. There is an Irish reluctance to face the grim realities; there are "pipe-dreams" of Tir na nOg, of a Land of the Blest beyond the horizon. But in the theatre, we can accept his searing message that man lives by his illusions, that no one is ever conclusively right or wrong, that no one is finally hateful or lovable, and that forgiveness is all. It is a typical if not exclusively Irish conclusion.

Because of his early familiarity and admiration for the work of the Abbey Company, it is regrettable that the Irish theatre did not forge stronger links with O'Neill, who once declared: "One thing that explains more than anything about me is the fact that I am Irish." He was not unappreciative of the Abbey's interest in staging plays like *Days Without End* at a period when he was given scanty recognition in the States. With a little more sympathy and foresight, Ireland might have filled the role that Sweden played in the establishment of O'Neill as one of the world's great playwrights. The European premiere of *The Iceman Cometh* and *A Moon for the Misbegotten* were staged in Stockholm and Malmo respectively. Before he died he asked that his unstaged work be bequeathed to the Royal Dramatic Theatre, Stockholm, in gratitude for the excellent performance of his plays over the years. So it transpired that no less than four world premieres of O'Neill plays were staged at the Royal Dramatic Theatre, Stockholm, between 1956 and 1962—*Long Day's Journey into Night, A Touch of the Poet, Hughie,* and *More Stately Mansions.*

However, as O'Neill had been an associate member of the Irish Academy of Letters, his widow, Carlotta O'Neill, agreed to a production of *Long Day's Journey* at the Abbey on condition that the play was produced uncut—a stipulation which was honored.

The Abbey, after a faltering start, has derived artistic and financial rewards from its tours in the United States, including its last visit in the bicentennial year with its Golden Jubilee production of O'Casey's *The Plough and the Stars.* The Abbey had also a large share in the Broadway success of Brendan Behan's *Borstal Boy,* directed by Tomas MacAnna. But in return it has spread its players throughout the English-speaking world. To the States went Dudley Digges, the Fay Brothers, J. M. Kerrigan, Maire O'Neill, Sara Allgood, Arthur Sinclair, Barry Fitzgerald, and his brother Arthur Shields. Later visitors include Jack McGowran, Cyril Cusack, Siobhan McKenna, and others. Of course the cinema, and nowadays television, have sheltered many of the Abbey's wild geese; but although these media made some of these players famous, it can fairly be said that success spoiled others.

FOR FURTHER READING

The earlier Irish theatrical impact on America awaits study both of its leaders, Power, Brougham, Williams (born Bernard Flaherty), and Florence (born Bernard Conlin) and of its context, the Dublin-London theatrical axis which fed emergent American theatre in the period after 1800. One of its early playwrights is treated in R. E. Blanc, *James McHenry (1785–1845), Playwright* (Philadelphia, 1939). The mid-century period and after has had deeper study, notably in Ely J. Kahn, *The Merry Partners: The Age and Stage of Harrigan and Hart* (New York, 1955); Robert Hogan, *Dion Boucicault* (New York, 1969); David Krause, ed., *The Dolmen Boucicault* (Dublin, 1964); and Marvin Feldheim, *The Theater of Augustin Daly* (Harvard, 1956). The conventions were studied in G. C. Duggan, *The Stage Irishman* (London, 1937), and K. R. Rossman, *The Irish in American Drama in the Nineteenth Century* (New York, 1939), with related light shed in S. G. Bolger, *The Irish Character in American Fiction, 1830–1860* (New York, 1976). The age of Shaw, Yeats, Gregory, and Synge coincided with the maturing of Irish America in social terms, and hence with a new readiness by Americans to reconsider the Irish afresh. Irish Americans, however, in their new role, found the new theater less palatable than were the engaging images of

Boucicault: their new acceptance (and perhaps self-acceptance) was too precarious to stand realistic portrayal of their Irish background. Ultimately, however, the new drama, and its vehicle, the Abbey, had greater impact than had the works of Boucicault or Brougham in their day. Una Ellis Fermor, *The Irish Dramatic Movement* (London, 1939); Lennox Robinson, *The Irish Theatre* (London, 1939); and his *Ireland's Abbey Theatre: A History, 1899–1951* (London, 1951); Michael O' hAodha, *The Abbey— Then and Now* (Dublin, 1969); Robert O'Driscoll, *Theatre and Nationalism in Twentieth Century Ireland* (Toronto, 1971); and Robert Hogan, *After the Irish Renaissance* (Minneapolis, 1967), study various aspects, with material on American tours and influence. Estimates of its impact may be gauged by statements of American critics like Ludwig Lewisohn, *The Modern Drama* (New York, 191?); James Huneker, *The Pathos of Distance* (New York, 1922), pp. 219–44; J. Wood Krutch, *"Modernism" in Modern Drama* (Ithaca, N.Y., 1953), pp. 88–103; and Van Wyck Brooks, *From the Shadow of the Mountain* (New York, 1961). There are reminiscences and reflections on American experiences in the memoirs of participants: Katherine Tynan, *Twenty-Five Years* (London, 1913); Lennox Robinson, *Curtain Up* (London, 1942); W. B. Yeats, *Autobiographies* (London, 1955); and Ann Saddlemayer, ed., *Theatre Business: Management of Men* (New York, 1971).

The new Irish-American drama, culminating in O'Neill's *Long Day's Journey into Night* (New Haven, Conn., 1955), is problematically Irish, certainly American: the impact of Irish realistic theatre, as seen here, being as great as that of Irish inheritance. Harry Cronin, *Eugene O'Neill: Irish and American: A Study in Cultural Context* (New York, 1976), and J. H. Raleigh, "O'Neill's *Long Day's Journey into Night* and New England Irish-Catholicism," *Partisan Review* 26 (1959): 573–92, make the case for major continuities, which is implicit in J. H. Raleigh, *The Plays of Eugene O'Neill* (Carbondale, Ill., 1965), and in Louis Sheaffer, *O'Neill: Son and Playwright* (London, 1968). Joseph Roppolo, *Philip Barry* (New York, 1965), studies a dramatic voice more clearly rooted in the Irish-American mainstream, whereas Paul Nolan, *Marc Connolly* (New York, 1969), studies another in whom the stream of ancestry, if conscious, runs thin.

CONCLUSION: SOME COUNTERTHEMES

OWEN DUDLEY EDWARDS

"To every thing there is a season, and a time to every purpose under the heaven . . . a time to be born, and a time to die, a time to weep , and a time to laugh, a time to mourn, and a time to dance . . . a time to keep silence and a time to speak. . . ." The opening verses of the third chapter of Ecclesiastes have a symbolic place in the story of the connection between Ireland and the United States, for they were spoken at the moment in time when the two countries held together a common grief that brought them closer together than they ever had been before, and probably ever would be again. John Fitzgerald Kennedy loved those verses, and they were spoken over his body during those terrible days when Irishmen and Americans united in a grief greater for both of them than for any other of the nations that mourned throughout the world.

It takes nothing from the cruel reality of that grief to say that both were united in mourning the death of a dream, although neither fully realized it, and although the unity of grief disguised the fact that the dreams were different dreams. To the Irish, Kennedy represented the end of a long and hard road, the fulfillment of the promise for which so many had struggled and died, while so many more had remained at home not choosing to venture to the promised land, yet enlarged by the thought that they could if they chose and the future might then be theirs. For the Irish Americans he was the end of all the miserable counting of names, and hunting through genealogies, and pathetic little lies deceiving nobody but their authors, designed to make a demeaned ethnic group appear great according to the rather vulgar standards of the ruling elites. He was the end of the brutalized and frustrated politics which, after the defeat of Al Smith in 1928, drove so many Irish Catholics into vehement championship of Franco and Father Coughlin, isolationism and witch-hunt, McCarthyism and McCarranism. To be sure, shadows of these things went on, but the symbolic exclusion was ended, and with it the psychological basis for them.

Time and historians were inevitably to raise questions about Kennedy's achievement as a statesman, most notably as to whether he was not glitter rather than gold; but as a symbol his place is secure. And in his own easygoing and rather sardonic way, he knew it. When he came into office, Irish diplomats in Washington, D.C., with memories of old Joe Kennedy's fury at being called Irish, assumed the new president would fight shy of excessive identification with the old country: in fact, he went there with an unmistakable pleasure, so confident in his Americanism that he could luxuriate in being Irish. Illness had deepened his devotion to reading, and Ireland discovered its glorious descendant knew his lost fatherland far more by its history and literature than by a distorted and dwindling heritage of grievances. He intended the Irish to be startled: "I think," remarked Pierre Salinger to me with a grin on the eve of the visit, "you folks are going to be surprised by the amount the President has read about Ireland." And in so doing he was enabled to bridge a critical gap existing in Ireland no less than in Irish America: the conflict between the intellectuals and conventional society.

He died, and that Irish dream was over, in its long aspiration and in its final realization. The world after Kennedy was a colder world, and one in which reality left less and less place for the making of other dreams. But the Americans, also, lost a dream of their own when he died. He had radiated confidence, conviction, charisma: the world which would follow became rapidly bankrupt on all three fronts and questioned the efficacy of all of them. The Kennedy assurance in retrospect seemed like inability to acknowledge ignorance; the Kennedy style came to appear a papering over the thinness of the Kennedy substance; the lightheartedness of Camelot ended in the military and moral disgrace of Vietnam. Like Gerard Manley Hopkins's Margaret, it was ourselves we were mourning, our dreams which had ended, our innocence which was lost, however little we perceived it through our grief in those days.

But Kennedy's symbolic achievement remains true, and it was a conscious achievement. He established himself not only as the symbol that an Irish-American Catholic from the most successful of the "undesirable" undergroups, could win the presidency, but also that all such undergroups could. As a Tennessee priest summed it up to us on Christmas Day, 1960, "we've got a Catholic President, and two Jews in the cabinet." Kennedy could—and did —jocularly tell an Italian-American audience on Columbus Day that his middle name was really Geraldini, and his fellow Irish Americans roared with laughter; the Italians laughed too, not believing him, but appreciating the identification with them that the frivolous claim represented. (Did it arise, one wonders, from Kennedy's memory of desperate and equally baseless Irish-American efforts to show the Irish Catholic identity of Shakespeare and the Duke of Wellington, such as Eugene O'Neill sardonically recalled in *Long Day's Journey into Night*? But the symbolism went further than Kennedy knew: he could claim an Italian ancestry he did not have, but his predecessor as an Irish-American political idol, Al Smith, went to his grave without revealing, perhaps without knowing, the secret that his followers could not be told—that his father was not of Irish, but of Italian, origin. American assimilationism tells us of the Irish who passed for WASPs: but we have much more to learn of other ethnic groups who passed for Irish.)

It was the King James version of the verses from Ecclesiastes that Kennedy liked; he was ecumenical enough to prefer the finest language, and there, too, he symbolized a new world rejecting the ghetto conformities, themselves often passion over shadows and blindness to substance. And it is the best tribute to him and what he represented to note that there is a time to praise, and a time to cease from praising. This book is a tribute to the United States in the years of its revolutionary bicentennial, but after one, two, or three cheers have been given according to personal inclination, the next stages call for cool heads. And although the notion of the donor of a gift horse looking it in the mouth seems a little odd, especially given the place of horse dealing in Irish life in and out of Somerville and Ross, it is fair to point out weaknesses in the present work. Inevitably it reads too much like a story of achievement; the Irish are shown to have a place here, there, and almost everywhere in American life. There must have been many who bitterly lamented their abandonment of their birthright for a mess of highly indigestible and hardly substantial pottage. Mrs Frances Trollope, watching a dead Irish immigrant on a canal bank, told herself that in Ireland there would at least be someone to close his eyes. (This was in the decade before the Great Famine: subsequently, lonely death could no longer be seen as alien to the Irish experience.)

Perhaps the shade of Thomas D'Arcy McGee is the most formidable of famous Irish ghosts typifying such a rejection. The war of realism and romanticism in his soul was one common to countless Irish, across the ethnic and religious divides, though perhaps few have swung quite so dramatically from an extremity of romanticism to its polar opposite. And his progress, which to many Irish and many Americans, hurts too much to be acknowledged as progress, led him to reject both the Irish nationalism of his youth and the American dream to which he so vigorously subscribed in the early 1850s. It is certainly easy to postulate an Irish American who rejects Ireland in one form or in another: Joseph P. Kennedy was one, and Judge Cohalan, at the heart of his crisis with de Valera in 1920, was surely another, and the quiet assimilationists who abandoned their tell-tale religion and nomenclature provide innumerable more. Edwin O'Connor's novel *All in the Family* gives us the reaction of an Irish American briefly on the old sod: "I'm about fed up with these home-grown Micks: there's not a quarter in the crowd."

And there are some very distinguished Irishmen who were sour enough about American pretensions: Theobald Wolfe Tone, in 1795–96 was one, James Stephens before and during the American Civil War was another,

James Connolly in 1903–09 was a notable, if better integrated, third. But a figure who rejects both his Irish and his American dreams seems alien to the ethos of much of this volume. Yet Thomas D'Arcy McGee found a positive faith in Canada, and his ideas of multiethnic culture had much to teach both the Irish and the American elites and local ethnic majorities. The lessons may have their application today, as Ireland and the United States are painfully learning; and so does the cause for which D'Arcy McGee gave his life, that of resisting the pretensions of murderous chauvinism. Canada is *terra incognita* to most Americans, though the converse is anything but true. The Irish connection with the United States must be explored both comparatively and otherwise in its Canadian context, and D'Arcy McGee should remind us that neither the Irish nor the American yardsticks will necessarily supply all the answers. In so doing we can bear in mind not only the pioneer work in D'Arcy McGee's own writings, where he illuminated much of the contrasts of the three societies, but also another nineteenth-century work, John F. Maguire's *The Irish in America*, which takes all of North America for its oyster.

If we need to remember Canada, are we not also in danger of forgetting Europe? England, after all, supplies one of the most significant links between Ireland and the United States, both as cultural agency, and as political interlocutor. And many of the Irish emigrants to the United States had a British dimension to their experience before the last and longest voyage, albeit few careers were as exotic as that of the agrarian rebel Thomas Ainge Devyr, who ended his days as a writer for Patrick Ford's *Irish World* in New York, but who had come to the United States from antilandlord agitation in Donegal via a fling in the Chartist movement in Britain such that he arrived, with perfect timing, as a vital contributor to the antirent warriors in Rensselaer County, New York. The diversity of the Scottish experience in America, Highland and Lowland, has many parallels and contrasts with Irish America, and may warn against excessive homogenization of the Irish emigration; and the special Scottish connection with Ulster poses specific problems, as does the intensity of American friendship and hostility toward the Scots. The more obviously Celtic emigrations from Wales and Cornwall also suggest profitable lines of comparison, particularly given the work that is being done for both emigrations by Professor Maldwyn Jones and Dr. John Rowe, respectively.

As we move to the continental landmass, a host of critical factors crowds around us. Irish responses to European events were vital to Irish history, but, at times more pointedly, also to the history of the Irish abroad. Italy, for instance, played a singular part in the alienation of the Irish Catholics from their environment in Britain, the Empire, and, to a lesser extent, the United States. In the twentieth century G. M. Trevelyan's historiographical oscillation between the Whig interpretation of English history and a three-volume panegyric on Garibaldi, well epitomized the contemporary response of the liberal intelligentsia of the period. If British Protestantism was declining in positive faith, its negative roots of antipapalism were as vigorous as ever, and Garibaldi appealed to these as well as to the spirit of liberty. Indeed, in 1860, as in 1688 and in 1774, antipapalism and liberty seemed to many Whiggish minds to be synonymous. Obviously the United States, in 1860, was moving very rapidly toward a crisis of liberty of its own: Americans were hardly to be blamed for turning more rapidly to the news of Mr. Lincoln, Senator Douglas, Vice-President Breckinridge, and their presidential campaigns than to that of Castelfidardo. But the 1850s had involved one desperate effort by American politicians to prove that the sectional conflict was not, after all, irrepressible by making the most of rising hostility to the immigrant, a less nationally divisive scapegoat. (The scheme crumbled as nativists split on whether they were proslavery anti-immigrants or antislavery anti-immigrants: As they say in Northern Ireland, are you a Protestant Jew or a Catholic Jew?) The American Civil War kept down the Garibaldi cult in the United States, at least below the level of British adulation, but when it surfaced in American minds, Garibaldi would have been seen as the European Americanizer *par excellence*. He even resembled Washington in his readiness to resign the command of his devoted army where lesser men—such as Cromwell and Napoleon—proved incapable of so doing. On the other hand to be an Irish Catholic, whatever one's feelings about Italian fellow immigrants, was, by definition, to be propapal and anti-Garibaldi. Archbishop John Hughes of New York and his Irish American coreligionists had been chilly enough to the antislavery doctrines of Pope Gregory XVI, but when his successor, Pius IX, compared the absorption of the papal state by the Kingdom of Italy to the rending of the seamless garment of Christ, they could happily wallow in his rhetoric. Victor Emmanuel's encirclement of the Pope's last redoubt in the 1860s, and the Pope's status as prisoner in the Vatican from 1870, would supply an analogy to the self-conscious Irish Catholics encircled by hostile Protestant admirers of the Risorgimento. If the formal expression of anti-Catholic politics in America was even less successful in the 1890s than in the 1850s, the triumph of the Risorgimento added a new contemporary vigor to American literary identification of the American ethos with the cause of anti-papalism. The sense of cultural siege was much less obvious than the formal attacks of anti-Catholic movements, but it was much more corrosive in its effects.

We can generalize from this example. Like American Jews, American Catholics had a European sense and a set of European sympathies which often brought them into conflict with the native Protestant culture. But although the American Catholics were generally less perceptive than the American Jews in their estimate of European states—Catholics were too ready to shut their eyes to the shortcomings of Catholic states, Jews needed to be told little about the shortcomings of *all* European states—both religious groups knew more about Europe than most of their Protestant counterparts, and cared more about it, quite apart from the precise European point of origin they might have. Irish Americans might be parochial, but the parish could from time to time become enormous. And for all of the sealing off of immigration in the 1920s, the hostility of Communists to Catholicism swayed Irish-American politics as drastically as Nazi persecution of the European Jews affected the politics of American Jews. The Irish-American resort to domestic witch-hunting becomes a little more comprehensible, if no less inexcusable, when we consider the longevity of the liberal anti-Catholic tradition in American culture; if Fordham University questioned the American loyalty of the Ivy League, it was partly with memories of Ivy League enshrinement of anti-Catholicism in conventional American elitist literary and historiographical tradition. The folk memory of American liberal support for the antipapalist Garibaldi induced a natural suspicion as to potential liberal support for the latest European leader of anti-Catholicism, Stalin.

Irish-American awareness of European pulls on loyalty owed much to another matter rather neglected in our book: the very extensive inroads made by the Irish in America, Catholic and Protestant, into the communications field from the time of the American Revolution. The emigrant Irish reporter won his audience, native and fellow Irish, and the Catholic diocesan newspapers possessed a much more impressive standard in the nineteenth century than could be said for them in the twentieth. A press which boasted editors such as Thomas D'Arcy McGee, Orestes Brownson, John Boyle O'Reilly, and James Jeffrey Roche needed to make few apologies.

As for the immigrant press, the Irish played their vigorous part in the roaring crescendo of publications which cascaded into greater and greater size, volume, and popularity as the century neared its close, a world in which as P. G. Wodehouse said in 1915, if an Eskimo landed in New York, the first thing he would find would be a paper written by Eskimos for Eskimos. The Irish-American Catholics in the general newspapers found their religious loyalties transmitted a European sense to their journalism. If the Americans of Ulster Protestant descent lack this—although, as the example of E. L. Godkin of the New York *Nation* and *Evening Post* shows, many did not lack it—they compensated by an early establishment of close-knit links in publications as well as business enterprise with their fellow ethnics at home. They may have lacked the rapport of the Catholics with Europe, but their individual signals across the Atlantic were clearer and deeper. And at certain points, notably during the era of the French Revolution, those individual signals gave a powerful urgency to such European awareness as they had.

If we can be faulted on our non-American and non-Irish dimensions, we would also need to stress how much remains unsaid here on the Irish experience in specific regions of the United States. The very studies here discussing Boston and San Francisco acknowledge by their content how individual those experiences often were. If Chicago contributors are more ready to generalize from their own experience, they also would confess the utter individuality of such Irish Chicago types as Daley and Dooley. Between those two there is an epitome of much of Irish America; yet considered in themselves there can be but one of each of them. There remain critical matters such as the often forgotten story of the Irish in the American South: the "Scotch-Irish" of North Carolina, so similar in appearance to, yet so different in conduct from, their brothers in Pennsylvania; the mighty and factious Pierce Butler clan of Georgia and South Carolina, slaveholders to the end in the teeth of marriage with the actress Fanny Kemble and of vituperation from the statesman Charles Sumner; Senator Charles William Jones of Florida, the Irish immigrant carpenter, who quietly championed the cause of Parnell; James F. Byrnes, scion of South Carolina Catholicism (which he abandoned) and U.S. congressman, senator, Supreme Court justice, and secretary of state; the O'Haras of Tara—steady on, you say, that is fiction. Fiction *Gone with the Wind* certainly is, and often highly unrealistic fiction at that. Yet it is of importance to us that in the novel (and film), which did so much to perpetuate the southern white myth of Reconstruction, the symbol chosen was an Irish-American family; and their almost insane worship of land ownership spoke truly of the Irish, however much the rest of the book talked nonsense about the white and black South. The white South, then, chose an Irish identity whence to realize its most popular portrait of its own imaginary martyrdom. And it is noteworthy, surely, that even though countless students have repeated one another on the indifference of the once-rural Irish concerning the land, once they arrived in America, they have failed to reckon with the blazing figure of Scarlett O'Hara.

So all you have here is a down payment, and there are many further installments that have to be made. The historiographical climate in which they are to appear has its own new fair and foul pockets. Scholarship in the old days of assimilationism belittled the Irish dimension of the Irish-American experience; it was at best seen as a caterpillar's skin to be shed before the contemplation of a truly American butterfly. The Irish, like other ethnic groups, might or might not be handled kindly by scribes, but all agreed that Americanization was the ideal. The new ethnicity invites a celebration of differences of experience. Orange and Green are beautiful. But once again we are in danger of an excess of filiopietism. In former days, filiopietism enlarged the egos of writers and readers by maximizing Irish contributions and stressing how American their Irishness was. Today we may be in for a further round of the same thing, save that the mode stresses how excitingly different this Irishness was. Our new techniques and skills blind us to the danger of our being as tribalist as our forebears. Chips on the shoulder become epaulettes when you know the right sociologese.

The old filiopietism was concerned to discover what were the desirable American values, and then to claim preeminence in them. The new filiopietism is not, in that sense, assimilationist, yet in another, perhaps it is. The new liberationist ethic is a better and more altruistic one than the tight, self-stratified, rung-crawling ethic of the past, but it exercises its own conformities at the expense of the truth. The Irish now do not have to have been militarists, but they do have to have been liberal. God knows there is much to arouse one's sympathy in the ideal of converting people to a faith by telling them they have it; yet it does create the danger of neo-mythologizing, and with new myths come new dangers. Ireland, Irish America, America at large, humanity at large, have a permanent need of what the poet AE called "the golden heresy of Truth." And is that older assimilationist world quite as dead as we think? Are we not in danger, in glorifying our ethnicities, of doing down the achievements of others, including, above all, the much-abused WASPs? Let us remember the warning of one Irish emigrant, Oscar Wilde, that the danger of being modern is that one becomes old-fashioned quite suddenly. And let us remember also the last words of the greatest Irish-American novel, *The Great Gatsby*: "So we beat on, boats against the current, borne back ceaselessly into the past."

CONCLUSION: SOME FURTHER THEMES

DAVID NOEL DOYLE

Recent studies by two research teams, organized and written by E. E. Davis and by Michael MacGreil, have demonstrated clearly how contemporary is the mental landscape of the overwhelming majority of Irish people. Over 70 percent of them subscribe to a value system committed to free enterprise, to democracy, to Christianity, and to lawful social order. The sometimes inertial, even fatalistic, character of the responses, rooted in the conviction that there seems no better alternative, rather than in positive enthusiasm, may lend an Irish twist to these findings; but otherwise they parallel remarkably the findings of attitudinal studies in the United States. Even the unexpected discovery that over 80 percent of Irish people believe their fellows would take advantage of them given a chance, so unlike the formal courtesies of their ways, yet exemplifies the same realism by which American law, public opinion, and policy assume that self-interest and self-regard so generally characterize men that they must be adequately catered for in the ongoing construction of the common good.[1] Optimistically, Americans have believed since Franklin, Madison, and Hamilton that adequate political representation and open economic opportunity will defuse the ills of narrower self-interest, and harmonize individual ambitions and public energies. The Irish may be less sanguine; yet their actual behavior, as much as their values, increasingly express a similar consensus: this despite the great differences in scope and scale, history and custom, between the two societies. Of course such parallels are those of today only, perhaps less surprising when the homogenizing effects of internationalized business, media, sciences, and popular styles are considered. But they surely point also to deeper meeting grounds, and should caution us against overly counterpointing the traditionalist Irish countryman and the enterprising American democrat of the past. In our search for a usable variety in the past to color the bold monochromes of the present, we too often forget the commonplaces that ease our own daily relationships and business, commonplaces which we find, as Irishmen or Americans, in dealing with each other, as well as among ourselves. These prosaic commonplaces of human expectation have for two centuries been the elemental component in the interaction of these two peoples, the mutual guarantor of a common humanity commonly understood. In Edward McSorley's novel *Our Own Kind* (1946), the aging Rhode Island iron molder and Leitrim immigrant Ned McDermott finds companionship and a fellow spirit in Kit Somerville, the Yankee farmer, sheriff, river pilot, and small politician from offshore Block Island. The novel is autobiographical, the instance substantially true. It cautions us against always opposing the one (Democratic, proletarian, Catholic, un-educated) against the other (Republican, affluent enough, Protestant, well educated), Irish against American. Both men loved cockfighting. Both sought just outcomes amid the thickets of their wary realism.

This symposium has come closer to realizing this commonness than has been the case with most of the past literature of Irish-American connections. Nonetheless, it has also benefited much from the accumulating studies of the field since 1940. A provisional listing of scholars active in the history of Irish America alone discovered over 100, quite apart from those whose studies in Irish and separately in American history had Ireland–United States implications. A listing in literature, political science, and sociology would prove as long again. A less selective, if more representative symposium, would have run to several volumes! Can any central themes be discerned in all this work which might point up the sources of certain reflections in these papers, and which might indicate fertile ground for future thought and writing?

Both the commemorative and adversary impulses fueled much work on the field before 1940; the Irish were a great people who had virtually made America, from its Revolution to its nineteenth-century economy (Thomas D'Arcy Magee, Patrick Ford, Michael O'Brien), or they were a race of ignorant peasants who subverted its republican purity (writers from Samuel Morse to Albert Bushnell Hart). These impulses are now so safely dead, and even their shadows remaining have been so clothed in scholarship's costume, that recent works stand independent of any residual animus or affection.[2] Yet there remain positions of feeling and principle to feed most of the new work. Scholars do not study the Irish, the Americans, or both if they are moved by a scientific curiosity which would better demonstrate its intuitions by a methodical study of the Lithuanians or the Brazilians. These impulses are the more covert for being nonnationalistic. Even traditional motives are covert when residual nationalism is not a matter of celebratory loyalty, but of ranging, comparative, and tentative curiosity. Peoples today are shattered into invigorating kaleidoscope by the contemporary explosion of knowledge and events. All scholars today are more likely to be trying to discover whether any clear points might be established about an equally kaleidoscopic past, than trying to prove points self-assuredly about a supposedly stable national tradition. In that sense even the ordinary reader, sensitized to complication by his routine day, suspects all that is not closely reasoned when he glances back at the past. Yet he will accept underlying motivation when it produces sensible positions scrupulously evidenced, and responsive to the alterations imposed by the recovered past itself. Since most of the literature of Irish-American connection now adheres to such standards, examination of it in terms of these partially instigative ideas is instructive.

American scholars in the fields of urban and labor history usually study Irish America with an eye to considerably wider matters than the fate of their subjects. The same broad interests that enticed some of the best English minds to study the earlier history of industrialization draw them to nineteenth-century Irish America. Does early industrialism necessitate the creation of an underpaid, casually employed, slum-housed working class? Are its early human results due to inherent economic forces or to miscalculation, ignorance, and greed? Because in 1860, Irish Americans were four-fifths urban, when native Americans were five-sixths rural, concentration upon Irish America in this context has been logical, delayed only by the tendency of American historians before the later 1920s to feel that such problems could be honestly investigated only with reference to Americans themselves. John R. Commons, the founder of U.S. industrial and labor history, took the view generally that the ethnic groups had largely themselves to blame if they failed to realize the promise of the country's high wage patterns. Today the leading scholars in such fields concentrate in great measure upon Irish subjects; their scholarship and humanity leads the majority of them to the conclusion that they must treat the Irish on their own terms, and not in terms of either nineteenth-century managerial, or modern narrowly Marxist preconceptions. There is a danger, however, that certain scholars, in a blanket enthusiasm for "modernization" theory, may slight the peasant, Gaelic, and Christian components of their subjects' identities as inimical to their rebirth as self-possessed partners of the new industrial culture. Ironically, it is historians of more leftward bent, such as Herbert Gutman, David Montgomery, and Michael Gordon, who seem more inclined to see the human continuities in the Irish Americans as workers, than do more conservative disciples of C. E. Black, Walt Rostow, and other proponents of the dynamic stages of economic growth. Oliver MacDonagh and Emmett Larkin, both preeminent historians of nineteenth-century Ireland, in dealing with emigration, stress as beneficial only those aspects of the countryman's Irish formation which accord with his future in America: literacy, respectability, political savvy, English, and economic individualism. Contemporary educational theory would rather concur with Gutman and others that even the range of anglicized or Gaelic folktales and folk song learned in Ireland, largely forgotten in America, would yet have broadened and made flexible and responsive minds to be reeducated amid the smelters and fly shuttles of the new America; and may even have furnished an inward cocoon of memory to preserve principle and self-respect against poverty and insecurity. Such topics need prolonged inquiry, as Kerby Miller shows. And there is no question that the two million "new" Irish immigrants who came to America from 1880 to 1920 had to start all over again as slum-housed, unskilled workers for the most part. The achievements of unionized or middle-class Irish Americans were insufficient to protect their incoming cousins from the "old country" from the cold logic of industrial society. The newcomers either fought back or cautiously held their ground, both often in groups.[3]

On the other hand, emphasis upon early industrialization, and its implications for the "American Dream," can lead U.S. scholars on several false trajectories. Pursuing an early industrialized group such as the Irish through to their later fortunes, as I myself have done, among others, can create a false impression that the original stratification which characterized the society is no longer a force to depress the fortunes of the many. But the unquestionable progression of most of the Irish from the impoverished and casually employed of the 1850s, through the skilled and unionized and well-paid worker elite of 1880–1920s, through to the white-collar ethnicity of more recent years, disguises the fact that until lately, their place was taken by others below them, and distorts the very dependence of Irish progression upon this central fact. In the 1840s, the Irishwomen and Irish children of New England spun and wove the fabric later tailored to clothe the cities and farms. In 1920, their offspring wore clothes woven by underpaid labor in the American South, and often tailored in New York and Philadelphia sweatshops manned by poor Russian Jews and Italians. Moreover, technological innovation and regional reconcentration has continuously altered the extent and location of America's working people and poor, and simultaneously accelerated the social progress of the well-schooled children of factory workers now living in areas of expanding opportunities in insurance, marketing, and wholesale distribution. Not until the 1930s, did Irish Americans find an opportunity to support national policies which would benefit the classes from which they sprang, as well as those in which they found themselves. Again, early locales have been overstudied: New England, with less than one-fifth of the Irish-born and their children in 1900, was more untypical of the nation than was California itself. In Massachussetts, 17 percent of them were middle and white-collar class, against 36 percent of the native-born of native parentage. Nationally, 21 percent of the Irish, and 18 percent of the native-born of native parentage, were so! False group and regional trajectories have greatly deepened our knowledge of Irish America itself, given the depth of detail expended upon them, but they obscure the central matters which these scholars first took up the Irish Americans to illuminate, as examples, rather than as closed subjects. Yet we may well be grateful for this subsequent overemphasis![4]

The Irish have also been studied closely because of the renewed and urgent interest of American scholars in the fate of the cities and the plight of rural-to-urban migrants. The cities deteriorate as large numbers of migrants fail to establish a hold in their industrial and service economies, a somewhat different issue than that of those who make themselves part of an indispensable, if underpaid, work force. The Irish passed through both stages, but the former only initially, or during recession. Nonetheless, they furnish a key study in the confusion and thence reorganization of uprooted strangers. Moreover, they were present at the creation of the modern metropolis, when cities were expanding chaotically yet confidently. In 1870, the Irish-born ranged from 5 percent to 25 percent of the inhabitants of the key industrial cities, and thus figure disproportionately in nineteenth-century urban history. Overly pessimistic diagnoses of current urban conditions and of their confused inhabitants' role in them has prompted wide-reaching investigation of what made these early cities work, notwithstanding their vast flux of strangers, wide poverty, and often hopeless civic government. Again, because so many complex variables are at work in such a situation, historians have sometimes taken refuge in an ever-more careful delineation of the politics, churches, organization, and progress of one group within the city, the Irish. This once more enriches our knowledge of Irish America: but one remains unconvinced that it offers a shortcut to the broader understanding of city life, then or now. However, as Dennis Clark notes, such studies are surely an indication of the resilience and adaptability of the apparently least equipped of town dwellers, the Irish countryman, and contain the implicit suggestion that there may have been more of a "hidden hand" operating through the "concourse of individual wills" in cities then, than modern urban governments would dare dream. Their weakness is precisely the failure to uncover the fugitive personality of the urbanizing American Irishman, except by extrapolation from his tracks, politics, and public clichés. And it leaves the more strong-stomached practitioners of urban history, such as Zane Miller and Sam Bass Warner, Jr., with the conviction that *then* is not *now*. If we cannot recover the substance of the Brooklyn Kennedy or Sullivan of 1850, there is little point in asking the contemporary Brooklynite to sit at the feet of his shadow; and there is even less in asking today's city comptroller or housing executives to go to school to the ward boss of yesterday, lovable rogue though he may have been. The boss offered contacts in a shifting world; we expect more from our officials. As in immigration and labor studies, however, scholarship has been so fertile of new approaches, and adept in turning prosaic survivals into revealing evidence, that we may yet enjoy a real breakthrough on this front: Mr. Fanning has pointed some sources and directions in his remarkable essay on Martin Dooley.[5]

If American scholars are interested in ordinary Irish immigrants and their children, Irish scholars are more interested in the exceptional and the articulate. This is not that they are uninterested in the fate of the usual migrant. Quite the contrary; but they lack the sources to pursue his American progress meticulously, and local variation within America cannot be an end in itself for them. Further, pressing contemporary issues incline them to seek out the exceptional. This does not mean that they subscribe to the notion that a people only become meaningful when they demonstrate a capacity for success (that undertone of certain social mobility, American Dream studies, leaves them cold). Rather, there is a certain legitimate nationalism prompting their interest, but one given force and edge by genuine concern as to whether those of Irish culture and background, reared in a circumscribed landscape even when comfortably off, are adequate to the challenges of a continent-wide society, to the opportunities of a vast industrial-market economy, to the political test of pressing their interests in a competitive arena. Membership in the European Community has made these questions of real import. Secondly, most Irish people, regardless of ideology or pattern of life, whether employees in state-controlled, state-sponsored, private, or multi-national bodies, share a belief that initiative, innovation, and enterprise in every context have vital social consequences in a country that must live by its wits as well as by its crops; that, in short, the exceptional are necessary to the ordinary. Hence the interest of studies such as E. R. R. Green's on Irish-American business, or Thomas N. Brown on the political entrepreneurs of the cities. What reads as acquiescence in "success mythology" to certain Americans reads very differently to Irishmen.

Thirdly, with regard to the articulate rather than the achievers, there is the related interest in those who in America were forced to frame an acceptably "Irish" response to the newer world, and to encompass in a framework of continuity what Irish Americans were actually doing with lives more and more indistinguishable from those of others. A Dublin accountant working for a computer import company, relaxing with Irving Wallace, and watching Perry Mason on TV, may have more in common with his Irish-American counterpart, than either does the Irish-speaking West Limerick dairyman, or English-speaking Wexford cultivator of 1840 who is their ancestor. But elusive threads of common identity still tie him more closely to the past than is the case with his American cousin. Articulate Irish Americans—journalists, politicians, novelists—faced similar dilemmas in the past, created usefully "Irish" ways of looking at these realities of an urban, marketplace existence. If their solutions were not always convincing, they often indicated themes which, when taken up at the deeper levels literature and perhaps religion suggest, manage to relativize the whole problem. The demon of supposed discontinuity may be exorcised if the ground of continuity is more deeply based, as Peggy O'Brien suggests. The very study of Irish America, illuminating both the drastic "severances" to which many immigrants were subject, and yet also the vitality with which they made much of their new culture, itself should reassure those who would see Irish humanity as a frail species, incapable of radical alteration, mortally wounded when separated from the rural community, from isolate nationalism, and from the patterns of thought and speech of the past.

Most of these articulate reactions to change were the ad hoc responses of men faced with the problems of the Irish workingmen's communities. The church preempted systematic reflection, and was too involved in apologetic defense in a new culture, to do much more than repeat conservative and stock responses in fields other than the narrowly religious. The principal exception was its generous response to America's republican institutions. The first *Catholic Encyclopedia* (New York, 1907–13) was almost baroque in its recurrent avoidance of the culture and problems of modernity. But the long lists of its lay sponsors, embracing several titans of finance and industry, represented a significant cross section of the entrepreneurial and professional Irish-American middle class. The real thought of the community was thus found in editorials, stump speeches, legal decisions, legislative proposals, trade union motions. By the depression of 1893, these reveal a community shifting decisively to a pragmatic politics of interclass betterment. Anticipated by Patrick Ford and others in the 1870s recession, now the middle class generally championed such schemes, appalled by the severity with which the new depression affected one quarter of Irish-American workers. Although their congressmen pressed ideas such as a federal income tax in that decade, not until after 1900 did the urban Irish machines move decisively to press for legislative regulation of the factory and city in the state assemblies, led by men such as Edmund Dunne in Illinois, Charles Murphy in New York, and Martin Lomasney in Massachussetts. Eventually, Monsignor John A. Ryan and others moved churchmen into formally sustaining the positions implicit in these moves, by building on their early acceptance of trade unionism (in the 1880s) and their acceptance of democratic politics. The liberalism of church leaders in certain Irish communities, notably that of Archbishops Thomas Carr of Melbourne and Henry Manning of Westminster, had long been used by Irish-American laymen to prod them toward such a commitment. The community was thus largely united in time to support the early New Deal.[6]

Irish Americans were at the heart of almost all the realities transforming America, even before the majority of native-stock WASP Americans: immigration, ethnicity, caste, proletariat, pluralism, industry, city growth, labor rationalization, the new politics, and racial friction. If their self-perceptions had been clear, between 1860 and 1930, they might have better helped abbreviate the nation's century-long quest for redefinition. Fearful of being accused of un-Americanism, they concentrated instead, perhaps more beneficially, upon actual improvement of urban conditions. Their incidental formulas to justify their work, however, were often quite bold. When fully studied, their activities and words may even give the newly urban, EEC–related Ireland as usable a past as that of the tired clichés of Anglo-Irish contention. America itself deeply affected the very definition they gave these questions, for its ideals, constantly expounded in the public schools, in press and in politics, enhanced Irish Americans' expectations of life, on the grounds of a basic and immutable human dignity.

It is often forgotten that almost all Irish Americans went to public schools before the 1880s; and thereafter, a very considerable portion. As late as 1900, one-half of the children of Irish-born fathers were attending public schools in the leading cities, over three quarters in Boston. One-fifth of public school teachers in northern cities were Irish American at the same time. Conservative Catholic Irish priests and laymen believed that these schools gave the Irish ideas above their predestined station, and unfitted them for their humble lives; Patrick Hickey praised the new Catholic schools as obviating this tendency, by producing children who were docile, shy, and quiet. Actually, as Harold Weisz has shown, Irish parents forced upon the Catholic schools the same curriculum and values as helped ensure that public schools produced children attuned to American life. Many opposed the recruitment of religious teachers from Ireland for these schools on the same grounds. Just as did interethnic neighborhoods and workplaces, the public schools and their Catholic copies went far to diversify the horizons of Irish Americans, undermine the fatalism of the mid-century immigrants, shown in Handlin and Dolan, and produce a people who might combine independence, initiative, and tradition.[7]

Exposure to American life and institutions thereby drastically modified the antipathy of Irish Americans to all that was associated with Protestant, "Anglo-Saxon" culture. The need to get on in the world, and to get on with the world, thus broke them away from the classic Irish associations of the nineteenth century, English and Protestant equals exploitation, materialism, and immorality. Conservative churchmen and propagandists might still attempt to sustain these connections in an American context, as Robert Cross has shown, exploiting a collective inferiority complex and a residual agrarian romanticism to lead the Irish-American working folk in a psychic revolt against the American city. But practical experience caused most Irish Americans to resist statements such as the clerical assertion that "If Catholicism is the true Church of Christ, then Protestantism is the foe of Christianity" (Indianapolis *Catholic Record*, 5 January 1899). As a French priest working in New Orleans noted in the 1880s, if Anglo-Saxon ruthlessness had created the tragedy of the Irish in the old country, Anglo-Saxon genius had created the means of their livelihood and advancement in the new (anon., *Irish Faith in America*, New York, 1881). Later community leaders like Bourke Cochran, Archbishop John Ireland, and Maurice F. Egan were so open to this fact, that under their auspices, the imperial federalism implicit in the Home Rule propaganda of Parnell and John Dillon came more naturally to Irish America than did the minority extremism of separatists under John Devoy: hence the wall between de Valera and most Irish Americans in 1919. The "ideological matrix" which Oliver MacDonagh and Oscar Handlin have shown affecting the Famine generation, an alienation from English-speaking, Protestant tradition and hence a great ambivalence about its material civilization, had evaporated for the most part by the 1880s, except as a ground of argument, or a theological position amongst conservative (especially immigrant Irish) clergy. As Thomas Beer noted, their polarizations were all but incomprehensible to the prosperous AmerIrish (as he called them). Unskilled relative newcomers were more likely to be radical nationalists than were established older immigrants.[8]

The wider results of this were vital, if largely unnoted. As late as 1898, in a series of letters to the *Irish World*, Irish archbishops and bishops evinced a profound distrust of industrial civilization, a distrust which found refuge in a romantic agrarian distributism. Irish Americans, on the other hand, in seeking to reform it from within, had overcome the ambivalent response to its Anglo-Protestant roots in America and Britain. The problem posed by the identification of the modernizing process with a conquering power, so intense in Ireland, as elsewhere in the twentieth century, was thus solved for Irish Americans in their American experience. Conservative liberals like John Dillon's Chicago brother William might wish that the optimum industrial and urban population be one-third of a nation, but they did not deny that the preeminent Irish Americans were the urban businessmen, nor that the future of their own community was in the city. Ireland itself achieved independence in a context of rural resurgence, which postponed similar recognition for two generations at home.

A second result was a reestimate of Catholic culture elsewhere. Irish Catholics traditionally romanticized France, Spain, and Italy. Irish Americans broke with that tradition fully and completely. In the 1820s and 1830s, they identified with the egalitarian strain in American politics which was most hostile to the illiberal and clerical regimes of continental Europe. In the 1840s, they sent large numbers to the war against Mexico, only a handful of whom deserted on the grounds of Catholic solidarity, despite extensive Mexican propaganda. They threw themselves enthusiastically into the war against Spain in 1898 despite the misgivings of the higher clergy. They reacted coldly to the attempts of the American Federation of Catholic Societies to create a united front in defense of the Spanish clergy in Cuba and the Philippines, so much the Irish-dominated organizations such as the Knights of Columbus and Ancient Order of Hibernians refused cooperation. In the

1920s and 1930s the majority resisted attempts to create a campaign against the radical regimes in Mexico, and over 30 percent of Catholics were reported as favoring the republic, not Franco, with 31 percent neutral, in the Spanish Civil War, as J. D. Valaik and R. E. Quigley have shown. Throughout the later nineteenth century, the cause of the temporal sovereignty of the papacy found them in embarrassed silence. In short, the fusion of American lay and republican traditions with their Catholicism, caused them to distrust and even despise regimes which combined social backwardness, political illiberalism, and Catholicism. Local Italo-Irish tensions in a host of American cities accelerated this severance from their Irish Latinophilism. By the 1930s, indeed, American Irish Catholics were often better equipped to understand the developing pluralism of European continental Catholicism than were more proximate Irish Catholics. In this too, they anticipated Irish development after Vatican II.[9]

Sadly, however, they provide little precedent for the fusion of Ireland's Catholic and Protestant traditions, despite the great impact of secularization, of public schools, and of the reestimate of Protestantism among them. This might cause some sober second thought about the possible progress of the latter trends among Irish Catholics today. Apart from a brief and important period from the 1790s to the 1830s, largely under United Irish emigré auspices, the Protestant and Catholic Irish traditions in America remained separate, so separate, as Dennis Clark has warned, that common treatment would falsify them. As William Shannon pointed out, Protestant Irish predominance in the flow from Ireland ceased in the early years of the republic. But the flow itself did not cease. It was overshadowed by a dramatic native Irish flow. Once the Irish Catholics in America sought to create their own leadership structures, after 1830, rather than using those of Anglo-Irish Protestants as a bridge to the wider America, the two communities separated so completely, that the Protestant immigrants decided on a low profile which would save them from identification with their migrant fellow countrymen. Yet it is probable, given S. H. Cousens's findings on continuing migration from Ulster, that as many as 1.3 million Irish Protestants came to America between 1783 and 1930, roughly a fifth of the total flow. The connecting link of relatives, uncles inviting nephews out, continued to link Ulster townlands with Pennsylvania and the Carolinas, with New York and Chicago, from the latter eighteenth century through to recent times. The whole migration needs full study; most of us have underestimated its dimensions. Irish Protestants such as John MacMannes, boss of Philadelphia in the 1860s; Tom Taggert, Progressive senator from Indiana; David Croly, cofounder of positivism in America; E. L. Godkin, the reformer and editor; William McAdoo, Cleveland's navy secretary; R. Ellis Thompson, the protectionist economist; and George Pepper, the leading Ohio Methodist minister and U.S. consul, indicate that the community was neither powerless, insubstantial, nor ill equipped for American life. That most took up a politics contrary to that of the urban Irish Catholics (Republican as against Democratic) underscores the depth of the continuing historical alienation. Nonetheless, McAdoo, Pepper, Thompson, Godkin, and Croly, among others, supported Irish Home Rule: they were far from unsympathetic to the cause of Irish nationalism, and unafraid of the political upheaval which should result for their Protestant relatives at home. It is possible that their experience of Irish Catholic politics and business enterprise in America helped them to trust their fellow countrymen's capacities and ultimate liberality.[10]

If Shannon has stressed the Irish contribution to America, it is appropriate for an Irish editor, as it were in reply, to stress the contribution of America to Ireland and its emigrants. Ultimately, America acted as a solvent on the fatalisms of the mind, urging men to rethink their scheme of human possibilities, of politics, of the geography of the mind. It could do so with a strange sudden finality. Father Eugene O'Growney, exponent of Irish traditionalism and a founder of the Gaelic League, went to Arizona suffering from tuberculosis. Conversations with Irish mine owners, workers, and others changed his view of things, as did his American reading. He wrote a friend in May 1899, "as competition increases, and the margin of profit dwindles away, people will be driven to co-operation of some kind. It is merely the selfish device of the ordinary man to get more than his share that prevents moderate socialism coming today." (The letter was published by William Dillon in the Chicago *New World*, 23 December 1899.) John Boyle O'Reilly, in many respects a romantic conservative, a manly preacher of an Irish American "Genteel Tradition," had accepted the inevitability of sharp social distinctions while he craved justice for the poor. Yet he wrote in 1883:

Socialism is the great problem of the present and the future; how to raise humanity to a higher and more equitable civilization. . . . The shallow reasoners of Europe who have dissociated Socialism and Religion have committed an unpardonable sin. With the deepest equities underlying the social order, the Catholic Church must always be in the deepest sympathy.[11]

Such statements were no endorsement of a general bureaucratization of life, a concentration of national power, as their contexts clarify. Their influence was marginal; as Humphrey Desmond of Milwaukee noted, "Religion has influence only with the laboring element: it can allay violence. . . . In moving capital to do equity, and in teaching the duties that are correlative of rights, it is powerless. Capital is a soulless aggregation." Nonetheless, they did create a common Irish-American stance, an abandonment of Irish priorities, and a recognition that "the Irish-American question" was "the social elevation of the vast mass of the American Irish" (Milwaukee *Catholic*

Citizen, 15 December 1894, 4 April 1896). This consensus achieved, and the Irish Americans gaining increasing political power after 1900, it was possible to ensure that American capitalism no longer develop as "a soulless aggregation" but as a force disciplined by social need while conserving its creative energies, as these writers had wished.

The successive new beginnings of Irish Americans, rooted ultimately in the moral imagination and political equities of their culture, are surely suggestive of the possibility of new beginnings elsewhere, even in an Ireland multiply divided.

NOTES

1. E. E. Davis, "Irish Social Attitudes and Views Towards Poverty," unpublished seminar paper, Educational and Social Research Council of Ireland, October 1977, forthcoming; M. MacGreil, *Prejudice and Tolerance in Ireland* (Dublin, 1977).

2. Edward Saveth, *American Historians and European Immigrants* (New York, 1948); J. P. Rodechko, *Patrick Ford and His Search for America* (New York, 1976); Isabel Skelton, *Life of Thomas D'Arcy Magee* (Toronto, 1925); Michael O'Brien, *A Hidden Phase of American History* (New York, 1919); J. J. O'Shea, "The Irish Leaven in American Progress," *Forum* 27 (April 1899): 285–96.

3. John R. Commons, *Races and Immigrants in America* (New York, 1907), a strange qualification to undertake his *History of Labor in the United States*, 4 vols. (New York, 1918–35); Herbert Gutman, *Work, Culture and Industrialising Society* (New York, 1976); Emmett Larkin, "The Devotional Revolution in Ireland," *American Historical Review* 77 (June 1972): 625–52; David N. Doyle, "Inimircigh nua agus Meiriceá tionsclaíoch, 1870–1910," in Stiofán Ó hAnnracháin, *Go Meiriceá Siar* (Dublin, 1979); Estelle F. Feinstein, *Stamford in the Gilded Age* (Stamford, 1973); Michael Gordon, "Studies in Irish and Irish American Thought and Behavior in Gilded Age New York City," Ph.D., University of Rochester, 1977; Philip R. Silvia, "The Spindle City: Labor, Politics and Religion in Fall River, 1870–1905," Ph.D., New York: Fordham University, 1973; Daniel J. Walkowitz, *Worker City, Company Town: Troy and Cohoes, 1855–1884* (Chicago, 1978).

4. Occupational advancement as shown in Doyle, "Social Structure of an Immigrant Faith," in *Irish Americans, Native Rights, National Empires* (New York, 1976), pp. 38–90; Bruce Laurie and Ted Hershberg, "Immigrants and Industry: The Philadelphia Experience, 1850–1880," *Journal of Social History* 9 (December 1975); Peter Hill, "Relative Skill and Income Levels of Foreign Born Workers in the United States," *Explorations in Economic History* 12 (1975): 47–60; Stephen Thernstrom, "Immigrants and WASPs . . . 1880–1940," in Richard Sennett and S. Thernstrom, *Nineteenth Century Cities* (New Haven, Conn., 1969); earlier in Isaac Hourwich, *Immigration and Labor*, 2nd ed. (New York, 1922); and for later advances to white-collar class generally, Liston Pope, "Religion and the Class Structure," *Annals of the American Academy of Political and Social Science* 256 (1948): 85 ff; Niles Carpenter, *Nationality, Color and Economic Opportunity in the City of Buffalo* (New York, 1927). For a refreshing skepticism, see David Montgomery, "The New Urban History," *Reviews in American History*, 2 (1974), 498–504.

5. David Ward, *Cities and Immigrants* (New York, 1971); Sam Bass Warner, Jr., *The Private City: Philadelphia* (Philadelphia, 1968) and his *Urban Wilderness: A History of the American City* (1972); Zane Miller, *The Urbanization of America* (New York, 1973); Dennis Clark, "The Urban Irishman," in his *Irish in Philadelphia* (Philadelphia, 1973); Lynn Lees and John Modell, "The Irish Countryman Urbanized," *Journal of Urban History*, 3 (1977): 391–408; Theodore Hershberg, "The New Urban History," ibid., 5 (1978): 3–40.

6. James E. Roohan, *American Catholics and the Social Question, 1865–1900* (New York, 1976); Francis Broderick, *Right Rev. New Dealer, John A. Ryan* (New York, 1963); Stephen Bell, *Rebel, Priest and Prophet: Edward McGlynn* (New York, 1937); John D. Buenker, "Edward F. Dunne," *Mid-America* 50 (1968): 3–21, "The Mahatma and Progressive Reform: Martin Lomasney as Lawmaker, 1911–17," *New England Quarterly* 44 (1971): 397–419, and "Urban, New Stock Liberalism and Progressive Reform in New Jersey," *New Jersey History* 87 (1969): 79–104; Dorothy Wayman, *David I. Walsh* (Milwaukee, 1952); John M. Blum, *Joe Tumulty and the Wilson Era* (Boston, 1951); Marc Karson, *American Labor Unions and Politics, 1900–1918* (Boston, 1965), esp. pp. 212–306.

7. Harold Weisz, "Public Schools for Irish Americans?" in his *Irish-American and Italian-American Educational Views and Activities* (New York, 1976), 47–96, and *passim*; J. A. Burns and B. F. Kohlbrenner, *History of Catholic Education in the United States* (New York, 1937); Ruth M. Ellson, *Guardians of Tradition* (Lincoln, Nebr., 1964); Harold A. Buetow, *Of Singular Benefit* (New York, 1970).

8. Robert D. Cross, "The Changing Image of the City Among American Catholics," *Catholic Historical Review* 48 (April 1962): 33–52; James McGurrin, *Bourke Cochran* (New York, 1948), and Bourke Cochran, *In the Name of Liberty* (New York, 1925); John Ireland, *The Church and Modern Society*, 2 vols. (New York, 1903); M. F. Egan, *Recollections of a Happy Life* (New York, 1925); Thomas Beer, *Mauve Decade* (New York, 1926), pp. 109–13.

9. R. E. Quigley, "American Catholic Opinion and Mexican Anti-Clericalism," Ph.D. (University of Pennsylvania, 1965); Frank Reuter, *American Catholic Influence on American Colonial Policies, 1898–1904* (Austin, Tex., 1967); J. D. Valaik, "Catholics, Neutrality and the Spanish Embargo, 1938–39," *Journal of American History* 54 (1967): 73–85.

10. S. H. Cousens, "Emigration and Demographic Change," *Economic History Review*, 2nd ser., 10 (1961): 275–88, and "The Regional Variation in Population Changes in Ireland, 1861–1881,"*Economic History Review* 17 (1964): 301–21. Kerby Miller, "Emigrants and Exiles," Ph.D., Berkeley: University of California, 1976, shows Protestant migration as do works of Doyle on 1740–1820 and Adams, *Ireland and Irish Emigration 1815 to the Famine*. Between 1851 and 1921, to take the later period, 300,000 emigrated from Protestant County Antrim and 165,000 left largely Protestant County Down: Nicholas Nolan, "A Celtic Exodus," M.Sc. thesis (Dublin: University College, 1933), p. 228.

11. F. G. MacManamin, *The American Years of John Boyle O'Reilly, 1870–1890* (New York, 1976), p. 200. Other quotations are directly from the journals concerned. Lest the work end on a mutually parochial note, however, it ought to be agreed with Owen Edwards that a body of research is discerning similar themes of tension and adjustment in the relations of Anglo-Protestant and Irish Catholic cultures in the

history of England, Australia, Canada and New Zealand. Only when these have been properly absorbed will the singularity of Irish/American relations be fully assessed. These works include Lynn H. Lees, *Exiles of Erin: Irish Migrants in Victorian London* (Manchester, 1979); Sheridan Gilley, "Papists, Protestants and the Irish in London, 1835–70," in *Studies in Church History*, 8 (1972): 259–66; W.J.Lowe, "The Irish in Lancashire, 1846–71: A Social History," Ph.D., University of Dublin, 1975; Harrington W. Benjamin, "The London Irish: A Study in Political Activism," Ph.D., Princeton University, 1976; [on Australia]: Denis Grundy, *'Secular, Compulsory and Free': The Education Act of 1872* (Melbourne, 1972); R.B. Madwick, *Immigration into Eastern Australia 1788-1851* (Sydney, 1969); Patrick O'Farrell, *The Catholic Church in Australia, 1788-1967* (Melbourne, 1969); Frances O'Kane, *A Path Is Set* (Melbourne, 1976); T. L. Suttor, *Hierarchy and Democracy in Australia, 1788-1870* (Melbourne, 1965); James Waldersee, *Catholic Society in New South Wales, 1788-1860* (Sydney, 1974); David Fitzpatrick, "Irish Emigration in the Later Nineteenth Century," [emphasizing Australia], *Irish Historical Studies*, 21 (1979): in press; Celia Hamilton, "Irish Catholics of New South Wales and the Labour Party, 1890-1910," *Historical Studies* [Melbourne], 8 (1958): 254–67; Oliver MacDonagh, "The Irish in Victoria, 1851–91," *Historical Studies* [Ireland], 8 (1971): 67–92; George Rudé, "Early Irish Rebels in Australia," *Historical Studies* [Melbourne], 16 (1974): 17–35; [on Canada]: Paul Crunican, *Priests and Politicians: Manitoba Schools and the Election of 1896* (Toronto, 1974); J. J. Mannion, *Irish Settlements in Eastern Canada* (Toronto, 1974); J. S. Moir, *Church and State in Canada West* (Toronto, 1959); Hereward Senior, *Fenians and Canada* (Toronto, 1978); Susan E. Houston, "Politics, Schools and Social Change in Upper Canada,"*Canadian Historical Review*, 53 (1972): 249–71; Michael Katz, "The People of a Canadian City, 1851–52,"ibid., 53 (1972): 402–26 [32% Irish born]; J. T. Copp, "The Conditions of the Working Class in Montreal, 1897–1920," *Historical Papers* (1972) 157–80 [Canadian Historical Association]; William M. Nolte, "The Irish in Canada, 1815–1867," Ph.D., University of Maryland, 1975; [on New Zealand]: Richard P. Davis, *Irish Issues in New Zealand Politics* (Dunedin, 1974).

AFTERWORD
CON HOWARD

Cumann Merriman went outside its usual kind of summer school to honor the U.S. Bicentennial. There were good reasons for this departure, not least the fact that America's relationship with Ireland in the words of U.S. Ambassador Walter Curley was probably closer than with any other nation on earth. But in spite of this the ambassador pointed to an information gap between the two countries. This school and the publication of the proceedings will have gone some way toward filling the gap.

It is right also that a cultural body such as Cumann Merriman should do all honor to the ties that exist between Ireland and the United States.

These ties have been forged by the large-scale emigration from Ireland to America and the contribution in every field made by the Irish in America. The political contribution is perhaps the best known, and it is worth repeating that it has been an all-Ireland contribution—Catholic and Protestant , orange and green.

Ireland and America share, perhaps to a unique degree, in a republican culture which *inter alia* is manifested in a populist informality in personal relations and in institutional work life. America made the idea of a republic meaningful in the modern world, and this idea has become an integral part of the Irish national outlook.

Inevitably the scholars of this school were concerned with the past. It is from the past however and from the work of our forebears that we learn how to build for the future. As President Kennedy remarked, "the past is prologue." So the school was concerned with the present and the future —with the living city and with the living Atlantic Community.

The Irish-American connection has a long and strong future. The Irish are an Atlantic people and have had from the very beginning a relationship of intimacy with the American people that is certain to continue. This does not conflict with Ireland's European responsibilities but perhaps, to some degree at least, gives the country a bridge-building role between the two continents.

The economic ties between Ireland and America remain strong; since 1960 America has supplied almost half of the foreign investment in Ireland which is vital to the creation of employment and the building up of our industrial sector. This trend has actually intensified in recent years. Both countries have been important trading partners since colonial times, and this relationship continues to flourish. Similarily tourism between the countries is expanding.

The intellectual and cultural interchange between both countries is also lively and flourishing—as is evidenced by the knowledge and fluency in Irish-American affairs displayed at this school. Irish studies in American universities and schools are in a healthy and expanding state, and the same is true of American studies in Ireland, though the impetus here is of a more recent origin. There is, however, no reason for complacency, and much work remains to be done.

The 1976 Merriman Summer School was a great occasion, intellectually and socially, and it has been saluted by American scholars as one of Europe's most outstanding contributions to the U.S. bicentennial. I would like particularly to express my appreciation to the American and Irish scholars and poets who participated in this school. Serious though their academic and cultural endeavors were, they were a fun-loving lot and they succeeded in common with everyone else who attended the school in maintaining a high level of cheerfulness. Thomas Jefferson would surely have approved of the school's dedication to "Life, Liberty and the Pursuit of Happiness." The participants also made the work of the director easy and pleasant. I also wish to thank the National Library of Ireland for mounting an excellent exhibition on Ireland and Irishmen in the American Revolution in the beautiful De Valera Library and Museum in Ennis. Cumann Merriman followed up the school with a visit to America in March 1978. They proudly marched up Fifth Avenue on St. Patrick's Day with the Clarmens Association and indeed with many other county associations. We were greatly honored by receptions in Washington by speaker Thomas P. O'Neill and Senator Edward Kennedy. Other receptions by the Irish Embassy and the EEC Embassy in Washington and by the Irish consulates and state bodies in New York and Boston and by Irish-American organizations, the Massachussetts Institute of Technology, which perhaps with little poetic license could be classified as an Irish-American organization, since it was founded by the son of Patrick Kerr Rodgers, who had to flee to America from Dublin in 1798 because of his support for the United Irishmen, and a splendid dinner at Stonehill College, Massachusetts, combined to make the visit a most memorable occasion.

Since the Merriman U.S. Bicentennial Summer School took place in Ennis, County Clare, it is fitting that we should close this volume with a rather fiery poem written by Tómas O'Miodhachain (Thomas Meehan), an Ennis schoolteacher and Irish language poet, in praise of George Washington on his hearing of the evacuation of Boston by Howe (17 March 1776). This song was set to a traditional folk tune renamed "Washington's Frolic." A translation by Dr. Tom Peete Cross and Professor F. N. Robinson, both of Harvard University, is also appended. The following material is quoted from the proceedings of the Colonial Society of Massachusetts, February Meeting 1911. We are grateful to Mr. John Smith of Trinity College, Dublin, for its rediscovery.

TRANSLITERATION OF THE IRISH TEXT

Tómas Ó Miodhachain *cecinit*. Air Washington's Frolic. Ar an sean fhonn Sir (?) Súd an Fear B[ ] gan Bríste.

A chraobha comainn na nGaoidhel ccomas do shaoircheap mhuireannach Mhíledh
Tá tréathlag tuirseach a plae le bruscar gan réim fé urchall cíosa
Sin scéala sonais do théarnaigh chugainn a ccéin tar dhromaibh na díleann
Go bhfuil méirligh mustair go déighenach gonta na bhéile fiolar is faoileann.

Is fonn s'is aitheas leam Howe s'na Sagsanaigh tabhartha trascartha choidhche
Sa crobhaire Washington cabharthach calma a cceann s'a cceannas a righeacht
Sin amhais ag screadadh gan chúil gan chathair gan trúip gan barcaibh ar taoide
Is fé samhain go dearbhthe búir na Breataine a b-punc fá thearmain Laoisigh.

D'eis an chluithche-si Éire léigfear da céile dlightheach ceart díleas
An féinedh fuinneamach faobhrach fulangach Séarlas soinneannta Stíobhard
Biaidh réim ag filedh s'go saoghal an fhiolair cead féir is uisge ag Gaoidhelaibh
Gacg géag ag filledh le h-éigeann duilledh s'na h-éisg ag lingedh asa lintibh.

Go saor am fhochair le méin dom fhocalaibh ag dhéanadh an ghortha
  Ó Mhaoidheachan
An té gan dochma nach n-gléasfaigh portaibh go séidtear gotaibh a pípe
Taosgam srutha don daor-phunch torainn is reabam cornaibh crínbhreach
A Thoirdhealbhaigh brostaigh lead Mhéidhbh inghin Chrotaigh is claon do chosa
  chum rincedh.

TRANSLATION

Thomas O'Meehan cecinit. Air, Washington's Frolic, to the old tune of "Seek Yonder the Fine Fellow without Breeches" (?).

1. O branches of the league of the mighty Gaels, of the noble, longhaired stem of Milesius, who are exhausted, tired, in their struggle with the rabble, without power, under shackle of tribute!

Those are stories of good fortune that have come to us from afar over the ridges of the sea,—that the arrogant robbers are wounded at last, the food of eagles and seagulls.

2. It is a source of joy and triumph in my eyes that Howe and the Saxons are taken and overthrown forever, and that the sturdy Washington, helpful and brave, is at the head and command of his realm.
The hirelings are screeching, without shelter, without city, without army, without ships on the tide. Verily the boors of Britain before November Day suddenly will be under the bondage of Louis.

3. After this exploit, Ireland will be given to her lawful spouse just, beloved, the vigorous champion, sharp, patient, the innocent Charles Stuart.
Courage shall be with the poet, and, for the lifetime of the eagle, permission to use grass and water shall belong to the Gael, every branch returning with the power of the leaves (i.e. bursting out into fresh leafage), and the fish jumping out of their waters.

4. Freely beside me, with good will to my words, kindling the heat, (sits) O'Meehan, the man without weakness, who will not make ready with tunes till it is blown with the sounds of his pipe. Let us drain rivers of good flowing punch and flourish the ancient drinking-horns.
O Turlough, make hast with thy Maeve daughter of Crotach, and bend thy legs to the dance!

Con Howard

Director

Merriman U.S. Bicentennial Summer School 1976

INDEX

ABOUT THE
CONTRIBUTORS

Thomas N. Brown, Professor of History, University of Massachusetts, Boston. His works include: *Irish American Nationalism, 1870–90* (1966); "The Irish Layman," in *A History of Irish Catholicism*, ed. P. J. Corish, vol. 6 (1970).

Michael J. Costello, Lieutenant General in the Irish army, retired Staff Officer, Irish War of Independence. Irish Military Mission to the United States, 1926–27. Graduated from the U.S. Command and General Staff School, Fort Leavenworth. Established the Irish Military College. Commanding officer, Southern Command, 1939–45. General Manager of the Irish Sugar Company, 1947–66. He has written and lectured on the U.S. Civil War, making a special study of General Philip Sheridan.

Denis Donoghue, Henry James Professor of Literature, New York University, and Professor of English and American Literature, University College, Dublin. His works include: *The Third Voice (1959); Connoisseur of Chaos* (1965); *The Ordinary Universe* (1968); *Jonathan Swift* (1969); *Emily Dickinson* (1969); *Yeats* (1971); *Thieves of Fire* (1974); *The Sovereign Ghost (1977)*. He is editor of *The Integrity of Yeats* (1964) and a *Swift Revisited* (1968).

David N. Doyle, Lecturer in American History, University College, Dublin. His works include: *Irish Americans, Native Rights and National Empires, 1890–1901* (1976); *Irishmen and Revolutionary America, 1740–1820* (1979). He is coeditor of *The Irish Americans*, 42 vols. (1976).

Owen Dudley Edwards, Lecturer in American History, Edinburgh University. His works include: *The Sins of Our Fathers: The Roots of Conflict in Northern Ireland* (1970); *The Mind of an Activist: James Connolly* (1971); *P. G.*

Wodehouse: A Critical and Historical Essay (1977). He is coeditor of *1916: The Easter Rising* (1968), coauthor of *Celtic Nationalism* (1968), and editor of *C. C. O'Brien Introduces Ireland* (1970).

Charles Fanning, Assistant Professor of English, Bridgewater State College, Massachusetts. His works include: *Mr. Dooley and the Chicago Irish* (1976).

Andrew M. Greeley, Director, National Opinion Research Center, Chicago. Publications in the sociology of ethnicity, education, and Catholicism include *Religion and Career* (1963); (with Peter Rossi), *The Education of Catholic Americans* (1966); *Priests in the United States* (1974); *Catholic Schools in a Declining Church* (1975); *The American Catholic: A Social Portrait* (1977). He has also written extensively upon religious topics and pastoral issues. Works germane to his present contribution are included in its bibliographic note.

E. R. R. Green, Director, Institute of Irish Studies, Queen's University of Belfast. His works include: *The Lagan Valley, 1800–1850* (1949); *The Industrial Archaeology of Co. Down* (1963); "Agriculture," in T. D. Edwards and R. D. Williams, eds., *The Great Famine* (1956); "Early Industrial Belfast," in J. C. Beckett and R. E. Glasscock, eds., *Belfast: Origins and Growth* (1967). He is editor and coauthor of *Essays in Scotch-Irish History* (1969).

Lawrence J. McCaffrey, Professor of History, Loyola University of Chicago. His works include: *Irish Federalism in the 1870s* (1962); *Daniel O'Connell and the Repeal Year* (1966); *The Irish Question, 1800–1922* (1968); *The Irish Diaspora in America* (1976). He is editor of *Irish Nationalism and the American Contribution* (1976), and of *The Irish Americans*, 42 vols. (1976).

William C. McCready, Senior Studies Director, National Opinion Research Center, Chicago. He is coauthor of *The Ultimate Values of the American Population* (1976).

Alasdair C. MacIntyre, Professor of Philosophy and Political Science, Boston University. His works include: *Marxism and Christianity*, rev. ed. (1968); *The Unconscious: A Conceptual Analysis* (1958); *Short History of Ethics* (1965); *Marcuse: An Exposition and Polemic* (1970); *Against the Self-Images of the Age* (1971). He is editor of *Metaphysical Belief* (1956), and *Social Theory and Philosophical Analysis* (1971).

David Montgomery, Professor of History, Yale University. His works include: *Beyond Equality: Labor and the Radical Republicans, 1862–1872* (1967); essays on early Philadelphia workingmen in *Labor History*, 1968, and the *Journal of Social History*, 1972. He is consultant editor of the *Biographical Dictionary of American Labor leaders* (Westport, Conn., 1974).

John A. Murphy, Professor of Irish History, University College, Cork. His works include: *Justin McCarthy, Lord Mountcashel* (1959); *Ireland in the Twentieth Century* (1975). He is editor of *Religion and Irish Society* (forthcoming).

Conor Cruise O'Brien, Senior Editor, *The Observer* (London) and formerly an Irish Cabinet Minister, 1973–77. His works include: *Maria Cross* (1954); *Parnell and His Party, 1880–1890* (1957); *To Katanga and Back* (1962); *Writers and Politics* (1965); *Murderous Angels* (1969); *Albert Camus* (1970); *The Suspecting Glance* (1972); *States of Ireland* (1972); *Herod—Reflections on Political Violence* (1978); (with Maire Cruise O'Brien), *A Concise History of Ireland* (1972). He is editor of: *Edmund Burke, Reflections on the Revolution in France* (1968); (with W. D. Vanech), *Power and Consciousness* (1967); *The Shaping of Modern Ireland* (1960).

Peggy O'Brien, Lecturer in American Literature, Trinity College, Dublin. She is author of a forthcoming study of Nathaniel Hawthorne.

León Ó Broin, Vice-President of the Royal Irish Academy and formerly Permanent Secretary to the Irish Department of Posts and Telegraphs, 1946–67. A noted Irish historian, his books include *Parnell: beathaisnéis* (1937); *The Unfortunate Mr. Robert Emmet* (1958); *Dublin Castle and the 1916 Rising* (1966); *Charles Gavan Duffy* (1967); *The Chief Secretary: Augustine Birrell in Ireland* (1969); *An Máidineach* (1971); *The Prime Informer* (1971); *Fenian Fever* (1971); *Revolutionary Underground* (1976).

Cormac Ó Gráda, Lecturer in Economic History, University College, Dublin. Extensive work upon nineteenth-century Irish agrarian, demographic, social, and economic history includes papers in *Economic History Review* (1975); *Agricultural History Review* (1975); *Population Studies* (1975); *Studia Hibernica* (1973); *Annales de Démographie Historique* (1978); *Comparative Aspects of Irish and Scottish Economic History* (1977), edited by L. M. Cullen and T. C. Smout.

Michéal Ó hAodha, Director, Abbey Theatre, Dublin, and formerly assistant controller of programmes, Radio Telefis Eireann. His radio dramatization of Seamas O'Kelly's *The Weaver's Grave* won the Italia Prize in 1961. Other books include *Plays and Places* (1960); *Dlí na Feirme* (1965); and *Theatre in Ireland* (1973).

William V. Shannon, U.S. Ambassador to Ireland, formerly on the editorial board of the *New York Times*. His works include: *The American Irish* (1963; rev. ed., 1966); *The Heir Apparent: Robert Kennedy and the Struggle for Power* (1967); (with R. S. Allen), *Our Sovereign State* (1949), and *The Truman Merry-Go-Round* (1950).

James P. Walsh, Professor of History, San José State University. He is editor of *The Irish: America's Political Class* (1976); *The San Francisco Irish, 1850–1976* (1978); and coeditor of *The Irish Americans*, 42 vols (1976). He is author of *Ethnic Militancy: An Irish Catholic Prototype* (1972).

William H. A. Williams, Associate Professor of History, Arizona State University, Tempe, formerly visiting lecturer in American History, University College, Dublin.

Robin W. Winks, Professor of Commonwealth History, Yale University, formerly U.S. Cultural Attaché, London, 1969–71. His works include: *Canada and the United States: The Civil War Years* (1960); *British Imperialism* (1963); *The Historiography of the British Empire and Commonwealth* (1966); *The Historian as Detective* (1970) *Blacks in Canada* (1971). He is editor or coeditor of *Malaysia* (1967); *Pastmasters* (1969); *Four Fugitive Slave Narratives* (1969); *Slavery: A Comparative Perspective* (1972); *Myth of the American Frontier* (1971).